James Joseph Baxter

Manual of Bible Truths and Histories

Adapted to the Questions of the Baltimore Catechism...

James Joseph Baxter

Manual of Bible Truths and Histories
Adapted to the Questions of the Baltimore Catechism...

ISBN/EAN: 9783337258955

Printed in Europe, USA, Canada, Australia, Japan

Cover: Foto ©Lupo / pixelio.de

More available books at **www.hansebooks.com**

MANUAL

OF

BIBLE TRUTHS AND HISTORIES

ADAPTED TO THE QUESTIONS OF

THE BALTIMORE CATECHISM

TOGETHER WITH

A LIFE OF CHRIST

FROM THE FOUR GOSPELS

COMPILED AND ARRANGED BY
REV. JAMES J. BAXTER, D. D.

NEW YORK:
P. J. KENEDY,
Publisher to the Holy Apostolic See,
EXCELSIOR CATHOLIC PUBLISHING HOUSE,
3. AND 5 BARCLAY STREET.

1898.

NIHIL OBSTAT.

PREFACE.

The chief aim of this Book is to contribute something, howsoever little, to the great work of popularizing the Sacred Scriptures. To this end, all of the more important and interesting passages are here presented, apart from their less attractive surroundings, while the text, though losing nothing of its original simplicity, is reduced, for brevity's sake, to the merest narrative. The volume is designed to accommodate at least three classes of persons, viz: Catechists, students in a general way of the Holy Bible, and Preachers of the Word of God.

Experience amply proves that in the Academy, and Parochial, as well as in the Sunday school, the ideal Teacher of Christian Doctrine must be equally ready to instruct and to entertain. The natural passion of children for stories should be so utilized that the story become the vehicle of truth. Doctrine thus imparted is grasped more easily and more eagerly and is longer remembered. The only difficulty in this method is, that it taxes so severely the inventive genius of the Teacher that the "Sunday school story" is usually either entirely irrelevant, or so utterly devoid of point and truth as to have become a byword and a reproach. Here then is an opportunity to diffuse a knowledge of the Bible by means of these charming little histories that foreshadow or assert or beautifully illustrate the chief truths of our Religion.

It is a deplorable fact that to very many of our people the Holy Scriptures are a sealed Book, and the Life of Christ, a mass of events confused and vague. Howsoever eager they may be to learn, the ponderous family Bible is a powerful discouragement to personal research. The result is that in sermons and instructions allusions are being constantly made which are lost on the hearers, and the broad and firm foundations of our Religion in Holy Writ are rarely appreciated. Protestants, too, already fairly conversant with the Scriptures, and desirous of becoming Catholics, are strongly impressed on finding that, as the two Cherubim gazed ever one upon the other and joined their wings over the Ark of the Covenant, so the two Testaments reflect each other and find their natural centre in the Catholic Church.

It is hoped also that this volume may prove convenient in the Pulpit. A striking text or pertinent story often serves to rouse the flagging interest of a congregation. "Search the Scriptures," says the Apostle, "for every Scripture inspired of God is profitable to teach, to reprove, to correct, to instruct in justice, that the man of God may be perfect, furnished to every good work." THE COMPILER.

CATECHISM.

LESSON FIRST.

ON THE END OF MAN.

Q. Who made the world?

(Acts 17 : 27.) God made the world, and all things therein, and being Lord of heaven and earth He dwelleth not in temples made with hands.

Q. Who is God?

(Acts 14 : 14. A. M. 1.) God made the heaven, and the earth, and the sea, and all things that are in them, upholding all things by the word of his power. It is God who worketh in you, both to will and to accomplish. He is the Alpha and Omega, the first and the last, the beginning and the end.

(Ex. 3 : 14-15. A. M. 2513.) God said to Moses : I AM WHO AM. He said : Thus shalt thou say to the children of Israel : HE WHO IS, hath sent me to you. And God said again to Moses : Thus shalt thou say to the children of Israel : The Lord God of your fathers, the God of Abraham, the God of Isaac, and the God of Jacob, hath sent me to you : This is my name for ever, and this is my memorial unto all generations.

(Ex. 6 : 2-3.) And the Lord spoke to Moses, saying : I am the Lord, that appeared to Abraham, to Isaac, and to Jacob, by the name of God Almighty ; and my name ADONAI I did not shew them.

Q. What is man?

(Gen. 2 : 7. A. M. 1.) The Lord God formed man of the slime of the earth : and breathed into his face the breath of life, and man became a living soul.

(Gen. 1 : 27.) And God created man to his own image : to the image of God he created him : male and female he created them.

(Job 14 : 1-2.) Man born of a woman, living for a short time, is filled with many miseries. Who cometh forth like a flower, and is destroyed, and fleeth as a shadow, and never continueth in the same state.

(Job 14 : 10-12.) But man

when he shall be dead, and stripped and consumed, I pray you where is he? As if the waters should depart out of the sea, and an emptied river should be dried up: so man when he is fallen asleep shall not rise again till the heavens be broken.

(Job 19: 25-27.) But I know that my Redeemer liveth, and in the last day I shall rise out of the earth. And I shall be clothed again with my skin, and in my flesh I shall see my God. Whom I myself shall see, and my eyes shall behold, and not another: this my hope is laid up in my bosom.

Q. Is this likeness in the body or in the soul?

(Gen. 1: 26.) God saw that it was good. And he said: Let us make man to our image and likeness.

Q. How is the soul like to God?

(Wisd. 2: 23.) God created man incorruptible, and to the image of his own likeness he made him.

Q. Why did God make you?
See "L. of C.," p. 76, No. 18.

(Rom. 9: 18-23.) He hath mercy on whom he will; and whom he will, he hardeneth. Thou wilt say therefore to me: Why doth he then find fault? for who resisteth his will? O man, who art thou that repliest against God? Shall the thing formed say to him that formed it: Why hast thou made me thus? Or hath not the potter power over the clay, of the same lump, to make one vessel unto honour, and another unto dishonour? What if God, willing to shew his wrath, and to make his power known, endured with much patience vessels of wrath, fitted for destruction. That he might shew the riches of his glory on the vessels of mercy, which he hath prepared unto glory?

(Deut. 10: 12-14.) And now, Israel, what doth the Lord thy God require of thee, but that thou fear the Lord thy God, and walk in his ways, and love him, and serve the Lord thy God, with all thy heart, and with all thy soul: and keep the commandments of the Lord, and his ceremonies, which I command thee this day, that it may be well with thee? Behold heaven is the Lord's thy God, and the heaven of heaven, the earth and all things that are therein.

Q. Of which must we take more care, our soul or our body?
See "L. of C.," p. 50, No. 11; p. 65, No. 28.

(Jer. 17: 5-8.) Thus saith the Lord: Cursed be the man that trusteth in man, and maketh flesh his arm, and whose heart departeth from the Lord. For he shall be like tamaric in the desert, and he shall not see when good shall come: but he shall dwell in dryness in the desert in a salt land, and not inhabited. Blessed be the man that trusteth in the Lord, and the Lord shall be his confidence. And he shall be as a tree that is planted by the waters, that spreadeth out its roots towards moisture: and it shall not fear when the heat cometh. And the leaf thereof shall be green, and in the time of drought it shall not be solicitous, neither shall it cease at any time to bring forth fruit.

Q. Why must we take more care of our soul than of our body?

See "L. of C.," p. 87, No. 19.

(Jer. 18: 1–10.) The word that came to Jeremias from the Lord, saying: Arise, and go down into the potter's house, and there thou shalt hear my words. And I went down into the potter's house, and behold he was doing a work on the wheel. And the vessel was broken which he was making of clay with his hands: and turning he made another vessel, as it seemed good in his eyes to make it. Then the word of the Lord came to me, saying: Cannot I do with you, as this potter, O house of Israel, saith the Lord? behold as clay *is* in the hand of the potter, so are you in my hand, O house of Israel. I will suddenly speak against a nation, and against a kingdom, to root out, and to pull down, and to destroy it. If that nation against which I have spoken, shall repent of their evil, I also will repent of the evil that I have thought to do to them. And I will suddenly speak of a nation and of a kingdom, to build up and plant it. If it shall do evil in my sight, that it obey not my voice: I will repent of the good that I have spoken to do unto it.

(Jer. 19: 1, 10–11.) Thus said the Lord: Go, and take a potter's earthen bottle, *and take* of the ancients of the people, and of the ancients of the priests: and thou shalt break the bottle in the sight of the men that shall go with thee. And thou shalt say to them: Thus saith the Lord of hosts: Even so will I break this people, and this city, as the potter's vessel is broken, which cannot be made whole again.

Q. What must we do to save our souls?

See "L of C.," p. 55, No. 7; p. 81, No. 7.

(2 Esdras 4: 16–20. A.M. 3550.) Now it came to pass from that day forward, that half of their young men did the work, and half were ready for to fight, with spears, and shields, and bows, and coats of mail, and the rulers were behind them in all the house of Juda. Of them that built on the wall and that carried burdens, and that laded: with one of his hands he did the work, and with the other he held a sword. For every one of the builders was girded with a sword about his reins. And they built, and sounded with a trumpet by me. And I said to the nobles, and to the

magistrates, and to the rest of the common people: The work is great and wide, and we are separated on the wall one far from another: in what place soever you shall hear the sound of the trumpet, run all thither unto us: our God will fight for us.

(Num. 32: 1–7. A. M. 2553.) Now the sons of Ruben and Gad had many flocks of cattle, and their substance in beasts was infinite. And when they saw the lands of Jazer and Galaad fit for feeding cattle, they came to Moses and Eleazar the priest, and the princes of the multitude, and said: We pray thee, if we have found favour in thy sight, that thou give it to us thy servants in possession, and make us not pass over the Jordan. And Moses answered them: What, shall your brethren go to fight, and will you sit here? Why do ye overturn the minds of the children of Israel, that they may not dare to pass into the place which the Lord hath given them?

(III. King 6: 7.) Now the house, when it was in building, was built of stones hewed and made ready: so that there was neither hammer nor axe nor any tool of iron heard in the house when it was in building.

Q. How shall we know the things which we are to believe?

(Luke 10: 16.) He that heareth you, heareth me; and he that despiseth you, despiseth me; and he that despiseth me, despiseth him that sent me.

(II. Tim. 3.) But continue thou in those things which thou hast learned, and which have been committed to thee: knowing of whom thou hast learned *them;* and because from thy infancy thou hast known the holy scriptures, which can instruct thee to salvation, by the faith which is in Christ Jesus. All scripture, inspired of God, is profitable to teach, to reprove, to correct, to instruct in justice, that the man of God may be perfect furnished to every good work.

(Mic. 4.) It shall come to pass in the last days that the mountain of the house of the Lord shall be prepared in the top of mountains, and high above the hills: and people shall flow to it. And many nations shall come in haste and say: Come, let us go up to the mountain of the Lord, and to the house of the God of Jacob: and he will teach us of his ways, and we will walk in his paths: for the law shall go forth out of Sion, and the word of the Lord out of Jerusalem.

LESSON SECOND.

ON GOD AND HIS PERFECTIONS.

Q. What is God?

(Heb. 12.) Our God is a consuming fire.

(Wisd. 13.) All men are vain, in whom there is not the knowledge of God: and who by these good things that are seen, could not understand him that is, neither by attending to the works have acknowledged who was the workman: but have imagined either the fire, or the wind, or the swift air, or the circle of the stars, or the great water, or the sun and moon, to be the gods that rule the world. With whose beauty if they being delighted, took them to be gods: let them know how much the Lord of them is more beautiful than they: for the first author of beauty made all those things. Or if they admired their power and their effects, let them understand by them, that he that made them, is mightier than they: for by the greatness of the beauty, and of the creature, the creator of them may be seen, so as to be known thereby.

Q. Had God a beginning?

See "L. of C.," p. 60, No. 19.

(Apoc. 1.) I am Alpha and Omega, the beginning and the end, saith the Lord God, who is, and who was, and who is to come, the Almighty.

Q. Where is God?

(Ps. 138.) Whither shall I go from thy spirit? or whither shall I flee from thy face? If I ascend into heaven, thou art there: if I descend into hell, thou art present. If I take my wings early in the morning, and dwell in the uttermost parts of the sea: even there also shall thy hand lead me: and thy right hand shall hold me. And I said: Perhaps darkness shall cover me: and night shall be my light in my pleasures. But darkness shall not be dark to thee, and night shall be light as the day: the darkness thereof, and the light thereof are alike *to thee*.

Q. If God is everywhere, why do we not see Him?

(I. Tim. 1.) Now to the king of ages, immortal, invisible, the only God, be honour and glory for ever and ever. Amen.

(I. Tim. 6.) Keep thou the commandment without spot, blameless, unto the coming of our Lord Jesus Christ, which in his times he shall shew who is the Blessed and only Mighty, the King of kings, and Lord of lords; who only hath immortality, and inhabiteth light inaccessible, whom no man hath seen, nor can see: to whom be honour and empire everlasting. Amen.

Q. Does God see us?

(Matt. 6.) I say to you, be not solicitous for your life, what you shall eat, nor for your body what you shall put on. Is not the life more than the meat: and the body more than the raiment? Behold the birds of the air, for they neither sow, nor do they reap, nor gather into barns: and your heavenly Father feedeth them. Are not you of much more value than they? And which of you by taking thought, can add to his stature one cubit? And for raiment why are you solicitous? Consider the lilies of the field how they grow: they labour not, neither do they spin. But I say to you, that not even Solomon in all his glory was arrayed as one of these. And if the grass of the field, which is to-day, and to-morrow is cast into the oven, God doth so clothe: how much more you, O ye of little faith? Be not solicitous therefore, saying, What shall we eat: or what shall we drink, or wherewith shall we be clothed? For after all these things do the heathens seek. For your Father knoweth that you have need of all these things.

(Deut. 4.) Neither is there any other nation so great, that hath God so nigh them, as our God is present to all our petitions.

Q. Does God know all things?

(Eccltus. 23.) Darkness compasseth me about, and the walls cover me, and no man seeth me: whom do I fear? the most High will not remember my sins. And he understandeth not that his eye seeth all things, for such a man's fear driveth from him the fear of God, and the eyes of men fearing him: and he knoweth not that the eyes of the Lord are far brighter than the sun, beholding round about all the ways of men, and the bottom of the deep, and looking into the hearts of men, into the most hidden parts. For all things were known to the Lord God, before they were created: so also after they were perfected he beholdeth all things.

Q. Can God do all things?
See "L. of C.," p. 8, No. 4.

(Judith 15.) O Adonai Lord, great art thou, and glorious in thy power, and no one can overcome thee: Let all thy creatures serve thee: because thou hast spoken, and they were made: thou didst send forth thy Spirit, and they were created; and there is no one that can resist thy voice.

Q. Is God just, holy and merciful?

(Job 34.) Ye men of understanding, hear me: far from God be wickedness, and iniquity from the Almighty. For he will render to a man his work, and according to the ways of every one he will reward them. For in very deed God will not condemn without cause, neither will the Almighty pervert judgment. The Lord is patient and full of mercy.

LESSON THIRD.

ON THE UNITY AND TRINITY OF GOD.

Q. Is there but one God?

(Isa. 45.) I am the Lord, and there is none else: there is no God besides me.

Q. Why can there be but one God?

(Isa. 44.) I am the first, and I am the last, and besides me there is no God. Who is like to me? let him call and declare: and let him set before me the order since I appointed the ancient people: and the things to come, and that shall be hereafter, let them shew unto them.

Q. How many persons are there in God?

(I. John 5.) And there are three who give testimony in heaven, the Father, the Word, and the Holy Ghost. And these three are one. And there are three that give testimony on earth: the spirit, and the water, and the blood: and these three are one.

Q. Is the Father God?

(John 20:17.) I ascend to My Father and to your Father, to My God and your God.

Q. Is the Son God?

See "L. of C.," p. 59, No 15; p. 17, No. 1.

(Col. 1:12-20.) Give thanks to God the Father, who hath made us worthy to be partakers of the lot of the saints in light, who hath delivered us from the power of darkness, and hath translated us into the kingdom of the Son of his love. In whom we have redemption through his blood, the remission of sins; who is the image of the invisible God, the first-born of every creature: for in him were all things created in heaven and on earth, visible and invisible, whether thrones, or dominations, or principalities, or powers: all things were created by him and in him. And he is before all, and by him all things consist. And he is the head of the body, the church, who is the beginning, the first-born from the dead; that in all things he may hold the primacy: because in him it hath well-pleased *the Father*, that all fulness should dwell; and through him to reconcile all things unto himself, making peace through the blood of his cross, both as to the things that are on earth, and the things that are in heaven.

Q. Is the Holy Ghost God?

(John 15.) When the Paraclete cometh, whom I will send you from the Father, the Spirit of truth, who proceedeth from the Father, he shall give testimony of me.

Q. What do you mean by the Blessed Trinity?

See "L. of C.," p. 106, No. 10.

Q. Are the three Divine Persons equal in all things?

See "L. of C.," p. 103, No. 8.

Q. Are the three Divine Persons one and the same God?
See "L. of C.," p. 58, No. 14; p. 102, No. 1.

Q. Can we fully understand how the three Divine Persons are one and the same God?
See "L. of C.," p. 53, No. 16.

(Rom. 11.) O the depth of the riches of the wisdom and of the knowledge of God! How incomprehensible are his judgments, and how unsearchable his ways! For who hath known the mind of the Lord? Or who hath been his counsellor? Or who hath first given to him, and recompense shall be made him? For of him, and by him, and in him, are all things: to him be glory for ever. Amen.

Q. What is a mystery?

We know in part, and we prophesy in part. But when that which is perfect is come, that which is in part shall be done away. When I was a child, I spoke as a child, I understood as a child, I thought as a child. But, when I became a man, I put away the things of a child. We see now through a glass in a dark manner; but then face to face. Now I know in part; but then I shall know even as I am known.

LESSON FOURTH.

ON CREATION.

Q. Who created heaven and earth, and all things?

(Gen. 1. A. M. 1.) In the beginning God created heaven, and earth. And the earth was void and empty, and darkness was upon the face of the deep; and the spirit of God moved over the waters. And God said: Be light made. And light was made. And he called the light Day, and the darkness Night; and there was evening and morning one day. And God made a firmament, and divided the waters that were under the firmament, from those that were above the firmament, and it was so. And God called the firmament, Heaven; and the evening and morning were the second day. God also said: Let the waters that are under the heaven, be gathered together into one place: and let the dry land appear. And it was so done. And he said: Let the earth bring forth the green herb, and such as may seed, and the fruit tree yielding fruit after its kind, which may have seed in itself upon the earth. And it was so done. And the evening and the morning were the third day. And God made two great lights: a greater light to rule the day; and a lesser light to rule the night; and the stars. And the evening and morning were the fourth day. And God created the great whales, and every living and moving creature, which the waters brought forth, according to their kinds, and every winged fowl according to its kind. And God saw that it was good. And he blessed them, saying: Increase and multiply, and fill the waters of the sea: and let the birds be multiplied upon the earth. And the evening and morning were the fifth day. And God made the beasts of the earth according to their kinds, and cattle, and every thing that creepeth on the earth after its kind. And God saw that it was good. And God created man to his own image: to the image of God he created him: male and female he created them. And God blessed them, saying: Increase and multiply, and fill the earth, and subdue it, and rule over the fishes of the sea, and the fowls of the air, and all living creatures that move upon the earth. And the evening and morning were the sixth day.

Q. How did God create heaven and earth?

(Ps. 32.) By the word of the Lord the heavens were established; and all the power of them by the spirit of his mouth: gathering together the waters of the sea, as in a vessel; laying up the depths in store-houses. Let all the earth fear the Lord, and let all the inhabitants of the world be in awe of him. For he spoke and they were made: he commanded and they were created.

Q. Which are the chief creatures of God?

(Col. 1.) For in him were all things created in heaven and on earth, visible and invisible, whether thrones, or dominations, or principalities, or powers: all things were created by him and in him.

(Gen. 1.) And he said: Let us make man to our image and likeness: and let him have dominion over the fishes of the sea, and the fowls of the air, and the beasts, and the whole earth, and every creeping creature that moveth upon the earth.

Q. What are angels?

(Ezek. 28.) Thou wast the seal of resemblance, full of wisdom, and perfect in beauty, thou wast in the pleasures of the paradise of God: thou a cherub stretched out, and protecting, and I set thee in the holy mountain of God, thou hast walked in the midst of the stones of fire. Thou wast perfect in thy ways from the day of thy creation, until iniquity was found in thee.

Q. Were the angels created for any other purpose?
See " L. of C.," p. 7, Nos. 1-2-3; p. 72, No. 8.

(Acts 12. A. D. 42.) Peter was kept in prison. But prayer was made without ceasing by the church unto God for him. And when Herod would have brought him forth, the same night Peter was sleeping between two soldiers, bound with two chains: and the keepers before the door kept the prison. And behold an Angel of the Lord stood by him: and a light shined in the room: and he striking Peter on the side, raised him up, saying: Arise quickly. And the chains fell off from his hands. And the Angel said to him: Gird thyself, and put on thy sandals. And he did so. And he said to him: Cast thy garment about thee, and follow me. And going out, he followed him, and he knew not that it was true which was done by the Angel: but thought he saw a vision. And passing through the first and the second ward, they came to the iron gate that leadeth to the city, which of itself opened to them. And going out, they passed on through one street: and immediately the Angel departed from him. And Peter coming to himself, said: Now I know in very deed, that the Lord hath sent his Angel, and hath delivered me out of the hand of Herod, and from all the expectation of the people of the Jews.

(Gen. 18–19. A. M. 2157.) The Lord appeared to Abraham in the vale of Mambre as he was sitting at the door of his tent, in the very heat of the day. And when he had lifted up his eyes, there appeared to him three men standing near him: and as soon as he saw them he ran to meet them from the door of his tent, and adored down to the ground. And he said: Lord, if I have found favour in thy sight, pass not away from thy servant: and when they had eaten, they said unto him: Where is Sara thy wife? He answered: Lo, she is in the tent. And he said to him: I will return and come to thee at this time, life accompanying, and Sara thy wife shall have a son. And the two angels came to Sodom in the evening, and Lot was sitting in the gate of the city. And they said to Lot: Hast thou here any of thine? son-in-law, or sons, or daughters, all that are thine bring them out of this city: for we will destroy this place, because their cry is grown loud before the Lord, who hath sent us to destroy them. So Lot went out, and spoke to his sons-in-law that were to have his daughters, and said: Arise: get you out of this place, because the Lord will destroy this city. And he seemed to them to speak as it were in jest. And when it was morning, the angels pressed him, saying: Arise, take thy wife, and the two daughters which thou hast: lest thou also perish in the wickedness of the city. And as he lingered, they took his hand, and the hand of his wife, and of his two daughters, because the Lord spared him. And they brought him forth, and set him without the city: and there they spoke to him, saying: Save thy life: look not back, neither stay thou in all the country about: but save thyself in the mountain, lest thou be also consumed. And Lot entered into Segor. And his wife looking behind her, was turned into a statue of salt. And the Lord rained upon Sodom and Gomorrha brimstone and fire from the Lord out of heaven.

(Ps. 90.) There shall no evil come to thee: nor shall the scourge come near thy dwelling. For he hath given his Angels charge over thee; to keep thee in all thy ways. In their hands they shall bear thee up; lest thou dash thy foot against a stone.

Q. Were the angels, as God created them, good and happy?

(III. Kings 10. A. M. 3023.) When the queen of Saba saw all the wisdom of Solomon, and the house which he had built, and the meat of his table, and the apartments of his servants, and the order of his ministers, and their apparel, and the cupbearers, and the holocausts, which he offered in the house of the Lord: she had no longer any spirit in her, and she said to the king: The report is true, which I heard in my own country, concerning thy words, and concerning thy wisdom. And I did not believe them that told me, till I came myself, and saw with my own eyes, and have found that the half hath not been told me: thy wisdom and thy works, exceed the fame which I heard. Blessed are thy men, and blessed are thy servants, who stand before thee always, and hear thy wisdom.

Q. Did all the angels remain good and happy?

(Apoc. 12.) There was a great battle in heaven, Michael and his angels fought with the dragon, and the dragon fought and his angels: and they prevailed not, neither was their place found any more in heaven. And that great dragon was cast out, that old serpent, who is called the devil and satan, who seduceth the whole world; and he was cast unto the earth, and his angels were thrown down with him.

(Luke 10.) The seventy-two returned with joy, saying: Lord, the devils also are subject to us in thy name. And he said to them: I saw satan like lightning falling from heaven.

(Jude 3.) The angels who kept not their principality, but forsook their own habitation, he hath reserved under darkness in everlasting chains, unto the judgment of the great day.

(II. Peter 2.) For if God spared not the angels that sinned, but delivered them, drawn down by infernal ropes to the lower hell, unto torments, to be reserved unto judgment: the Lord knoweth how to deliver the godly from temptation, but to reserve the unjust unto the day of judgment to be tormented.

LESSON FIFTH.

ON OUR FIRST PARENTS AND THE FALL.

Q. Who were the first man and woman?

(Gen. 2. A. M. 1.) The Lord God formed man of the slime of the earth and breathed into his face the breath of life, and man became a living soul. And the Lord God said. It is not good for man to be alone: let us make him a help like unto himself. Then the Lord God cast a deep sleep upon Adam: and when he was fast asleep, he took one of his ribs, and filled up flesh for it. And the Lord God built the rib which he took from Adam into a woman: and brought her to Adam. And Adam said: This now is bone of my bones, and flesh of my flesh; she shall be called woman, because she was taken out of man. Wherefore a man shall leave father and mother, and shall cleave to his wife: and they shall be two in one flesh.

(Gen. 3.) And Adam called the name of his wife Eve: because she was the mother of all the living.

Q. Were Adam and Eve innocent and holy when they came from the hand of God?

(Wisd. 1.) God made not death, neither hath he pleasure in the destruction of the living. For he created all things that they might be: and he made the nations of the earth for health: and there is no poison of destruction in them, nor kingdom of hell upon the earth. For justice is perpetual and immortal.

(Wisd. 2.) For God created man incorruptible, and to the image of his own likeness he made him. But by the envy of the devil, death came into the world.

(Gen. 2.) And they were both naked: to wit, Adam and his wife: and were not ashamed.

Q. Did God give any command to Adam and Eve?

(Gen. 2.) The Lord God took man, and put him into the paradise of pleasure, to dress it, and to keep it. And he commanded him, saying: Of every tree of paradise thou shalt eat: but of the tree of knowledge of good and evil, thou shalt not eat. For in what day soever thou shalt eat of it, thou shalt die the death.

Q. Which were the chief blessings intended for Adam and Eve had they remained faithful to God?

(Gen. 2.) The Lord God had planted a paradise of pleasure from the beginning: wherein he placed man whom he had formed. And the Lord God brought forth of the ground all manner of trees, fair to behold, and pleasant to eat of: the tree of life also in the midst of paradise: and the tree of knowledge of good and evil. And the

Lord God took man, and put him into the paradise of pleasure, to dress it, and to keep it. And the Lord God having formed out of the ground all the beasts of the earth, and all the fowls of the air, brought them to Adam to see what he would call them: for whatsoever Adam called any living creature the same is its name. And Adam called all the beasts by their names, and all the fowls of the air, and all the cattle of the field.

(Gen. 1.) And God said: Behold I have given you every herb bearing seed upon the earth, and all trees that have in themselves seed of their own kind, to be your meat: and to all beasts of the earth, and to every fowl of the air, and to all that move upon the earth, and wherein there is life, that they may have to feed upon. And it was so done.

Q. Did Adam and Eve remain faithful to God?

(Gen. 3.) Now the serpent was more subtle than any of the beasts of the earth which the Lord God had made. And he said to the woman: Why hath God commanded you, that you should not eat of every tree of paradise? And the woman answered him, *saying:* Of the fruit of the trees that are in parndise we do eat: but of the fruit of the tree which is in the midst of paradise, God hath commanded us that we should not eat; and that we should not touch it, lest perhaps we die. And the serpent said to the woman: No, you shall not die the death. For God doth know that in what day soever you shall eat thereof, your eyes shall be opened: and you shall be as Gods, knowing good and evil. And the woman saw that the tree was good to eat, and fair to the eyes, and delightful to behold: and she took of the fruit thereof, and did eat, and gave to her husband who did eat.

Q. What befell Adam and Eve on account of their sin?

(Gen. 3.) The eyes of them both were opened: and when they perceived themselves to be naked, they sewed together fig-leaves, and made themselves aprons. And when they heard the voice of the Lord God walking in paradise at the afternoon air, Adam and his wife hid themselves from the face of the Lord God, amidst the trees of paradise. And the Lord God called Adam, and said to him: Where art thou? And he said: I heard thy voice in paradise; and I was afraid, because I was naked, and I hid myself. And he said to him: And who hath told thee that thou wast naked, but that thou hast eaten of the tree whereof I commanded thee that thou shouldst not eat? And Adam said: The woman, whom thou gavest me to be my companion, gave me of the tree, and I did eat. And the Lord God said to the woman: Why hast thou done this? And she answered: The serpent deceived me, and I did eat. And the Lord God said to the serpent: Because thou hast done this thing, thou art cursed among all cattle, and beasts of the earth: upon thy breast shalt thou go, and earth shalt thou eat all the days of thy life. I will put enmities between thee and the woman, and thy seed and her seed: she shall crush thy head, and thou shalt lie in wait for her heel. To the woman also he said: I will multiply thy sorrows, and thy conceptions: in sorrow shalt thou bring forth children, and thou shalt be under thy husband's power, and he shall have dominion over thee. And to Adam he said: Because thou hast hearkened to the voice of thy wife, and has eaten of the tree, whereof I commanded thee that thou shouldst not eat, cursed is the earth in thy work; with labour and toil shalt thou eat thereof all the days of thy life. Thorns and thistles shall it bring forth to thee; and thou shalt eat the herbs of the earth. In the sweat of thy face shalt thou eat bread till thou return to the earth, out of which thou wast taken: for dust thou art, and into dust thou shalt return. And the Lord God made for Adam and his wife, garments of skins, and clothed them. And he said: Behold Adam is become as one of us, knowing good and evil: now, therefore, lest perhaps he put forth his hand, and take also of the tree of life, and eat, and live for ever. And the Lord God sent him out of the paradise of leasure, to till the earth from which he was taken. And he cast out Adam; and placed before the paradise of pleasure Cherubims, and a flaming sword, turning every way, to keep the way of the tree of life.

(Isa. 5.) I will sing to my beloved the canticle of my cousin concerning his vineyard. My beloved had a vineyard on a hill in a fruitful place. And he fenced it in, and picked the stones out of it, and planted it with the choicest wines, and built a tower in the midst thereof, and set up a wine-press therein: and he looked that it should bring forth grapes, and it brought forth wild grapes. And now, O ye inhabitants of Jerusalem, and ye men of Juda, judge between me and my vineyard. What is there that I ought to do more to my vineyard, that I have not done to it? was it that I looked that it should bring forth grapes, and it hath brought forth wild grapes? And now I will shew you what I will do to my vineyard. I will take away the hedge thereof, and it shall be wasted: I will break down the wall thereof, and it shall be trodden down. And I will make it desolate: it shall not be pruned, and it shall not be digged: but briers and thorns shall come up: and I will command the clouds to rain no rain upon it. For the vineyard of the Lord of hosts is the house of Israel: and the man of Juda, his pleasant plant: and I looked that he should do judgment, and behold iniquity: and do justice, and behold a cry.

Q. What evil befell us on account of the disobedience of our first parents?

(Ex. 5. A. M. 2513.) Pharao said: The people of the land is numerous: you see that the multitude is increased: how much more if you give them rest from their works? Therefore he commanded the same day the overseers of the works, and the task-masters of the people, saying: You shall give straw no more to the people to make brick, as before: but let them go and gather straw. And you shall lay upon them the task of bricks, which they did before, neither shall you diminish any thing thereof: for they are idle, and therefore they cry, saying: Let us go and sacrifice to our God. Let them be oppressed, with works, and let them fulfil them: that they may not regard lying words. And the overseers of the works and the task-masters went out and said to the people: Thus saith Pharao, I allow you no straw: go, and gather it where you can find it: neither shall anything of your work be diminished. And the people was scattered through all the land of Egypt to gather straw. And the overseers of the works pressed them, saying: Fulfil your work every day as before you were wont to do when straw was given you. And they that were over the works of the children of Israel were scourged by Pharao's task-masters, saying: Why have you not made up the task of bricks both yesterday and to-day as before?

Q. What other effects followed from the sin of our first parents?

(Eccltus. 40.) Great labour is created for all men, and a heavy yoke is upon the children of Adam, from the day of their coming out of their mother's womb, until the day of their burial into the mother of all. Their thoughts, and fears of the heart, their imagination of things to come, and the day of their end: from him that sitteth on a glorious throne, unto him that is humbled in earth and ashes: from him that weareth purple, and beareth the crown, even to him that is covered with rough linen: wrath, envy, trouble, unquietness, and the fear of death, continual anger, and strife, such things happen to all flesh, from man even to beast, and upon sinners are sevenfold more. Moreover, death, and bloodshed, strife, and sword, oppressions, famine, and affliction, and scourges: all these things are created for the wicked.

Q. What is the sin called which we inherit from our first parents?

(I. Tim. 2.) In like manner women also in decent apparel: adorning themselves with modesty and sobriety, not with plaited hair, or gold, or pearls, or costly attire, but as it becometh women professing godliness, with good works. Let the woman learn in silence, with all subjection. But I suffer not a woman to teach, nor to use authority over the man: but to be in silence. For Adam was first formed; then Eve. And Adam was not seduced; but the woman being seduced, was in the transgression.

Q. Why is this sin called original?

(Rom. 5.) As by one man sin entered into this world, and by sin death; and so death passed upon all men, in whom all have sinned. For until the law sin was in the world; but sin was not imputed, when the law was not. But death reigned from Adam unto Moses, even over them also who have not sinned after the similitude of the transgression of Adam, who is a figure of him who was to come.

Q. Does this corruption of our nature remain in us after original sin is forgiven?

(II. Cor. 12.) Lest the greatness of the revelations should exalt me, there was given me a sting of my flesh, an angel of satan, to buffet me. For which thing thrice I besought the Lord, that it might depart from me. And he said to me: My grace is sufficient for thee: for power is made perfect in infirmity. Gladly therefore will I glory in my infirmities, that the power of Christ may dwell in me.

(Rom. 7.) I am delighted with the law of God, according to the inward man: but I see another law in my members, fighting against the law of my mind, and captivating me in the law of sin, that is in my members. Unhappy man that I am, who shall deliver me from the body of this death? The grace of God, by Jesus Christ our Lord. Therefore, I myself, with the mind, serve the law of God; but with the flesh, the law of sin.

Q. Was any one ever preserved from original sin?

See "L. of C.," p. 8, No. 5; p. 36, No. 26.

(Apoc. 12.) A great sign appeared in heaven: A woman clothed with the sun, and the moon under her feet, and on her head a crown of twelve stars.

(Cant. 5: Cant. 6.) Who is she that cometh forth as the morning rising, fair as the moon, bright as the sun, terrible as an army set in array?

(Gen. 6. A. M. 1536.) Noe found grace before the Lord. But the earth was corrupted before God, and was filled with iniquity. And when God had seen that the earth was corrupted (for all flesh had corrupted its way upon the earth,) he said to Noe: The end of all flesh is come before me, the earth is filled with iniquity through them, and I will destroy them with the earth. Make thee an ark of timber planks: thou shalt make little rooms in the ark, and thou shalt pitch it within and without. And thus shalt thou make it: The length of the ark shall be three hundred cubits: the breadth of it fifty cubits, and the height of it thirty cubits. Thou shalt make a window in the ark, and in a cubit shalt thou finish the top of it: and the door of the ark thou shalt set in the side: with lower, middle chambers, and third stories shalt thou make it. Behold I will bring the waters of a great flood upon the earth, to destroy all flesh, wherein is the breath of life, under heaven. All things that are in the earth shall be consumed. And I will establish my covenant with thee, and thou shalt enter into the ark, thou and thy sons, and thy wife, and the wives of thy sons with thee.

(Gen. 7.) And Noe went in and his sons, his wife and the wives of his sons with him into the ark, because of the waters of the flood. And of beasts clean and unclean, and of fowls, and of everything that moveth upon the earth. Two and two went in to Noe into the ark, male and female, as the Lord had commanded Noe. And after the seven days were passed, the waters of the flood overflowed the earth. And the rain fell upon the earth forty days and forty nights. The water was fifteen cubits higher than the mountains which it covered. And all flesh was destroyed that moved upon the earth, both of fowl, and of cattle, and of beasts, and of all creeping things that creep upon the earth: and all men. And all things wherein there is the breath of life on the earth, died, and the waters prevailed upon the earth a hundred and fifty days.

(Gen. 8.) And God remembered Noe, and all the living creatures, and all the cattle which were with him in the ark, and brought a wind upon the earth, and the waters were abated. And the waters were going and decreasing until the tenth month: for in the tenth month, the first day of the month, the tops of the mountains appeared. And after that forty days were passed, Noe, opening the window of the ark which he had made, sent forth a raven: which went forth and did not return, till the waters were dried up upon the earth. He sent forth also a dove after him, to see if the waters had now ceased upon the face of the earth. But she, not finding where her foot might rest, returned to him into the ark: for the waters were upon the whole earth: and he put forth his hand, and caught her, and brought her into the ark. And having waited yet seven other days, he again sent forth the dove out of the ark. And she came to him in the evening, carrying a bough of an olive tree, with green leaves, in her mouth. Noe therefore understood that the waters were ceased upon the earth. And he stayed yet other seven days: and he sent forth the dove, which returned not any more unto him. So Noe went out, he and his sons: his wife, and the wives of his sons with him. And all living things, and cattle, and creeping things that creep upon the earth, according to their kinds, went out of the ark.

(Gen. 9.) And God blessed Noe and his sons. And he said to them: Increase and multiply, and fill the earth. I will establish my covenant with you, and all flesh shall be no more destroyed with the waters of a flood, neither shall there be from henceforth a flood to waste the earth. And God said: This is the sign of the covenant which I give between me and you, and to every living soul that is with you, for perpetual generations. I will set my bow in the clouds, and it shall be the sign of a covenant between me, and between the earth. And when I shall cover the sky with clouds, my bow shall appear in the clouds: and I will remember my covenant with you, and with every living soul that beareth flesh: and there shall no more be waters of a flood to destroy all flesh. And the bow shall be in the clouds, and I shall see it, and shall remember the everlasting covenant, that was made between God and every living soul of all flesh which is upon the earth. And God said to Noe: This shall be the sign of the covenant which I have established between me and all flesh upon the earth.

(Ex. 14. A. M. 2513.) When Moses had stretched forth his hand over the sea, the Lord took it away by a strong and burning wind blowing all the night, and turned it into dry ground: and the water was divided. So Mary the prophetess the sister of Aaron, took a timbrel in her hand: and all the women went forth after her with timbrels and with dances: and the children of Israel went in through the midst of the sea dried up: for the water was as a wall on their right hand and on their left. And the Egyptians pursuing went in after them, and all Pharao's horses, his chariots and horsemen through the midst of the sea. And the Lord said to Moses: Stretch forth thy hand over the sea, that the waters may come again upon the Egyptians, upon their chariots and horsemen. And when Moses had stretched forth his hand towards the sea, it returned at the first break of day to the former place: and as the Egyptians were fleeing away, the waters came upon them, and the Lord shut them up in the middle of the waves. And the waters returned, and covered the chariots and the horsemen of all the army of Pharao, who had come into the sea after them, neither did there so much as one of them remain. But the children of Israel marched through the midst of the sea upon dry land, and the waters were to them as a wall on the right hand and on the left: and the Lord delivered Israel on that day out of the hands of the Egyptians.

(Judg. 4. A. M. 2570.) The Lord delivered the Israelites up into the hands of Jabin king of Chanaan, who reigned in Asor: and he had a general of his army named Sisara, and he dwelt in Haroseth of the Gentiles. And there was at that time Debbora a prophetess the wife of Lapidoth, who judged the people. And she sent and called Barac the son of Abinoem out of Cedes in Nephtali: and she said to him: The Lord God of Israel hath commanded thee: Go, and lead an army to mount Thabor, and thou shalt take with thee ten thousand fighting men of the children of Nephtali, and of the children of Zabulon: and I will bring unto thee in the place of the torrent Cison, Sisara the general of Jabin's army, and his chariots, and all his multitude, and will deliver them into thy hand. And Barac said to her: If thou wilt come with me, I will go: if thou wilt not come with me, I will not go. She said to him: I will go indeed with thee, but at this time the victory shall not be attributed to thee, because Sisara shall be delivered into the hand of a woman. Debbora therefore arose, and went with Barac to Cedes. And the Lord struck a terror into Sisara, and all his chariots, and all his multitude, with the edge of the sword, at the sight of Barac, insomuch that Sisara leaping down from off his chariot, fled away on foot. And Barac pursued after the fleeing chariots and the army unto Haroseth of the Gentiles, and all the multitude of the enemies was utterly destroyed. But Sisara fleeing came to the tent of Jahel the wife of Haber the Cinite, for there was peace between Jabin the king of Asor, and the house of Haber the Cinite. And Jahel went forth to meet Sisara, and said to him: Come in to me, my lord, come in, fear not. He went in to her tent, and being covered by her with a cloak, said to her: Give me, I beseech thee, a little water, for I am very thirsty. She opened a bottle of milk, and gave him to drink, and covered him. And Sisara said to her: Stand before the door of the tent, and when any shall come and inquire of thee, saying: Is there any man here? thou shalt say:

There is none. So Jahel Haber's wife took a nail of the tent, and taking also a hammer: and going in softly, and with silence, she put the nail upon the temples of his head, and striking it with the hammer, drove it through his brain fast into the ground: and so passing from deep sleep to death, he fainted away and died. And behold Barac came pursuing after Sisara: and Jahel went out to meet him, and said to him: Come, and I will shew thee the man whom thou seekest. And when he came into her tent, he saw Sisara lying dead, and the nail fastened in his temples.

(Judg. 6. A. M. 2759.) Gedeon said to God: If thou wilt save Israel by my hand, as thou hast said, I will put this fleece of wool on the floor: if there be dew on the fleece only, and it be dry on all the ground beside, I shall know that by my hand, as thou hast said, thou wilt deliver Israel. And it was so. And rising before day wringing the fleece, he filled a vessel with the dew. And he said again to God: Let not thy wrath be kindled against me if I try once more, seeking a sign in the fleece. I pray that the fleece only may be dry, and all the ground wet with dew. And God did that night as he had requested: and it was dry on the fleece only, and there was dew on all the ground.

(Judith A. M. 3347.) Nabuchodonosor king of the Assyrians, sent messengers to the nations. But they all with one mind refused, and sent them back empty, and rejected them without honour. Then king Nabuchodonosor being angry against all that land, swore by his throne and kingdom that he would revenge himself of all those countries. And he said that his thoughts were to bring all the earth under his empire. And when this saying pleased them all, Nabuchodonosor, the king, called Holofernes the general of his armies, and said to him: Go out against all the kingdoms of the west, and against them especially that despised my commandment. Thy eye shall not spare any kingdom, and all the strong cities thou shalt bring under my yoke. Then Holofernes went forth, he and all the army, with the chariots, and horsemen, and archers, who covered the face of the earth, like locusts. Then the children of Israel, who dwelt in the land of Juda, hearing these things, were exceedingly afraid of him. Dread and horror seized upon their minds, lest he should do the same to Jerusalem and to the temple of the Lord, that he had done to other cities and their temples. And they sent into all Samaria round about, as far as Jericho, and seized upon all the tops of the mountains: and they compassed their towns with walls, and gathered together corn for provision for war. And it was told Holofernes the general of the army of the Assyrians, that the children of Israel prepared themselves to resist, and had shut up the ways of the mountains. And he was transported with exceeding great fury and indignation. But Holofernes on the next day gave orders to his army, to go up against Bethulia. Now Holofernes, in going round about, found that the fountain which supplied them with water, ran through an aqueduct without the city on the south side: and he commanded their aqueduct to be cut off. Nevertheless there were springs not far from the walls, out of which they were seen secretly to draw water, to refresh themselves a little rather than to drink their fill. Then he placed all round about a hundred men at every spring. And when they had kept this watch for full twenty days, the cisterns, and the reserve of waters failed among all the inhabitants of Bethulia, so that there was not within the city, enough to satisfy them, no not for one day, for water was daily given out to the people by measure. Then all the men and women, young men, and children, gathering themselves together to Ozias, all together with one voice, said: God be judge between us and thee, for thou hast done evil against us, in that thou wouldst not speak peaceably with the Assyrians, and for this cause God hath sold us into their hands. And now assemble ye all that are in the city, that we may of our own accord yield ourselves all up to the people of Holofernes. Ozias rising up all in tears, said: Be of good courage, my brethren, and let us wait these five days for mercy from the Lord. For perhaps he will put a stop to his indignation, and will give glory to his own name. But if after five days be past there come no aid, we will do the things which you have spoken. Now Judith was a widow now three years and six months. And she made herself a private chamber in the upper part of her house, in which she abode shut up with her maids, and she wore haircloth upon her loins, and fasted all the days of her life, except the sabbaths, and new-moons, and the feasts of the house of Israel. And she was exceedingly beautiful, and her husband left her great riches, and very many servants, and large possessions of herds of oxen, and flocks of sheep. And she was greatly renowned among all, because she feared the Lord very much, neither was there any one that spoke an ill word of her. Now it came to pass, when Judith had heard these words she went into her oratory: and putting on hair-cloth, laid ashes on her head: and falling down prostrate before the Lord, she cried to the Lord. And it came to pass, when she had ceased to cry to the Lord, that she rose from the place wherein she lay prostrate before the Lord. And she called her maid, and going down into her house she took off her hair-cloth, and put away the garments of her widowhood, and she washed her body, and anointed herself with the best ointment, and plaited the hair of her head, and put a bonnet upon her head, and clothed herself with the garments of her gladness, and put sandals on her feet, and took her bracelets, and lilies, and earlets, and rings, and adorned herself with all her ornaments. And the Lord also gave her more beauty: because all this dressing up did not proceed from sensuality, but from virtue: and therefore the Lord increased this her beauty, so that she appeared to all men's eyes incomparably lovely. And she gave to her maid a bottle of wine to carry, and a vessel of oil, and parched corn, and dry figs, and bread and cheese, and went out. But Judith praying to the Lord, passed through the gates, she and her maid. And it came to pass, when she went down the hill, about break of day, that the watchmen of the Assyrians met her, and stopped her, saying: Whence comest thou? or whither goest thou? And she answered: I am a daughter of the Hebrews, and I am fled from them, because I knew they would be made a prey to you, because they despised you, and would not of their own accord yield themselves, that they might find mercy in your sight. And they brought her to the tent of Holofernes, telling him of her. And when she was come into his presence, forthwith Holofernes was caught by his eyes. And Judith said to him: Receive the words of thy handmaid, for if thou wilt follow the words of thy handmaid, the Lord will do with thee a perfect thing. For it is certain that our God is so offended with sins, that he hath sent word by his prophets to the people, that he will deliver them up for their sins. And because the children of Israel know they have offended their God, thy dread is upon them. And because God is angry with them, I am sent to tell these very things to thee. And all these words pleased Holofernes, and his servants, and they admired her wisdom, and they said one to another: There is not such another woman upon earth in look, in beauty, and in sense of words. Then he ordered that she should go in where his treasures were laid up, and bade her tarry there, and he appointed what should be given her from his own table. Judith answered him and said: Now I can not eat of these things which thou commandest to be given me, lest sin come upon me: but I will eat of the things which I have brought. Holofernes said to her: If these things which thou hast brought with thee, fail thee, what shall we do for thee? And Judith said: As thy soul liveth, my Lord, thy handmaid shall not spend all these things till God do by my hand that which I have purposed. And his servants brought her into the tent which he had commanded. Now when she was going in, she desired that she might have liberty to go out at night and before day to prayer, and to beseech the Lord. And he commanded his chamberlains, that she might go out and in, to adore her God as she pleased, for three days. And it came to pass on the fourth day, that Holofernes made a supper for his servants, and said to Vagao his eunuch: Go, and persuade that Hebrew woman, to consent of her own accord to dwell with me. And Judith answered him: Who am I, that I should gainsay my lord? All that shall be good and best before his eyes, I will do. And whatsoever shall please him, that shall be best to me all the days of my life. And she arose and dressed herself out with her garments, and going in she stood before his face. And the heart of Holofernes was smitten, and when it was grown late, his servants made haste to their lodgings, and Vagao shut the chamber-doors, and went his way. And they were all overcharged with wine. And Judith was alone in the chamber. But Holofernes lay on his bed, fast asleep, being exceedingly drunk. And Judith spoke to her maid to stand without before the chamber, and to watch: and Judith stood before the bed praying with tears, and the motion of her lips in silence. Then she went to the pillar that was at his bed's head, and loosed his sword that hung tied upon it. And when she had drawn it out, she took him by the hair of his head, and said: Strengthen me, O Lord God, at this hour. And she struck twice upon his neck, and cut off his head, and took off his canopy from the pillars, and rolled away his headless body. And after a while she went out, and delivered the head of Holofernes to her maid, and bade her put it into her wallet. And they two went out according to their custom, as it were to prayer, and they passed the camp, and having compassed the valley, they came to the gate of the city. And all ran to meet her from the least to the greatest: for they now had no hopes that she would come. And when all had held their peace, Judith said: Praise ye the Lord our God, who hath not forsaken them that hope in him. And that thou mayst find that it is so, behold the head of Holofernes, who in the contempt of his pride despised the God of Israel: and threatened thee with death. But after they had recovered their spirits they fell down at her feet, and reverenced her, and said: Blessed art thou by thy God in every tabernacle of Jacob, for in every nation which shall hear thy name, the God of Israel shall be magnified on occasion of thee. And immediately at break of day, they hung up the head of Holofernes upon the walls, and every man took his arms, and they went out with a great noise and shouting. And the watchmen seeing this, ran to the tent of Holofernes. But when with harkening, he perceived no motion of one lying, he came near to the curtain, and lifting it up, and seeing the body of Holofernes, lying upon the ground, without the head, weltering in his blood, he cried out with a loud voice, with weeping, and rent his garments. And he went into the tent of Judith, and not finding her, he run out to the people, and said: One Hebrew woman hath made confusion in the house of king Nabuchodonosor: for behold Holofernes lieth upon the ground, and his head is not upon him. And when all the army heard that Holofernes was beheaded, courage and counsel fled from them, and being seized with trembling and fear they thought only to save themselves by flight: so the children of Israel seeing them fleeing, followed after them. And they went down sounding with trumpets and shouting after them. And thirty days were scarce sufficient for the people of Israel to gather up the spoils of the Assyrians. And Joachim the high priest came from Jerusalem to Bethulia with all his ancients to see Judith. And when she was come out to him, they all blessed her with one voice, saying: Thou art the glory of Jerusalem, thou art the joy of Israel, thou art the honour of our people. And she abode in her husband's house a hundred and five years, and made her handmaid free, and she died, and was buried with her husband in Bethulia.

LESSON SIXTH.

ON SIN AND ITS KINDS.

Q. Is original sin the only kind of sin?

(Gal. 5.) Now the works of the flesh are manifest, which are fornication, uncleanness, immodesty, luxury, idolatry, witchcrafts, enmities, contentions, emulations, wraths, quarrels, dissensions, sects, envies, murders, drunkenness, revellings, and such like. Of the which I foretell you, as I have foretold to you, that they who do such things shall not obtain the kingdom of God.

Q. What is actual sin?
See "L. of C.," p. 59, No. 17.

(I. John 2.) Love not the world, nor the things which are in the world. If any man love the world, the charity of the

Father is not in him. For all that is in the world, is the concupiscence of the flesh, and the concupiscence of the eyes, and the pride of life, which is not of the Father, but is of the world. And the world passeth away, and the concupiscence thereof: but he that doth the will of God, abideth for ever.

Q. How many kinds of actual sin are there?

(I. Cor. 3.) Other foundation no man can lay, but that which is laid; which is Christ Jesus. Now if any man build upon this foundation, gold, silver, precious stones, wood, hay, stubble: every man's work shall be manifest; for the day of the Lord shall declare it, because it shall be revealed in fire; and the fire shall try every man's work, of what sort it is. If any man's work abide, which he hath built thereupon, he shall receive a reward. If any man's work burn, he shall suffer loss; but he himself shall be saved, yet so as by fire. Know you not, that you are the temple of God, and that the Spirit of God dwelleth in you? But if any man violate the temple of God, him shall God destroy. For the temple of God is holy, which you are.

Q. What is mortal sin?
See "L. of C.," p. 68, No. 37.

(James 1.) Every man is tempted by his own concupiscence, being drawn away and allured. Then when concupiscence hath conceived, it bringeth forth sin. But sin, when it is completed, begetteth death.

Q. Why is this sin called mortal?
See "L. of C.," p. 84, No. 13.

(I. John 5.) All iniquity is sin. And there is a sin unto death.

Q. How many things are necessary to make a sin mortal?

(Prov. 2.) They leave the right way, and walk by dark ways: who are glad when they have done evil, and rejoice in most wicked things: whose ways are perverse, and their steps infamous.

Q. What is venial sin?
See "L. of C.," p. 109, No. 4.

(Prov. 24.) A just man shall fall seven times and shall rise again: but the wicked shall fall down into evil.
(Eccltus. 19.) And he that contemneth small things, shall fall by little and little.

Q. Which are the effects of venial sin?
See "L. of C.," p. 110, No. 2; p. 111, No. 5.

(Eccltus. 19.) He that contemneth small things, shall fall by little and little.

Q. Which are the chief sources of sin?

(Gen. 11. A. M. 1800.) Now the earth was of one tongue, and of the same speech. And when they removed from the east, they found a plain in the land of Sennaar, and dwelt in it. And each one said to his neighbour: Come, let us make brick, and bake them with fire. And they had brick instead of stones, and slime instead of mortar. And they said: Come, let us make a city and a tower, the top whereof may reach to heaven: and let us make our name famous before we be scattered abroad into all lands. And the Lord came down to see the city and the tower, which the children of Adam were building. And he said: Behold, it is one people, and all have one tongue: and they have begun to do this, neither will they leave off from their designs, till they accomplish them in deed. Come ye, therefore, let us go down, and there confound their tongue, that they may not understand one another's speech. And so the Lord scattered them from that place into all lands, and they ceased to build the city. And therefore the name thereof was called Babel, because there the language of the whole earth was confounded: and from thence the Lord scattered them abroad upon the face of all countries.

(Eccltus. 5.) A covetous man shall not be satisfied with money; and he that loveth riches shall reap no fruit from them: so this also is vanity. Where there are great riches, there are also many to eat them. And what doth it profit the owner, but that he seeth the riches with his eyes? Sleep is sweet to a labouring man, whether he eat little or much: but the fulness of the rich will not suffer him to sleep. There is also another grievous evil, which I have seen under the sun: riches kept to the hurt of the owner. For they are lost with very great affliction: he hath begotten a son, who shall be in extremity of want. As he came forth naked from his mother's womb, so shall he return, and shall take nothing away with him of his labour. A most deplorable evil: as he came, so shall he return. What then doth it profit him that he hath laboured for the wind? All the days of his life he eateth in darkness, and in many cares, and in misery, and sorrow. This therefore hath seemed good to me, that a man should eat and drink, and enjoy the fruit of his labour, wherewith he hath laboured under the sun, all the days of his life, which God hath given him: and this is his portion. And every man to whom God hath given riches, and substance, and hath given him power to eat thereof, and to enjoy his portion, and to rejoice of his labour: this is the gift of God.

(Prov. 7.) She entangled him with many words, and drew him away with the flattery of her lips. Immediately he followeth her as an ox led to be a victim, and as a lamb playing the wanton, and not knowing that he is drawn like a fool to bonds. Till the arrow pierce his liver: as if a bird should make haste to the snare, and knoweth not that his life is in danger.

(Gen. 4. A. M. 2.) Abel was a shepherd, and Cain a husbandman. And it came to pass after many days, that Cain offered, of the fruits of the earth, gifts to the Lord. Abel also offered of the firstlings of his flock, and of their fat: and the Lord had respect to Abel, and to his offerings. But to Cain and his offerings he had no respect: and Cain was exceedingly angry, and his countenance fell. And the Lord said to him: Why art thou angry? and why is thy countenance fallen? If thou do well, shalt thou not receive? but if ill, shall not sin forthwith be present at the door? but the lust thereof shall be under thee, and thou shalt have dominion over it. And Cain said to Abel his brother: Let us go forth abroad. And when they were in the field, Cain rose up against his brother Abel, and slew him. And the Lord said to Cain: Where is thy brother Abel? And he answered, I know not: am I my brother's keeper? And he said to him: What hast thou done? the voice of thy brother's blood crieth to me from the earth. Now, therefore, cursed shalt thou be upon the earth, which hath opened her mouth and received the blood of thy brother at thy hand.

(Gen. 9. A. M. 1656.) Now the sons of Noe who came out of the ark, were Sem, Cham, and Japheth: and Cham is the father of Chanaan. These three are the sons of Noe: and from these was all mankind spread over the whole earth. And Noe, a husbandman began to till the ground, and planted a vineyard. And drinking of the wine was made drunk, and was uncovered in his tent. Which when Cham the father of Chanaan had seen, to wit, that his father's nakedness was uncovered, he told it to his two brethren without. But Sem and Japheth put a cloak upon their shoulders, and going backward, covered the nakedness of their father: and their faces were turned away, and they saw not their father's nakedness. And Noe awaking from the wine, when he had learned what his younger son had done to him, He said: Cursed be Chanaan, a servant of servants shall he be unto his brethren.

(Gen. 37. A. M. 2276.) Joseph, when he was sixteen years old, was feeding the flock with his brethren, being *but* a boy: and he was with the sons of Bala and of Zelpha his father's wives: and he accused his brethren to his father of a most wicked crime. Now Israel loved Joseph above all his sons, because he had him in his old age: and he made him a coat of divers colours. And his brethren seeing that he was loved by his father, more than all his sons, hated him, and could not speak peaceably to him. Now it fell out also that he told his brethren a dream, that he had dreamed: which occasioned them to hate him the more. And he said to them: Hear my dream which I dreamed. I thought we were binding sheaves in the field: and my sheaf arose as it were, and stood, and your sheaves standing about, bowed down before my sheaf. His brethren answered: Shalt thou be our king? or shall we be subject to thy dominion? Therefore this matter of his dreams and words ministered nourishment to *their* envy and hatred. And when his brethren abode in Sichem, feeding their father's flocks, Israel said to him: Thy brethren feed the sheep in Sichem: come, I will send thee to them. And when he answered: I am ready: he said to him: Go, and see if all things be well with thy brethren, and the cattle: and bring me word again what is doing. So being sent from the vale of Hebron, he came to Sichem: and when they saw him afar off, before he came nigh them, they thought to kill him. And said one to another: Behold the dreamer cometh. Come, let us kill him, and cast him into some old pit: and we will say: Some evil beast hath devoured him: and then it shall appear what his dreams avail him: and Ruben hearing this, endeavoured to deliver him out of their hands, and said: Do not take away his life, nor shed *his* blood: but cast him into this pit, that is in the wilderness, and keep your hands harmless; now he said this, being desirous to deliver him out of their hands and to restore him to his father. And as soon as he came to his brethren, they forthwith stript him of his outside coat, that was of divers colours: and cast him into an old pit, where there was no water. And Juda said to his brethren: what will it profit us to kill our brother, and conceal his blood? It is better that he be sold to the Ismaelites, and that our hands be not defiled: for he is our brother and our flesh. His brethren agreed to his words. And when the Madianite merchants passed by, they drew him out of the pit, and sold him to the Ismaelites, for twenty pieces of silver: and they led him into Egypt. And they took his coat, and dipped it in the blood of a kid, which they had killed: sending some to carry it to their father, and to say: This we have found: see whether it be thy son's coat, or not. And the father acknowledging it, said: It is my son's coat, an evil wild beast hath eaten him, a beast hath devoured Joseph. And tearing his garments, he put on sackcloth, mourning for his son a long time.

(Num. 21. A. M. 2253.) Now the people began to be weary of their journey and labour: and speaking against God and Moses, they said: Why didst thou bring us out of Egypt, to die in the wilderness? There is no bread, nor have we any waters: our soul now loatheth this very light food. Wherefore the Lord sent among the people fiery serpents, which bit them and killed many of them.

LESSON SEVENTH.

ON THE INCARNATION AND REDEMPTION.

Q. Did God abandon man after he fell into sin?

See "L. of C.," p. 89, No. 28.

(Gen. 3. A. M. 1.) The Lord God said to the serpent: Because thou hast done this thing, thou art cursed among all cattle, and beasts of the earth: upon thy breast shalt thou go, and earth shalt thou eat all the days of thy life. I will put enmities between thee and the woman, and thy seed and her seed: she shall crush thy head, and thou shalt lie in wait for her heel.

(Gen. 50. A. M. 2369.) Joseph returned into Egypt with his brethren, and all that were in his company, after he had buried his father. Now he being dead, his brethren were afraid, and talked one with another: Lest perhaps he should remember the wrong he suffered, and requite us all the evil that we did to him. And they sent a message to him, saying: Thy father commanded us before he died, that we should say thus much to thee from him: I beseech thee to forget the wickedness of thy brethren, and the sin and malice they practised against thee: we also pray thee, to forgive the servants of the God of thy father this wickedness. And when Joseph heard this, he wept. And his brethren came to him: and worshipping prostrate on the ground they said: We are thy servants. And he answered them: Fear not: can we resist the will of God? You thought evil against me: but God turned it into good, that he might exalt me, as at present you see, and might save many people. Fear not: I will feed you and your children. And he comforted them, and spoke gently and mildly.

(Ex. 2. A. M. 2433.) There went a man of the house of Levi; and took a wife of his own kindred. And she bore a son; and seeing him a goodly *child*, hid him three months. And when she could hide *him* no longer, she took a basket made of bulrushes, and daubed it with slime and pitch: and put the little babe therein, and laid him in the sedges by the river's brink, his sister standing afar off, and taking notice what would be done. And behold the daughter of Pharao came down to wash herself in the river: and her maids walked by the river's brink. And when she saw the basket in the sedges, she sent one of her maids for it: and when it was brought, she opened it and seeing within it an infant crying, having compassion on it she said: This is one of the babes of the Hebrews. And the child's sister said to her: Shall I go and call to thee a Hebrew woman, to nurse the babe? She answered: Go. The maid went and called her mother. And Pharao's daughter said to her: Take this child and nurse him for me: I will give thee thy wages. The woman took, and nursed the child: and when he was grown up, she delivered him to Pharao's daughter. And she adopted him for a son, and called him Moses, saying: Because I took him out of the water.

(I. Kings 25. A. M. 2947.) Now the name of the man was Nabal: and the name of his wife was Abigail. And when David heard in the wilderness, that Nabal was shearing his sheep, he sent ten young men, and said to them: Go up to Carmel, and go to Nabal, and salute him in my name with peace. And when David's servants came, they spoke to Nabal all these words in David's name: and then held their peace. But Nabal answering the servants of David, said: Who is David? and what is the son of Isai? servants are multiplied now a days who flee from their masters. So the servants of David went back their way, and returning came and told him all the words that he said. Then David said to his young men: Let every man gird on his sword. And they girded on every man his sword. And David also girded on his sword: and there followed David about four hundred men: and two hundred remained with the baggage. But one of the servants told Abigail the wife of Nabal, saying: Behold David sent messengers out of the wilderness, to salute our master: and he rejected them. These men were very good to us, and gave us no trouble: neither did we ever lose any thing all the time that we conversed with them in the desert. They were a wall unto us both by night and day, all the while we were with them keeping the sheep. Wherefore consider, and think what thou hast to do: for evil is determined against thy husband, and against thy house. Then Abigail made haste and coming down to the foot of the mountain, David and his men came down over-against her, and she met them. And she fell at his feet, and said: Upon me let this iniquity be, my Lord: let thy handmaid speak, I beseech, in thy ears: and hear the words of thy servant. This shall not be an occasion of grief to thee, and a scruple of heart to my lord, that thou hast shed innocent blood, or hast revenged thyself: and when the Lord shall have done well by my lord, thou shalt remember thy handmaid. And David said to Abigail: Blessed be the Lord the God of Israel, who sent thee this day to meet me, and blessed be thy speech: and blessed be thou, who hast kept me to-day, from coming to blood, and revenging me with my own hand.

Q. Who is the Redeemer?
See "L. of C.," p. 70, No. 1.

(Apoc. 19.) I saw heaven opened, and behold a white horse; and he that sat upon him was called faithful and true, and with justice doth he judge and fight. And his eyes were as a flame of fire, and on his head were many diadems, and he had a name written, which no man knoweth but himself. And he was clothed with a garment sprinkled with blood; and his name is called, The Word of God. And the armies that are in heaven followed him on white horses, clothed in fine linen, white and clean. And out of his mouth proceedeth a sharp two-edged sword; that with it he may strike the nations. And he shall rule them with a rod of iron; and he treadeth the wine-press of the fierceness of the wrath of God the Almighty. And he hath on his garment, and on his thigh written: King of Kings, and Lord of Lords. And I saw an Angel standing in the sun, and he cried with a loud voice, saying to all the birds that did fly through the midst of heaven: Come, gather yourselves together to the great supper of God: that you may eat the flesh of kings and the flesh of tribunes, and the flesh of mighty men, and the flesh of horses, and of them that sit on them, and the flesh of all freemen and bondmen, and of little and of great. And I saw the beast, and the kings of the earth, and their armies gathered together to make war with him that sat upon the horse, and with his army. And the beast was taken, and with him the false prophet, who wrought signs before him, wherewith he seduced them who received the character of the beast, and who adored his image. These two were cast alive into the pool of fire, burning with brimstone. And the rest were slain by the sword of him that sitteth upon the horse, which proceedeth out of his mouth; and all the birds were filled with their flesh.

(Gen. 42–45. A. M. 2296.) Jacob hearing that food was sold in Egypt, said to his sons: Go ye down, and buy us necessaries, that we may live, and not be consumed with want. So the ten brethren of Joseph went down, to buy corn in Egypt: whilst Benjamin was kept at home by Jacob. Now Joseph was governor in the land of Egypt, and corn was sold by his direction to the people. And when his brethren had bowed down to him, and he knew them, he spoke as it were to strangers somewhat roughly, asking them: Whence came you? They answered: From the land of Chanaan, to buy necessaries of life. And though he knew his brethren, he was not known by them. He saith: This is it that I say: You are spies. If you be peaceable men, let one of your brethren be bound in prison: and go ye your ways and carry the corn that you have bought, unto your houses. And bring your youngest brother to me, that I may find your words to be true, and you may not die. They did as he had said. And they talked one to another: We deserve to suffer these things, because we have sinned against our brother, seeing the anguish of his soul, when he besought us, and we would not hear: therefore is this affliction come upon us. And they knew not that Joseph understood, because he spoke to them by an interpreter. And he turned himself away a little while, and wept: and returning he spoke to them. And taking Simeon, and binding him in their presence, he commanded his servants to fill their sacks with wheat, and to put every man's money again in their sacks, and to give them besides provisions for the way: and they did so. And they came to Jacob their father in the land of Chanaan, and they told him all things that had befallen them. When they had told this, they poured out their corn, and every man found his money tied in the mouth of his sack: and all being astonished together, their father Jacob said: My son shall not go down with you: his brother is dead, and he is left alone: if any mischief befall him in the land to which you go, you will bring down my gray hairs with sorrow to hell. In the meantime the famine was heavy upon all the land. And Juda said to his father: Send the boy with me, that we may set forward, and may live: lest both we and our children perish. Then Israel said to them: If it must needs be so, do what you will: take of the best fruits of the land in your vessels, and carry down presents to the man. So the men took the presents, and double money, and Benjamin: and went down into Egypt, and stood before Joseph. And Joseph commanded the steward of his house, saying: Fill their sacks with corn, as much as they can hold: and put the money of every one in the top of his sack. And in the mouth of the younger's sack put my silver cup, and the price which he gave for the wheat. And it was so done. And when they were now departed out of the city, and had gone forward a little way; Joseph sending for the steward of his house, said: Arise, and pursue after the men: and when thou hast overtaken them, say to them: Why have you returned evil for good? The cup which you have stolen, is that in which my lord drinketh, and in which he is wont to divine: you have done a very evil thing. He did as he had commanded him. And having overtaken them, he spoke to them the same words. Which when he had searched, begining at the eldest and ending at the youngest, he found the cup in Benjamin's sack. And Juda at the head of his brethren went in to Joseph (for he was not yet gone out of the place) and they altogether fell down before him on the ground. And Juda said to him: What shall we answer my lord? or what shall we say, or be able justly to allege? God hath found out the iniquity of thy servants: behold, we are all bondmen to my lord, both we, and he with whom the cup was found. Joseph answered: God forbid that I should do so: he that stole the cup, he shall be my bondman: and go you away free to your father. Then Juda coming nearer, said boldly: I thy servant will stay instead of the boy in the service of my lord, and let the boy go up with his brethren. For I cannot return to my father without the boy, lest I be a witness of the calamity that will oppress my father. Joseph could no longer refrain himself before many that stood by: whereupon he commanded that all should go out, and no stranger be present at their knowing one another. And he lifted up his voice with weeping, which the Egyptians and all the house of Pharao heard. And he said to his brethren: I am Joseph: is my father yet living? His brethren could not answer him, being struck with exceeding great fear. And he said mildly to them: Come nearer to me. And when they were come near him, he said: I am Joseph, your brother, whom you sold into Egypt. And Joseph kissed all his brethren, and wept upon every one of them: after which they were emboldened to speak to him. And they went up out of Egypt, and came into the land of Chanaan to their father Jacob. And they told him, saying: Joseph thy son is living: and he is ruler in all the land of Egypt. Which when Jacob heard, he awaked as it were out of a deep sleep. And he said: It is enough for me, if Joseph my son be yet living: I will go and see him before I die.

(II. Kings 24. A. M. 2987.) When the angel of the Lord had stretched out his hand over Jerusalem to destroy it, the Lord had pity on the affliction, and said to the angel that slew the people: It is enough: now hold thy hand. And David said to the Lord, when he saw the angel striking the people: It is I, I am he that have sinned, I have done wickedly: these that are the sheep, what have they done? let thy hand, I beseech thee, be turned against me, and against my father's house. And Gad came to David that day, and said: Go up, and build an altar to the Lord in the thrashing floor of Areuna the Jebusite. And David went up according to the word of Gad which the Lord had commanded him. And Areuna said to David: Let my lord the king take, and offer, as it seemeth good to him: thou hast here oxen for a holocaust, and the wain, and the yokes of the oxen for wood. All these things Areuna as a king gave to the king: and Areuna said to the king: The Lord thy God receive thy vow. And the king answered him, and said: Nay, but I will buy it of thee at a price, and I will not offer to the Lord my God holocausts free-cost. So David bought the floor, and the oxen, for fifty sicles of silver: and David built there an altar to the Lord, and offered holocausts and peace-offerings: and the Lord became merciful to the land, and the plague was stayed from Israel.

Q. **What do you believe of Jesus Christ?**
See "L. of C.," p. 35, No. 25.

(Gen. 25. A. M. 2183.) Abraham gave all his possessions to Isaac. And to the children of the concubines he gave gifts, and separated them from Isaac his son, while he yet lived, to the east country.

(Gen. 28. A. M. 2252.) Jacob being departed from Bersabee, went on to Haran. And when he was come to a certain place, and would rest in it after sunset, he took of the stones that lay there, and putting under his head, slept in the same place. And he saw in his sleep a ladder standing upon the earth, and the top thereof touching heaven: the angels also of God ascending and descending by it. And the Lord leaning upon the ladder, saying to him: I am the Lord God of Abraham thy father, and the God of Isaac; The land, wherein thou sleepest, I will give to thee and to thy seed. And thy seed shall be as the dust of the earth: thou shalt spread abroad to the west, and to the east, and to the north, and to the south: and in thee and thy seed all the tribes of the earth shall be blessed. And I will be thy keeper whithersoever thou goest, and will bring thee back into this land: neither will I leave thee, till I shall have accomplished all that I have said.

(III. King 6. A. M. 3000.) Solomon made in the oracle two cherubims of olive-tree, of ten cubits in height. One wing of the cherub was five cubits, and the other wing of the cherub was five cubits: that is, in all ten cubits, from the extremity of one wing to the extremity of the other wing. The second cherub also was ten cubits: and the measure, and the work was the same in both the cherubims: that is to say, one cherub was ten cubits high, and in like manner the other cherub. And he set the cherubims in the midst of the inner temple: and the cherubims stretched forth their wings, and the wing of the one touched one wall, and the wing of the other cherub touched the other wall: and the other wings in the midst of the temple touched one another.

Q. Why is Jesus Christ true God?

See "L. of C.," p. 17, No. 1.

(Ex. 4. A. M. 2513.) Moses answered and said: They will not believe me, nor hear my voice, but they will say: The Lord hath not appeared to thee. Then he said to him: What is that thou holdest in thy hand? He answered: A rod. And the Lord said: Cast it down upon the ground. He cast it down, and it was turned into a serpent: so that Moses fled from it. And the Lord said: Put out thy hand and take it by the tail. He put forth his hand, and took hold of it, and it was turned into a rod. That they may believe, saith he, that the Lord God of their fathers, the God of Abraham, the God of Isaac, and the God of Jacob, hath appeared to thee. And the Lord said again: Put thy hand into thy bosom. And when he had put it into *his* bosom, he brought it forth leprous as snow. And he said: Put back thy hand into thy bosom. He put it back, and brought it out again, and it was like the other flesh. If they will not believe thee, saith he, nor hear the voice of the former sign, they will believe the word of the latter sign. But if they will not even believe these two signs, nor hear thy voice: take of the river water, and pour it out upon the dry land, and whatsoever thou drawest out of the river, shall be turned into blood.

(III. Kings 17. A. M. 3092.) Elias the Thesbite of the inhabitants of Galaad said to Achab: As the Lord liveth the God of Israel, in whose sight I stand, there shall not be dew nor rain these years, but according to the words of my mouth. And going, he dwelt by the torrent Carith, which is over-against the Jordan. And the ravens brought him bread and flesh in the morning, and bread and flesh in the evening, and he drank of the torrent. But after some time the torrent was dried up, for it had not rained upon the earth. Then the word of the Lord came to him, saying: Arise, and go to Sarephta of the Sidonians, and dwell there: for I have commanded a widow-woman there to feed thee. He arose, and went to Sarephta. And when he was come to the gate of the city, he saw the widow-woman gathering sticks, and he called her, and said to her: Give me a little water in a vessel, that I may drink. And when she was going to fetch it he called after her, saying: Bring me also, I beseech thee, a morsel of bread in thy hand. And she answered: As the Lord thy God liveth, I have no bread, but only a handful of meal in a pot, and a little oil in a cruse: behold I am gathering two sticks that I may go in and dress it, for me and my son, that we may eat it, and die. And Elias said to her: Fear not, but go, and do as thou hast said: but first make for me of the same meal a little hearth-cake, and bring it to me: and after make for thyself and thy son. For thus saith the Lord the God of Israel: The pot of meal shall not waste, nor the cruse of oil be diminished, until the day wherein the Lord will give rain upon the face of the earth. She went and did according to the word of Elias: and he eat, and she, and her house: and from that day the pot of meal wasted not, and the cruse of oil was not diminished, according to the word of the Lord, which he spoke in the hand of Elias. And it came to pass after this that the son of the woman, the mistress of the house, fell sick, and the sickness was very grievous, so that there was no breath left in him. And she said to Elias: What have I to do with thee, thou man of God? art thou come to me that my iniquities should be remembered, and that thou shouldst kill my son? And Elias said to her: Give me thy son. And he took him out of her bosom, and carried him into the upper chamber where he abode, and laid him upon his own bed. And he cried to the Lord, and said: O Lord my God, hast thou afflicted also the widow, with whom I am after a sort maintained, so as to kill her son? And he stretched, and measured himself upon the child three times, and cried to the Lord, and said: O Lord my God, let the soul of this child, I beseech thee, return into his body. And the Lord heard the voice of Elias: and the soul of the child returned into him, and he revived. And Elias took the child, and brought him down from the upper chamber to the house below, and delivered him to his mother, and said to her: Behold thy son liveth. And the woman said to Elias: Now, by this I know that thou art a man of God, and the word of the Lord in thy mouth is true.

Q. Why is Jesus Christ true man?

See "L. of C.," p. 42, No. 44.

(Jer. 31. A. M. 3406.) Thus saith the Lord: A voice was heard on high of lamentation, of mourning, and weeping, of Rachel weeping for her children, and refusing to be comforted for them, because they are not. Thus saith the Lord: Let thy voice cease from weeping, and thy eyes from tears: for there is a reward for thy work, saith the Lord: and they shall return out of the land of the enemy. And there is hope for thy last end, saith the Lord: and the children shall return to their own borders. How long wilt thou be dissolute in deliciousness, O wandering daughter? (for the Lord hath created a new thing upon the earth: A woman shall compass a man.)

Q. How many natures are there in Jesus Christ?

See "L. of C.," p. 25, No. 10; p. 56, Nos. 9, 10.

Q. Is Jesus Christ more than one person?

See "L. of C.," p. 91, No. 33.

Q. Was Jesus Christ always God?

See "L. of C.," p. 51, No. 12; p. 60, No. 18.

(Ex. 3. A. M. 2513.) Now Moses fed the sheep of Jethro his father-in-law, the priest of Madian: and he drove the flock to the inner parts of the desert, and came to the mountain of God, Horeb. And the Lord appeared to him in a flame of fire out of the midst of a bush: and he saw that the bush was on fire and was not burnt. And Moses said: I will go and see this great sight, why the bush is not burnt. And when the Lord saw that he went forward to see, he called to him out of the midst of the bush, and said: Moses, Moses. And he answered: Here I am. And he said: Come not nigh hither, put off the shoes from thy feet: for the place, whereon thou standest is holy ground. And he said: I am the God of thy father, the God of Abraham, the God of Isaac, and the God of Jacob. Moses hid his face: for he durst not look at God. And the Lord said to him: I have seen the affliction of my people in Egypt, and I have heard their cry because of the rigour of them that are over the works: and knowing their sorrow, I am come down to deliver them out of the hands of the Egyptians, and to bring them out of that land into a good and spacious land, into a land that floweth with milk and honey, to the places of the Chanaanite, and Hethite, and Amorrhite, and Pherezite, and Hevite, and Jebusite. For the cry of the children of Israel is come unto me: and I have seen their affliction, wherewith they are oppressed by the Egyptians. But come, and I will send thee to Pharao, that thou mayst bring forth my people the children of Israel out of Egypt.

Q. Was Jesus Christ always man?

(Gal. 4.) Now I say, as long as the heir is a child, he differeth nothing from a servant, though he be lord of all: but is under tutors and governors until the time appointed by the father: so we also, when we were children, were serving under the elements of the world. But when the fulness of the time was come, God sent his Son, made of a woman, made under the law: that he might redeem them who were under the law: that we might receive the adoption of sons. And because you are sons, God hath sent the Spirit of his Son into your hearts, crying: Abba, Father. Therefore now he is not a servant, but a son. And if a son, an heir also through God.

Q. What do you mean by the Incarnation?

See "L. of C.," p. 89, No. 29.

(Phil. 2.) Christ being in the form of God, thought it not robbery to be equal with God: but emptied himself, taking the form of a servant, being made in the likeness of men, and in habit found as a man.

Q. How was the Son of God made man?

See "L of C.," p. 8, No. 4; p. 10, No. 8.

(Ruth A. M. 2706.) In the days of one of the judges, when the judges ruled, there came a famine in the land. And a certain man of Bethlehem Juda, went to sojourn in the land of Moab with his wife and his two sons. And Elimelech the husband of Noemi died: and she remained with her sons. And they took wives of the women of Moab, of which one was called Orpha, and the other Ruth. And they dwelt there ten years. And they both died, to wit, Mahalon and Chelion: and the woman was left alone, having lost both her sons and her husband. And she arose to go from the land of Moab to her own country with both her daughters-in-law: she said to them: Go ye home to your mothers, the Lord deal mercifully with you, as you have dealt with the dead and with me. And she kissed them. And they lifted up their voice and began to weep, and to say: We will go on with thee to thy people. But she answered them: Return, my daughters, why come ye with me? And they lifted up their voice, and began to weep again: Orpha kissed her mother-in-law and returned: Ruth stuck close to her mother-in-law. And Ruth the Moabitess said to her mother-in-law: Be not against me, to desire that I should leave thee and depart: for whithersoever thou shalt go, I will go: and where thou shalt dwell, I also will dwell. Thy people *shall be* my people, and thy God my God. So Noemi came with Ruth the Moabitess her daughter-in-law, from the land of her sojournment: and returned into Bethlehem, in the beginning of the barley harvest. And Ruth the Moabitess said to her mother-in-law: If thou wilt, I will go into the field, and glean the ears of corn that escape the hands of the reapers. She went therefore. And it happened that the owner of that field was Booz, who was of the kindred of Elimelech. And Booz said to Ruth: Hear me, daughter, do not go to glean in any other field, and do not depart from this place: but keep with my maids. And she said: I have found grace in thy eyes, my lord, who hast comforted me and hast spoken to the heart of thy handmaid, who am not like to one of thy maids. And Booz commanded his servants, saying: If she would even reap with you, hinder her not: and let fall some of your handfuls of purpose, and leave them, that she may gather them without shame, and let no man rebuke her when she gathereth them. She gleaned therefore three bushels, which she took up and returned into the city, and showed it to her mother-in-law: moreover she brought out, and gave her of the remains of her meat, wherewith she had been filled. And when Booz had eaten, and drunk, and was merry, he went to sleep by the heap of sheaves, and she came softly and uncovering his feet, laid herself down. And he said to her: Who art thou? And she answered: I am Ruth thy handmaid: spread thy coverlet over thy servant, for thou art a near kinsman. And he said: Fear not therefore, but whatsoever thou shalt say to me I will do to thee. For all the people that dwell within the gates of my city, know that thou art a virtuous woman. Neither do I deny myself to be near of kin, but there is another nearer than I. Rest thou this night: and when morning is come, if he will take thee by the right of kindred, all is well: but if he will not, I will undoubtedly take thee, *as* the Lord liveth. And again he said: Spread thy mantle, wherewith thou art covered, and hold it with both hands. And when she spread it and held it, he measured six measures of barley, and laid it upon her. And she carried it and went into the city. Then Booz went up to the gate, and sat there. And when he had seen the kinsman going by, of whom he had spoken before, he said to him, calling him by his name: Turn aside for a little while, and sit down here. They sat down, and he spoke to the kinsman: Noemi, who is returned from the country of Moab, will sell a parcel of land that belonged to our brother Elimelech. When thou shalt buy the field at the woman's hand, thou must take also Ruth the Moabitess, who was the wife of the deceased: to raise up the name of thy kinsman in his inheritance. He answered: I yield up my right of next akin: for I must not cut off the posterity of my own family. Do thou make use of my privilege, which I profess I do willingly forego. Booz therefore took Ruth, and married her: and the Lord gave her to bear a son. And Noemi taking the child laid it in her bosom, and she carried it, and was a nurse unto it. And the women her neighbours, congratulated with her.

Q. Is the Blessed Virgin Mary truly the Mother of God.

See "I. of C.," p. 13, No 16; p. 38, No. 25; p. 64, No. 25; p. 116, No. 7.

(Num. 36. A. M. 2553.) Moses answered the children of Israel, and said by the command of the Lord: this is the law promulgated by the Lord touching the daughters of Salphaad: Let them marry to whom they will, only so that it be to men of their own tribe. Lest the possession of the children of Israel be mingled from tribe to tribe. For all men shall marry wives of their own tribe and kindred: and all women shall take husbands of the same tribe: that the inheritance may remain in the families, and that the tribes be not mingled one with another, but remain so, as they were separated by the Lord.

(III. Kings 2. A. M. 2000.) Adonias the son of Haggith came to Bethsabee the mother of Solomon. And she said to him: Is thy coming peaceable? he answered: Peaceable. And he added: I have a word to speak with thee. She said to him: Speak. And he said: I pray thee speak to king Solomon (for he cannot deny thee any thing) to give me Abisag the Sunamitess to wife. And Bethsabee said: Well, I will speak for thee to the king. Then Bethsabee came to king Solomon, to speak to him for Adonias: and the king arose to meet her, and bowed to her, and sat down upon his throne: and a throne was set for the king's mother, and she sat on his right hand. And she said to him: I desire one small petition of thee, do not put me to confusion. And the king said to her: My mother, ask: for I must not turn away thy face.

(Cant. 2.) Behold my beloved speaketh to me: Arise, make haste, my love, my dove, my beautiful one, and come. For winter is now past, the rain is over and gone. The flowers have appeared in our land, the time of pruning is come: the voice of the turtle is heard in our land: the fig-tree hath put forth her green figs: the vines in flower yield their sweet smell. Arise, my love, my beautiful one, and come.

(Isa. 7. A. M. 3262.) The Lork spoke to Achaz, saying: Ask thee a sign of the Lord thy God, either unto the depth of hell, or unto the height above. And Achaz said: I will not ask, and I will not tempt the Lord. And he said: Hear ye therefore, O house of David: Is it a small thing for you to be grievous to men, that you are grievous to my God also? Therefore the Lord himself shall give you a sign. Behold a virgin shall conceive, and bear a son, and his name shall be called Emmanuel.

Q. Did the Son of God become man immediately after the sin of our first parents?

See "L. of C.," p. 87. No. 22; p. 88. Nos. 24, 25.

(Heb. 9.) Jesus is not entered into the Holies made with hands, the patterns of the true: but into heaven itself, that he may appear now in the presence of God for us. Nor yet that he should offer himself often, as the high priest entereth into the Holies, every year with the blood of others: for then he ought to have suffered often from the beginning of the world: but now once at the end of ages, he hath appeared for the destruction of sin, by the sacrifice of himself. And as it is appointed unto men once to die, and after this the judgment: so also Christ was offered once to exhaust the sins of many; the second time he shall appear without sin to them that expect him unto salvation.

Q. How could they be saved who lived before the Son of God became man?

See "L. of C.," p. 15, No. 1.

(Gen. 21. A. M. 2113.) When Sara had seen the son of Agar the Egpytian playing with Isaac her son, she said to Abraham: Cast out this bondwoman, and her son: for the son of the bondwoman shall not be heir with my son Isaac. Abraham took this grievously for his son. And God said to him: Let it not seem grievous to thee for the boy, and for thy bondwoman: in all that Sara hath said to thee, hearken to her voice: for in Isaac shall thy seed be called. But I will make the son also of the bond-woman a great nation, because he is thy seed. So Abraham rose up in the morning, and taking bread and a bottle of water, put it upon her shoulder, and delivered the boy, and sent her away. And she departed, and wandered in the wilderness of Bersabee. And when the water in the bottle was spent, she cast the boy under one of the trees that were there. And she went her way, and sat overagainst him a great way off as far as a bow can carry, for she said: I will not see the boy die: and sitting over-against, she lifted up her voice and wept. And God heard the voice of the boy: and an angel of God called to Agar from heaven, saying: What art thou doing, Agar? fear not: for God hath heard the voice of the boy, from the place wherein he is. Arise, take up the boy, and hold him by the hand: for I will make him a great nation. And God opened her eyes: and she saw a well of water, and went and filled the bottle, and gave the boy to drink. And *God* was with him: and he grew and dwelt in the wilderness.

Q. On what day was the Son of God conceived and made man?

See "L. of C.," p. 8, No. 4.

Q. On what day was Christ born?

See "L. of C.," p. 10, No. 9.

(Mic. 5.) And thou, Bethlehem Ephrata, art a little one among the thousands of Juda: out of thee shall he come forth unto me that is to be the ruler in Israel: and his going forth *is* from the beginning, from the days of eternity.

Q. How long did Christ live on earth?

See "L. of C.," p. 12, No. 12; p. 13, Nos. 13, 15; p. 54, No. 2.

(Gen. 39. A. M. 2286.) Joseph was brought into Egypt, and Putiphar an eunuch of Pharao, chief captain of the army, an Egyptian, bought him of the Ismaelites, by whom he was brought. And the Lord was with him, and he was a prosperous man in all things: and he dwelt in his master's house, who knew very well that the Lord was with him, and made all that he did to prosper in his hand. And Joseph found favour in the sight of his master, and ministered to him: and being set over all by him, he governed the house committed to him, and all things that were delivered to him: and the Lord blessed the house of the Egyptian for Joseph's sake, and multiplied all his substance, both at home, and in the fields. Neither knew he any other thing, but the bread which he ate. And Joseph was of a beautiful countenance, and comely to behold.

Q. Why did Christ live so long on earth?

See "L. of C.," p. 23, No. 8; p. 25, No. 11; p. 27, No. 15; p. 47, No. 1; p. 53, No. 20.

LESSON EIGHTH.

ON OUR LORD'S PASSION, DEATH, RESURRECTION, AND ASCENSION.

Q. What did Jesus Christ suffer?

See "L. of C.," p. 52, No. 14; p. 97, No. 45; p. 99, No. 3; p. 108, Nos. 1, 2; p. 109, No. 3; p. 110, No. 1; p. 111, No. 6; p. 113, Nos. 3, 4; p. 114, No. 5; p. 115, Cpt. vii., Nos. 1, 2.

(Isa. 53.) He shall grow up as a tender plant before him, and as a root out of a thirsty ground: there is no beauty in him, nor comeliness: and we have seen him, and there was no sightliness, that we should be desirous of him: despised, and the most abject of men, a man of sorrows, and acquainted with infirmity: and his look *was* as it were hidden and despised, whereupon we esteemed him not. Surely he hath borne our infirmities and carried our sorrows: and we have thought him as it were a leper, and as one struck by God and afflicted. But he was wounded for our iniquities, he was bruised for our sins: the chastisement of our peace *was* upon him, and by his bruises we are healed. All we like sheep have gone astray, every one hath turned aside into his own way: and the Lord hath laid on him the iniquity of us all. He was offered because it was his own will, and he opened not his mouth: he shall be led as a sheep to the slaughter, and shall be dumb as a lamb before his shearer, and he shall not open his mouth. He was taken away from distress, and from judgment: who shall declare his generation? because he is cut off out of the land of the living: for the wickedness of my people have I struck him.

Q. On what day did Christ die?

See "L. of C.," p. 116, No. 8.

Q. Why do you call that day "good" on which Christ died so sorrowful a death?

See "L. of C.," p. 59, No. 16.

(Num. 20. A. M. 2252.) The children of Israel, and all the multitude came into the desert of Sin, in the first month: and the people abode in Cades. And Mary died there, and was buried in the same place. And the people wanting water, came together against Moses and Aaron: and making a sedition, they said: Would God we had perished among our brethren before the Lord. Moses therefore took the rod, which was before the Lord, as he had commanded him, and having gathered together the multitude before the rock, he said to them: Hear, ye rebellious and incredulous: Can we bring you forth water out of this rock? When Moses had lifted up his hand, and struck the rock twice with the rod, there came forth water in great abundance, so that the people and their cattle drank.

Q. Where did Christ die?

See "L. of C.," p. 115, Cpt. vii., No. 1.

Q. How did Christ die?

See "L. of C." p. 87, No. 21; p. 115, Cpt. vii., Nos. 2, 3; p. 116, Nos. 4-8.

(Num. 21. A. M. 2553.) The Israelites marched from mount Hor, by the way that leadeth to the Red Sea, to compass the land of Edom. And the people began to be weary of their journey and labour: and speaking against God and Moses, they said: Why didst thou bring us out of Egypt, to die in the wilderness? There is no bread, nor have we any waters: our soul now loatheth this very light food. Wherefore the Lord sent among the people fiery serpents, which bit them and killed many of them. Upon which they came to Moses, and said: We have sinned, because we have spoken against the Lord and thee; pray that he may take away these serpents from us. And Moses prayed for the people. And the Lord said to him: Make a brazen serpent, and set it up for a sign: whosoever being struck shall look on it, shall live. Moses therefore made a brazen serpent, and set it up for a sign: which when they that were bitten looked upon, they were healed.

(Josh. 10. A. M. 2553.) Then Josue spoke to the Lord, in the day that he delivered the Amorrhite in the sight of the children of Israel, and he said before them: Move not, O sun, toward Gabaen, nor thou, O moon, toward the valley of Ajalon. And the sun and the moon stood still, till the people revenged themselves of their enemies. Is not this written in the book of the just? So the sun stood still in the midst of heaven, and hasted not to go down the space of one day. There was not before nor after so long a day, the Lord obeying the voice of a man, and fighting for Israel.

Q. Why did Christ suffer and die?

See "L. of C.," p. 70, No. 3.

(Gen. 22. A. M. 2135.) After these things, God tempted Abraham, and said to him: Abraham, Abraham. And he answered: Here I am. He said to him: Take thy only begotten son Isaac, whom thou lovest, and go into the land of vision: and there thou shalt offer him for an holocaust upon one of mountains which I will shew thee. So Abraham rising up in the night, saddled his ass: and took with him two young men, and Isaac his son: and when he had cut wood for the holocaust he went his way to the place which God had commanded him. And on the third day, lifting up his eyes, he saw the place afar off. And he said to his young men: Stay you here with the ass: I and the boy will go with speed as far as yonder, and after we have worshipped, will return to you. And he took the wood for the holocaust, and laid it upon Isaac his son and he himself carried in his hands fire and a sword. And as they two went on together, Isaac said to his father: My father. And he answered: What wilt thou, son? Behold, saith he, fire and wood: where is the victim for the holocaust? And Abraham said: God will provide himself a victim for an holocaust, my son. So they went on together. And they came to the place which God had shewn him, where he built an altar, and laid the wood in order upon it: and when he had bound Isaac his son, he laid him on the altar upon the pile of wood. And he put forth his hand and took the sword, to sacrifice his son. And behold an Angel of the Lord from heaven called to him, saying: Abraham, Abraham. And he answered: Here I am. And he said to him: Lay not thy hand upon the boy, neither do thou anything to him: now I know that thou fearest God, and hast not spared thy only begotten son for my sake. Abraham lifted up his eyes, and saw behind his back a ram amongst the briars sticking fast by the horns, which he took and offered for a holocaust instead of his son.

(Ex. 17.) So the people were thirsty there for want of water, and murmured against Moses, saying: Why didst thou make us go forth out of Egypt, to kill us and our children, and our beasts with thirst? And Moses cried to the Lord, saying: What shall I do to this people? Yet a little more and they will stone me. And the Lord said to Moses: Go before the people, and take with thee of the ancients of Israel: and take in thy hand the rod wherewith thou didst strike the river, and go. Behold I will stand there before thee, upon the rock Horeb: and thou shalt strike the rock, and water shall come out of it that the people may drink. Moses did so before the ancients of Israel.

(IV. Kings 6. A. M. 3116.) The sons of the prophets said to Eliseus: Behold the place where we dwell with thee is too strait for us. Let us go as far as the Jordan and take out of the wood every man a piece of timber, that we may build us there a place to dwell in. And he said: Go. And one of them said: But come thou also with thy servants. He answered: I will come. So he went with them. And when they were come to the Jordan they cut down wood. And it happened, as one was felling some timber, that the head of the axe fell into the water: and he cried out, and said: Alas, alas, alas, my lord, for this same was borrowed. And the man of God said: Where did it fall? and he shewed him the place. Then he cut off a piece of wood, and cast it in thither: and the iron swam.

Q. What lessons do we learn from the sufferings and death of Christ?

See "L. of C.," p. 78, No. 22.

(Titus 2.) The grace of God our Saviour hath appeared to all men; instructing us, that, denying ungodliness and worldly desires, we should live soberly, and justly, and godly in this world, looking for the blessed hope and coming of the glory of the great God and our Saviour Jesus Christ, who gave himself for us, that he might redeem us from all iniquity, and might cleanse to himself a people acceptable, a pursuer of good works.

Q. Whither did Christ's soul go after His Death?

(Apoc. 6. A. D. 64.) When he had opened the fifth seal, I saw under the altar the souls of them that were slain for the word of God, and for the testimony which they held. And they cried with a loud voice, saying: How long, O Lord (holy and true) dost thou not judge and revenge our blood on them that dwell on the earth? And white robes were given to every one of them one; and it was said to them, that they should rest for a little time, till their fellow-servants, and their brethren, who are to be slain, even as they, should be filled up.

Q. Did Christ's soul descend into the hell of the damned?

See "L. of C.," p. 126, No. 25.

Q. Why did Christ descend into Limbo?

(Apoc. 7.) One of the ancients answered, and said to me: These that are clothed in white robes, who are they? and whence came they? And I said to him: My Lord, thou knowest. And he said to me: These are they who are come out of great tribulation, and have washed their robes, and have made them white in the blood of the Lamb. Therefore they are before the throne of God, and they serve him day and night in his temple: and he, that sitteth on the throne, shall dwell over them. They shall no more hunger nor thirst, neither shall the sun fall on them, nor any heat. For the Lamb, which is in the midst of the throne, shall rule them, and shall lead them to the fountains of the waters of life, and God shall wipe away all tears from their eyes.

Q. Where was Christ's body while his soul was in Limbo?
See "L. of C.," p. 117, No. 10.

Q. On what day did Christ rise from the dead?
See "L. of C.," p. 118, No. 11; p. 119, No. 1.

(Zach. 3. A. M. 3485.) The Lord shewed me Jesus the high priest standing before the Angel of the Lord: and satan stood on his right hand to be his adversary. And the Lord said to satan: The Lord rebuke thee, O satan: and the Lord that chose Jerusalem rebuke thee: Is not this a brand pluckt out of the fire? And Jesus was clothed with filthy garments: and he stood before the face of the Angel. Who answered, and said to them that stood before him, saying: Take away the filthy garments from him. And he said to him: Behold I have taken away thy iniquity, and have clothed thee with change of garments. And he said: Put a clean mitre upon his head: and they put a clean mitre upon his head, and clothed him with garments.

Q. How long did Christ stay on earth after His resurrection?
See "L. of C.," p. 119, No. 2; p. 120, Nos. 3, 4; p. 121, No. 7; p. 122, Nos. 9, 10; p. 124, Nos. 14-16; p. 128, No. 28.

Q. After Christ had remained forty days on earth whither did He go?
See "L. of C.," p. 124, No. 18; p. 125, Nos. 19, 20.

(Gen. 47. A. M. 2300.) Then Joseph went in and told Pharao, saying: My father and brethren, their sheep and their herds, and all that they possess, are come out of the land of Chanaan: and behold they stay in the land of Gessen. Five men also the last of his brethren, he presented before the king: and he asked them: What is your occupation? They answered: We thy servants are shepherds, both we, and our fathers. We are come to sojourn in thy land, because there is no grass for the flocks of thy servants, the famine being very grievous in the land of Chanaan: and we pray thee to give orders that we thy servants may be in the land of Gessen. The king therefore said to Joseph: Thy father and thy brethren are come to thee. The land of Egypt is before thee: make them dwell in the best place, and give them the land of Gessen. And if thou knowest that there are industrious men among them, make them rulers over my cattle.

Q. Where is Christ in heaven?

(Acts 7. A. D. 33.) Stephen, full of grace and fortitude, did great wonders and signs among the people, saying: You stiff-necked and uncircumcised in heart and ears, you always resist the Holy Ghost: as your fathers *did*, so *do* you also. Which of the prophets have not your fathers persecuted? And they have slain them who foretold of the coming of the Just One; of whom you have been now the betrayers and murderers: who have received the law by the disposition of Angels, and have not kept it. Now hearing these things, they were cut to the heart, and they gnashed with their teeth at him. But he, being full of the Holy Ghost, looking up steadfastly to heaven, saw the glory of God, and Jesus standing on the right hand of God. And he said: Behold, I see the heavens opened, and the Son of man standing on the right hand of God. And they crying out with a loud voice, stopped their ears, and with one accord ran violently upon him. And casting him forth without the city, they stoned him; and the witnesses laid down their garments at the feet of a young man, whose name was Saul. And they stoned Stephen, invoking and saying: Lord Jesus, receive my spirit. And falling on his knees, he cried with a loud voice, saying: Lord, lay not this sin to their charge. And when he had said this, he fell asleep in the Lord. And Saul was consenting to his death.

Q. What do you mean by saying that Christ sits at the right hand of God?

See "L. of C.," p. 111, No 7.

LESSON NINTH.

ON THE HOLY GHOST AND HIS DESCENT UPON THE APOSTLES.

Q. Who is the Holy Ghost?

(Rom. 5.) Being justified therefore by faith, let us have peace with God, through our Lord Jesus Christ: by whom also we have access through faith into this grace, wherein we stand, and glory in the hope of the glory of the sons of God. And not only so; but we glory also in tribulations, knowing that tribulation worketh patience; and patience trial; and trial hope; and hope confoundeth not: because the charity of God is poured forth in our hearts, by the Holy Ghost, who is given to us.

Q. From whom does the Holy Ghost proceed?
See "L. of C.," p. 105, No. 7.

Q. Is the Holy Ghost equal to the Father and the Son?
(I. John 5.) It is the Spirit which testifieth, that Christ is the truth. And there are three who give testimony in heaven, the Father, the Word, and the Holy Ghost. And these three are one.

Q. On what day did the Holy Ghost come down upon the Apostles?
See "L. of C.," p. 125, No. 23.

Q. How did the Holy Ghost come down upon the Apostles?
See "L. of C.," p. 125, No. 23.

Q. Who sent the Holy Ghost upon the Apostles?
(Gen. 50. A. M. 2369.) Joseph returned into Egypt with his brethren, and all that were in his company, after he had buried his father. After which he told his brethren: God will visit you after my death, and will make you go up out of this land, to the land which he swore to Abraham, Isaac, and Jacob.

Q. Why did Christ send the Holy Ghost?
(Isa. 60.) Arise, be enlightened, O Jerusalem: for thy light is come, and the glory of the Lord is risen upon thee. For behold darkness shall cover the earth, and a mist the people: but the Lord shall arise upon thee, and his glory shall be seen upon thee. And the Gentiles shall walk in thy light, and kings in the brightness of thy rising. Iniquity shall no more be heard in thy land, wasting nor destruction in thy borders, and salvation shall possess thy walls, and praise thy gates. Thou shalt no more have the sun for thy light by day, neither shall the brightness of the moon enlighten thee: but the Lord shall be unto thee for an everlasting light and thy God for thy glory. Thy sun shall go down no more, and thy moon shall not decrease: for the Lord shall be unto thee for an everlasting light, and the days of thy mourning shall be ended. And thy people *shall be* all just, they shall inherit the land for ever, the branch of my planting, the work of my hand to glorify *me*. The least shall become a thousand, and a little one a most strong nation: I the Lord will suddenly do this thing in its time.

(Ezek. 34. A. M. 3417.) The word of the Lord came to me, saying: Son of man, prophesy concerning the shepherds of Israel: prophesy, and say to the shepherds: Thus saith the Lord God: Wo to the shepherds of Israel, that fed themselves: should not the flocks be fed by the shepherds? The weak you have not strengthened, and that which was sick you have not healed, that which was broken you have not bound up, and that which was driven away you have not brought again, neither have you sought that which was lost: but you ruled over them with rigour, and with a high hand. And my sheep were scattered, because there was no shepherd: and they became the prey of all the beasts of the field, and were scattered. My sheep have wandered in every mountain, and in every high hill: and my flocks were scattered upon the face of the earth, and there was none that sought them, there was none, I say, that sought them. But thus saith the Lord God: Behold I myself will seek my sheep, and will visit them. As the shepherd visiteth his flock in the day when he shall be in the midst of his sheep that were scattered, so will I visit my sheep, and will deliver them out of all the places where they have been scattered in the cloudy and dark day. And I will bring them out from the peoples, and will gather them out of the countries, and will bring them to their own land: and I will feed them in the mountains of Israel, by the rivers, and in all the habitations of the land. I will feed them in the most fruitful pastures, and their pastures shall be in the high mountains of Israel: there shall they rest on the green grass, and be fed in fat pastures upon the mountains of Israel. I will feed my sheep: and I will cause them to lie down, saith the Lord God. I will seek that which was lost: and that which was driven away, I will bring again: and I will bind up that which was broken, and I will strengthen that which was weak, and that which was fat and strong I will preserve: and I will feed them in judgment.

Q. Will the Holy Ghost abide with the Church for ever?

See " L. of C.," p. 103, No. 2.

LESSON TENTH.

ON THE EFFECTS OF THE REDEMPTION.

Q. Which are the chief effects of the Redemption?

(Titus 2.) The grace of God our Saviour hath appeared to all men; instructing us, that, denying ungodliness and worldly desires, we should live soberly, and justly, and godly in this world, looking for the blessed hope and coming of the glory of the great God and our Saviour Jesus Christ, who gave himself for us, that he might redeem us from all iniquity, and might cleanse to himself a people acceptable, a pursuer of good works.

Q. What do you mean by grace?

See "L. of C.," p. 21, No 6.

Q. How many kinds of grace are there?

(Ezek. 36.) I will give you a new heart, and put a new spirit within you: and I will take away the stony heart out of your flesh, and will give you a heart of flesh. And I will put my spirit in the midst of you: and I will cause you to walk in my commandments, and to keep my judgments, and do them.

Q. What is sanctifying grace?

See "L. of C.," p. 104, No. 4.

Q. What do you call those graces or gifts of God by which we believe in Him, hope in Him, and love Him?

See "L. of C.," p. 45, No. 50.

(Rom. 5.) Being justified by faith, let us have peace with God, through our Lord Jesus Christ: by whom also we have access through faith into this grace, wherein we stand, and glory in the hope of the glory of the sons of God. And not only so; but we glory also in tribulations, knowing that tribulation worketh patience; and patience trial; and trial hope; and hope confoundeth not: because the charity of God is poured forth in our hearts, by the Holy Ghost, who is given to us.

Q. What is Faith?

See "L. of C.," p. 35, No. 23; p. 42, Nos. 42, 45; p. 76, No. 17.

(Heb. 11.) Now faith is the substance of things to be hoped for, the evidence of things that appear not.

(James 2.) What shall it profit, my brethren, if a man say he hath faith, but hath not works? Shall faith be able to save him? And if a brother or sister be naked, and want daily food: and one of you say to them: Go in peace, be ye warmed and filled; yet give them not those things that are necessary for the body, what shall it profit? So faith also, if it have not works, is dead in itself. But some man will say: Thou hast faith, and I have works: shew me thy faith without works; and I will shew thee, by works, my faith. Thou believest that there is one God. Thou dost well: the devils also believe and tremble.

(Josh. 2. A. M. 2553.) Josue the son of Nun sent from Setim two men, to spy secretly: and said to them: Go, and view the land and the city of Jericho. They went and entered into the house of a woman named Rahab, and lodged with her. And the king of Jericho sent to Rahab, saying: Bring forth the men that came to thee, and are entered into thy house: for they are spies, and are come to view all the land. And the woman taking the men, hid them, and said: I confess they came to me, but I knew not whence they were: And at the time of shutting the gate in the dark, they also went out together. I know not whither they are gone: pursue after them quickly, and you will overtake them. Now the men that were hidden were not yet asleep, when behold the woman went up to them, and said: I know that the Lord hath given this land to you: for the dread of you is fallen upon us, and all the inhabitants of the land have lost all strength. Now therefore swear ye to me by the Lord, that as I have shewn mercy to you, so you also will shew mercy to my father's house: and give me a true token, that you will save my father and mother, my brethren and sisters, and all things that are theirs, and deliver our souls from death. And they said to her: We shall be blameless of this oath, which thou hast made us swear: if when we come into the land, this scarlet cord be a sign, and thou tie it in the window, by which thou hast let us down: and gather together thy father and mother, and brethren and all thy kindred into thy house. Whosoever shall go out of the door of thy house, his blood shall be upon his own head, and we shall be quit. But the blood of all that shall be with thee in the house, shall light upon our head, if any man touch them. But if thou wilt betray us, and utter this word abroad, we shall be quit of this oath which thou hast made us swear. And she answered: As you have spoken, so be it done. And sending them on their way, she hung the scarlet cord in the window.

Q. What is Hope?

(Rom. 8.) We are saved by hope. But hope that is seen, is not hope. For what a man seeth, why doth he hope for? But if we hope for that which we see not, we wait for it with patience. What shall we then say to these things? If God be for us, who is against us? He that spared not even his own Son, but delivered him up for us all, how hath he not also, with him, given us all things?

Q. What is Charity?

(I. Cor. 13.) If I speak with the tongues of men, and of angels, and have not charity, I am become as sounding brass, or a tinkling cymbal. And if I should have prophecy and should know all mysteries, and all knowledge, and if I should have all faith, so that I could remove mountains, and have not charity, I am nothing. And if I should distribute all my goods to feed the poor, and if I should deliver my body to be burned, and have not charity, it profiteth me nothing. Charity is patient, is kind: charity envieth not, dealeth not perversely; is not puffed up; is not ambitious, seeketh not her own, is not provoked to anger, thinketh no evil; rejoiceth not in iniquity, but rejoiceth with the truth; beareth all things, believeth all things, hopeth all things, endureth all things. Charity never falleth away: whether prophecies shall be made void, or tongues shall cease, or knowledge shall be destroyed. For we know in part, and we prophesy in part. But when that which is perfect is come, that which is in part shall be done away. When I was a child, I spoke as a child, I understood as a child, I thought as a child. But, when I became a man, I put away the things of a child. We see now through a glass in a dark manner; but then face to face. Now I know in part; but then I shall know even as I am known. And now there remain faith, hope, charity, these three; but the greater of these is charity.

(IV. Kings 2. A. M. 3108.) It came to pass, when the Lord would take up Elias into heaven by a whirlwind, that Elias and Eliseus were going from Galgal. And Elias said to him: Stay here, because the Lord hath sent me as far as the Jordan. And he said: As the Lord liveth, and as thy soul liveth, I will not leave thee; and they two went on together. Soon they two stood by the Jordan. And Elias took his mantle and folded it together, and struck the waters, and they were divided hither and thither, and they both passed over on dry ground. And when they were gone over, Elias said to Eliseus: Ask what thou wilt have me to do for thee, before I be taken away from thee. And Eliseus said: I beseech thee that in me may be thy double spirit. And as they went on, walking and talking together, behold a fiery chariot, and fiery horses parted them both asunder: and Elias went up by a whirlwind into heaven. And Eliseus took up the mantle of Elias, that fell from him: and going back, he stood upon the bank of the Jordan, and he struck the waters with the mantle of Elias, that had fallen from him, and they were not divided. And he said: Where is now the God of Elias? And he struck the waters, and they were divided, hither and thither, and Eliseus passed over.

Q. **What is actual grace?**
See "L. of C.," p. 50, No. 9.

Q. **Is grace necessary to salvation?**
(Ex. 5. A. M. 2513.) Pharao commanded the same day the overseers of the works, and the task-masters of the people, saying: You shall give straw no more to the people to make brick, as before: but let them go and gather straw. And you shall lay upon them the task of

bricks, which they did before, neither shall you diminish any thing thereof: for they are idle, and therefore they cry, saying: Let us go and sacrifice to our God. Let them be oppressed, with works, and let them fulfil them: that they may not regard lying words.

Q. Can we resist the grace of God?

(I. Kings 5. A. M. 2888.) The Philistines took the ark of God and brought it into the temple of Dagon, and set it by Dagon. And when the Azotians arose early the next day, behold Dagon lay upon his face on the ground before the ark of the Lord: and they took Dagon, and set him again in his place. And the next day again, when they arose in the morning, they found Dagon lying upon his face on the earth before the ark of the Lord: and the head of Dagon, and both the palms of his hands were cut off upon the threshold: and only the stump of Dagon remained in its place. For this cause neither the priests of Dagon, nor any that go into the temple tread on the threshold of Dagon in Azotus unto this day. And the hand of the Lord was heavy upon the Azotians, and he destroyed them. And while they were carrying it about, the hand of the Lord came upon every city with an exceeding great slaughter: and he smote the men of every city, both small and great, and they had emerods.

And the Gethrites consulted together. Therefore they sent the ark of God into Accaron. And when the ark of God was come into Accaron, the Accaronites cried out, saying: They have brought the ark of the God of Israel to us, to kill us and our people. They sent therefore and gathered together all the lords of the Philistines: and they said: Send away the ark of the God of Israel, and let it return into its own place, and not kill us and our people. For there was the fear of death in every city, and the hand of God was exceeding heavy.

(I. Kings 19. A. M. 2944.) David fled and escaped, and came to Samuel in Ramatha, and told him all that Saul had done to him: and he and Samuel went and dwelt in Najoth. And it was told Saul by some, saying: Behold David is in Najoth in Ramatha. So Saul sent officers to take David: and when they saw a company of prophets prophesying, and Samuel presiding over them, the Spirit of the Lord came also upon them, and they likewise began to prophesy. And when this was told Saul, he sent other messengers: but they also prophesied. And again Saul sent messengers the third time: and they prophesied also. And Saul being exceedingly angry, went also himself to Ramatha, and came as far as the great cistern, which is in Socho, and he asked, and said: In what place are Samuel and David?

And it was told him: Behold they are in Najoth in Ramatha. And he went to Najoth, in Ramatha, and the Spirit of the Lord came upon him also, and he went on, and prophesied till he came to Najoth in Ramatha.

(Isa. 6. A. M. 3246.) One of the Seraphims flew to me, and in his hand was a live coal, which he had taken with the tongs off the altar. And he touched my mouth, and said: Behold this hath touched thy lips, and thy iniquities shall be taken away, and thy sin shall be cleansed. And I heard the voice of the Lord, saying: Whom shall I send? and who shall go for us? And I said: Lo, here am I, send me. And he said: Go, and thou shalt say to this people: Hearing hear, and understand not: and see the vision, and know it not. Blind the heart of this people, and make their ears heavy, and shut their eyes: lest they see with their eyes, and hear with their ears, and understand with their heart, and be converted and I heal them.

(Jonas A. M. 3179.) Now the word of the Lord came to Jonas the son of Amathi, saying: Arise, and go to Ninive the great city, and preach in it: for the wickedness thereof is come up before me. And Jonas rose up to flee into Tharsis from the face of the Lord, and he went down to Joppe, and found a ship going to Tharsis: and he paid the fare thereof, and went down into it, to go with them to Tharsis from the face of the Lord. But the Lord sent a great wind into the sea: and a great tempest was raised in the sea, and the ship was in danger to be broken. And the mariners were afraid, and the men cried to their god: and they cast forth the wares that were in the ship, into the sea, to lighten it of them: and Jonas went down into the inner part of the ship, and fell into a deep sleep. And the ship-master came to him, and said to him: Why art thou fast asleep? rise up, call upon thy God, if so be that God will think of us, that we may not perish. And they said every one to his fellow: Come, and let us cast lots, that we may know why this evil is upon us. And they cast lots, and the lot fell upon Jonas. And he said to them: Take me up, and cast me into the sea, and the sea shall be calm to you: for I know that for my sake this great tempest is upon you. And they took Jonas, and cast him into the sea, and the sea ceased from raging. Now the Lord prepared a great fish to swallow up Jonas: and Jonas was in the belly of the fish three days and three nights. And Jonas prayed to the Lord his God out of the belly of the fish. And the Lord spoke to the fish: and it vomited out Jonas upon the dry land. And Jonas arose, and went to Ninive, according to the word of the Lord: now Ninive was a great city of three days' journey. And Jonas began to enter into the city one day's journey: and he cried, and said: Yet forty days, and Ninive shall be destroyed. And the men of Ninive believed in God: and they proclaimed a fast, and put on sackcloth from the greatest to the least. And the word came to the king of Ninive; and he rose up out of his throne, and cast away his robe from him, and was clothed with sackcloth, and sat in ashes. And God saw their works, that they were turned from their evil way: and God had mercy with regard to the evil which he had said that he would do to them, and he did it not. And Jonas was exceedingly troubled, and was angry: and the Lord said: Dost thou think thou hast reason to be angry? Then Jonas went out of the city, and sat toward the east side of the city: and he made himself a booth there, and he sat under it in the shadow, till he might see what would befall the city. And the Lord God prepared an ivy, and it came up over the head of Jonas, to be a shadow over his head, and to cover him (for he was fatigued): and Jonas was exceeding glad of the ivy. But God prepared a worm, when the morning arose on the following day: and it struck the ivy and it withered. And when the sun was risen, the Lord commanded a hot and burning wind: and the sun beat upon the head of Jonas, and he broiled with the heat: and he desired for his soul that he might die, and said: It is better for me to die than to live. And the Lord said to Jonas: Dost thou think thou hast reason to be angry, for the ivy? And he said: I am angry with reason even unto death. And the Lord said: Thou art grieved for the ivy, for which thou hast not laboured, nor made it to grow, which in one night came up, and in one night perished. And shall not I spare Ninive, that great city, in which there are more than a hundred and twenty thousand persons that know not how to distinguish between their right hand and their left.

Q. What is the grace of perseverance?

See "L. of C.," p. 64, No. 24.

(Gen. 48. A. M. 2315.) Joseph set Ephraim on his right hand, that is, towards the left hand of Israel; but Manasses on his left hand, to wit, towards his father's right hand, and brought them near to him. But he stretching forth his right hand, put it upon the head of Ephraim the younger brother; and the left upon the head of Manasses who was the elder, changing his hands. And Jacob blessed the sons of Joseph, and said: God, in whose sight my fathers Abraham and Isaac walked, God that feedeth me from my youth until this day; the angel that delivereth me from all evils, bless these boys: and let my name be called upon them, and the names of my fathers Abraham, and Isaac, and may they grow into a multitude upon the earth. And Joseph seeing that his father had put his right hand upon the head of Ephraim, was much displeased: and taking his father's hand he tried to lift it from Ephraim's head, and to remove it to the head of Manasses. And he said to his father: It should not be so, my father: for this is the first-born, put thy right hand upon his head. But he refusing, said: I know, my son, I know: and this also shall become peoples, and shall be multiplied: but this younger brother shall be greater than he: and his seed shall grow into nations.

LESSON ELEVENTH.

ON THE CHURCH.

Q. Which are the means instituted by our Lord to enable men at all times to share in the fruits of the Redemption?

See "L. of C.," p. 127, Nos. 26, 27.

(James 2.) My brethren, have not the faith of our Lord Jesus Christ of glory with respect of persons. For if there shall come into your assembly a man having a golden ring, in fine apparel, and there shall come in also a poor man in mean attire, and you have respect to him that is clothed with the fine apparel, and shall say to him: Sit thou here well; but say to the poor man: Stand thou there, or sit under my footstool: do you not judge within yourselves, and are become judges of unjust thoughts? Hearken, my dearest brethren: hath not God chosen the poor in this world, rich in faith, and heirs of the kingdom which God hath promised to them that love him? But you have dishonoured the poor man. Do not the rich oppress you by might? and do not they draw you before the judgment-seats? Do not they blaspheme the good name that is invoked upon you? If then you fulfil the royal law, according to the scriptures, *Thou shalt love thy neighbour as thyself;* you do well. But if you have respect to persons, you commit sin, being reproved by the law as transgressors.

(Gen. 25. A. M. 2148.) Isaac besought the Lord for his wife, because she was barren; and he heard him, and made Rebecca to conceive. But the children struggled in her womb: and she said: If it were to be so with me, what need was there to conceive? And she went to consult the Lord. And he answering said: Two nations are in thy womb, and two peoples shall be divided out of thy womb, and one people shall overcome the other, and the elder shall serve the younger. And when her time was come to be delivered, behold twins were found in her womb. And when they were grown up, Esau became a skilful hunter, and a husbandman: but Jacob a plain man dwelt in tents. Isaac loved Esau, because he eat of his hunting: and Rebecca loved Jacob. And Jacob boiled pottage: to whom Esau, coming faint out of the field, said: Give me of this red pottage, for I am exceeding faint. For which reason his name was called Edom. And Jacob said to him: Sell me thy first birth-right. He answered: Lo I die, what will the first birth-right avail me. Jacob said: Swear therefore to me. Esau swore to him, and sold his first birth-right. And so taking bread and the pottage of lentils, he ate, and drank, and went his way; making little account of having sold his first birth-right.

Q. What is the Church?
See "L. of C.," p. 18. No. 2; p. 40, No. 36.

(Ezek. 47. A. M. 3430.) An angel brought me again to the gate of the house, and behold waters issued out from under the threshold of the house, towards the east: and when the man that had the line in his hand went out towards the east, he measured a thousand cubits: and he brought me through the water up to the ankles. And again he measured a thousand, and he brought me through the water up to the knees. And he measured a thousand, and he brought me through the water up to the loins. And he measured a thousand, *and it was* a torrent, which I could not pass over: for the waters were risen so as to make a deep torrent, which could not be passed over. And he said to me: These waters that issue forth toward the hillocks of sand to the east, and go down to the plains of the desert, shall go into the sea, and shall go out, and the water shall be healed. And every living creature that creepeth whithersoever the torrent shall come, shall live: and there shall be fishes in abundance after these waters shall come thither, and they shall be healed, and all things shall live to which the torrent shall come. And the fishers shall stand over these *waters*, from Engaddi even to Engallim there shall be drying of nets: there shall be many sorts of the fishes thereof, as the fishes of the great sea, a very great multitude: but on the shore thereof, and in the fenny places they shall not be healed, because they shall be turned into salt-pits. And by the torrent on the banks thereof on both sides shall grow all trees that bear fruit: their leaf shall not fall off, and their fruit shall not fail: every month shall they bring forth first-fruits, because the waters thereof shall issue out of the sanctuary: and the fruits thereof shall be for food, and the leaves thereof for medicine.

Q. Who is the invisible Head of the Church?
See "L. of C.," p. 62, No. 21.

(Eph. 1.) Now therefore you are no more strangers and foreigners: but you are fellow-citizens with the saints, and the domestics of God, built upon the foundation of the apostles and prophets, Jesus Christ himself being the chief corner-stone: in whom all the building, being framed together, groweth up into an holy temple in the Lord. In whom you also are built together, into an habitation of God in the Spirit.

Q. Who is the visible Head of the Church?
See "L. of C.," p. 24, No. 9; p. 50, No. 10.

(IV. Kings 25. A. M. 3414.) It came to pass in the ninth year of his reign, in the tenth month, the tenth day of the month, that Nabuchodonosor king of Babylon came, he and all his army against Jerusalem: and they surrounded it: and raised works round about it. And the city was shut up and besieged till the eleventh year of king Sedecias. The ninth day of the month: and a famine prevailed in the city, and there was no bread for the people of the land. And a breach was made into the city: and all the men of war fled in the night between the two walls by the king's garden (now the Chaldees besieged the city round about,) and Sedecias fled by the way that leadeth to the plains of the wilderness. And the army of the Chaldees pursued after the king, and overtook him in the plains of Jericho: and all the warriors that were with him were scattered, and left him: so they took the king, and brought him to the king of Babylon to Reblatha, and he gave judgment upon him. And he slew the sons of Sedecias before his face, and he put out his eyes, and bound him with chains, and brought him to Babylon.

Q. Why is the Pope, the Bishop of Rome, the visible Head of the Church?
See "L. of C.," p. 102. No. 8; p. 123, Nos. 11, 12.

(Apoc. 4.) In the sight of the throne was, as it were, a sea of glass like to crystal; and in the midst of the throne, and round about the throne, were four living creatures, full of eyes before and behind. And the first living creature was like a lion; and the second living creature like a calf: and the third living creature, having the face, as it were, of a man; and the fourth living creature was like an eagle flying.

Q. Who are the successors of the other Apostles?
See "L. of C.," p. 30. No. 5; p. 54, No. 5; p. 94, No. 89.

(Acts 19. A. D. 56.) Now some also of the Jewish exorcists who went about, attempted to invoke over them that had evil spirits, the name of the Lord

Jesus, saying: I conjure you by Jesus, whom Paul preacheth. And there were certain men, seven sons of Sceva, a Jew, a chief priest, that did this. But the wicked spirit, answering, said to them: Jesus I know, and Paul I know; but who are you? And the man in whom the wicked spirit was, leaping upon them, and mastering them both, prevailed against them, so that they fled out of that house naked and wounded. And this became known to all the Jews and the gentiles that dwelt at Ephesus; and fear fell on them all, and the name of the Lord Jesus was magnified. And many of them that believed, came confessing and declaring their deeds.

(I. Cor. 1.) See your vocation, brethren, that *there are* not many wise according to the flesh, not many mighty, not many noble: but the foolish things of the world hath God chosen, that he may confound the wise; and the weak things of the world hath God chosen, that he may confound the strong. And the base things of the world, and the things that are contemptible hath God chosen, and things that are not, that he might bring to nought things that are; that no flesh should glory in his sight.

(Ezek. 1. A. M. 3409.) I saw, and behold a whirlwind came out of the north: and a great cloud, and a fire infolding *it*, and brightness was about. (And in the midst thereof the likeness of four living creatures: and this was their appearance: there was the likeness of a man in them. Every one had four faces, and every one four wings. And the wings of one were joined to the wings of another. They turned not when they went: but every one went straight forward. And as for the likeness of their faces: there was the face of a man, and the face of a lion on the right side of all the four: and the face of an ox, on the left side of all the four: and the face of an eagle over all the four. And their faces, and their wings were stretched upward: two wings of every one were joined, and two covered their bodies: and every one of them went straight forward: whither the impulse of the spirit was to go, thither they went: and they turned not when they went.)

Q. Why did Christ found the Church?
See "L. of C.," p. 25, No. 12.

(Gen. 27. A. M. 2245.) Now Isaac was old, and his eyes were dim, and he could not see: and he called Esau his elder son, and said to him: Take thy arms, thy quiver, and bow, and go abroad: and when thou hast taken some thing by hunting, make me savoury meat thereof, as thou knowest I like, and bring it, that I may eat: and my soul may bless thee before I die. And when Rebecca had heard this, and he was gone into the field to fulfil his father's commandment, she said to her son Jacob: now, therefore, my son, follow my counsel: and go thy way to the flock, bring me two kids of the best, that I may make of them meat for thy father, such as he gladly eateth: which when thou hast brought in, and he hath eaten, he may bless thee before he die. And she put on him very good garments of Esau, which she had at home with her: and the little skins of the kids she put about his hands, and covered the bare of his neck. And she gave him the savoury meat, and delivered him bread that she had baked. Which when he had carried in, he said: my father? But he answered: I hear. Who art thou, my son? And Jacob said: I am Esau thy first-born: I have done as thou didst command me: arise, sit, and eat of my venison, that thy soul may bless me. He came near, and kissed him. And immediately as he smelled the fragrant smell of his garments, blessing him, he said: Behold the smell of my son is as the smell of a plentiful field, which the Lord hath blessed. God give thee the dew of heaven, and of the fatness of the earth, abundance of corn and wine. And let peoples serve thee, and tribes worship thee: be thou lord of thy brethren, and let thy mother's children bow down before thee. Cursed be he that curseth thee: and let him that blesseth thee be filled with blessings. Isaac had scarce ended his words, when Jacob being now gone out abroad, Esau came, and he said: Thy brother came deceitfully and got thy blessing. And Esau said to him: Hast thou only one blessing, father? I beseech thee bless me also. And when he wept with a loud cry, Isaac being moved, said to him: In the fat of the earth, and in the dew of heaven from above, shall thy blessing be. Thou shalt live by the sword and shalt serve thy brother: and the time shall come, when thou shalt shake off and loose his yoke from thy neck.

(Josh. 6. A. M. 2553.) Now Jericho was close shut up and fenced, for fear of the children of Israel, and no man durst go out or come in. And the Lord said to Josue: Behold I have given into thy hands Jericho, and the king thereof, and all the valiant men. Go round about the city all ye fighting men once a day: so shall ye do for six days. And on the seventh day the priests shall take the seven trumpets, which are used in the jubilee, and shall go before the ark of the covenant: and you shall go about the city seven times, and the priests shall sound the trumpets. And when the voice of the trumpet shall give a longer and broken tune, and shall sound in your ears, all the people shall shout together with a very great shout, and the walls of the city shall fall to the ground, and they shall enter in every one at the place against which they shall stand. So they did six days. And when in the seventh going about the priests sounded with the trumpets, Josue said to all Israel: Shout: for the Lord hath delivered the city to you: so all the people making a shout, and the trumpets sounding, when the voice and the sound thundered in the ears of the multitude, the walls forthwith fell down: and every man went up by the place that was over-against him: and they took the city. At that time, Josue made an imprecation, saying: Cursed be the man before the Lord, that shall raise up and build the city of Jericho.

Q. Are all bound to belong to the Church?
See "L. of C.," p. 34. No. 21; p. 39, No. 34; p. 40, No. 35.

(Num. 16. A. M. 2535.) Core the son of Isaar, the son of Caath, the son of Levi, and Dathan and Abiron the sons of Eliab, and Hon the son of Pheleth of the children of Ruben, rose up against Moses, and *with them* two hundred and fifty others of the children of Israel, leading men of the synagogue, and who in the time of assembly were called by name. And when they had stood up against Moses and Aaron, they said: Let it be enough for you, that all the multitude consisteth of holy ones, and the Lord is among them: Why lift you up yourselves above the people of the Lord? Then Moses sent to call Dathan and Abiron the sons of Eliab. But they answered: We will not come. Is it a small matter to thee, that thou hast brought us out of a land that flowed with milk and honey, to kill us in the desert, except thou rule also like a lord over us? And the Lord said to Moses: Command the whole people to separate themselves from the tents of Core and Dathan and Abiron. And Moses arose, and went to Dathan and Abiron: and the ancients of Israel following him, he said to the multitude: Depart from the tents of these wicked men, and touch nothing of theirs, lest you be involved in their sins. And when they were departed from their tents round about, Dathan and Abiron coming out stood in the entry of their pavilions with their wives and children, and all the people. And immediately the earth broke asunder under their feet: and opening her mouth, devoured them with their tents and all their substance. And they went down alive into hell, the ground closing upon them, and they perished from among the people. The following day all the multitude of the children of Israel murmured against Moses and Aaron, saying: You have killed the people of the Lord. And when there arose a sedition, and the tumult increased, Moses and Aaron fled to the tabernacle of the covenant. And the Lord said to Moses: Get you out from the midst of this multitude, this moment will I destroy them. And as they were lying on the ground, Moses said to Aaron: Take the censer, and putting fire in it from the altar, put incense upon it, and go quickly to the people to pray for them: for already wrath is gone out from the Lord, and the plague rageth. When Aaron had done this, and had run to the midst of the multitude which the burning fire was now destroying, he offered the incense: and standing between the dead and the living, he prayed for the people, and the plague ceased.

(Deut. 12.) Beware lest thou offer thy holocausts in every place that thou shalt see: but in the place which the Lord shall choose in one of thy tribes shalt thou offer sacrifices, and shalt do all that I command thee. Thou mayst not eat in thy towns the tithes of thy corn, and thy wine, and thy oil, the first-born of thy herds and thy cattle, nor any thing that thou vowest, and that thou wilt offer voluntarily, and the first fruits of thy hands: but thou shalt eat them before the Lord thy God in the place which the Lord thy God shall choose, thou and thy son, and thy daughter, and thy man-servant, and maid-servant, and the Levite that dwelleth in thy cities: and thou shalt rejoice and be refreshed before the Lord thy God in all things, whereunto thou shalt put thy hand.

(II. Parl. 26. A. M. 3194.) Ozias was sixteen years old when he began to reign. And he sought the Lord in the days of Zacharias that understood and saw God: and as long as he sought the Lord, he directed him in all things. But when he was made strong, his heart was lifted up to his destruction, and he neglected the Lord his God: and going into the temple of the Lord, he had a mind to burn incense upon the altar of incense. And immediately Azarias the priest going in after him, and with him fourscore priests of the Lord, most valiant men, withstood the king and said: It doth not belong to thee, Ozias, to burn incense to the Lord, but to the priests, that is, to the sons of Aaron, who are consecrated for this ministry: go out of the sanctuary, do not despise: for this thing shall not be accounted to thy glory by the Lord God. And Ozias was angry, and holding in his hand the censer to burn incense, threatened the priests. And presently there rose a leprosy in his forehead before the priests, in the house of the Lord at the altar of incense. And Ozias the king was a leper unto the day of his death, and he dwelt in a house apart being full of the leprosy, for which he had been cast out of the house of the Lord.

(Isa. 2. A. M. 3219.) The word that Isaias the son of Amos saw, concerning Juda and Jerusalem. And in the last days the mountain of the house of the Lord shall be prepared on the top of mountains, and it shall be exalted above the hills, and all nations shall flow unto it. And many people shall go, and say: Come and let us go up to the mountain of the Lord, and to the house of the God of Jacob, and he will teach us his ways, and we will walk in his paths: for the law shall come forth from Sion, and the word of the Lord from Jerusalem. And he shall judge the Gentiles, and rebuke many people: and they shall turn their swords into plough-shares, and their spears into sickles: nation shall not lift up sword against nation, neither shall they be exercised any more to war.

LESSON TWELFTH.

ON THE ATTRIBUTES AND MARKS OF THE CHURCH.

Q. Which are the attributes of the Church?

(Matt. 28.) Jesus coming, spoke to them, saying: All power is given to me in heaven and in earth. Going therefore, teach ye all nations; baptizing them in the name of the Father, and of the Son, and of the Holy Ghost. Teaching them to observe all things whatsoever I have commanded you: and behold I am with you all days, even to the consummation of the world.

Q. What do you mean by the authority of the Church?

See "L. of C.," p. 114, No. 6.

(Deut. 17.) If thou perceive that there be among you a hard and doubtful *matter* in judgment between blood and blood, cause and cause, leprosy and leprosy: and thou see that the words of the judges within thy gates do vary: arise, and go up to the place, which the Lord thy God shall choose. And thou shalt come to the priests of the Levitical race, and to the judge, that shall be at that time: and thou shalt ask of them, and they shall shew thee the truth of the judgment. And thou shalt do whatsoever they shall say, that preside in the place, which the Lord shall choose, and what they shall teach thee, according to his law; and thou shalt follow their sentence: neither shalt thou decline to the right hand nor to the left hand. But he that will be proud, and refuse to obey the commandment of the priest, who ministereth at that time to the Lord thy God, and the decree of the judge, that man shall die, and thou shalt take away the evil from Israel.

Q. What do you mean by the infallibility of the Church?

See "L of C.," p. 50, No. 10.

(I. Tim. 3.) These things I

write to thee, hoping that I shall come to thee shortly. But if I tarry long, that thou mayest know how thou oughtest to behave thyself in the house of God, which is the church of the living God, the pillar and ground of the truth.

(III. Kings 7. A. M. 3000.) Solomon set up the two pillars in the porch of the temple: and when he had set up the pillar on the right hand, he called the name thereof Jachin: in like manner he set up the second pillar, and called the name thereof Booz.

Q. When does the Church teach infallibly?

See "L. of C.," p. 106, No. 11.

Q. What do you mean by the indefectibility of the Church?

(II. Kings 7. A. M. 2960.) When thy days shall be fulfilled, and thou shalt sleep with thy fathers, I will raise up thy seed after thee, which shall proceed out of thy bowels, and I will establish his kingdom. He shall build a house to my name, and I will establish the throne of his kingdom for ever. I will be to him a father, and he shall be to me a son: and thy house shall be faithful, and thy kingdom for ever before thy face, and thy throne shall be firm for ever.

(IV. Kings 6. A. M. 3116.) The servant of the man of God rising early, went out, and saw an army round about the city, and horses and chariots: and he told him, saying: Alas, alas, alas, my lord, what shall we do? But he answered: fear not: for there are more with us than with them. And Eliseus prayed, and said: Lord, open his eyes, that he may see. And the Lord opened the eyes of the servant, and he saw: and behold the mountain *was* full of horses, and chariots of fire round about Eliseus. And the enemies came down to him, but Eliseus prayed to the Lord, saying: Strike, I beseech thee, this people with blindness. And the Lord struck them with blindness, according to the word of Eliseus. And Eliseus said to them: This is not the way, neither is this the city: follow me, and I will shew you the man whom you seek. So he led them into Samaria. And a great provision of meats was set before them, and they eat and drank, and he let them go, and they went away to their master, and the robbers of Syria came no more into the land of Israel.

(Jer. 31. A. M. 3406.) Behold the days shall come, saith the Lord, and I will make a new covenant with the house of Israel, and the house of Juda: not according to the covenant which I made with their fathers, in the day that I took them by the hand to bring them out of the land of Egypt: the covenant which they made void, and I had dominion over them, saith the Lord. But this shall be the covenant, that

I will make with the house of Israel, after those days, saith the Lord: I will give my law in their bowels, and I will write it in their heart: and I will be their God, and they shall be my people. If these ordinances shall fail before me, saith the Lord: then also the seed of Israel shall fail, so as not to be a nation before me for ever.

Q. In whom are these attributes found in their fulness?

(Dan. 2. A. M. 3401.) In the second year of the reign of Nabuchodonosor, Nabuchodonoser had a dream, and his spirit was terrified, and his dream went out of his mind. Then the king commanded to call together the diviners and the wise men, and the magicians, and the Chaldeans: to declare to the king his dreams: so they came and stood before the king. And the king said to them: I saw a dream: and being troubled in mind I know not what I saw. The thing is gone out of my mind: unless you tell me the dream, and the meaning thereof, you shall be put to death, and your houses shall be confiscated. But if you tell the dream, and the meaning of it, you shall receive of me rewards, and gifts, and great honour: therefore tell me the dream, and the interpretation thereof. Then the Chaldeans answered before the king, and said: The thing that thou askest, O king, is difficult: nor can any one be found that can shew it before the king, except the gods, whose conversation is not with men. Upon hearing this, the king in fury, and in great wrath, commanded that all the wise men of Babylon should be put to death. And the decree being gone forth, the wise men were slain: and Daniel and his companions were sought for, to be put to death. Then was the mystery revealed to Daniel by a vision in the night: and Daniel blessed the God of heaven. Then Arioch in haste brought in Daniel to the king, and said to him: I have found a man of the children of the captivity of Juda, that will resolve the question to the king. The king answered, and said to Daniel, whose name was Baltassar: Thinkest thou indeed that thou canst tell me the dream that I saw, and the interpretation thereof? And Daniel made answer before the king, and said: Thou, O king, sawest, and behold *there was* as it were a great statue: this statue, which was great and high, tall of stature, stood before thee, and the look thereof was terrible. The head of this statue was of fine gold, but the breast and the arms of silver, and the belly and the thighs of brass: and the legs of iron, the feet part of iron and part of clay. Thus thou sawest, till a stone was cut out of a mountain without hands: and it struck the statue upon the feet thereof that were of iron and of clay, and broke them in pieces; but the stone that struck the statue, became a great mountain, and filled the whole earth. This is the dream: we will also tell the interpretation thereof before thee, O king. Thou art a king of kings: and the God of heaven hath given thee a kingdom, and strength, and power, and glory: thou therefore art the head of gold. And after thee shall rise up another kingdom, inferior to thee, of silver: and another third kingdom of brass, which shall rule over all the world. And the fourth kingdom shall be as iron. As iron breaketh into pieces, and subdueth all things, so shall that break and destroy all these. And whereas thou sawest the feet, and the toes, part of potter's clay, and part of iron: the kingdom shall be divided. But in the days of those kingdoms the God of heaven will set up a kingdom that shall never be destroyed, and his kingdom shall not be delivered up to another people, and it shall break in pieces, and shall consume all these kingdoms, and itself shall stand for ever. Then the king advanced Daniel to a high station, and gave him many and great gifts: and he made him governor over all the provinces of Babylon, and chief of the magistrates over all the wise men of Babylon.

Q. Has the Church any marks by which it may be known?

(Eph. 4.) I therefore, a prisoner in the Lord, beseech you that you walk worthy of the vocation in which you are called, with all humility and mildness, with patience, supporting one another in charity. Careful to keep the unity of the Spirit in the bond of peace. One body and one Spirit; as you are called in one hope of your calling. One Lord, one faith, one baptism. One God and Father of all, who is above all, and through all, and in us all. But to every one of us is given grace, according to the measure of the giving of Christ.

Q. How is the Church One?
See "L. of C.," p. 37, No. 28; p. 48, No. 4; p. 53, No. 17.

Q. How is the Church Holy?
(I. Peter 1.) Wherefore having the loins of your mind girt up, being sober, trust perfectly in the grace which is offered you in the revelation of Jesus Christ, as children of obedience, not fashioned according to the former desires of your ignorance: but according to him that hath called you, who is Holy, be you also in all manner of conversation holy: because it is written: *You shall be holy, for I am holy.*

Q. How is the Church Catholic or universal?
See "L. of C.," p. 69, No. 39.
(Zach. 2. A. M. 3485.) I lifted up my eyes, and saw, and behold a man, with a measuring line in his hand. And I said: Whither goest thou? and

he said to me: To measure Jerusalem, and to see how great is the breadth thereof, and how great the length thereof. And behold the Angel that spoke in me went forth, and another Angel went out to meet him. And he said to him: Run, speak to this young man, saying: Jerusalem shall be inhabited without walls, by reason of the multitude of men, and of the beasts in the midst thereof. And I will be to it, saith the Lord, a wall of fire round about: and I will be in glory in the midst thereof.

Q. How is the Church Apostolic?
See "L. of C.," p. 117, No. 9.

Q. In which Church are these attributes and marks found?
See "L. of C.," p. 124, No. 17.

(Gal. 1.) Though we, or an angel from heaven, preach a gospel to you besides that which we have preached to you, let him be anathema. As we said before, so now I say again: If any one preach to you a gospel, besides that which you have received, let him be anathema.

Q. From whom does the Church derive its undying life and infallible authority?

(Acts 5. A. D. 33.) When they had brought them, they set them before the council. And the high priest asked them, saying: Commanding we commanded you, that you should not teach in this name; and behold, you have filled Jerusalem with your doctrine, and you have a mind to bring the blood of this man upon us. But Peter and the apostles answering, said: We ought to obey God, rather than men. But one in the council rising up, a Pharisee, named Gamaliel, a doctor of the law respected by all the people, commanded the men to be put forth a little while. And he said to them: Ye men of Israel, take heed to yourselves what you intend to do, as touching these men. And now, therefore, I say to you, refrain from these men, and let them alone; for if this council or this work be of men, it will come to naught: but if it be of God, you cannot overthrow it, lest perhaps you be found even to fight against God. And they consented to him.

(Isa. 54.) Fear not, for thou shalt not be confounded, nor blush: for thou shalt not be put to shame. For he that made thee shall rule over thee, the Lord of hosts is his name: and thy Redeemer, the holy one of Israel, shall be called the God of all the earth. For the mountains shall be moved, and the hills shall tremble; but my mercy shall not depart from thee, and the covenant of my peace shall not be moved: said the Lord that hath mercy on thee. O poor little one, tossed with tempest, without all comfort, behold I will lay thy stones in order, and will lay thy foundations with sapphires, and I will make thy bulwarks of jasper: and thy gates of graven stones, and all thy borders of desirable stones. All thy children *shall be* taught of the Lord: and great shall be the peace of thy children. And thou shalt be founded in justice: depart far from oppression, for thou shalt not fear; and from terror, for it shall not come near thee. No weapon that is formed against thee shall prosper: and every tongue that resisteth thee in judgment, thou shalt condemn. This is the inheritance of the servants of the Lord, and their justice with me, saith the Lord.

Q. By whom is the Church made and kept One, Holy, and Catholic?

(Judg. 7. A. M. 2759.) The Lord said to Gedeon: The people that are with thee are many, and Madian shall not be delivered into their hands: lest Israel should glory against me, and say: I was delivered by my own strength. Speak to the people, and proclaim in the hearing of all, Whosoever is fearful and timorous let him return. So two and twenty thousand men went away from mount Galaad and returned home, and only ten thousand remained. And the Lord said to Gedeon: The people are still too many, bring them to the waters, and there I will try them: and of whom I shall say to thee, This shall go with thee, let him go: whom I shall forbid to go, let him return. And when the people were come down to the waters, the Lord said to Gedeon: They that shall lap the water with their tongues, as dogs are wont to lap, thou shalt set apart by themselves: but they that shall drink bowing down their knees, shall be on the other side. And the number of them that had lapped water, casting it with the hand to their mouth, was three hundred men: and all the rest of the multitude had drunk kneeling. And the Lord said to Gedeon: By the three hundred men, that lapped water, I will save you, and deliver Madian into thy hand: but let all the rest of the people return to their place.

LESSON THIRTEENTH.

ON THE SACRAMENTS IN GENERAL.

Q. What is a Sacrament?

(Num. 35. A. M. 2553.) The Lord spoke these things also to Moses in the plains of Moab by the Jordan, over-against Jericho: Command the children of Israel that they give to the Levites out of their possessions, cities to dwell in, and their suburbs round about: that they may abide in the towns, and the suburbs may be for their cattle and beasts: and among the cities, which you shall give to the Levites, seven shall be separated for refuge to fugitives, that he who hath shed blood may flee to them: and besides these there shall be other forty-two cities, and when the fugitive shall be in them, the kinsman of him that is slain may not have power to kill him, until he stand before the multitude, and his cause be judged. And of those cities, that are separated for the refuge of fugitives, three shall be beyond the Jordan, and three in the land of Chanaan, as well for the children of Israel as for strangers and sojourners, that he may flee to them, who hath shed blood against his will.

Q. How many Sacraments are there?

(Gen. 17. A. M. 2098.) This is my covenant which you shall observe, between me and you, and thy seed after thee: All the male kind of you shall be circumcised: an infant of eight days old shall be circumcised among you, every man child in your generations: he that is born in the house, as well as the bought servant shall be circumcised, and whosoever is not of your stock: and my covenant shall be in your flesh for a perpetual covenant. The male, who shall not be circumcised, that soul shall be destroyed out of his people: because he hath broken my covenant.

(Lev. 12. A. M. 2514.) The Lord spoke to Moses, saying: Speak to the children of Israel, and thou shall say to them: If a woman shall bear a man-child, she shall be unclean seven days. But if she shall bear a maid-child, she shall be unclean two weeks, and when the days of her purification are expired, for a son, or for a daughter, she shall bring to the door of the tabernacle of the testimony, a lamb of a year old for a holocaust, and a young pigeon or a turtle for sin, and shall deliver them to the priest: who shall offer them before the Lord, and shall pray for her, and so she shall be cleansed from the issue of her blood. This is the law for her that beareth a man-child or a maid-child. And if her hand find not sufficiency, and she is not able to offer a lamb, she shall take two turtles, or two young pigeons, one for a holocaust, and another for sin: and the priest shall pray for her, and so she shall be cleansed.

(Ex. 12. A. M. 2513.) The Lord said to Moses and Aaron in the land of Egypt: Speak ye to the whole assembly of the children of Israel, and say to them: On the tenth day of this month let every man take a lamb by their families and houses. But if the number be less than may suffice to eat the lamb, he shall take unto him his neighbor that joineth to his house, according to the number of souls which may be enough to eat the lamb. And it shall be a lamb without blemish, a male, of one year: according to which rite also you shall take a kid. And you shall keep it until the fourteenth day of this month: and the whole multitude of the children of Israel shall sacrifice it in the evening. And they shall take of the blood thereof, and put it upon both the side posts, and on the upper door-posts of the houses, wherein they shall eat it. And they shall eat the flesh that night roasted at the fire, and unleavened bread with wild lettuce. You shall not eat thereof anything raw, nor boiled in water, but only roasted at the fire: you shall eat the head with the feet and entrails thereof. Neither shall there remain any thing of it until morning. If there be any thing left, you shall burn it with fire. And thus you shall eat it: you shall gird your reins, and you shall have shoes on your feet, holding staves in your hands, and you shall eat in haste: for it is the Phase (that is the Passage) of the Lord.

(Ex. 29.) Thou shalt also do this, but they may be consecrated to me in priesthood. Thou shalt bring Aaron to the door of the tabernacle of the testimony. And when thou hast washed him with water, thou shalt clothe Aaron with his vestments, that is, with the linen garment and the tunick, and the ephod and the rational, which thou shalt gird with the girdle. And thou shalt put the mitre upon his head, and the holy plate upon the mitre, and thou shalt pour the oil of unction upon his head: and by this rite shall he be consecrated.

Q. Whence have the Sacraments the power of giving grace?

(Acts 3-4. A. D. 33.) Now Peter and John went up into the temple at the ninth hour of prayer. And a certain man who was lame from his mother's womb, was carried: whom they laid every day at the gate of the temple, which is called Beautiful, that he might ask alms of them that went into the temple. He, when he had seen Peter and John about to go into the temple, asked to receive an alms. But Peter with John fastening his eyes upon him, said: Look upon us. But he looked earnestly upon them, hoping that he should receive something of them. But Peter said: Silver and gold I have none; but what I have, I give thee: In the name of Jesus Christ of Nazareth, arise, and walk. And taking him by the right hand, he lifted him up, and forthwith his feet and soles received strength. And he leaping up, stood, and walked, and went in with them into the temple, walking, and leaping, and praising God. And all the people saw him walking and praising God. And they knew him, that it was he who sat begging alms at the beautiful gate of the temple: and they were filled with wonder and amazement at that which had happened to him. And as he held Peter and John, all the people ran to them to the porch which is called Solomon's, greatly wondering. But Peter seeing, made answer to the people: If we this day are examined concerning the good deed done to the infirm man, by what means he hath been made whole: be it known to you all, and to all the people of Israel, that by the name of our Lord Jesus Christ of Nazareth, whom you crucified, whom God hath raised from the dead, even by him this man standeth here before you whole. This is *the stone which was rejected by you the builders, which is become the head of the corner.* Neither is there salvation in any other. For there is no other name under heaven given to men, whereby we must be saved.

Q. What grace do the Sacraments give?

(Acts 16. A. D. 51.) Upon the sabbath-day, we went forth without the gate by a riverside, where it seemed that there was prayer; and sitting down, we spoke to the women that were assembled. And a certain woman named Lydia, a seller of purple, of the city of Thyatira, one that worshipped God, did hear: whose heart the Lord opened to attend to those things which were said by Paul. And when she was baptized, and her household, she besought us, saying: If you have judged me to be faithful to the Lord, come into my house, and abide there. And she constrained us. And it came to pass, as we went to prayer, a certain girl, having a pythonical spirit, met us, who brought to her masters much gain by divining. This same following Paul and us, cried out, saying: These men are the servants of the most high God, who preach unto you the way of salvation. And this she did many days. But Paul being grieved, turned, and said to the spirit: I command thee, in the name of Jesus Christ, to go out from her. And he went out the same hour. But her masters, seeing that the hope of their gain was gone, apprehending Paul and Silas, brought them into the marketplace to the rulers. And when they had laid many stripes upon them, they cast them into prison, charging the gaoler to keep them diligently. Who having received such a charge, thrust them into the inner prison, and made their feet fast in the stocks. And at midnight, Paul and Silas praying, praised God. And they that were in prison, heard them. And suddenly there was a great earthquake, so that the foundations of the prison were shaken. And immediately all the doors were opened, and the bands of all were loosed. And the keeper of the prison, awaking out of his sleep, and seeing the doors of the prison open, drawing his sword, would have killed himself, supposing that the prisoners had been fled. But Paul cried with a loud voice, saying: Do thyself no harm, for we all are here. Then calling for a light, he went in, and trembling, fell down at the feet of Paul and Silas. And bringing them out, he said: Masters, what must I do, that I may be saved? But they said: Believe in the Lord Jesus, and thou shalt be saved, and thy house. And they preached the word of the Lord to him and to all that were in his house. And he, taking them the same hour of the night, washed their stripes, and himself was baptized, and all his house immediately.

Q. Which are the Sacraments that give sanctifying grace?

(Acts 9. A. D. 34.) Saul, as yet breathing out threatenings and slaughter against the disciples of the Lord, went to the high priest, and asked of him letters to Damascus, to the synagogues: that if he found any men and women of this way, he might bring them bound to Jerusalem. And as he went on his journey, it came to pass that he drew nigh to Damascus; and suddenly a light from heaven shined round about him. And falling on the ground, he heard a voice saying to him: Saul, Saul, why persecutest thou me? Who said: Who art thou, Lord? And he: I am Jesus whom thou persecutest. It is hard for thee to kick against the goad. And he trembling and astonished, said: Lord, what wilt thou have me to do? And the Lord said to him: Arise, and go into the city, and there it shall be told thee what thou must do. Now the men who went in company with him, stood amazed, hearing indeed a voice, but seeing no man. And Saul arose from the ground; and when his eyes were opened, he saw nothing. But they leading him by the hands, brought him to Damascus. And he was there three days, without sight, and he did neither eat nor drink. Now there was a certain disciple at Damascus, named Ananias. And the Lord said to him in a vision: Ananias. And he said: Behold I am here, Lord. And the Lord *said* to him: Arise, and go into the street that is called Strait, and seek in the house of Judas, one named Saul of Tarsus. For behold he prayeth. And Ananias went his way, and entered into the house. And laying his hands upon him, he said: Brother Saul, the Lord Jesus hath sent me. he that appeared to thee in the way as thou camest; that thou mayest receive thy sight and be filled with the Holy Ghost. And immediately there fell from his eyes as it were scales, and he received his sight; and rising up, he was baptized. And when many days were passed, the Jews consulted together to kill him. But their laying in wait was made known to Saul. And they watched the gates also day and night, that they might kill him. But the disciples taking him in the night, conveyed him away by the wall, letting him down in a basket.

Q. Why are Baptism and Penance called Sacraments of the dead?

See "L. of C.," p. 127, No. 26.

Q. Which are the Sacraments that increase sanctifying grace in our soul?

(Apoc. 22. A. D. 64.) The Angel saith to me: Seal not the words of the prophecy of this book: for the time is at hand. He that hurteth, let him hurt still: and he that is filthy, let him be filthy still: and he that is just, let him be justified still: and he that is holy, let him be sanctified still. Behold, I come quickly; and my reward is with me, to render to every man according to his works.

Q. Why are Confirmation, Holy Eucharist, Extreme Unction, Holy Orders, and Matrimony called Sacraments of the living?

(Phil. 1.) Grace be unto you, and peace from God our Father, and from the Lord Jesus Christ. I give thanks to my God in every remembrance of you, being confident of this very thing, that he, who hath begun a good work in you, will perfect it unto the day of Christ Jesus.

Q. What sin does he commit who receives the Sacraments of the living in mortal sin?

(I. Cor. 11.) Whosoever shall eat this bread, or drink the chalice of the Lord unworthily, shall be guilty of the body and of the blood of the Lord.

Q. Besides sanctifying grace do the Sacraments give any other grace?

(Ps. 22.) The Lord hath brought me up, on the water of refreshment: he hath converted my soul. He hath led me on the path of justice, for his own name's sake. For though I should walk in the midst of the shadow of death, I will fear no evils, for thou art with me. Thy rod and thy staff, they have comforted me. Thou hast prepared a table before me, against them that afflict me. Thou hast anointed my head with oil; and my chalice which inebriateth *me*, how goodly is it! And thy mercy will follow me all the days of my life. And that I may dwell in the house of the Lord unto length of days.

Q. What is sacramental grace?

(Phil. 1.) I give thanks to my God in every remembrance of you, always in all my prayers making supplication for you all, with joy. For your communication in the gospel of Christ from the first day until now. Being confident of this very thing, that he, who hath begun a good work in you, will perfect it unto the day of Christ Jesus.

Q. Do the Sacraments always give grace?

See "L. of C.," p. 34, No. 19; p. 89, No. 20.

(Isa. 55.) All you that thirst, come to the waters: and you that have no money make haste, buy, and eat: come ye, buy wine and milk without money, and without any price. Seek ye the Lord, while he may be found: call upon him, while he is near. Let the wicked forsake his way, and the unjust man his thoughts, and let him return to the Lord, and he will have mercy on him, and to our God: for he is bountiful to forgive. For my thoughts are not your thoughts: nor your ways my ways, saith the Lord. For as the heavens are exalted above the earth, so are my ways exalted above your ways, and my thoughts above your thoughts. And as the rain and the snow come down from heaven, and return no more thither, but soak the earth, and water it, and make it to spring, and give seed to the sower, and bread to the eater: so shall my word be, which shall go forth from my mouth: it shall not return to me void, but it shall do whatsoever I please, and shall prosper in the things for which I sent it.

Q. Can we receive the Sacraments more than once?

(Prov. 24.) A just man shall fall seven times and shall rise again: but the wicked shall fall down into evil.

Q. Why can we not receive Baptism, Confirmation, and Holy Orders more than once?

(Ezek. 9. A. M. 3410.) The Lord said to him: Go through the midst of the city, through the midst of Jerusalem: and mark Thau upon the foreheads of the men that sigh, and mourn for all the abominations that are committed in the midst thereof. And to the others he said in my hearing: Go ye after him through the city, and strike: let not your eyes spare, nor be ye moved with pity. Utterly destroy old and young, maidens, children and women: but upon whomsoever you shall see Thau, kill him not, and begin ye at my sanctuary.

Q. What is the character which these Sacraments imprint in the soul?

(Apoc. 7.) I saw another Angel ascending from the rising of the sun, having the sign of the living God; and he cried with a loud voice to the four Angels, to whom it was given to hurt the earth and the sea, saying: Hurt not the earth, nor the sea, nor the trees, till we sign the servants of our God in their foreheads.

Q. Does this character remain in the soul even after death?

(Apoc. 14.) The third Angel followed them, saying with a loud voice: If any man shall adore the beast and his image, and receive his character in his forehead, or in his hand; he also shall drink of the wine of the wrath of God, which is mingled with pure wine in the cup of his wrath, and shall be tormented with fire and brimstone in the sight of the holy Angels, and in the sight of the Lamb. And the smoke of their torments shall ascend up for ever and ever: neither have they rest day nor night, who have adored the beast, and his image, and whoever receiveth the character of his name.

(Heb. 7.) For he testifieth: *Thou art a priest for ever, according to the order of Melchisedech.*

LESSON FOURTEENTH.

ON BAPTISM.

Q. What is Baptism?

(Isa. 44.) Fear not, O my servant Jacob, and thou most righteous whom I have chosen. For I will pour out waters upon the thirsty ground, and streams upon the dry land: I will pour out my spirit upon thy seed, and my blessing upon thy stock.

(Num. 9. A. M. 2514.) Now on the day that the tabernacle was reared up, a cloud covered it. But from the evening there was over the tabernacle, as it were, the appearance of fire until the morning. So it was always: by day the cloud covered it, and by night as it were the appearance of fire. And when the cloud that covered the tabernacle was taken up, then the children of Israel marched forward: and in the place where the cloud stood still, there they camped. At the commandment of the Lord they marched, and at his commandment they pitched the tabernacle. All the days that the cloud abode over the tabernacle, they remained in the same place: and if it was so that it continued over it a long time, the children of Israel kept the watches of the Lord, and marched not, for as many days soever as the cloud staid over the tabernacle. At the commandment of the Lord they pitched their tents, and at his commandment they took them down. If the cloud tarried from evening until morning, and immediately at break of day left the tabernacle, they marched forward: and if it departed after a day and a night, they took down their tents. But if it remained over the tabernacle for two days or a month or a longer time, the children of Israel remained in the same place, and marched not: but immediately as soon as it departed, they removed the camp. By the word of the Lord they pitched their tents, and by his word they marched: and kept the watches of the Lord according to his commandment by the hand of Moses.

Q. Are actual sins ever remitted by Baptism?

(Ezek. 36.) I will pour upon you clean water, and you shall be cleansed from all your filthiness, and I will cleanse you from all your idols. And will give you a new heart, and put a new spirit within you: and I will take away the stony heart out of your flesh, had will give you a heart of flesh. And I will put my spirit in the midst of you: and I will cause you to walk in my commandments, and to keep my judgments, and do them. And you shall dwell in the land which I gave to your fathers, and you shall be my people, and I will be your God.

Q. Is Baptism necessary to salvation?

See "L. of C.," p. 11, No. 10; p. 16, No. 4; p. 20, No. 3.

(Ex. 14. A. M. 2513.) The Lord hardened the heart of Pharao king of Egypt, and he pursued the children of Israel: But they were gone forth in a mighty hand. And when the Egyptians followed the steps of them who were gone before, they found them encamped at the sea side: and the Lord said to Moses: Why criest thou to me? Speak to the children of Israel to go forward. But lift thou up thy rod, and stretch forth thy hand over the sea, and divide it: that the children of Israel may go through the midst of the sea on dry ground. And when Moses had stretched forth his hand over the sea, the Lord took it away by a strong and burning wind blowing all the night, and turned it into dry ground: and the water was divided. And the children of Israel went in through the midst of the sea dried up: for the water was as a wall on their right hand and on their left. And the Egyptians pursuing went in after them, and all Pharao's horses, his chariots and horsemen through the midst of the sea. And when Moses had stretched forth his hand towards the sea, it returned at the first break of day to the former place: and as the Egyptians were fleeing away, the waters came upon them, and the Lord shut them up in the middle of the waves.

Q. Who can administer Baptism?

See "L. of C.," p. 17, No. 6; p. 21, No. 4.

CATECHISM. 81

Q. How is Baptism given?
See "L. of C., p." 16, No. 3; p. 48, No. 5.

Q. How many kinds of Baptism are there?

(I. John 5.) This is he that came by water and blood, Jesus Christ: not by water only, but by water and blood. And it is the Spirit which testifieth, that Christ is the truth. And there are three that give testimony on earth: the spirit, and the water, and the blood: and these three are one.

Q. What is Baptism of water?
See "L. of C." p. 28, No. 1.

Q. What is Baptism of desire?

(Acts 11. A. D. 40.) When Peter was come up to Jerusalem, they that were of the circumcision contended with him, saying: Why didst thou go into men uncircumcised, and didst eat with them? But Peter began and declared to them the *matter in* order, saying: I was in the city of Joppe praying, and I saw in an ecstasy of mind a vision, a certain vessel descending, as it were a great sheet let down from heaven by four corners, and it came even unto me. Into which looking, I considered, and saw fourfooted creatures of the earth, and beasts, and creeping things, and fowls of the air: and I heard also a voice saying to me: Arise, Peter: kill and eat. And I said: Not so, Lord; for nothing common or unclean hath ever entered into my mouth. And the voice answered again from heaven: What God hath made clean, do not thou call common. And this was done three times: and all were taken up again into heaven. And behold, immediately there were three men come to the house wherein I was, sent to me from Cesarea. And the Spirit said to me, that I should go with them, nothing doubting. And these six brethren went with me also: and we entered into the man's house. And he told us how he had seen an angel in his house, standing, and saying to him: Send to Joppe, and call hither Simon, who is surnamed Peter, who shall speak to thee words, whereby thou shalt be saved, and all thy house. And when I had begun to speak, the Holy Ghost fell upon them, as upon us also in the beginning. And I remembered the word of the Lord, how that he said: *John indeed baptized with water, but you shall be baptized with the Holy Ghost.* If then God gave them the same grace, as to us also who believed in the Lord Jesus Christ; who was I, that could withstand God?

Q. What is Baptism of blood?
See "L. of C.," p. 13, No. 14.

(Ex. 4. A. M. 2513.) When Moses was in his journey, in the inn, the Lord met him, and would have killed him. Immediately Sephora took a very sharp stone, and circumcised her son, and touched his feet, and said: A bloody spouse art thou to me. And he let him go after she had said: A bloody spouse thou art to me, because of the circumcision.

Q. Is Baptism of desire or of blood sufficient to produce the effects of Baptism of water?

(Acts 8. A. D. 34.) Now an Angel of the Lord spoke to Philip, saying: Arise, go towards the south, to the way that goeth down from Jerusalem into Gaza: this is desert. And rising up, he went. And behold a man of Ethiopia, an eunuch, of great authority under Candace the queen of the Ethiopians, who had charge over all her treasures, had come to Jerusalem to adore. And he was returning, sitting in his chariot, and reading Isaias the prophet; then Philip, opening his mouth, and beginning at this scripture, preached unto him Jesus. And as they went on their way they came to a certain water; and the eunuch said: See, here is water: what doth hinder me from being baptized? And Philip said: If thou believest with all thy heart, thou mayest. And he answering, said: I believe that Jesus Christ is the Son of God. And he commanded the chariot to stand still; and they went down into the water, both Philip and the eunuch: and he baptized him. And when they were come up out of the water, the spirit of the Lord took away Philip; and the eunuch saw him no more.

(Rom. 4.) This blessedness then doth it remain in the circumcision only, or in the uncircumcision also? For we say that unto Abraham faith was reputed to justice. How then was it reputed? *When he was in circumcision, or in uncircumcision?* Not in circumcision, but in uncircumcision. And he received the sign of circumcision, a seal of the justice of the faith, which he had, being uncircumcised.

Q. What do we promise in Baptism?
See "L. of C.," p. 15, No. 2.

Q. Why is the name of a saint given in Baptism?
See "L. of C.," p. 9, No. 7; p. 11; No. 10.

Q. Why are godfathers and godmothers given in Baptism?
See "L. of C.," p. 11, No. 11.

Q. What is the obligation of a godfather and a godmother?

(Mark 10: 14.) Suffer the little children to come to Me, and forbid them not: for of such is the Kingdom of God.

LESSON FIFTEENTH.

ON CONFIRMATION.

Q. What is Confirmation?

See "L. of C.," p. 125, No. 23; p. 126, No. 24.

(Acts 4. A. D. 33.) As the apostles were speaking to the people, the priests, and the officer of the temple, and the Sadducees, came upon them, being grieved that they taught the people, and preached in Jesus the resurrection from the dead: and calling them, they charged them not to speak at all, nor teach in the name of Jesus. But Peter and John answering, said to them: If it be just in the sight of God, to hear you rather than God, judge ye. For we cannot but speak the things which we have seen and heard. And when they had prayed, the place was moved wherein they were assembled; and they were all filled with the Holy Ghost, and they spoke the word of God with confidence.

(Job 7.) The life of man upon earth is a warfare, and his days are like the days of a hireling. As a servant longeth for the shade, as the hireling looketh for the end of his work. So I also have had empty months, and have numbered to myself wearisome nights. If I lie down to sleep, I shall say: When shall I arise? and again I shall look for the evening, and shall be filled with sorrows even till darkness. What is a man that thou shouldst magnify him? or why dost thou set thy heart upon him? Thou visitest him early in the morning and thou provest him suddenly.

Q. Who administers Confirmation?

(Acts 8. A. D. 33.) Now *there was* a certain man named Simon, who before had been a magician in that city, seducing the people of Samaria, giving out that he was some great one: to whom they all gave ear, from the least to the greatest, saying: This man is the power of God, which is called great. And they were attentive to him, because, for a long time, he had bewitched them with his magical practices. But when they had believed Philip preaching of the kingdom of God, in the name of Jesus Christ, they were baptized, *both* men and women. Then Simon himself believed also; and being baptized, he stuck close to Philip. And being astonished, wondered to see the signs and exceeding great miracles which were done. Now when the apostles, who were in Jerusalem, had heard that Samaria had received the word of God, they sent unto them Peter and John. Who, when they were come, prayed for them, that they might receive the Holy Ghost. For he was not as yet come upon any of them; but they were only baptized in the name of the Lord Jesus. Then they laid their hands upon them, and they received the Holy Ghost. And when Simon saw, that by the imposition of the hands of the apostles, the Holy Ghost was given, he offered them money, saying: Give me also this power, that on whomsoever I shall lay *my* hands, he may receive the Holy Ghost. But Peter said to him: Keep thy money to thyself, to perish with thee, because thou hast thought that the gift of God may be purchased with money.

Q. How does the bishop give Confirmation?

(I. Kings 10. A. M. 2909.) Samuel took a little vial of oil, and poured it upon Saul's head, and kissed him, and said: Behold, the Lord hath anointed thee to be prince over his inheritance, and thou shalt deliver his people out of the hands of their enemies, that are round about them. And this shall be a sign unto thee, that God hath anointed thee to be prince. And the Spirit of the Lord shall come upon thee, and thou shalt prophesy with them, and shalt be changed into another man. Saul then departed to his own house in Gabaa: and there went with him a part of the army, whose hearts God had touched. But the children of Belial said: Shall this fellow be able to save us? And they despised him, and brought him no presents, but he dissembled as though he heard not.

Q. What is holy chrism?

(Ex. 30. A. M. 2513.) The Lord spoke to Moses, saying: Take spices, of principal and chosen myrrh five hundred sicles, and of cinnamon half so much, that is, two hundred and fifty sicles, of calamus in like manner two hundred and fifty. And of cassia five hundred sicles by the weight of the sanctuary, of oil of olives the measure hin: and thou shalt make the holy oil of unction, an ointment compounded after the art of the perfumer, and therewith thou shalt anoint the tabernacle of the testimony, and the ark of the testament, and the table with the vessels thereof, the candlestick and furniture thereof, the altars of incense, and of holocaust, and all the furniture that belongeth to the service of them. And thou shalt sanctify all, and they shall be most holy: he that shall touch them shall be sanctified. Thou shalt anoint Aaron and his sons, and shalt sanctify them, that they may do the office of priesthood unto me. And thou shalt say to the children of Israel: This oil of unction shall be holy unto me throughout your generations. The flesh of man shall not be anointed therewith, and you shall make none other of the same composition, because it is sanctified, and shall be holy unto you. What man soever shall compound such, and shall give thereof to a stranger, he shall be cut off from his people.

Q. What does the bishop say in anointing the person he confirms?

(II. Cor. 1.) Now he that confirmeth us with you in Christ, and that hath anointed us, is God: who also hath sealed us, and given the pledge of the Spirit in our hearts.

Q. What is meant by anointing the forehead with chrism in the form of a cross?

(Ezek. 9.) The Lord said to him: Go through the midst of the city, through the midst of Jerusalem: and mark Thau upon the foreheads of the men.

Q. Why does the bishop give the person he confirms a slight blow on the cheek?

(Rom. 8.) The Spirit himself giveth testimony to our spirit, that we are the sons of God. And if sons, heirs also; heirs indeed of God, and joint-heirs with Christ: yet so, if we suffer with him, that we may be also glorified with him. For I reckon that the sufferings of this time are not worthy to be compared with the glory to come, that shall be revealed in us. Who then shall separate us from the love of Christ? Shall tribulation? or distress? or famine? or nakedness? or danger? or persecution? or the sword? (As it is written: *For thy sake we are put to death all the day long. We are accounted as sheep for the slaughter.*) But in all these things we overcome, because of him that hath loved us. For I am sure that neither death, nor life, nor Angels, nor principalities, nor powers, nor things present, nor things to come, nor might, nor height, nor depth, nor any other creature, shall be able to separate us from the love of God, which is in Christ Jesus our Lord.

Q. To receive Confirmation worthily is it necessary to be in the state of grace?

(Wisd. 1.) Wisdom will not enter into a malicious soul, nor dwell in a body subject to sins. For the Holy Spirit of discipline will flee from the deceitful, and will withdraw himself from thoughts that are without understanding, and he shall not abide when iniquity cometh in.

Q. What special preparation should be made to receive Confirmation?

(Acts 19. A. D. 54.) It came to pass, while Apollo was at Corinth, that Paul having passed through the upper coasts, came to Ephesus, and found certain disciples. And he said to them: Have you received the Holy Ghost since ye believed? But they said to him: We have not so much as heard whether there be a Holy Ghost. And he said: In what then were you baptized? Who said: In John's baptism. Then

Paul said: John baptized the people with the baptism of penance, saying: That they should believe in him who was to come after him, that is to say, in Jesus. Having heard these things, they were baptized in the name of the Lord Jesus. And when Paul had imposed his hands on them, the Holy Ghost came upon them, and they spoke with tongues and prophesied.

Q. Is it a sin to neglect Confirmation?

(I. Cor. 12.) I give you to understand, that no man, speaking by the spirit of God, saith Anathema to Jesus. And no man can say the Lord Jesus, but by the Holy Ghost.

LESSON SIXTEENTH.

ON THE GIFTS AND FRUITS OF THE HOLY GHOST.

Q. **Which are the effects of Confirmation?**

See "L. of C.," p. 105, No. 7.

(Ps. 67.) Thou has ascended on high, thou hast led captivity captive; thou hast received gifts in men.

(Judg. 14. A. M. 2867.) Samson went down with his father and mother to Thamnatha. And when they were come to the vineyards of the town, behold a young lion met him raging and roaring. And the spirit of the Lord came upon Samson, and he tore the lion as he would have torn a kid in pieces, having nothing at all in his hand: and he would not tell this to his father and mother. And he went down and spoke to the woman that had pleased his eyes. And after some days returning to take her, he went aside to see the carcass of the lion, and behold there was a swarm of bees in the mouth of the lion and a honey-comb. And when he had taken it in his hands, he went on eating: and coming to his father and mother, he gave them of it, and they ate: but he would not tell them, that he had taken the honey from the body of the lion.

(Judg. 15. A. M. 2868.) The sons of Judas said to him, we are come to bind thee and to deliver thee into the hands of the Philistines. And Samson said to them: Swear to me, and promise me, that you will not kill me. They said: We will not kill thee: but we will deliver thee up bound. And they bound him with two new cords, and brought him from the rock Etam. Now when he was come to the place of the Jaw-bone, and the Philistines shouting went to meet him, the Spirit of the Lord came strongly upon him: and as the flax is wont to be consumed at the approach of fire, so the bands with which he was bound were broken and loosed. And finding a jaw-bone, even the jaw-bone of an ass which lay there, catching it up, he slew therewith a thousand men. And he said: With the jaw-bone of an ass, with the jaw of the colt of asses I have destroyed them, and have slain a thousand men. And when he had ended these words singing, he threw the jaw-bone out of his hand, and called the name of that place Ramathlechi, which is interpreted the lifting up of the jaw-bone. And being very thirsty, he cried to the Lord, and said: Thou hast given this very great deliverance and victory into the hand of thy servant: and behold I die for thirst, and shall fall into the hands of the uncircumcised. Then the Lord opened a great tooth in the jaw of the ass, and waters issued out of it. And when he had drank them he refreshed his spirit, and recovered his strength.

Q. Which are the gifts of the Holy Ghost?

(IV. Kings 13. A. M. 3165.) Eliseus said to Joas: Bring a bow and arrows. And when he had brought him a bow, and arrows, he said: Take the arrows. And when he had taken them, he said to him: Strike with an arrow upon the ground. And he struck three times and stood still. And the man of God was angry with him, and said: If thou hadst smitten five or six or seven times, thou hadst smitten Syria even to utter destruction: but now three times shalt thou smite it.

(Isa. 11.) The spirit of the Lord shall rest upon him: the spirit of wisdom, and of understanding, the spirit of counsel, and of fortitude, the spirit of knowledge, and of godliness. And he shall be filled with the spirit of the fear of the Lord.

Q. Why do we receive the gift of Fear of the Lord?

(Eccltus. 1.) The fear of the Lord is honour, and glory, and gladness, and a crown of joy. The fear of the Lord shall delight the heart, and shall give joy, and gladness, and length of days. With him that feareth the Lord, it shall go well in the latter end, and in the day of his death he shall be blessed. The fear of the Lord driveth out sin: for he that is without fear, cannot be justified: for the wrath of his high spirits is his ruin.

Q. Why do we receive the gift of Piety?

See "L. of C.," p. 103, No. 2.

Q. Why do we receive the gift of Knowledge?

See "L. of C.," p. 85, No. 14.

Q. Why do we receive the gift of Fortitude?

(II. Maccbs. 6. A. M. 3837.) Eleazar one of the chief of the scribes, a man advanced in years, and of a comely countenance, was pressed to open his mouth to eat swine's flesh. But he, choosing rather a most glorious death than a hateful life, went forward voluntarily to the torment. And considering in what manner he was come to it, patiently bearing, he determined not to do any unlawful things for the love of life. But they that stood by, being moved with wicked pity, for the old friendship they had with the man, taking him aside, desired that flesh might be brought, which it was lawful for him to eat, that he might make as if he had eaten, as the king had commanded of the flesh of the sacrifice: that by so doing he might be delivered from death: and for the sake of their old friendship with the man they did him this courtesy. But he began to consider the dignity of his age, and his ancient years, and the inbred honour of his grey head, and his good life and conversation from a child: and he answered without delay, according to the ordinances of the holy law made by God, saying, that he would rather be sent into the other world. For it doth not become our age, said he, to dissemble: whereby many young persons might think that Eleazar, at the age of fourscore and ten years, was gone over to the life of the heathens: and so they, through my dissimulation, and for a little time of a corruptible life, should be deceived, and hereby I should bring a stain and a curse upon my old age. For though, for the present time, I should be delivered from the punishments of men, yet should I not escape the hand of the Almighty neither alive nor dead. Wherefore by departing manfully out of this life, I shall show myself worthy of my old age: and I shall leave an example of fortitude to young men, if with a ready mind and constancy I suffer an honourable death, for the most venerable and most holy laws. Thus did this man die, leaving not only to young men, but also to the whole nation, the memory of his death for an example of virtue and fortitude.

Q. Why do we receive the gift of Counsel?

(Eccltus. 32.) My son, do thou nothing without counsel, and thou shalt not repent when thou hast done.

Q. Why do we receive the gift of Understanding?

(Isa. 42.) The Lord shall go forth as a mighty man, as a man of war shall he stir up zeal: he shall shout and cry: I will lead the blind into the way which they know not: and in the paths which they were ignorant of I will make them walk: I will make darkness light before them, and crooked things straight: these things have I done to them, and have not forsaken them.

Q. Why do we receive the gift of Wisdom?

(III. Kings 3. A. M. 2991.)

Then there came two women to the king, and stood before him: and one of them said: I beseech thee, my lord, I and this woman dwelt in one house, and I was delivered of a child with her in the chamber. And the third day, after that I was delivered, she also was delivered, and we were together, and no other person with us in the house, only we two. And this woman's child died in the night: for in her sleep she overlaid him. And rising in the dead time of the night, she took my child from my side, while I thy handmaid was asleep, and laid it in her bosom: and laid her dead child in my bosom. And when I rose in the morning to give my child food, behold it was dead: but considering him more diligently when it was clear day, I found that it was not mine which I bore. And the other woman answered: It is not so as thou sayest, but thy child is dead and mine is alive. On the contrary she said; Thou liest: for my child liveth, and thy child is dead. And in this manner they strove before the king. Then said the king: The one saith, My child is alive, and thy child is dead. And the other answereth: Nay, but thy child is dead, and mine liveth. The king therefore said: Bring me a sword. And when they had brought a sword before the king. divide, said he, the living child in two, and give half to the one, and half to the other. But the woman whose child was alive, said to the king (for her pity was moved upon her child) I beseech thee, my lord, give her the child alive, and do not kill it. But the other said: Let it be neither mine nor thine, but divide it. The king answered, and said: Give the living child to this woman, and let it not be killed, for she is the mother thereof.

Q. Which are the Beatitudes?

See "L. of C," p. 81, No. 7.

(I. Tim. 6.) Charge the rich of this world not to be high-minded, nor to trust in the uncertainty of riches, but in the living God, (who giveth us abundantly all things to enjoy,) to do good, to be rich in good works, to live easily, to communicate to others, to lay up in store for themselves a good foundation against the time to come, that they may lay hold on the true life.

(Job 21.) Why then do the wicked live, are they advanced, and strengthened with riches? Their seed continueth before them, a multitude of kinsmen, and of children's children in their sight. Their houses are secure and peaceable, and the rod of God is not upon them. Their cattle have conceived, and failed not: their cow has calved, and is not deprived of her fruit. Their little ones go out like a flock, and their children dance and play. They take the timbrel, and the harp, and rejoice at the sound of the organ. They spend their days in wealth, and in a moment they go down to hell. Who have said to God: Depart from us, we desire not the knowledge of thy ways. Who is the Almighty, that we should serve him? and what doth it profit us if we pray to him? Yet because their good things are not in their hand, may the counsel of the wicked be far from me. How often shall the lamp of the wicked be put out, and a deluge come upon them, and he shall distribute the sorrows of his wrath? They shall be as chaff before the face of the wind, and as ashes which the whirlwind scattereth. God shall lay up the sorrow of the father for his children: and when he shall repay, then shall he know. His eyes shall see his own destruction, and he shall drink of the wrath of the Almighty. Because the wicked man is reserved to the day of destruction, and he shall be brought to the day of wrath.

See "L. of C.," p. 55, No. 6; p. 83, No. 10.
  See "L. of C.," p. 106, No. 8.
  See "L. of C.," p. 57, No. 11.
See "L. of C.," p. 34, No. 18; p. 53, No. 18; p. 116, No. 6.
  See "L. of C.," p. 86, No. 18.
  See "L. of C.," p. 67, No. 32.
  See "L. of C.," p. 68, No. 36.

(Job 2. A. M. 2520.) Now it came to pass, when on a certain day the sons of God came, and stood before the Lord, and Satan came among them, and stood in his sight, that the Lord said to Satan: Whence comest thou?. And he answered and said: I have gone round about the earth, and walked through it. And the Lord said to Satan: Hast thou considered my servant Job, that there is none like him in the earth, a man simple, and upright, and fearing God, and avoiding evil, and still keeping his innocence? But thou hast moved me against him, that I should afflict him without cause. And Satan answered, and said: Skin for skin, and all that a man hath he will give for his life: but put forth thy hand, and touch his bone and his flesh, and then thou shalt see that he will bless thee to thy face. And the Lord said to Satan: Behold he is in thy hand, but yet save his life. So Satan went forth from the presence of the Lord, and struck Job with a very grievous ulcer, from the sole of the foot even to the top of his head: and he took a potsherd and scraped the corrupt matter, sitting on a dunghill. And his wife said to him: Dost thou still continue in thy simplicity? bless God, and die. And he said to her: Thou hast spoken like one of the foolish women: if we have received good things at the hand of God, why should we not receive evil? In all these things Job did not sin with his lips. The Lord also was turned at the penance of Job, when he prayed for his friends. And the Lord gave Job twice as much as he had before. And the Lord blessed the latter end of Job more than his beginning.

Q. Which are the twelve fruits of the Holy Ghost?

(Gal. 5.) The fruit of the Spirit is, charity, joy, peace, patience, benignity, goodness, longanimity, mildness, faith, modesty, continency, chastity.

(Josh. 4. A. M. 2553.) Josue called twelve men, whom he had chosen out of the children of Israel, one out of every tribe, and he said to them: Go before the ark of the Lord your God to the midst of the Jordan, and carry from thence every man a stone on your shoulders, according to the number of the children of Israel, that it may be a sign among you: and when your children shall ask you to-morrow, saying: What mean these stones? You shall answer them: The waters of the Jordan ran off before the ark of the covenant of the Lord, when it passed over the same: therefore were these stones set for a monument of the children of Israel for ever. The children of Israel therefore did as Josue commanded them, carrying out of the channel of the Jordan twelve stones, as the Lord had commanded him, according to the number of the children of Israel, unto the place wherein they camped, and there they set them. And Josue put other twelve stones in the midst of the channel of the Jordan, where the priests stood that carried the ark of the covenant: and they are there until this present day.

LESSON SEVENTEENTH.

ON THE SACRAMENT OF PENANCE.

Q. What is the Sacrament of Penance?
See "L. of C.," p. 19, No. 1; p. 40, No. 38.

(IV. Kings 5. A. M. 3115.) Naaman, general of the army of the king of Syria, was a great man with his master, and honourable: for by him the Lord gave deliverance to Syria: and he was a valiant man and rich, but a leper. Now there had gone out robbers from Syria, and had led away captive out of the land of Israel a little maid, and she waited upon Naaman's wife. And she said to her mistress: I wish my master had been with the prophet, that is in Samaria: he would certainly have healed him of the leprosy which he hath. And Eliseus sent a messenger to him, saying: Go, and wash seven times in the Jordan, and thy flesh shall recover health, and thou shalt be clean. Then he went down, and washed in the Jordan seven times:

according to the word of the man of God, and his flesh was restored, like the flesh of a little child, and he was made clean. And returning to the man of God with all his train, he came, and stood before him, and said: In truth, I know there is no other God in all the earth, but only in Israel: I beseech thee therefore take a blessing of thy servant. But he answered: As the Lord liveth, before whom I stand, I will receive none. And when he pressed him, he still refused. But Giezi the servant of the man of God said: My master hath spared Naaman this Syrian, in not receiving of him that which he brought: as the Lord liveth, I will run after him, and take some thing of him: then he went in, and stood before his master. And Eliseus said: Whence comest thou, Giezi? He answered: Thy servant went no whither. But he said: Was not my heart present, when the man turned back from his chariot to meet thee? So now thou hast received money, and received garments, to buy olive-yards, and vineyards, and sheep, and oxen, and men-servants, and maid-servants. But the leprosy of Naaman shall also stick to thee, and to thy seed for ever. And he went out from him a leper as white as snow.

Q. How does the Sacrament of Penance remit sin, and restore to the soul the friendship of God?
See " L. of C.," p. 26, No. 13.

(Ezek. 18.) The soul that sinneth, the same shall die: but if the wicked do penance for all his sins which he hath committed, and keep all my commandments, and do judgment, and justice, living he shall live, and shall not die. I will not remember all his iniquities that he hath done: in his justice which he hath wrought, he shall live. Is it my will that a sinner should die saith the Lord God, and not that he should be converted from his ways, and live? But if the just man turn himself away from his justice, and do iniquity according to all the abominations which the wicked man useth to work, shall he live? all his justices which he hath done, shall not be remembered: in the prevarication, by which he hath prevaricated, and in his sin, which he hath committed, in them he shall die.

Q. How do you know that the priest has the power of absolving from the sins committed after Baptism?
See " L. of C.," p. 26, No. 14; p. 75, No. 14; p. 122, No. 8.

Q. How do the priests of the Church exercise the power of forgiving sins?
See " L. of C.," p. 35, No. 24

(Ezek. 33. A. M. 3417.) The word of the Lord came to me, saying: Son of man, speak to the children of thy people, and say to them: When I bring the sword upon a land, if the people of the land take a man, one of their meanest, and make him a watchman over them. And he see the sword coming upon the land, and sound the trumpet, and tell the people: then he that heareth the sound of the trumpet, whosoever he be, and doth not look to himself, if the sword come, and cut him off: his blood shall be upon his own head. And if the watchman see the sword coming, and sound not the trumpet: and the people look not to themselves, and the sword come, and cut off a soul from among them: he indeed is taken away in his iniquity, but I will require his blood at the hand of the watchman. So thou, O son of man, I have made thee a watchman to the house of Israel: therefore thou shalt hear the word from my mouth, and shalt tell it them from me. When I say to the wicked: O wicked man, thou shalt surely die: if thou dost not speak to warn the wicked man from his way: that wicked man shall die in his iniquity, but I will require his blood at thy hand. But if thou tell the wicked man, that he may be converted from his ways, and he be not converted from his way: he shall die in his iniquity: but thou hast delivered thy soul. Thou therefore, O son of man, say to the house of Israel: *As* I live, saith the Lord God, I desire not the death of the wicked, but that the wicked turn from his way, and live. Turn ye, turn ye from your evil ways: and why will you die, O house of Israel? Yea, if I shall say to the just that he shall surely live, and he, trusting in his justice, commit iniquity: all his justices shall be forgotten, and in his iniquity, which he hath committed, in the same shall he die. And if I shall say to the wicked: Thou shalt surely die: and he do penance for his sin, and do judgment and justice, and if that wicked man restore the pledge, and render what he had robbed, *and* walk in the commandments of life, and do no unjust thing: he shall surely live, and shall not die. None of his sins, which he hath committed, shall be imputed to him: he hath done judgment and justice, he shall surely live.

Q. What must we do to receive the Sacrament of Penance worthily?
See "L. of C.," p. 73, No. 9; p. 79, No. 1.

Q. What is the examination of conscience?
See "L. of C.," p. 72, No. 7.

Q. How can we make a good examination of conscience?
(II. Kings 12. A. M. 2971.) The Lord sent Nathan to David: and when he was come to him, he said to him: There were two men in one city, the one rich, and the other poor. The rich man had exceeding many sheep and oxen. But the poor man had nothing at all but one little ewe-lamb, which he had bought and nourished up, and which had grown up in his house together with his children, eating of his bread,

and drinking of his cup, and sleeping in his bosom: and it was unto him as a daughter. And when a certain stranger was come to the rich man, he spared to take of his own sheep and oxen, to make a feast for that stranger, who was come to him, but took the poor man's ewe, and dressed it for the man that was come to him. And David's anger being exceedingly kindled against that man, he said to Nathan: As the Lord liveth, the man that hath done this is a child of death. He shall restore the ewe fourfold, because he did this thing, and had no pity. And Nathan said to David: Thou art the man. Thus saith the Lord the God of Israel: I anointed thee king over Israel, and I delivered thee from the hand of Saul, and gave thee thy master's house and thy master's wives into thy bosom, and gave thee the house of Israel and Juda: and if these things be little, I shall add far greater things unto thee. Why therefore hast thou despised the word of the Lord, to do evil in my sight? Thou hast killed Urias the Hethite with the sword, and hast taken his wife to be thy wife, and hast slain him with the sword of the children of Ammon. Therefore the sword shall never depart from thy house, because thou hast despised me, and hast taken the wife of Urias the Hethite to be thy wife.

Q. What should we do before beginning the examination of conscience?

(Apoc. 3.) To the angel of the church of Laodicea, write: These things saith the Amen, the faithful and true witness, who is the beginning of the creation of God: I know thy works, that thou art neither cold, nor hot. I would thou wert cold, or hot. But because thou art lukewarm, and neither cold, nor hot, I will begin to vomit thee out of my mouth.

LESSON EIGHTEENTH.

ON CONTRITION.

Q. What is contrition, or sorrow for sin?

(IV. Kings 20. A. M. 3291.) In those days Ezechias was sick unto death: and Isaias the son of Amos the prophet came and said to him: Thus saith the Lord God: Give charge concerning thy house, for thou shalt die, and not live. And he turned his face to the wall, and prayed to the Lord, saying: I beseech thee, O Lord, remember how I have walked before thee in truth, and with a perfect heart, and have done that which is pleasing before thee. And Ezechias wept with much weeping. And before Isaias was gone out of the middle of the court, the word of the Lord came to him, saying: Go back, and tell Ezechias the captain of my people: Thus saith the Lord the God of David thy father: I have heard thy prayer, and I have seen thy tears: and behold I have healed thee, on the third day thou shalt go up to the temple of the Lord. And Ezechias said to Isaias: What shall be the sign that the Lord will heal me, and that I shall go up to the temple of the Lord the third day? And Isaias said to him: This shall be the sign from the Lord, that the Lord will do the word which he hath spoken: Wilt thou that the shadow go forward ten lines, or that it go back so many degrees? And Ezechias said: It is an easy matter for the shadow to go forward ten lines: and I do not desire that this be done, but let it return back ten degrees. And Isaias the prophet called upon the Lord, and he brought the shadow ten degrees backwards by the lines, by which it had already gone down in the dial of Achaz.

Q. What kind of sorrow should we have for our sins?

(II. Cor. 7.) Although I made you sorrowful by my epistle, I do not repent; and if I did repent, seeing that the same epistle (although but for a time) did make you sorrowful; now I am glad: not because you were made sorrowful; but because you were made sorrowful unto penance. For you were made sorrowful according to God, that you might suffer damage by us in nothing. For the sorrow that is according to God worketh penance, steadfast unto salvation: but the sorrow of the world worketh death. For behold this self-same thing, that you were made sorrowful according to God, how great carefulness it worketh in you; yea defence, yea indignation, yea fear, yea desire, yea zeal, yea revenge: in all things you have shewed yourselves to be undefiled in the matter.

Q. What do you mean by saying that our sorrow should be interior?

(Deut. 30.) Now when all these things shall be come upon thee, the blessing or the curse, which I have set forth before thee, and thou shalt be touched with repentance of thy heart among all the nations, into which the Lord thy God shall have scattered thee, and shalt return to him, and obey his commandments, as I command thee this day, thou and thy children, with all thy heart, and with all thy soul: the Lord thy God will bring back again thy captivity, and will have mercy on thee, and gather thee again out of all the nations, into which he scattered thee before. If thou be driven as far as the poles of heaven, the Lord thy God will fetch thee back from thence, and will take thee to himself, and bring thee into the land which thy fathers possessed, and thou shalt possess it: and blessing thee, he will make thee more numerous than were thy fathers. Yet so if thou hear the voice of the Lord thy God, and keep his precepts and ceremonies, which are written in this law: and return to the Lord thy God with all thy heart, and with all thy soul.

Q. **What do you mean by saying that our sorrow should be supernatural?**

See "L. of C.," p. 83, No. 11; p. 108, No. 12.

Q. **What do you mean by saying that our sorrow should be universal?**

(Num. 33. A. M. 2553.) The Lord said to Moses: Command the children of Israel, and say to them: When you shall have passed over the Jordan, entering into the land of Chanaan, destroy all the inhabitants of that land: beat down their pillars, and break in pieces their statues, and waste all their high places, cleansing the land, and dwelling in it. For I have given it you for a possession. But if you will not kill the inhabitants of the land: they that remain, shall be unto you as nails in *your* eyes, and spears in *your* sides, and they shall be your adversaries in the land of your habitation. And whatsoever I had thought to do to them, I will do to you.

(I. King 15. A. M. 2934.) And Saul smote Amalec from Hevila, until thou comest to Sur, which is over-against Egypt. And he took Agag the king of Amalec alive: but all the common people he slew with the edge of the sword. And Saul and the people spared Agag and the best of the flocks of sheep and of the herds, and the garments and the rams, and all that was beautiful, and would not destroy them: but every thing that was vile and good for nothing, that they destroyed. And Samuel said: When thou wast a little one in thy own eyes, wast thou not made the head of the tribes of Israel? And the Lord anointed thee to be king over Israel. And the Lord sent thee on the way, and said: Go, and kill the sinners of Amalec, and thou shalt fight against them until thou hast utterly destroyed them. Why then didst thou not hearken to the voice of the Lord: but hast turned to the prey, and hast done evil in the eyes of the Lord. And Saul said to Samuel: Yea I have hearkened to the voice of the Lord, and have walked in the way by which the Lord sent me, and have brought Agag the king of Amalec, and Amalec I have slain. But the people took of the spoils sheep and oxen, *as* the first-fruits of those things that were slain, to offer sacrifice to the Lord their God in Galgal. And Samuel said: Doth the Lord desire holocaust and victims, and not rather that the voice of the Lord should be obeyed? For obedience is better than sacrifices: and to hearken rather than to offer the fat of rams. Because it is like the sin of witchcraft, to rebel: and like the crime of idolatry, to refuse to obey. Forasmuch therefore as thou hast rejected the word of the Lord, the Lord hath *also* rejected thee from being king.

Q. What do you mean when you say that our sorrow should be sovereign?

See "L. of C.," p. 85, No. 15.

Q. Why should we be sorry for our sins?

See "L. of C.," p. 68, No. 35.

Q. How many kinds of contrition are there?

(Ecc. 2.) Ye that fear the Lord, wait for his mercy: and go not aside from him, lest ye fall. Ye that fear the Lord, believe him: and your reward shall not be made void. Ye that fear the Lord, hope in him: and mercy shall come to you for your delight. Ye that fear the Lord, love him, and your hearts shall be enlightened. For God is compassionate and merciful, and will forgive sins in the day of tribulation: and he is a protector to all that seek him in truth. They that fear the Lord, will not be incredulous to his word: and they that love him will keep his way. They that fear the Lord, will seek after the things that are well pleasing to him: and they that love him, shall be filled with his law.

(Jer. 17.) Let them be confounded that persecute me, and let not me be confounded: let them be afraid, and let not me be afraid: bring upon them the day of affliction, and with a double destruction, destroy them.

Q. What is perfect contrition?

See "L. of C.," p. 36, No. 27.

Q. What is imperfect contrition?

See "L. of C.," p. 81, No. 7.

Q. Is imperfect contrition sufficient for a worthy confession?

See "L of C.," p. 73, No. 9.

Q. What do you mean by a firm purpose of sinning no more?

See "L. of C.," p. 54, Nos. 3, 4; p. 85, No. 16.

(Gen. 19. A. M. 2107.) The sun was risen upon the earth, and Lot entered into Segor. And the Lord rained upon Sodom and Gomorrha brimstone and fire from the Lord out of heaven. And he destroyed these cities, and all the country about, all the inhabitants of the cities, and all things that spring from the earth. And his wife looking behind her, was turned into a statue of salt.

(Gen. 35.) In the mean time God said to Jacob: Arise, and go up to Bethel, and dwell there, and make there an altar to God, who appeared to thee when thou didst flee from Esau thy brother. And Jacob having called together all his household, said: Cast away the strange gods that are among you, and be cleansed and change your garments. Arise, and let us go up to Bethel, that we may make there an altar to God: who heard me in the day of my affliction, and accompany me in my journey. So they gave him all the strange gods they had, and the earrings which were in their ears: and he buried them under the turpentine-tree, that is behind the city of Sichem. And when they were departed, the terror of God fell upon all the cities round about, and they durst not pursue after them as they went away.

Q. What do you mean by the near occasions of sin?
See " L. of C.," p. 53, No. 19.

(Judg. 13. A. M. 2849.) Now there was a certain man of Saraa, and of the race of Dan, whose name was Manue, and his wife was barren. And an angel of the Lord appeared to her, and said: Behold thou shalt conceive and bear a son: beware thou drink no wine, nor strong drink, nor eat any unclean thing: for the child shall be a Nazarite of God from his infancy, from his mother's womb until the day of his death, and he shall begin to deliver Israel from the hands of the Philistines. And she bore a son, and called his name Samson. And the child grew, and the Lord blessed him. Then Samson went down to Thamnatha, and seeing there a woman of the daughters of the Philistines, he came up, and told his father and his mother, saying: I saw a woman in Thamnatha of the daughters of the Philistines: I beseech you, take her for me to wife. After this he loved a woman, who dwelt in the valley of Sorec, and she was called Dalila. And the princes of the Philistines came to her, and said: Deceive him, and learn of him wherein his great strength lieth, and how we may be able to overcome him, to bind and afflict him: which if thou shalt do, we will give thee every one of us eleven hundred pieces of silver. Then opening the truth of the thing, he said to her: The razor hath never come upon my head, for I am a Nazarite, that is to say, consecrated to God from my mother's womb: If my head be shaven, my strength shall depart from me, and I shall become weak, and shall be like other men. But she made him sleep upon her knees, and lay his head in her bosom. And she called a barber, and shaved his seven locks, and began to drive him away, and thrust him from her: for immediately his strength departed from him. And she said: The Philistines are upon thee, Samson. And awakening from sleep, he said in his mind: I will go out as I did before, not knowing that the Lord was departed from him. Then the Philistines seized upon him, and forthwith pulled out his eyes, and led him bound in chains to Gaza, and shutting him up in prison made him grind.

LESSON NINETEENTH.

ON CONFESSION.

Q. What is confession?

(Num. 5. A. M. 2514.) The Lord spoke to Moses, saying: Say to the children of Israel: When a man or woman shall have committed any of all the sins that men are wont to commit, and by negligence shall have transgressed the commandment of the Lord, and offended, they shall confess their sin, and restore the principal itself, and the fifth part over and above, to him against whom they have sinned. But if there be no one to receive it, they shall give it to the Lord, and it shall be the priest's.

Q. What sins are we bound to confess?

See " L. of C.," p. 74, No. 11.

(I. Kings 17. A. M. 2942.) Saul said to David: Thou art not able to withstand this Philistine, nor to fight against him: for thou art *but* a boy, but he is a warrior from his youth. And David said: The Lord who delivered me out of the paw of the lion, and out of the paw of the bear, he will deliver me out of the hand of this Philistine. And Saul said to David: Go, and the Lord be with thee. And David said to the Philistine: Thou comest to me with a sword, and with a spear, and with a shield: but I come to thee in the name of the Lord of hosts, the God of the armies of Israel, which thou hast defied this day, and the Lord will deliver thee into my hand, and I will slay thee, and take away thy head from thee: and I will give the carcasses of the army of the Philistines this day to the birds of the air, and to the beasts of the earth: that all the earth may know that there is a God in Israel. And all this assembly shall know, that the Lord saveth not with sword and spear: for it is his battle, and he will deliver you into our hands. And when the Philistine arose and was coming, and drew nigh to meet David, David made haste, and ran to the fight to meet the Philistine. And he put his hand into his scrip, and took a stone, and cast it with the sling, and fetching it about struck the Philistine in the forehead:

and the stone was fixed in his forehead, and he fell on his face upon the earth. And David prevailed over the Philistine, with a sling and a stone, and he struck, and slew the Philistine. And as David had no sword in his hand, he ran, and stood over the Philistine, and took his sword, and drew it out of the sheath, and slew him, and cut off his head. And the Philistines seeing that their champion was dead, fled away.

Q. Which are the chief qualities of a good Confession?

See "L. of C.," p. 68, Nos. 33, 34.

Q. When is our Confession humble?

See "L. of C.," p. 23, No. 7; p. 71, No. 5.

Q. When is our Confession sincere?

(Prov. 28.) He that hideth his sins, shall not prosper: but he that shall confess, and forsake them, shall obtain mercy.

Q. When is our Confession entire?

(Acts 4–5. A. D. 33.) With great power did the apostles give testimony of the resurrection of Jesus Christ our Lord; and great grace was in them all. For neither was there any one needy among them. For as many as were owners of lands or houses, sold them, and brought the price of the things they sold, and laid it down before the feet of the apostles. And distribution was made to every one, according as he had need, but a certain man named Ananias, with Saphira his wife, sold a piece of land, and by fraud kept back part of the price of the land, his wife being privy thereunto: and bringing a certain part of it, laid it at the feet of the apostles. But Peter said: Ananias, why hath satan tempted thy heart, that thou shouldst lie to the Holy Ghost, and by fraud keep part of the price of the land? Whilst it remained, did it not remain to thee? and after it was sold, was it not in thy power? Why hast thou conceived this thing in thy heart? Thou hast not lied to men, but to God. And Ananias hearing these words, fell down, and gave up the ghost. And there came great fear upon all that heard it. And the young men rising up, removed him, and carrying him out, buried him. And it was about the space of three hours after, when his wife, not knowing what had happened, came in. And Peter said to her: Tell me woman, whether you sold the land for so much? And she said: Yea, for so much. And Peter *said* unto her: Why have you agreed together to tempt the Spirit of the Lord? Behold the feet of them who have buried thy husband are at the door, and they shall carry thee out. Immediately she fell down before his feet, and gave up the ghost. And the young men coming in, found her dead: and carried her out, and buried her by her husband. And there came great fear upon the whole church, and upon all that heard these things.

Q. What should we do if we cannot remember the number of our sins?

(I. John 1.) This is the declaration which we have heard from him, and declare unto you: That God is Light, and in him there is no darkness. If we say that we have fellowship with him, and walk in darkness, we lie, and do not the truth. But, if we walk in the light, as he also is in the light, we have fellowship one with another, and the blood of Jesus Christ his Son cleanseth us from all sin. If we say that we have no sin, we deceive ourselves, and the truth is not in us. If we confess our sins, he is faithful and just, to forgive us our sins, and to cleanse us from all iniquity. If we say that we have not sinned, we make him a liar, and his word is not in us.

Q. Is our Confession worthy if, without our fault, we forget to confess a mortal sin?

See "L. of C.," p. 115, Cpt. vii., No. 2.

Q. Is it a grievous offense wilfully to conceal a mortal sin in Confession?

See "L. of C.," p 42, No. 43.

(II. Cor. 6.) Bear not the yoke with unbelievers, For what participation hath justice with injustice? Or what fellowship hath light with darkness? And what concord hath Christ with Belial? Or what part hath the faithful with the unbeliever? And what agreement hath the temple of God with idols? For you are the temple of the living God; as God saith: *I will dwell in them, and walk among them; and I will be their God, and they shall be my people.* Wherefore, *Go out from among them, and be ye separate*, saith the Lord, *and touch not the unclean thing: and I will receive you; and I will be a Father to you; and you shall be my sons and daughters, saith the Lord Almighty.*

(James 2.) Whosoever shall keep the whole law, but offend in one *point*, is become guilty of all. For he that said, thou shalt not commit adultery, said also, Thou shalt not kill. Now if thou do not commit adultery, but shalt kill, thou art become a transgressor of the law.

Q. What must he do who has wilfully concealed a mortal sin in Confession?

See "L. of C.," p. 92, No. 36.

Q. Why does the priest give us a penance after Confession?

See "L. of C.," p. 74, No. 10.

Q. Does not the Sacrament of Penance remit all punishment due to sin?

(II. Kings 12. A. M. 2970.) David said to Nathan: I have sinned against the Lord. And Nathan said to David: The Lord also hath taken away thy sin: thou shalt not die. Nevertheless, because thou hast given occasion to the enemies of the Lord to blaspheme, for this thing, the child that is born to thee, shall surely die.

Q. Why does God require a temporal punishment as a satisfaction for sin?
See "L. of C.," p. 82, No. 9.

Q. Which are the chief means by which we satisfy God for the temporal punishment due to sin?
See "L. of C.," p. 33. Nos. 14-16; p. 51, No. 13.

(Gen. 32. A. M. 2265.) The messengers returned to Jacob, saying: We came to Esau thy brother, and behold he cometh with speed to meet thee with four hundred men. Then Jacob was greatly afraid; and in his fear divided the people that was with him, and the flocks, and the sheep, and the oxen, and the camels, into two companies, saying: if Esau come to one company and destroy it, the other company that is left shall escape. And Jacob said: O God of my father Abraham, and God of my father Isaac, O Lord. Deliver me from the hand of my brother Esau, for I am greatly afraid of him: lest perhaps he come, and kill the mother with the children. And when he had slept there that night, he set apart, of the things which he had, presents for his brother Esau, and he sent them by the hands of his servants, every drove by itself, and he said to his servants: Go before me, and let there be a space between drove and drove. And he commanded the first, saying: If thou meet my brother Esau, and he ask thee: Whose art thou? or whither goest thou? or whose are these before thee? Thou shalt answer: Thy servant Jacob's: he hath sent them as a present to my lord Esau: and he cometh after us. In like manner he commanded the second and the third, and all that followed the droves, saying: Speak ye the same words to Esau, when ye find him. And ye shall add: Thy servant Jacob himself also followeth after us; for he said: I will appease him with the presents that go before, and afterwards I will see him, perhaps he will be gracious to me. He remained alone: and behold a man wrestled with him till morning. And when he saw that he could not overcome him, he touched the sinew of his thigh, and forthwith it shrank. And he said to him: Let me go, for it is break of day. He answered: I will not let thee go except thou bless me. And he said: What is thy name? He answered: Jacob. But he said: Thy name shall not be called Jacob, but Israel: for if thou hast been strong against God, how much more shalt thou prevail against men? Then Esau ran to meet his brother, and embraced him: and clasping him fast about the neck, and kissing him, wept. And Esau said: What are the droves that I met? He answered: That I might find favour before my lord. But he said: I have plenty, my brother keep what is thine for thyself. And Jacob said: Do not so I beseech thee, but if I have found favour in thy eyes, receive a little present at my hands: for I have seen thy face, as if I should have seen the countenance of God: be gracious to me, and take the blessing, which I have brought thee, and which God hath given me, who giveth all things. He took it with much ado at his brother's earnest pressing him.

Q. Which are the chief spiritual works of mercy?

See "L. of C.," p. 75, No. 14; p. 82, quest. 1; p. 91, quest. 2; p. 35, No. 24.

(Job 1. A. M. 2520.) There was a man in the land of Hus, whose name was Job, and that man was simple and upright, and fearing God, and avoiding evil. Now on a certain day when the sons of God came to stand before the Lord, Satan also was present among them. And the Lord said to him: Whence comest thou? And he answered and said: I have gone round about the earth, and walked through it. And the Lord said to him: Hast thou considered my servant Job, that there is none like him in the earth, a simple and upright man, and fearing God, and avoiding evil? And Satan answering, said: Doth Job fear God in vain? Hast not thou made a fence for him, and his house, and all his substance round about, blessed the works of his hands, and his possession hath increased on the earth? But stretch forth thy hand a little, and touch all that he hath, and see if he blesseth thee not to thy face. Then the Lord said to Satan: Behold, all that he hath is in thy hand; only put not forth thy hand upon his person. And Satan went forth from the presence of the Lord. Now upon a certain day when his sons and daughters were eating and drinking wine in the house of their eldest brother, there came a messenger to Job, and said: The oxen were plowing, and the asses feeding beside them, and the Sabeans rushed in, and took all away, and slew the servants with the sword, and I alone have escaped to tell thee. And while he was yet speaking, another came, and said: The fire of God fell from heaven, and striking the sheep and the servants, hath consumed them, and I alone have escaped to tell thee. And while he also was yet speaking, there came another, and said: The Chaldeans made three troops, and have fallen upon the camels, and taken them, moreover they have slain the servants with the sword, and I alone have escaped to tell thee. He was yet speaking, and behold another came in, and said: Thy sons and daughters were eating and drinking wine in the house of their elder brother, a violent wind came on a sudden from the side of the desert, and shook the four corners of the house, and it fell upon thy children and they are dead, and I alone have escaped to tell thee. Then Job rose up, and rent his garments, and having shaven his head fell down upon the ground and worshipped, and said: Naked came I out of my mother's womb, and naked shall I return thither: the Lord gave, and the Lord hath taken away; as it hath pleased the Lord so it is done: blessed be the name of the Lord. The Lord also was turned at the penance of Job, when he prayed for his friends. And the Lord gave Job twice as much as he had before. And the Lord blessed the latter end of Job more than his beginning.

See "L. of C.," p. 76, No. 16.

(I. Kings 24. A. M. 2946.) There was a cave, into which Saul went, to sleep: now David and his men lay hid in the inner part of the cave. And the servants of David said to him: Behold the day, of which the Lord said to thee: I will deliver thy enemy unto thee, that thou mayest do to him as it shall seem good in thy eyes. Then David arose, and secretly cut off the hem of Saul's robe. After which David's heart struck him, because he had cut off the hem of Saul's robe. And he said to his men: The Lord be merciful unto me, that I may do no such thing to my master the Lord's anointed, as to lay my hand upon him, because he is the Lord's anointed. And David stopped his men with his words, and suffered them not to rise against Saul: But Saul rising up out of the cave, went on his way.

(I. Kings 26. A. M. 2947.) David and Abisai came to the people by night, and found Saul lying and sleeping in the tent, and his spear fixed in the ground at his head: and Abner and the people sleeping round about him. And Abisai said to David: God hath shut up thy enemy this day into thy hands: now then I will run him through with my spear even to the earth at once, and there shall be no need of a second time. And David said to Abisai: Kill him not: for who shall put forth his hand against the Lord's anointed, and shall be guiltless? And David said: As the Lord liveth, unless the Lord shall strike him, or his day shall come to die, or he shall go down to battle and perish: the Lord be merciful unto me, that I extend not my hand upon the Lord's anointed. But now take the spear, which is at his head, and the cup of water, and let us go.

Q. Which are the chief corporal works of mercy?

(Tobias A. M. 3283.) Tobias daily went among all his kindred, and comforted them, and distributed to every one as he was able, out of his goods. he fed the hungry, and gave clothes to the naked, and was careful to bury the dead, and they that were slain. Now it happened one day, that being wearied with burying, he came to his house, and cast himself down by the wall and slept, and as he was sleeping he was made blind. Now Anna his wife went daily to weaving work, and she brought home what she could get for their living by the labour of her hands. Then Tobias sighed, and began to pray with tears. Now it happened on the same day, that Sara daughter of Raguel, in Rages a city of the Medes, received a reproach from one of her father's servant maids, because she had been given to seven husbands, and a devil named Asmodeus had killed them, so when she reproved the maid for her fault, she answered her, saying: May we never see son, or daughter of thee upon the earth, thou murderer of thy husbands. Wilt thou kill me also, as thou hast already killed seven husbands? At these words she went into an upper chamber of her house: and for three days and three nights did neither eat nor drink: but continuing in prayer with tears besought God, that he would deliver her from this reproach. And it came to pass on the third day, the prayers of them both were heard in the sight of the glory of the most high God: and the holy Angel of the Lord, Raphael, was sent to heal them both, whose prayers at one time were rehearsed in the sight of the Lord. Therefore when Tobias thought that his prayer was heard that he might die, he called to him Tobias his son, and said to him: Hear, my son, the words of my mouth, and lay them as a foundation in thy heart, bless God at all times: and desire of him to direct thy ways, and that all thy counsels may abide in him. I tell thee also, my son, that I lent ten talents of silver, while thou wast yet a child, to Gabelus, in Rages a city of the Medes, and I have a note of his hand with me: but go now, and seek thee out some faithful man, to go with thee for his hire: that thou mayst receive it, while I yet live. Then Tobias going forth, found a beautiful young man, standing girded, and as it were ready to walk. And not knowing that he was an Angel of God, he saluted him, and said: From whence art thou, good young man? But he answered: Of the children of Israel. And Tobias said to him: Knowest thou the way that leadeth to the country of the Medes? And he answered: I know it: and I have often walked through all the ways thereof, and I have abode with Gabelus our brother, who dwelleth at Rages a city of the Medes, which is situate in the mount of Ecbatana. And Tobias said to him: Stay for me, I beseech thee, till I tell these same things to my father. Then

Tobias going in told all these things to his father. Upon which his father being in admiration, desired that he would come in unto him. And Tobias said to him: Canst thou conduct my son to Gabelus at Rages, a city of the Medes? and when thou shalt return, I will pay thee thy hire. And the Angel said to him: I will conduct him thither, and bring him back to thee. Then all things being ready, that were to be carried in their journey, Tobias bid his father and his mother farewell, and they set out both together. And Tobias went forward, and the dog followed him, and he lodged the first night by the river of Tigris. And he went out to wash his feet, and behold a monstrous fish came up to devour him. And Tobias being afraid of him, cried out with a loud voice, saying: Sir, he cometh upon me. And the Angel said to him: Take him by the gill, and draw him to thee. And when he had done so, he drew him out upon the land, and he began to pant before his feet. Then the Angel said to him: Take out the entrails of this fish, and lay up his heart, and his gall, and his liver for thee: for these are necessary for useful medicines. Then Tobias asked the Angel, and said to him: I beseech thee, brother Azarias, tell me what remedies are these things good for which thou hast bid me keep of the fish? And the Angel, answering, said to him: If thou put a little piece of its heart upon coals, the smoke thereof driveth away all kinds of devils, either from man or from woman, so that they come no more to them. And the gall is good for anointing the eyes, in which there is a white speck, and they shall be cured. And Tobias said to him: Where wilt thou that we lodge? And the Angel answering, said: Here is one whose name is Raguel, a near kinsman of thy tribe, and he hath a daughter named Sara, but he hath no son nor any other daughter beside her. All his substance is due to thee, and thou must take her to wife. Then Tobias answered, and said: I hear that she hath been given to seven husbands, and they all died: moreover I have heard, that a devil killed them. Then the Angel Raphael said to him: Hear me, and I will shew thee who they are, over whom the devil can prevail. For they who in such manner receive matrimony, as to shut out God from themselves, and from their mind, and to give themselves to their lust, over them the devil hath power. But thou when thou shalt take her, go into the chamber, and for three days give thyself to nothing else but to prayers with her. And on that night lay the liver of the fish on the fire, and the devil shall be driven away. And they went into Raguel, and Raguel received them with joy. And

Raguel said to them: Do you know Tobias my brother? And they said: We know him. And when he was speaking many good things of him, the Angel said to Raguel: Tobias concerning whom thou inquirest is this young man's father. And Raguel went to him, and kissed him with tears, and Anna his wife, and Sara their daughter wept. And when he desired them to sit down to dinner, Tobias said: I will not eat nor drink here this day, unless thou first grant me my petition, and promise to give me Sara thy daughter. Now when Raguel heard this he was afraid, knowing what had happened to those seven husbands. The Angel said to him: Be not afraid to give her to this man, for to him who feareth God is thy daughter due to be his wife: therefore another could not have her. Then Raguel said: I doubt not but God hath regarded my prayers and tears in his sight. And taking the right hand of his daughter, he gave it into the right hand of Tobias, saying: The God of Abraham, and the God of Isaac, and the God of Jacob be with you, and may he join you together, and fulfil his blessing in you. And Tobias remembering the Angel's word, took out of his bag part of the liver and laid it upon burning coals. Then the Angel Raphael took the devil, and bound him in the desert of upper Egypt. Then Raphael took four of Raguel's servants, and two camels, and went to Rages the city of the Medes: and finding Gabelus, gave him his note of hand, and received of him all the money. And he told him concerning Tobias the son of Tobias, all that had been done: and made him come with him to the wedding. But as Tobias made longer stay upon occasion of the marriage, Tobias his father was solicitous, saying: Why thinkest thou doth my son tarry, or why is he detained there? Is Gabelus dead thinkest thou, and no man will pay him the money. And he began to be exceeding sad, both he and Anna his wife with him: and they began both to weep together: because their son did not return to them on the day appointed. But Raguel said to his son-in-law: Stay here, and I will send a messenger to Tobias thy father, that thou art in health. And Tobias said to him: I know that my father and mother now count the days, and their spirit is grievously afflicted within them. And when Raguel had pressed Tobias with many words, and he by no means would hearken to him, he delivered Sara unto him, admonishing her to honour her father and mother-in-law, to love her husband, to take care of the family, to govern the house, and to behave herself irreprehensibly. And as they were returning Raphael said to Tobias: As soon as thou shalt come into thy house, forthwith adore the Lord thy God: and giving thanks to him, go to thy father, and kiss him. And immediately anoint his eyes with this gall of the fish, which thou carriest with thee. Then the dog, which had been with them in the way, ran before, and coming as if he had brought the news, shewed his joy by his fawning and wagging his tail. And his father that was blind, rising up, began to run stumbling with his feet: and giving a servant his hand, went to meet his son. Then Tobias taking of the gall of the fish, anointed his father's eyes. And he stayed about half an hour: and a white skin began to come out of his eyes, like the skin of an egg. And Tobias took hold of it, and drew it from his eyes, and immediately he recovered his sight. And they glorified God, both he and his wife and all that knew him. Then Tobias called to him his son, and said to him: What can we give to this holy man, that is come with thee? So the father and the son calling him, took him aside: and began to desire him that he would vouchsafe to accept of half of all things that they had brought. Then he said to them secretly: Bless ye the God of heaven, give glory to him in the sight of all that live, because he hath shewn his mercy to you. When thou didst pray with tears, and didst bury the dead, and didst leave thy dinner, and hide the dead by day in thy house, and bury them by night, I offered thy prayer to the Lord. And because thou wast acceptable to God, it was necessary that temptation should prove thee. And now the Lord hath sent me to heal thee, and to deliver Sara thy son's wife from the devil. For I am the Angel Raphael, one of the seven, who stand before the Lord. And when they had heard these things, they were troubled, and being seized with fear they fell upon the ground on their face. And the Angel said to them: Peace be to you, fear not. For when I was with you, I was there by the will of God: bless ye him, and sing praises to him. I seemed indeed to eat and to drink with you: but I use an invisible meat and drink, which cannot be seen by men. It is time therefore that I return to him, that sent me: but bless ye God, and publish all his wonderful works. And when he had said these things, he was taken from their sight, and they could see him no more.

LESSON TWENTIETH.

ON THE MANNER OF MAKING A GOOD CONFESSION.

Q. What should we do on entering the confessional?

(I. Esdras 9. A. M. 3538.) At the evening sacrifice I rose up from my affliction, and having rent my mantle and my garment, I fell upon my knees, and spread out my hands to the Lord my God, and said: My God I am confounded and ashamed to lift up my face to thee: for our iniquities are multiplied over our heads, and our sins are grown up even unto heaven, from the days of our fathers: and we ourselves also have sinned grievously unto this day, and for our iniquities we and our kings, and our priests have been delivered into the hands of the kings of the lands, and to the sword, and to captivity, and to spoil, and to confusion of face, as it is at this day. And now as a little, and for a moment has our prayer been made before the Lord our God, that our God would enlighten our eyes, and would give us a little life in our bondage. For we are bondmen, and in our bondage our God hath not forsaken us, but hath extended mercy upon us. (And now, O our God, what shall we say after this?) for we have forsaken thy commandments, which thou hast commanded by the hand of thy servants the prophets, saying: The land which you go to possess, is an unclean land, according to the uncleanness of the people, and of other lands, with their abominations, who have filled it from mouth to mouth with their filth. And after all that is come upon us, for our most wicked deeds, and our great sin, seeing that thou our God hast saved us from our iniquity, and hast given us a deliverance as at this day, that we should not turn away, nor break thy commandments. Art thou angry with us unto utter destruction, not to leave us a remnant to be saved? O Lord God of Israel, thou art just: for we remain yet to be saved as at this day. Behold we are before thee in our sin, for there can be no standing before thee in this matter.

Q. Which are the first things we should tell the priest in Confession?

See "L. of C.," p. 74, No. 10.

Q. After telling the time of our last Confession and Communion what should we do?

(James 5.) Confess therefore your sins one to another: and pray one for another, that you may be saved.

Q. What must we do when the confessor asks us questions?

(Eccltus. 4.) Be not ashamed to confess thy sins, but submit not thyself to every man for sin. For there is a shame that bringeth sin, and there is a shame that bringeth glory and grace.

Q. What should we do after telling our sins?

(Prov. 13.) Poverty and shame to him that refuseth instruction: but he that yieldeth to reproof, shall be glorified.

Q. How should we end our Confession?

(Eph. 4.) Put off, according to former conversation, the old man, who is corrupted according to the desire of error. And be renewed in the spirit of your mind: and put on the new man, who according to God is created in justice and holiness of truth.

Q. What should we do while the priest is giving us absolution?

(II. Peter 2.) By whom a man is overcome, of the same also he is the slave. For if, flying from the pollutions of the world, through the knowledge of our Lord and Saviour Jesus Christ, they *be* again entangled in them and overcome: their latter state is become unto them worse than the former. For it had been better for them not to have known the way of justice, than after they have known it, to turn back from that holy commandment which was delivered to them. For, that of the true proverb has happened to them: The dog is returned to his vomit: and, The sow that was washed, to her wallowing in the mire.

LESSON TWENTY-SECOND.

ON THE HOLY EUCHARIST.

Q. What is the Holy Eucharist?

(Ex. 26. A. M. 2513.) The children of Israel said to Moses: Would to God we had died by the hand of the Lord in the land of Egypt, when we sat over the flesh-pots, and ate bread to the full. Why have you brought us into this desert? And the Lord spoke to Moses, saying: I have heard the murmuring of the children of Israel: say to them: In the evening you shall eat flesh, and in the morning you shall have your fill of bread: and you shall know that I am the Lord your God. So it came to pass in the evening, that quails coming up, covered the camp: and in the morning a dew lay round about the camp. And when it had covered the face of the earth, it appeared in the wilderness small, and as it were beaten with a pestle, like unto the hoarfrost on the ground. And when the children of Israel saw it, they said one to another: Manhu! which signifieth: What is this! for they knew not what it was. And Moses said to them: This is the bread, which the Lord hath given you to eat. This is the word, that the Lord hath commanded: Let every one gather of it as much as is enough to eat: a gomor for every man, according to the number of your souls that dwell in a tent, so shall you take of it. And the children of Israel did so: and they gathered, one more, another less. And they measured by the measure of a gomor: neither had he more that had gathered more: nor did he find less that had provided less: but every one had gathered, according to what they were able to eat. And the house of Israel called the name thereof Manna: and it was like coriander seed white, and the taste thereof like to flour with honey. And Moses said: This is the word, which the Lord hath commanded: Fill a gomor of it, and let it be kept unto generations to come hereafter, that they may know the bread, wherewith I fed you in the wilderness, when you were brought forth out of the land of Egypt. And Moses said to Aaron: Take a vessel, and put manna into it, as much as a gomor can hold: and lay it up before the Lord to keep unto your generations, as the Lord commanded Moses. And Aaron put it in the tabernacle to be kept. And the children of Israel ate manna forty years, till they came to a habitable land: with this meat were they fed, until they reached the borders of the land of Chanaan.

(IV. Kings 4. A. M. 3110.) A certain man came from Baalsalisa bringing to the man of God bread of the first fruits, twenty loaves of barley, and new corn in his scrip. And he said: Give to the people, that they may eat. And his servant answered him: How much is this, that I should set it before a hundred men? He said again: Give to the people, that they may eat: for thus saith the Lord: They shall eat, and there shall be left. So he set it before them: and they eat, and there was left according to the word of the Lord.

Q. When did Christ institute the Holy Eucharist?

See "L. of C.," p. 99, Nos. 1, 2.

(Gen. 14. A. M. 2092.) Which when Abram had heard, to wit, that his brother Lot was taken, he numbered of the servants born in his house, three hundred and eighteen well appointed: and pursued them to Dan. And dividing his company, he rushed upon them in the night: and defeated them, and pursued them as far as Hoba, which is on the left hand of Damascus. And he brought back all the substance, and Lot his brother, with his substance, the women also and the people. And the king of Sodom went out to meet him, after he returned from the slaughter of Chodorlahomor, and of the kings that were with him in the vale of Save, which is the king's vale. But Melchisedech the king of Salem, bringing forth bread and wine, for he was the priest of the most high God, blessed him, and said: Blessed be Abram by the most high God, who created heaven and earth. And blessed be the most high God, by whose protection the enemies are in thy hands. And he gave him the tithes of all.

Q. Who were present when our Lord instituted the Holy Eucharist?
See "L. of C.," p. 49, No. 6; p. 99, No. 2.

Q. How did our Lord institute the Holy Eucharist?
See "L. of C.," p. 99, Nos. 1, 2, 3; p. 100, No. 4.

Q. What happened when our Lord said, This is my body; this is my blood?
See "L. of C.," p. 43, No. 48.

Q. Is Jesus Christ whole and entire both under the form of bread and under the form of wine?
See "L. of C.," p. 46, No. 51; p. 120, No. 6.

Q. Did anything remain of the bread and wine after their substance had been changed into the substance of the body and blood of our Lord?

(I. Cor. 10.) I speak as to wise men: judge ye yourselves what I say. The chalice of benediction, which we bless, is it not the communion of the blood of Christ? And the bread, which we break, is it not the partaking of the body of the Lord? For we, being many, are one bread, one body, all that partake of one bread.

Q. What do you mean by the appearances of bread and wine?
See "L. of C.," p. 18, No. 3.

Q. What is the change of the bread and wine into the body and blood of our Lord called?

(Ex. 4. A. M. 2513.) Moses said to God: Who am I that I should go to Pharao, and should bring forth the children of Israel out of Egypt? And he said to him: I will be with thee: and this thou shalt have for a sign, that I have sent thee: take of the river water, and pour it out upon the dry land, and whatsoever thou drawest out of the river, shall be turned into blood.

Q. How was the substance of the bread and wine changed into the substance of the body and blood of Christ.

(I. Cor. 11.) I have received of the Lord that which also I delivered unto you, that the Lord Jesus, the same night in which he was betrayed, took bread, and giving thanks, broke, and said: Take ye, and eat: this is my body, which shall be delivered for you: this do for the commemoration of me. In like manner also the chalice, after he had supped, saying:

This chalice is the new testament in my blood: this do ye, as often as you shall drink, for the commemoration of me. For as often as you shall eat this bread, and drink the chalice, you shall shew the death of the Lord, until he come.

Q. Does this change of bread and wine into the body and blood of Christ continue to be made in the Church?

(Acts 2.) They were persevering in the doctrine of the Apostles, and in the communication of the Breaking of Bread.

(IV. Kings 4. A. M. 3109.) Now a certain woman of the wives of the prophets cried to Eliseus, saying: Thy servant my husband is dead, and thou knowest that thy servant was one that feared God, and behold the creditor is come to take away my two sons to serve him. And Eliseus said to her: What wilt thou have me do for thee? Tell me, what hast thou in thy house? And she answered: I thy handmaid have nothing in my house but a little oil, to anoint me. And he said to her: Go, borrow of all thy neighbours empty vessels not a few. And go in, and shut thy door, when thou art within, and thy sons: and pour out thereof into all those vessels: and when they are full take them away. So the woman went, and shut the door upon her, and upon her sons: they brought her the vessels, and she poured in. And when the vessels were full, she said to her son: Bring me yet a vessel. And he answered: I have no more. And the oil stood. And she came, and told the man of God. And he said: Go, sell the oil, and pay thy creditor: and thou and thy sons live of the rest.

Q. When did Christ give His priests the power to change bread and wine into His body and blood?

See "L. of C.," p. 100, No. 4.

Q. How do the priests exercise this power of changing bread and wine into the body and blood of Christ?

(I. Cor. 11.) This do ye, as often as you shall drink, for the commemoration of me. For as often as you shall eat this bread, and drink the chalice, you shall shew the death of the Lord, until he come.

LESSON TWENTY-THIRD.

ON THE ENDS FOR WHICH THE HOLY EUCHARIST WAS INSTITUTED.

Q. Why did Christ institute the Holy Eucharist?

(Num. 14. A. M. 2514.) The whole multitude crying wept that night. And all the children of Israel murmured against Moses and Aaron, saying: Would God that we had died in Egypt: and would God we may die in this vast wilderness, and that the Lord may not bring us into this land, lest we fall by the sword, and our wives and children be led away captives. Is it not better to return into Egypt? And they said one to another: Let us appoint a captain, and let us return into Egypt. And Moses sent twelve to view the land of Chanaan, and said to them: Go you up by the south side. And when you shall come to the mountains, view the land, of what sort it is: and the people that are the inhabitants thereof, whether they be strong or weak: few in number or many: and when they were gone up, they viewed the land from the desert of Sin, unto Rohob as you enter into Emath. And going forward as far as the torrent of the cluster of grapes, they cut off a branch with its cluster of grapes, which two men carried upon a lever. They took also of the pomegranates and of the figs of that place: and came to Moses and Aaron and to all the assembly of the children of Israel to the desert of Pharan, which is in Cades. And speaking to them and to all the multitude, they shewed them the fruits of the land: and they related and said: We came into the land to which thou sentest us, which in very deed floweth with milk and honey as may be known by these fruits: but it hath very strong inhabitants, and the cities are great and walled. We saw there the race of Enac. In the mean time Caleb, to still the murmuring of the people that rose against Moses, said: Let us go up and possess the land, for we shall be able to conquer it. But the others, that had been with him, said: No, we are not able to go up to this people, because they are stronger than we. And they spoke ill of the land, which they had viewed, before the children of Israel, saying: The land which we have viewed, devoureth its inhabitants: the people, that we beheld, are of a tall stature. There we saw certain monsters of the sons of Enac, of the giant-kind: in comparison of whom, we seemed like locusts.

(III. Kings 19. A. M. 3097.) Achab told Jezabel all that Elias had done, and how he had slain all the prophets with the sword. Then Elias was afraid, and rising up he went whithersoever he had a mind: and he came to Bersabee of Juda, and left his servant there, and he went forward, one day's journey into the desert. And when he was there, and sat under a juniper tree, he requested for his soul that he might die, and said: It is enough for me, Lord, take away my soul: for I am no better than my fathers. And he cast himself down, and slept in the shadow of the juniper tree: and behold an angel of the Lord touched him, and said to him: Arise and eat. He looked, and behold there was at his head a hearth-cake, and a vessel of water: and he eat and drank, and he fell asleep again. And the angel of the Lord came again the second time, and touched him, and said to him: Arise, eat: for thou hast yet a great way to go. And he arose, and eat, and drank, and walked in the strength of that food forty days and forty nights, unto the mount of God, Horeb.

Q. How are we united to Jesus Christ in the Holy Eucharist?
See "L. of C.," p. 104, No. 4.

Q. What is Holy Communion?
See "L. of C.," p. 46, No. 51.

Q. What is necessary to make a good Communion?
See "L. of C.," p. 90, No. 8.

(Acts 20. A. D. 58.) On the first day of the week, when we were assembled to break bread, Paul discoursed with them, being to depart on the morrow: and he continued his speech until midnight. And there was a great number of lamps in the upper chamber where we were assembled. And a certain young man named Eutychus, sitting on the window, being oppressed with a deep sleep (as Paul was long preaching,) by occasion of his sleep fell from the third loft down, and was taken up dead. To whom, when Paul had gone down, he laid himself upon him, and embracing him, said: Be not troubled, for his soul is in him. Then going up, and breaking bread and tasting, and having talked a long time to them, until daylight, so he departed. And they brought the youth alive, and were not a little comforted.

(I. Cor. 10.) The things which the heathens sacrifice, they sacrifice to devils, and not to God. And I would not that you should be made partakers with devils. You cannot drink the chalice of the Lord, and the chalice of devils: you cannot be partakers of the table of the Lord, and of the table of devils.

(I. Kings 21. A. M. 2944.) David came to Nobe to Achimelech the priest: and Achimelech was astonished at David's coming. And David said to Achimelech the priest: The king hath commanded me a business, and said: Let no man know the thing for which thou art sent by me, and what manner of commands I have given thee: and I have appointed my servants to such and such a place. Now therefore if thou have anything at hand, though it were but five loaves, give me, or whatsoever thou canst find. And the priest answered David, saying: I have no common bread at hand, but only holy bread, if the young men be clean. And David answered the priest, and said to him: Truly, we have refrained ourselves from yesterday and the day before, when we came out, and the vessels of the young men were holy. Now this way is defiled, but it shall also be sanctified this day in the vessels. The priest therefore gave him hallowed bread: for there was no bread there, but only the loaves of proposition, which had been taken away from before the face of the Lord, that hot loaves might be set up.

Q. Does he who received Communion in mortal sin receive the body and blood of Christ?
See " L. of C.," p. 86, No. 17.

(I. Cor. 11.) Let a man prove himself: and so let him eat of that bread, and drink of the chalice. For he that eateth and drinketh unworthily, eateth and drinketh judgment to himself, not discerning the body of the Lord.

Q. Is it enough to be free from mortal sin to receive plentifully the graces of Holy Communion?
See " L. of C.," p. 101, No. 5.

Q. What is the fast necessary for Holy Communion?

(Acts 13. A. D. 42.) Now there were in the church which was at Antioch, prophets and doctors, among whom was Barnabas, and Simon, who was called Niger, and Lucius of Cyrene, and Manahen, who was the foster-brother of Herod the tetrarch, and Saul. And as they were ministering to the Lord, and fasting, the Holy Ghost said to them: Separate me Saul and Barnabas, for the work whereunto I have taken them. Then they, fasting and praying, and imposing their hands upon them, sent them away.

Q. Is any one ever allowed to receive Holy Communion when not fasting?
See " L. of C.," p. 116, No. 8.

Q. When are we bound to receive Holy Communion?
See " L. of C.," p. 67, No. 31.

Q. Is it well to receive Holy Communion often?
See " L. of C.," p. 125, No. 20; p. 127, No. 26.

Q. What should we do after Holy Communion?
See " L of C.," p. 101, No. 6.

(Eph. 5.) Be ye filled with the holy Spirit, speaking to yourselves in psalms, and hymns, and spiritual canticles, singing and making melody in your hearts to the Lord; giving thanks always for all things, in the name of our Lord Jesus Christ, to God and the Father.

LESSON TWENTY-FOURTH.

ON THE SACRIFICE OF THE MASS.

Q. When and where are the bread and wine changed into the body and blood of Christ?

See "L. of C.," p. 100, No. 4; p. 120, No. 6.

Q. What is the Mass?

(Mal. 1.) Beseech ye the face of God, that he may have mercy on you, (for by your hand hath this been done,) if by any means he will receive your faces, saith the Lord of hosts. Who is there among you, that will shut the doors, and will kindle the fire on my altar gratis? I have no pleasure in you, saith the Lord of hosts: and I will not receive a gift of your hand. For from the rising of the sun even to the going down, my name is great among the Gentiles, and in every place there is sacrifice, and there is offered to my name a clean oblation: for my name is great among the Gentiles, saith the Lord of hosts.

Q. What is a sacrifice?

(Gen. 4. A. M. 2.) It came to pass after many days, that Cain offered, of the fruits of the earth, gifts to the Lord. Abel also offered of the firstlings of his flock, and of their fat; and the Lord had respect to Abel, and to his offerings.

(Gen. 8.) Noe built an altar unto the Lord: and taking of all cattle and fowls that were clean, offered holocausts upon the altar. And the Lord smelled a sweet savour, and said: I will no more curse the earth for the sake of man: for the imagination and thought of man's heart are prone to evil from his youth: therefore I will no more destroy every living soul as I have done. All the days of the earth, seed time and harvest, cold and heat, summer and winter, night and day, shall not cease.

Q. Is the Mass the same sacrifice as that of the Cross?

(Ex. 12. A. M. 2513.) The Lord said to Moses and Aaron in the land of Egypt: Speak ye to the whole assembly of the children of Israel, and say to them: On the tenth day of this month let every man take a lamb by their families and houses. But if the number be less than may suffice to eat the lamb, he shall take unto him his neighbour that joineth to his house, according to the number of souls which may be enough to eat the lamb. And it shall be a lamb without blemish, a male, of one year: according to which rite also you shall take a kid. And you shall keep it until the fourteenth day of this month: and the whole multitude of the children of Israel shall sacrifice it in the evening. And dip a bunch of hyssop in the blood that is at the door, and sprinkle the transom of the door therewith, and both the door cheeks: let none of you go out of the door of his house till morning. For the Lord will pass through striking the Egyptians; and when he shall see the blood on the transom, and on both the posts, he will pass over the door of the house, and not suffer the destroyer to come into your houses and to hurt *you*. And you shall eat the flesh that night roasted at the fire, and unleavened bread with wild lettuce. Neither shall there remain any thing of it until morning. If there be any thing left, you shall burn it with fire. In one house shall it be eaten, neither shall you carry forth of the flesh thereof out of the house, neither shall you break a bone thereof. And thus you shall eat it: you shall gird your reins, and you shall have shoes on your feet, holding staves in your hands, and you shall eat in haste: for it is the Phase (that is the Passage) of the Lord. And I will pass through the land of Egypt that night, and will kill every first-born in the land of Egypt both man and beast: and against all the gods of Egypt I will execute judgments: I *am* the Lord. And the blood shall be unto you for a sign in the houses where you shall be: and I shall see the blood, and shall pass over you: and the plague shall not be upon you to destroy you, when I shall strike the land of Egypt. And this day shall be for a memorial to you: and you shall keep it a feast to the Lord in your generations with an everlasting observance. All the assembly of the children of Israel shall keep it. And if any stranger be willing to dwell among you, and to keep the Phase of the Lord, all his males shall first be circumcised, and then shall he celebrate it according to the manner: and he shall be as he that is born in the land: but if any man be uncircumcised, he shall not eat thereof. Thou shalt keep this thing as a law for thee and thy children for ever.

Q. How is the Mass the same sacrifice as that of the Cross?

(I. Cor. 11: 26.) As often as you shall eat this Bread, and drink the Chalice, you shall show the death of the Lord, until He come.

Q. What were the ends for which the sacrifice of the Cross was offered?

(I. Kings 7. A. M. 2888.) The Philistines heard that the children of Israel were gathered together to Maspbath, and the lords of the Philistines went up against Israel. And when the children of Israel heard this, they were afraid of the Philistines. And they said to Samuel: cease not to cry to the Lord our God for us, that he may save us out of the hand of the Philistines. And Samuel took a sucking lamb, and offered it whole for a holocaust to the

Lord: and Samuel cried to the Lord for Israel, and the Lord heard him. And it came to pass, when Samuel was offering the holocaust, the Philistines began the battle against Israel: but the Lord thundered with a great thunder on that day upon the Philistines, and terrified them, and they were overthrown before the face of Israel.

Q. Is there any difference between the sacrifice of the Cross and the sacrifice of the Mass?

(Rom. 6.) Now if we be dead with Christ, we believe that we shall live also together with Christ: knowing that Christ rising again from the dead, dieth now no more, death shall no more have dominion over him. For in that he died to sin, he died once; but in that he liveth, he liveth unto God: so you also reckon, that you are dead to sin, but alive unto God, in Christ Jesus our Lord.

Q. How should we assist at Mass?

(Ex. 19. A. M. 2513.) Moses told the words of the people to the Lord. And he said to him: Go to the people, and sanctify them to-day, and to-morrow, and let them wash their garments. And let them be ready against the third day: for on the third day the Lord will come down in the sight of all the people upon mount Sinai, and thou shalt appoint certain limits to the people round about, and thou shalt say to them: Take heed you go not up into the mount, and that ye touch not the borders thereof: every one that toucheth the mount dying he shall die.

Q. Which is the best manner of hearing Mass?
See "L. of C.," p. 80, No. 4.

LESSON TWENTY-FIFTH.

ON EXTREME UNCTION AND HOLY ORDERS.

Q. What is the Sacrament of Extreme Unction?
See "L. of C.," p. 42, No. 46.

Q. When should we receive Extreme Unction?

(Eccltus. 38.) Honour the physician for the need thou hast of him: for the most High hath created him. For all healing is from God, and he shall receive gifts of the king. The skill of the physician shall lift up his head, and in the sight of great men he shall be praised. The most High hath created medicines out of the earth, and a wise man will not abhor them. Was not bitter water made sweet with wood? The virtue of these things *is come* to the knowledge of men, and the most High hath given knowledge to men, that he may be honoured in his wonders. By these he shall cure and shall allay their pains, and *of these* the apothecary shall make sweet confections, and shall make up ointments of health, and of his works there shall be no end. My son, in thy sickness neglect not thyself, but pray to the Lord, and he shall heal thee. Turn away from sin and order thy hands aright, and cleanse thy heart from all offence. Give a sweet savour, and a memorial of fine flour, and make a fat offering, and then give place to the physician. For the Lord created him: and let him not depart from thee, for his works are necessary. For there is a time when thou must fall into their hands: and they shall beseech the Lord, that he would prosper what they give for ease and remedy, for their conversation. He that sinneth in the sight of his Maker, shall fall into the hands of the physician. My son, shed tears over the dead, and begin to lament as if thou hadst suffered some great harm, and according to judgment cover his body, and neglect not his burial. And for *fear of* being ill spoken of weep bitterly for a day, and then comfort thyself in thy sadness. And make mourning for him according to his merit for a day, or two, for fear of detraction.

Q. Should we wait until we are in extreme danger before we receive Extreme Unction?

(James 5.) Is any man sick among you? Let him bring in the priests of the church, and let them pray over him, anointing him with oil in the name of the Lord. And the prayer of faith shall save the sick man: and the Lord shall raise him up: and if he be in sins, they shall be forgiven him. Confess therefore your sins one to another: and pray one for another, that you may be saved. For the continual prayer of a just man availeth much. Elias was a man passible like unto us: and with prayer he prayed that it might not rain upon the earth, and it rained not for three years and six months. And he prayed again: and the heaven gave rain, and the earth brought forth her fruit. My brethren, if any of you err from the truth, and one convert him: he must know that he who causeth a sinner to be converted from the error of his way, shall save his soul from death, and shall cover a multitude of sins.

Q. Which are the effects of the Sacrament of Extreme Unction?

(IV. Kings 4. A. M. 3109.) There was a day when Eliseus passed by Sunam: now there was a great woman there, who detained him to eat bread; and the woman brought forth a son. And her child grew. And on a certain day, when he went out to his father to the reapers, he said to his father: My head acheth, my head acheth. But he said to his servant: Take him, and carry him to his mother. And when he had taken him, and brought him to his mother, she set him on her knees until noon, and then he died. And she went up and laid him upon the bed of the man of God, and shut the door: and going out, she went forward, and came to the man of God to mount Carmel: and when the man of God saw her coming towards, he said to Giezi his servant: Behold that Sunamitess. And when she came to the man of God to the mount, she caught hold on his feet; and Giezi came to remove her. And the man of God said: Let her alone for her soul is in anguish, and the Lord hath hid it from me, and hath not told me. Then he said to Giezi: Gird up thy loins, and take my staff in thy hand, and go. If any man meet thee, salute him not: and if any man salute thee, answer him not: and lay my staff upon the face of the child. But the mother of the child said: As the Lord liveth, and as thy soul liveth, I will not leave thee. He arose, therefore, and followed her. But Giezi was gone before them, and laid the staff upon the face of the child, and there was no voice nor sense: and he returned to meet him, and told him, saying: The child is not risen. Eliseus therefore went into the house, and behold the child lay dead on his bed. And going in he shut the door upon him, and upon the child, and prayed to the Lord. And he went up, and lay upon the child: and put his mouth upon his mouth, and his eyes upon his eyes, and his hands upon his hands: and he bowed himself upon him, and the child's flesh grew warm. Then he returned and walked in the house, once to and fro: and he went up, and lay upon him: and the child gaped seven times, and opened his eyes. And he called Giezi, and said to him: Call this Sunamitess. And she being called, went in to him: and he said: Take up thy son. She came and fell at his feet, and worshipped upon the ground: and took up her son, and went out.

Q. **What do you mean by the remains of sin?**

See "L. of C.," p. 55, No. 7.

Q. **How should we receive the Sacrament of Extreme Unction?**

See "L. of C.," p. 41, Nos. 39, 40.

Q. **Who is the minister of the Sacrament of Extreme Unction?**

See "L. of C.," p. 125, Nos. 21, 22.

Q. **What is the Sacrament of Holy Orders?**

(Acts 6. A. D. 33.) In those days, the number of the disciples increasing, there arose a murmuring of the Greeks against the Hebrews, for that their widows were neglected in the daily ministration. Then the twelve calling together the multitude of the disciples, said: It is not reason that we should leave the word of God, and serve tables. Wherefore, brethren, look ye out among you seven men of good reputation, full of the Holy Ghost and wisdom, whom we may appoint over this business. But we will give ourselves continually to prayer, and to the ministry of the word. And the saying was liked by all the multitude. And they chose Stephen, a man full of faith, and of the Holy Ghost, and Philip, and Prochorus, and Nicanor, and Timon, and Parmenas, and Nicolas, a proselyte of Antioch. These they set before the apostles; and they praying, imposed hands upon them.

(I. Cor. 14.) Let women keep silence in the churches: for it is not permitted them to speak, but to be subject, as also the law saith. But if they would learn anything, let them ask their husbands at home. For it is a shame for a woman to speak in the church.

(Ezek. 3. A. M. 3409.) At the end of seven days the word of the Lord came to me, saying: Son of man, I have made thee a watchman to the house of Israel: and thou shalt hear the word out of my mouth, and shalt tell it them from me. If, when I say to the wicked, Thou shalt surely die: thou declare it not to him, nor speak *to him*, that he may be converted from his wicked way, and live: the same wicked man shall die in his iniquity, but I will require his blood at thy hand. But if thou give warning to the wicked, and he be not converted from his wickedness: and from his evil way: he indeed shall die in his iniquity, but thou hast delivered thy soul. Moreover if the just man shall turn away from his justice, and shall commit iniquity: I will lay a stumbling-block before him, he shall die, because thou hast not given him warning: he shall die in his sin, and his justices which he hath done, shall not be remembered: but I will require his blood at thy hand. But if thou warn the just man, that the just may not sin, and he doth not sin: living he shall live, because thou hast warned him, and thou hast delivered thy soul. And the hand of the Lord was upon me, and he said to me: Rise *and* go forth into the plain, and there I will speak to thee. And I rose up, and went forth into the plain: and behold the glory of the Lord stood there, like the glory which I saw by the river Chobar: and I fell upon my face. And the spirit entered into me, and set me upon my feet: and he spoke to me, and said to me: Go in; and shut thyself up in the midst of thy house. And thou, O son of man, behold they shall put bands upon thee, and they shall bind thee with them: and thou shalt not go forth from the midst of them.

Q. What is necessary to receive Holy Orders worthily?
See "L. of C.," p. 56, No. 8; p. 104, No. 5

(Heb. 5.) Every high-priest taken from among men, is ordained for men in the things that appertain to God, that he may offer up gifts and sacrifices for sins: who can have compassion on them that are ignorant and that err: because he himself also is compassed with infirmity. And therefore he ought, as for the people, so also for himself, to offer for sins. Neither doth any man take the honor to himself, but he that is called by God, as Aaron was.

(I. Kings 1. A. M. 2848.) There was a man of Ramathaim-sophim, of mount Ephraim, and his name was Elcana, the son of Jeroham, the son of Eliu, the son of Thohu, the son of Suph, an Ephraimite: and he had two wives, the name of one was Anna, and the name of the other Phenenna. Phenenna had children: but Anna had no children. Now the day came, and Elcana offered sacrifice, and gave to Phenenna his wife, and to all her sons and daughters, portions: but to Anna he gave one portion with sorrow, because he loved Anna. So Anna arose after she had eaten and drunk in Silo: And Heli the priest sitting upon a stool before the door of the temple of the Lord: as Anna had her heart full of grief, she prayed to the Lord, shedding many tears, and she made a vow, saying: O Lord of hosts, if thou wilt look down on the affliction of thy servant, and wilt be mindful of me, and not forget thy hand-maid, and wilt give to thy servant a man-child: I will give him to the Lord all the days of his life, and no razor shall come upon his head. And it came to pass, as she multiplied prayers before the Lord, that Heli observed her mouth. Now Anna spoke in her heart, and only her lips moved, but her voice was not heard at all. Then Heli said to her: Go in peace: and the God of Israel grant thee thy petition, which thou hast asked of him. And it came to pass when the time was come about, Anna bore a son, and called his name Samuel: because she had asked him of the Lord. And after she had weaned him, she carried him with her, with three calves, and three bushels of flour, and a bottle of wine, and she brought him to the house of the Lord in Silo. Now the child was as yet very young: and they immolated a calf, and offered the child to Heli. And Anna said: I beseech thee, my lord, as thy soul liveth, my lord: I am that woman who stood before thee here praying to the Lord. For this child did I pray, and the Lord hath granted me my petition, which I asked of him. Therefore I also have lent him to the Lord all the days of his life, he shall be lent to the Lord. And they adored the Lord there. Now the child Samuel ministered to the Lord before Heli, and the word of the Lord was precious in those days, there was no manifest vision. And it came to pass one day when Heli lay in his place, and his eyes were grown dim, that he could not see: before the lamp of God went out, Samuel slept in the temple of the Lord, where the ark of God was. And the Lord called Samuel. And he answered: Here am I. And he ran to Heli and said: Here am I: for thou didst call me. He said: I did not call: go back and sleep. And he went and slept. And the Lord called Samuel again. And Samuel arose and went to Heli, and said: Here am I: for thou calledest me. He answered: I did not call thee, my son: return and sleep. Now Samuel did not yet know the Lord, neither had the word of the Lord been revealed to him. And the Lord called Samuel again the third time. And he arose up and went to Heli, and said: Here am I: for thou didst call me. Then Heli understood that the Lord called the child, and he said to Samuel: Go, and sleep: and if he shall call thee any more, thou shalt say: Speak, Lord, for thy servant heareth. So Samuel went and slept in his place. And the Lord came and stood: and he called, as he had called the other times, Samuel, Samuel. And Samuel said: Speak, Lord, for thy servant heareth. And the Lord said to Samuel: I will raise me up a faithful priest, who shall do according to my heart, and my soul, and I will build him a faithful house, and he shall walk all days before my anointed. And the child Samuel advanced, and grew on, and pleased both the Lord and men.

(I. Kings 16. A. M. 2934.) And the Lord said to Samuel: How long wilt thou mourn for Saul, whom I have rejected from reigning over Israel? fill thy horn with oil, and come, that I may send thee to Isai the Bethlehemite: for I have provided me a king among his sons. Then Samuel did as the Lord had said to him. And he came to Bethlehem, and the ancients of the city wondered, and meeting him, they said: Is thy coming hither peaceable? And he said: *It is* peaceable: I am come to offer sacrifice to the Lord, be ye sanctified, and come with me to the sacrifice. And he sanctified Isai and his sons, and called them to the sacrifice. And when they were come in, he saw Eliab, and said: Is the Lord's anointed before him? And the Lord said to Samuel: Look not on his countenance, nor on the height of his stature: because I have rejected him, nor do I judge according to the look of man: for man seeth those things that appear, but the Lord beholdeth the heart. Isai therefore brought his seven sons before Samuel: and Samuel said to

Isai: The Lord hath not chosen any one of these. And Samuel said to Isai: Are here all thy sons? He answered: There remaineth yet a young one, who keepeth the sheep. And Samuel said to Isai: Send, and fetch him, for we will not sit down till he come hither. He sent therefore and brought him. Now he was ruddy and beautiful to behold, and of a comely face. And the Lord said: Arise, and anoint him, for this is he. Then Samuel took the horn of oil, and anointed him in the midst of his brethren: and the Spirit of the Lord came upon David from that day forward: and Samuel rose up, and went to Ramatha.

(Num. 17. A. M. 2530.) The Lord spoke to Moses, saying: Speak to the children of Israel, and take of every one of them a rod by their kindreds, of all the princes of the tribes, twelve rods, and write the name of every man upon his rod. And the name of Aaron shall be for the tribe of Levi, and one rod shall contain all their families: and thou shalt lay them up in the tabernacle of the covenant before the testimony, where I will speak to thee. Whomsoever of these I shall choose, his rod shall blossom: and I will make to cease from me the murmurings of the children of Israel, wherewith they murmur against you. And Moses spoke to the children of Israel: and all the princes gave him rods one for every tribe: and there were twelve rods besides the rod of Aaron. And when Moses had laid them up before the Lord in the tabernacle of the testimony: he returned on the following day, and found that the rod of Aaron for the house of Levi, was budded: and that the buds swelling it had bloomed blossoms, which spreading the leaves, were formed into almonds.

(Judg. 6. A. M. 2759.) An angel of the Lord came, and sat under an oak, that was in Ephra, and belonged to Joas the father of the family of Ezri. And when Gedeon his son was thrashing and cleansing wheat by the wine-press, to flee from Madian, the angel of the Lord appeared to him and said: The Lord is with thee, O most valiant of men. And Gedeon said to him: I beseech thee my lord, if the Lord be with us, why have these evils fallen upon us? Where are his miracles, which our fathers have told us of, saying: The Lord brought us out of Egypt? but now the Lord hath forsaken us, and delivered us into the hands of Madian. And the Lord looked upon him, and said: Go in this thy strength, and thou shalt deliver Israel out of the hand of Madian: know that I have sent thee. He answered and said: I beseech thee, my lord, wherewith shall I deliver Israel? Behold my family is the meanest in Manassas, and I am the least of my father's house. And the Lord said to him: I will be with thee: and thou shalt cut off Madian as one man. And he said: If I have found grace before thee, give me a sign that it is thou that speakest to me, and depart not hence, till I return to thee, and bring a sacrifice, and offer it to thee. And he answered: I will wait thy coming. So Gedeon went in, and boiled a kid, and made unleavened loaves of a measure of flour: and putting the flesh in a basket, and the broth of the flesh into a pot, he carried all under the oak, and presented to him. And the angel of the Lord said to him: Take the flesh and the unleavened loaves, and lay them upon that rock, and pour out the broth thereon. And when he had done so, the angel of the Lord put forth the tip of the rod, which he held in his hand, and touched the flesh and the unleavened loaves: and there rose a fire from the rock, and consumed the flesh and the unleavened loaves: And the angel of the Lord vanished out of his sight.

(Judg. 7.) And Gedeon returned to the camp of Israel, and said: Arise, for the Lord hath delivered the camp of Madian into our hands. And he divided the three hundred men into three parts, and gave them trumpets in their hands, and empty pitchers, and lamps within the pitchers. And he said to them: What you shall see me do, do you the same: I will go into one part of the camp, and do you as I shall do. When the trumpet shall sound in my hand, do you also blow the trumpets on every side of the camp. And Gedeon, and the three hundred men that were with him, went into part of the camp, at the beginning of the midnight watch, and the watchmen being alarmed, they began to sound their trumpets, and to clap the pitchers one against another. And when they sounded their trumpets in three places round about the camp, and had broken their pitchers, they held their lamps in their left hands, and with their right hands the trumpets which they blew, and they cried out: The sword of the Lord and of Gedeon: standing every man in his place round about the enemies' camp. So all the camp was troubled, and crying out and howling they fled away. And the three hundred men nevertheless persisted sounding the trumpets. And the Lord sent the sword into all the camp, and they killed one another.

(Jer. 1. A. M. 3375.) The word of the Lord came to me, saying: Before I formed thee in the bowels of thy mother, I knew thee: and before thou camest forth out of the womb, I sanctified thee, and made thee a prophet unto the nations. And I said: Ah, ah, ah, Lord God: behold, I cannot speak, for I am a child. And the Lord said to me: Say not: I am a child: for thou shalt go to all that I shall send thee: and whatsoever I shall command thee, thou shalt speak. Be not afraid at their presence: for I am with thee to deliver thee, saith the Lord. And the Lord put forth his hand, and touched my mouth: and the Lord said to me: Behold I have given my words in thy mouth: lo, I have set thee this day over the nations, and over kingdoms, to root up, and to pull down, and to waste, and to destroy, and to build, and to plant.

(Jer. 16.) And the word of the Lord came to me, saying: Thou shalt not take thee a wife, neither shalt thou have sons, and daughters in this place. For thus saith the Lord concerning the sons and daughters, that are born in this place, and concerning their mothers that bore them: and concerning their fathers, of whom they were born in this land: they shall die by the death of grievous illnesses: they shall not be lamented, and they shall not be buried, they shall be as dung upon the face of the earth: and they shall be consumed with the sword, and with famine: and their carcasses shall be meat for the fowls of the air, and for the beasts of the earth.

Q. How should Christians look upon the priests of the Church?

See "L. of C.," p. 31, No. 8.

(I. Cor. 4.) Let a man so account of us as of the ministers of Christ, and the dispensers of the mysteries of God. Here now it is required among the dispensers, that a man be found faithful. But to me it is a very small thing to be judged by you, or by man's day; but neither do I judge my own self. For I am not conscious to myself of any thing, yet am I not hereby justified; but he that judgeth me, is the Lord. Therefore judge not before the time; until the Lord come, who both will bring to light the hidden things of darkness, and will make manifest the counsels of the hearts; and then shall every man have praise from God.

(I. Tim. 5.) Let the priests that rule well, be esteemed worthy of double honour: especially they who labour in the word and doctrine: For the scripture saith: *Thou shalt not muzzle the ox that treadeth out the corn:* and, *The labourer is worthy of his reward.* Against a priest receive not an accusation, but under two or three witnesses.

(Josh. 3: 4. A. M. 2553.) Josue rose before daylight, and removed the camp: and they departed from Setim, and came to the Jordan, he, and all the children of Israel, and they abode there for three days. After which, the heralds went through the midst of the camp, and began to proclaim: When you shall see the ark of the covenant of the Lord your God, and the priests of the race of Levi carrying it, rise you up also, and follow them as they go before: And let there be between you and the ark the space of two thousand cubits: that you may see it afar off, and know which way you must go: for you have not gone this way before: and take care you come not near the ark. And when the priests, that carry the ark of the Lord the God of the whole earth, shall set the soles of their feet in the waters of the Jordan, the waters that are beneath shall run down and go off: and those that come from above, shall stand together upon a heap. And as soon as they came into the Jordan, and their feet were dipped in part of the water, (now the Jordan, it being harvest time, had filled the banks of its channel,) the waters that came down from above stood in one place, and swelling up like a mountain, were seen afar off from the city that is called Adom, to the place of Sarthan: but those that were beneath, ran down into the sea of the wilderness (which now is called the Dead sea) until they wholly failed. And the people marched over-against Jericho: and the priests that carried the ark of the covenant of the Lord, stood girded upon the dry ground in the midst of the Jordan, and all the people passed over through the channel that was dried up. Now the priests that carried the ark, stood in the midst of the Jordan till all things were accomplished which the Lord had commanded Josue to speak to the people, and Moses had said to him. And the people made haste and passed over. And when they that carried the ark of the covenant of the Lord, were come up, and began to tread on the dry ground, the waters returned into the channel, and ran as they were wont before.

(I. Kings 2. A. M. 2860.) There came a man of God to Heli, and said to him: Thus saith the Lord: Did I not plainly appear to thy father's house, when they were in Egypt in the house of Pharao? And I chose him out of all the tribes of Israel to be my priest, to go up to my altar, and burn incense to me, and to wear the ephod before me: and I gave to thy father's house of all the sacrifices of the children of Israel. Why have you kicked away my victims, and my gifts which I commanded to be offered in the temple: and thou hast rather honoured thy sons than me, to eat the first-fruits of every sacrifice of my people Israel? Wherefore thus saith the Lord the God of Israel: I said indeed that thy house, and the house of thy father should minister in my sight, for ever. But now saith the Lord: Far be this from me: but whosoever shall glorify me, him will I glorify: but they that despise me, shall be despised. Behold the days come: and I will cut off thy arm, and the arm of thy father's house, that there shall not be an old man in thy house. And thou shalt see thy rival in the temple, in all the prosperity of Israel, and there shall not be an old man in thy house for ever.

(IV. Kings 12. A. M. 3147.) Joas said to the priests: All the money of the sanctified things, which is brought into the temple of the Lord by those that pass, which is offered for the price of a soul, and which of their own accord, and of their own free heart they bring into the temple of the Lord: let the priests take it according to their order, and repair the house, wheresoever they shall see any thing that wanteth repairing.

(I. Kings 22. A. M. 2944.) The king sent to call for Achimelech the priest the son of Achitob, and all his father's house, the priests that were in Nobe, and they came all of them to the king. And the king said: dying thou shalt die, Achimelech, thou and all thy father's house. And the king said to the messengers that stood about him: Turn, and kill the priests of the Lord, for their hand is with David, because they knew that he was fled, and they told it not to me. And the king's servants would not put forth their hands against the priests of the Lord.

Q. Who can confer the Sacrament of Holy Orders?

(Ex. 29. A. M. 2514.) Thou shalt bring Aaron and his sons to the door of the tabernacle of the testimony. And when thou hast washed the father and his sons with water, thou shalt clothe Aaron with his vestments, that is, with the linen garment and the tunick, and the ephod and the rational, which thou shalt gird with the girdle. And thou shalt put the mitre upon his head, and the holy plate upon the mitre, and thou shalt pour the oil of unction upon his head: and by this rite shall he be consecrated. Thou shalt bring his sons also and shalt put on them the linen tunicks, and gird them with a girdle: to wit, Aaron and his children, and thou shalt put mitres upon them: and they shall be priests to me by a perpetual ordinance. After thou shalt have consecrated their hands, thou shalt take also the ram, upon whose head Aaron and his sons shall lay their hands. And when thou hast sacrificed him, thou shalt take of his blood, and put upon the tip of the right ear of Aaron and of his sons, and upon the thumbs and great toes of their right hand and foot, and thou shalt pour the blood upon the altar round about. And when thou hast taken of the blood, that is upon the altar, and of the oil of unction, thou shalt sprinkle Aaron and his vesture, his sons and their vestments.

(III. Kings 19. A. M. 3000.) Elias departing from thence, found Eliseus the son of Saphat, ploughing with twelve yoke of oxen: and he was one of them that were ploughing with twelve yoke of oxen: and when

Elias came up to him, he cast his mantle upon him. And he forthwith left the oxen and ran after Elias, and said: Let me, I pray thee, kiss my father and my mother, and then I will follow thee. And he said to him: Go, and return back: for that which was my part, I have done to thee. And returning back from him, he took a yoke of oxen, and killed them, and boiled the flesh with the plough of the oxen, and gave to the people, and they eat: and rising up he went away, and followed Elias, and ministered to him.

LESSON TWENTY-SIXTH.

ON MATRIMONY.

Q. What is the Sacrament of Matrimony?

(I. Cor. 7.) I say to the unmarried, and to the widows: It is good for them if they so continue, even as I. But if they do not contain themselves, let them marry. For it is better to marry than to be burnt. But to them that are married, not I but the Lord commandeth, that the wife depart not from her husband. And if she depart, that she remain unmarried, or be reconciled to her husband. And let not the husband put away his wife. Now concerning virgins, I have no commandment of the Lord; but I give counsel, as having obtained mercy of the Lord, to be faithful. I think therefore that this is good for the present necessity, that it is good for a man so to be. Art thou bound to a wife? seek not to be loosed. Art thou loosed from a wife? seek not a wife. But if thou take a wife, thou hast not sinned. But if a virgin marry, she hath not sinned: nevertheless, such shall have tribulation of the flesh. But I would have you to be without solicitude. He that is without a wife, is solicitous for the things that belong to the Lord, how he may please God. But he that is with a wife, is solicitous for the things of the world, how he may please his wife; and he it divided. And the unmarried woman and the virgin thinketh on the things of the Lord, that she may be holy both in body and in spirit. But she that is married thinketh on the things of the world, how she may please her husband. A woman is bound by the law as long as her husband liveth; but if her husband die, she is at liberty: let her marry to whom she will; only in the Lord. But more blessed shall she be, if she so remain, according to my counsel; and I think that I also have the spirit of God.

(Gen. 2. A. M. 1.) The Lord God cast a deep sleep upon Adam: and when he was fast asleep, He took one of his ribs, and filled up flesh for it.—And the Lord God built the rib which He took from Adam into a woman: and brought her to Adam.—And Adam said: This now is bone of my bones, and flesh of my flesh; she shall be called woman, because she was taken out of man.—Wherefore a man shall leave father and mother, and shall cleave to his wife: and they shall be two in one flesh. And God blessed them, saying: Increase and multiply, and fill the earth, and subdue it, and rule over the fishes of the sea, and the fowls of the air, and all living creatures that move upon the earth.

Q. Can a Christian man and woman be united in lawful marriage in any other way than by the Sacrament of Matrimony?

(Eph. 5.) Let women be subject to their husbands, as to the Lord: because the husband is the head of the wife, as Christ is the head of the church. He is the saviour of his body. Therefore as the church is subject to Christ, so also let the wives be to their husbands in all things. Husbands, love your wives, as Christ also loved the church, and delivered himself up for it. That he might sanctify it, cleansing it by the laver of water in the word of life: that he might present it to himself a glorious church, not having spot or wrinkle, or any such thing; but that it should be holy, and without blemish. So also ought men to love their wives as their own bodies. He that loveth his wife, loveth himself. For no man ever hated his own flesh; but nourisheth and cherisheth it, as also Christ doth the church: because we are members of his body, of his flesh, and of his bones. *For this cause shall a man leave his father and mother, and shall cleave to his wife, and they shall be two in one flesh.* This is a great sacrament; but I speak in Christ and in the church. Nevertheless let every one of you in particular love his wife as himself: and let the wife fear her husband.

Q. Can the bond of Christian marriage be dissolved by any human power?
See "L. of C.," p. 74, No. 12; p. 80, No. 5.

(Mal. 2. A. M. 3604.) This again have you done, you have covered the altar of the Lord with tears, with weeping, and bellowing, so that I have no more a regard to sacrifice, neither do I accept any atonement at your hands. And you have said: For what cause? Because the Lord hath been witness between thee, and the wife of thy youth, whom thou hast despised: yet she was thy partner, and the wife of thy covenant. Did not one make *her*, and she is the residue of his spirit? And what doth one seek, but the seed of God? Keep then your spirit, and despise not the wife of thy youth. When thou shalt hate her put her away, saith the Lord the God of Israel; but iniquity shall cover his garment, saith the Lord of hosts, keep your spirit, and despise not.

Q. Which are the effects of the Sacrament of Matrimony?

(I. Cor. 7.) To the rest I speak, not the Lord. If any brother have a wife that believeth not, and she consent to dwell with him, let him not put her away. And if any woman have a husband that believeth not, and he consent to dwell with her, let her not put away her husband. For the unbelieving husband is sanctified by the believing wife; and the unbelieving wife is sanctified by the believing husband: otherwise your children should be unclean; but now they are holy. But if the unbeliever depart, let him depart. For a brother or sister is not under servitude in such *cases.* But God hath called us in peace. For how knowest thou, O wife, whether thou shalt save thy husband? Or how knowest thou, O man, whether thou shalt save thy wife? But as the Lord hath distributed to every one, as God hath called every one, so let him walk; and so in all churches I teach.

Q. To receive the Sacrament of Matrimony worthily is it necessary to be in the state of grace?

(I. Peter 3.) In like manner also let wives be subject to their husbands: that if any believe not the word, they may be won without the word, by the conversation of the wives. Considering your chaste conversation with fear. Whose adorning let it not be the outward plaiting of the hair, or the wearing of gold, or the putting on of apparel: but the hidden man of the heart in the incorruptibility of a quiet and a meek spirit, which is rich in the sight of God. For after this manner heretofore the holy women also, who trusted in God, adorned themselves, being in subjection to their own husbands. As Sara obeyed Abraham, calling him lord: whose daughters you are, doing well, and not fearing any disturbance. Ye husbands, likewise dwelling with them according to knowledge, giving honour to the female as to the weaker vessel, and as to the coheirs of the grace of life: that your prayers be not hindered.

Q. Who has the right to make laws concerning the Sacrament of marriage?

See "L. of C.," p. 90, No. 30.

(Rom. 7.) Know you not, brethren, (for I speak to them that know the law,) that the law hath dominion over a man, as long as it liveth? For the woman that hath an husband, whilst her husband liveth is bound to the law. But if her husband be dead, she is loosed from the law of her husband. Therefore, whilst her husband liveth, she shall be called an adulteress, if she be with another man: but if her husband be dead, she is delivered from the law of her husband; so that she is not an adulteress, if she be with another man. Therefore, my brethren, you also are become dead to the law, by the body of Christ; that you may belong to another, who is risen again from the dead, that we may bring forth fruit to God.

Q. Does the Church forbid the marriage of Catholics with persons who have a different religion or no religion at all?

(Gen. 24. A. M. 2148.) Now Abraham was old; and advanced in age; and the Lord had blessed him in all things. And he said to the elder servant of his house, who was ruler over all he had: Swear by the Lord the God of heaven and earth, that thou take not a wife for my son, of the daughters of the Chanaanites, among whom I dwell: but that thou go to my own country and kindred, and take a wife from thence for my son Isaac. The servant answered: If the woman will not come with me into this land, must I bring thy son back again to the place, from whence thou camest out? And Abraham said: Beware thou never bring my son back again thither. The Lord God of heaven, who took me out of my father's house, and out of my native country, who spoke to me, and swore to me, saying: To thy seed will I give this land: he will send his Angel before thee, and thou shalt take from thence a wife for my son. But if the woman will not follow thee, thou shalt not be bound by the oath; only bring not my son back thither again. The servant therefore swore to him upon this word. And he took ten camels of his master's herd, and departed, carrying something of all his goods with him, and he set forward and went on to Mesopotamia to the city of Nachor. And when he had made the camels lie down without the town near a well of water in the evening, at the time when women are wont to come out to draw water, he said: O Lord the God of my master Abraham, meet me to-day, I beseech thee, and shew kindness to my master Abraham. Behold I stand nigh the spring of water, and the daughters of the inhabitants of this city will come out to draw water. Now, therefore, the maid to whom I shall say: Let down thy pitcher that I may drink: and she shall answer, Drink, and I will give thy camels drink also: let it be the same whom thou hast provided for thy servant Isaac: and by this I shall understand, that thou hast shewn kindness to my master. He had not yet ended these words within himself, and behold Rebecca came out, the daughter of Bathuel, son of Melcha, wife to Nachor the brother of Abraham, having a pitcher on her shoulder: an exceeding comely maid, and a most beautiful virgin: and she went down to the spring, and filled her pitcher and was coming back. And the servant ran to meet her, and said: Give me a little water to drink of thy pitcher. And she answered: Drink, my lord. And quickly she let down the pitcher upon her arm, and gave him drink. And when he had drunk, she said: I will draw water for thy camels also, till they all drink. And pouring out the pitcher into the troughs, she ran back to the well to draw water: and having drawn she gave to all the camels. And after that the camels had drunk, the man took out golden ear-rings, weighing two sicles: and as many bracelets of ten sicles weight. The man bowed himself down, and adored the Lord, saying: Blessed be the Lord God of my master Abraham, who hath not taken away his mercy and truth from my master, and hath brought me the straight way into the house of my master's brother. Then the maid ran, and told in her mother's house, all that she had heard. And Rebecca had a brother named Laban, who went out in haste to the man, to the well. And when he had seen the ear-rings and bracelets in his sister's hands, and had heard all that she related, saying: Thus and thus the man spoke to me: he came to the man who stood by the camels, and near to the spring of water, and said to him: Come in, thou blessed of the Lord: why standest thou without? I have prepared the house, and a place for the camels. And he brought him in into his lodging: and he unharnessed the camels and gave straw and hay, and water to wash his feet, and the feet of the men that were come with him. And bread was set before him. But he said: I will not eat, till I tell my message. He answered him: Speak. And he said: I am the servant of Abraham: and my master made me swear, saying: Thou shalt not take a wife for my son of the Chanaanites, in whose land I dwell: but thou shalt go to my father's house, and shalt take a wife of my own kindred for my son: and the Lord God of my master Abraham hath brought me the straight way to take the daughter of my master's brother for his son. Wherefore if you do according to mercy and truth with my master, tell me: but if it please you otherwise, tell me that also, that I may go to the right hand, or to the left. And Laban and Bathuel answered: Behold Rebecca is before thee, take her and go thy way, and let her be the wife of thy master's son, as the Lord hath spoken. Which when Abraham's servant heard, falling down to the ground he adored the Lord. And bringing forth vessels of silver and gold, and garments, he gave them to Rebecca for a present. He offered gifts also to her brothers, and to her mother. And a banquet was made, and they ate and drank together, and lodged there. And in the morning, the servant arose, and said: Let me depart, that I may go to my master. And they said: Let us call the maid, and ask her will. And they called her, and when she was come, they asked: Wilt thou go with this man? She said: I will go. So they sent her away, and her nurse, and Abraham's servant, and his company. So Rebecca, and her maids being set upon camels, followed the man: who with speed returned to his master. At the same time Isaac was walking along the way to the well which is called Of the living and the seeing: for he dwelt in the south country. And he was gone forth to meditate in the field, the day being now well spent: and when he had lifted up his eyes, he saw camels coming afar off. Rebecca also, when she saw Isaac, lighted off the camel, and said to the servant: Who is that man who cometh towards us along the field? And he said to her: That man is my master. But she quickly took *her* cloak, and covered herself. And the servant told Isaac all that he had done. Who brought her into the tent of Sara his mother, and took her to wife: and he loved her so much, that it moderated the sorrow which was occasioned by his mother's death.

Q. Why does the Church forbid the marriage of Catholics with persons who have a different religion or no religion at all?

(Gen. 34. A. M. 2273.) When Hemor the father of Sichem was come out to speak to Jacob, he said: The soul of my son Sichem has a longing for your daughter: give her him to wife: and let us contract marriages one with another: give us your daughters and take you our daughters, and dwell with us: the land is at your command, till, trade, and possess it. Sichem also said to her father and to her brethren: Let me find favor in your sight: and whatsoever you shall appoint I will give. Raise the dowry, and ask gifts, and I will gladly give what you shall demand: only give me this damsel to wife. The sons of Jacob answered Sichem and his father: We cannot do what you demand, nor give our sister to one that is uncircumcised, which with us is unlawful and abominable. But in this we may be allied with you, if you will be like us, and all the male sex among you be circumcised: then will we mutually give and take your daughters, and ours: and we will dwell with you, and will be one people: but if you will not be circumcised, we will take our daughter and depart.

Q. Why do many marriages prove unhappy?

(Tob. 6. A. M. 3299.) Then Tobias answered, and said: I hear that she hath been given to seven husbands, and they all died: moreover I have heard that a devil killed them.—Now I am afraid, lest the same thing should happen to me also: and whereas I am the only child of my parents, I should bring down their old age with sorrow to hell.—Then the Angel Raphael said to him: *Hear me, and I will show thee who they are, over whom the devil can prevail.—For they who in such manner receive matrimony, as to shut out God from themselves, and from their mind, and to give themselves to their lust, over them the devil hath power. But thou when thou shalt take her, go into the chamber, and for three days keep thyself continent from her, and give thyself to nothing else but to prayers with her.—And on that night lay the liver of the fish on the fire, and the devil shall be driven away.—But the second night thou shalt be admitted into the society of the holy Patriarchs.—And the third night thou shalt obtain a blessing that sound children may be born of you.*

Q. How should Christians prepare for a holy and happy marriage?

(Gen. 29. A. M. 2245.) Jacob went on in his journey, and came into the east country. And he saw a well in the field, and three flocks of sheep lying by it: for the beasts were watered out of it, and the mouth thereof was closed with a great stone. And behold Rachel came with her father's sheep: for she fed the flock. And when Jacob saw her, and knew her to be his cousin-german, and that they were the sheep of Laban, his uncle: he removed the stone wherewith the well was closed. And having watered the flock, he kissed her: and lifting up his voice, wept. And he told her that he was her father's brother, and the son of Rebecca: but she went in haste and told her father. Who, when he heard that Jacob his sister's son was come, ran forth to meet him: and embracing him, and heartily kissing him brought him into his house. And when he had heard the causes of his journey, he answered: Thou art my bone and my flesh. And after the days of one month were expired, he said to him: Because thou art my brother, shalt thou serve me without wages? Tell me what wages thou wilt have. Now he had two daughters, the name of the elder was Lia: and the younger was called Rachel. But Lia was blear-eyed: Rachel was well favored, and of a beautiful countenance. And Jacob being in love with her, said: I will serve thee seven years for Rachel thy younger daughter. Laban answered: It is better that I give her to thee than to another man; stay with me. So Jacob served seven years for Rachel: and they seemed *but* a few days, because of the greatness of his love.

(Judg. 21. A. M. 2890.) The Ancients commanded the children of Benjamin, and said: Go, and lie hid in the vineyards, and when you shall see the daughters of Silo come out, as the custom is, to dance, come ye on a sudden out of the vineyards, and catch you every man his wife among them, and go into the land of Benjamin. And when their fathers and their brethren shall come, and shall begin to complain against you, and to chide, we will say to them: Have pity on them: for they took them not away as by the right of war or conquest, but when they asked to have them, you gave them not, and the fault was committed on your part. And the children of Benjamin did, as they had been commanded: and according to their number, they carried off for themselves every man his wife of them that were dancing: and they went into their possession and built up their cities, and dwelt in them.

LESSON TWENTY-SEVENTH.

ON THE SACRAMENTALS.

Q. What is a sacramental?

(Num. 21. A. M. 2553.) The people came to Moses, and said: We have sinned, because we have spoken against the Lord and thee: pray that he may take away these serpents from us. And Moses prayed for the people. And the Lord said to him: Make a brazen serpent, and set it up for a sign: whosoever being struck shall look on it, shall live. Moses therefore made a brazen serpent, and set it up for a sign: which when they that were bitten looked upon, they were healed.

Q. What is the difference between the Sacraments and the sacramentals?

(Wisd. 16.) It is impossible to escape thy hand. For the wicked that denied to know thee, were scourged by the strength of thy arm, being persecuted by strange waters, and hail, and rain, and consumed by fire. And which was wonderful, in water, which extinguisheth all things, the fire had more force: for the world fighteth for the just. For at one time, the fire was mitigated, that the beasts which were sent against the wicked might not be burned, but that they might see and perceive that they were persecuted by the judgment of God. And at another time the fire, above its own power, burnt in the midst of water, to destroy the fruits of a wicked land. Instead of which things thou didst feed thy people with the food of Angels, and gavest them bread from heaven prepared without labour; having in it all that is delicious, and a sweetness of every taste. For thy sustenance shewed thy sweetness to thy children, and serving every man's will, it was turned to what every man liked.

Q. Which is the chief sacramental used in the Church?

(I. Cor. 1.) The word of the cross, to them indeed that perish, is foolishness; but to them that are saved, that is, to us, it is the power of god. For it is written: *I will destroy the wisdom of the wise, and the prudence of the prudent I will reject. Where is the wise? Where is the scribe? Where is the disputer of this world?* Hath not God made foolish the wisdom of this world? For seeing that in the wisdom of God the world, by wisdom, knew not God, it pleased God, by the foolishness of *our* preaching, to save them that believe. For both the Jews require signs, and the Greeks seek after wisdom: but we preach Christ crucified, unto the Jews indeed a stumbling-block, and unto the gentiles foolishness: but unto them that are called, both Jews and Greeks, Christ the power of God, and the wisdom of God. For the foolishness of God is wiser than men; and the weakness of God is stronger than men.

Q. How do we make the sign of the cross?

(Ezek. 9. A. M. 3410.) The Lord said to him: Go through the midst of the city, through the midst of Jerusalem: and mark Thau upon the foreheads of the men that sigh, and mourn for all the abominations that are committed in the midst thereof. And to the others he said in my hearing: Go ye after him through the city, and strike: let not your eyes spare, nor be ye moved with pity. Utterly destroy old and young, maidens, children and women: but upon whomsoever you shall see Thau, kill him not.

Q. Why do we make the sign of the cross?

(Gal. 6.) God forbid that I should glory, save in the cross of our Lord Jesus Christ: by whom the world is crucified to me, and I to the world. And whosoever shall follow this rule, peace on them, and mercy, and upon the Israel of God. From henceforth let no man be troublesome to me; for I bear the marks of the Lord Jesus in my body.

Q. How is the sign of the cross a profession of faith in the chief mysteries of our religion?

(I. Cor. 1.) We preach Christ crucified, unto the Jews indeed a stumbling-block, and unto the gentiles foolishness: but unto them that are called, both Jews and Greeks, Christ the power of God, and the wisdom of God. For the foolishness of God is wiser than men; and the weakness of God is stronger than men. For see your vocation, brethren, that *there are* not many wise according to the flesh, not many mighty, not many noble: but the foolish things of the world hath God chosen, that he may confound the wise; and the weak things of the world hath God chosen, that he may confound the strong. And the base things of the world, and the things that are contemptible hath God chosen, and things that are not, that he might bring to nought things that are: that no flesh should glory in his sight.

Q. How does the sign of the cross express the mystery of the Unity and Trinity of God?

(I. John 5.) There are three who give testimony in heaven, the Father, the word, and the Holy Ghost. And these three are one.

Q. How does the sign of the cross express the mystery of the Incarnation and death of our Lord?

(Ezek. 37. A. M. 3430.) The word of the Lord came to me, saying: And thou son of man, take thee a stick: and write upon it: Of Juda, and of the children of Israel his associates: and take another stick and write upon it: For Joseph the stick of Ephraim, and for all the house of Israel, and of his associates. And join them one to the other into one stick, and they shall become one in thy hand. And when the children of thy people shall speak to thee, saying: Wilt thou not tell us what thou meanest by this? Say to them: Thus saith the Lord God: Behold, I will take the stick of Joseph, which is in the hand of Ephraim, and the tribes of Israel that are associated with him, and I will put them together with the stick of Juda, and will make them one stick: and they shall be one in his hand. And the sticks whereon thou hast written, shall be in thy hand, before their eyes. And thou shalt say to them: Thus saith the Lord God: Behold, I will take the children of Israel from the midst of the nations whither they are gone: and I will gather them on every side, and will bring them to their own land. And I will make them one nation in the land on the mountains of Israel, and one king shall be king over them all: and they shall no more be two nations, neither shall they be divided any more into two kingdoms. And I will make a covenant of peace with them, it shall be an everlasting covenant with them: and I will establish them, and will multiply them, and will set my sanctuary in the midst of them for ever. And my tabernacle shall be with them: and I will be their God, and they shall be my people. And the nations shall know that I am the Lord the sanctifier of Israel, when my sanctuary shall be in the midst of them for ever.

Q. What other sacramental is in very frequent use?

(Num. 19.) They shall pour living waters into a vessel. And a man that is clean shall dip hyssop in them, and shall sprinkle therewith all the tent, and all the furniture, and the men that are defiled with touching any unclean thing: and in this manner he that is clean shall purify the unclean on the third and on the seventh day. And being expiated the seventh day, he shall wash both himself and his garments, and be unclean until the evening. If any man be not expiated after this rite, his soul shall perish out of the midst of the church: because he hath profaned the sanctuary of the Lord, and was not sprinkled with the water of purification.

Q. What is holy water?

(Num. 8. A. M. 2514.) The Lord spoke to Moses, saying: Take the Levites out of the midst of the children of Israel, and thou shalt purify them, according to this rite: Let them be sprinkled with the water of purification.

(IV. Kings 2.) The men of the city said to Eliseus: Behold the situation of this city is very good, as thou, my lord, seest: but the waters are very bad, and the ground barren. And he said: bring me a new vessel, and put salt into it. And when they had brought it, he went out to the spring of the waters, and cast the salt into it, and said: Thus saith the Lord: I have healed these waters, and there shall be no more in them death or barrenness. And the waters were healed unto this day, according to the word of Eliseus, which he spoke.

Q. Are there other sacramentals besides the sign of the cross and holy water?

(Lev. 6.) The fire on the altar shall always burn, and the priest shall feed it, putting wood on it every day in the morning, and laying on the holocaust, shall burn thereupon the fat of the peace-offerings. This is the perpetual fire which shall never go out on the altar.

(Gen. 2.) In the sweat of thy face shalt thou eat bread till thou return to the earth, out of which thou wast taken: for dust thou art, and into dust thou shalt return.

(John 12. A. D. 33.) On the next day a great multitude, that was come to the festival day, when they had heard that Jesus was coming to Jerusalem,—Took branches of palm-trees, and went forth to meet Him, and cried: Hosanna, blessed is He that cometh in the name of the Lord, the king of Israel.

(III. Kings 6. A.M. 3000.) All the walls of the temple round about he carved with divers figures and carvings: and he made in them cherubim and palm-trees, and divers representations as it were standing out, and coming forth from the wall.

(Apoc. 8.) Another angel came, and stood before the altar, having a golden censer: and there was given to him much incense, that he should offer of the prayers of all saints upon the golden altar, which is before the throne of God.—And the smoke of the incense of the prayers of the saints ascended up before God, from the hand of the angel.

(Apoc. 12.) A great sign appeared in heaven: A woman clothed with the sun, and the moon under her feet, and on her head a crown of twelve stars.

(Isa. 61.) I will greatly rejoice in the Lord, and my soul shall be joyful in my God: for He hath clothed me with the garments of salvation; and with the robe of justice he hath covered me, as a bridegroom decked with a crown, and as a bride adorned with her jewels.

LESSON TWENTY-EIGHTH.

ON PRAYER.

Q. Is there any other means of obtaining God's grace than the Sacraments?

(I. Kings 16. A. M. 2934.) The spirit of the Lord departed from Saul, and an evil spirit from the Lord troubled him. And Saul said to his servants: Provide me some man that can play well, and bring him to me. And one of the servants answering, said: Behold I have seen a son of Isai the Bethlehemite, a skilful player, and one of great strength, and a man fit for war, and prudent in his words, and a comely person: and the Lord is with him. Then Saul sent messengers to Isai, saying: Send me David thy son, who is in the pastures. And Isai took an ass laden with bread, and a bottle of wine, and a kid of the flock, and sent them by the hand of David his son to Saul. And David came to Saul, and stood before him: and he loved him exceedingly, and made him his armour-bearer. And Saul sent to Isai, saying: Let David stand before me: for he hath found favour in my sight. So whensoever the evil spirit from the Lord was upon Saul, David took his harp, and played with his hand, and Saul was refreshed, and was better, for the evil spirit departed from him.

Q. What is prayer?

(Col. 3.) All whatsoever you do in word or in work, do all in the name of the Lord Jesus Christ, giving thanks to God and the Father by him. Wives, be subject to your husbands, as it behoveth in the Lord. Husbands, love your wives, and be not bitter towards them. Children, obey your parents in all things: for this is well pleasing to the Lord. Fathers, provoke not your children to indignation, lest they be discouraged. Servants, obey in all things your masters according to the flesh, not serving to the eye, as pleasing men, but in simplicity of heart, fearing God. Whatsoever you do, do it from the heart, as to the Lord, and not to men: knowing that you shall receive of the Lord the reward of inheritance.

(Num. 10. A. M. 2514.) The Lord spoke to Moses, saying: Make thee two trumpets of beaten silver, wherewith thou mayest call together the multitude when the camp is to be removed. And when thou shalt sound the trumpets, all the multitude shall gather unto thee to the door of the tabernacle of the covenant. If thou sound but once, the princes and the heads of the multitude of Israel shall come to thee. But if the sound of the trumpets be longer, and with interruptions, they that are on the east side, shall first go forward. And at the second sounding and like noise of the trumpet, they who lie on the south side shall take up their tents. And after this manner shall the rest do, when the trumpets shall sound for a march. But when the people is to be gathered together, the sound of the trumpets shall be plain, and they shall not make a broken sound. And the sons of Aaron the priest shall sound the trumpets: and this shall be an ordinance for ever in your generations. If you go forth to war out of your land against the enemies that fight against you, you shall sound aloud with the trumpets, and there shall be a remembrance of you before the Lord your God, that you may be delivered out of the hands of your enemies. If at any time you shall have a banquet, and on your festival days, and on the first days of your months, you shall sound the trumpets over the holocausts, and the sacrifices of peace-offerings, that they may be to you for a remembrance of your God. I am the Lord your God.

(III. Kings 3. A. M. 2991.) The Lord appeared to Solomon in a dream by night, saying: Ask what thou wilt that I should give thee. And Solomon said: Thou hast shewn great mercy to thy servant David my father, even as he walked before thee in truth, and justice, and an upright heart with thee: and thou hast kept thy great mercy for him, and hast given him a son to sit on his throne, as it is this day. And now, O Lord God, thou hast made thy servant king instead of David my father: and I am but a child, and know not how to go out and come in. And thy servant is in the midst of the people which thou hast chosen, an immense people, which cannot be numbered nor counted for multitude. Give therefore to thy servant an understanding heart, to judge thy people, and discern between good and evil. For who shall be able to judge this people, thy people which is so numerous? And the word was pleasing to the Lord that Solomon had asked such a thing. And the Lord said to Solomon: Because thou hast asked this thing, and hast not asked for thyself long life or riches, nor the lives of thy enemies, but hast asked for thyself wisdom to discern judgment, behold I have done for thee according to thy words, and have given thee a wise and understanding heart, insomuch that there hath been no one like thee before thee, nor shall arise after thee. Yea and the things also which thou didst not ask, I have given thee: to wit, riches and glory, so that no one hath been like thee among the kings in all days heretofore. And if thou wilt walk in my ways, and keep my precepts, and my commandments, as thy father walked, I will lengthen thy days. And Solomon awaked, and perceived that it was a dream: and when he was come to Jerusalem, he stood before the ark of the covenant of the Lord, and offered holocausts, and sacrificed victims.

(Dan. 6. A. M. 3466.) It seemed good to Darius, and he appointed over the kingdom a hundred and twenty governors to be over his whole kingdom, and three princes over them, of whom Daniel was one. And Daniel excelled all the princes and governors: because a greater spirit of God was in him. And the king thought to set him over all the kingdom: whereupon the princes, and the governors sought to find occasion against Daniel with regard to the king. Then the princes, and the governors craftily suggested to the king, that an edict be published: That whosoever shall ask any petition of any god, or man, for thirty days, but of thee, O king, shall be cast into the den of lions. Now when Daniel knew this, that is to say, that the law was made, he went into his house: and opening the windows in his upper chamber towards Jerusalem, he knelt down three times a day, and adored, and gave thanks before his God, as he had been accustomed to do before. Wherefore those men carefully watching him, found Daniel praying and making supplication to his God. And they came and spoke to the king concerning the edict. Now when the king had heard these words, he was very much grieved, and in behalf of Daniel he set his heart to deliver him and even till sunset he laboured to save him. But those men perceiving the king's design, said to him: Know thou, O king, that the law of the Medes and Persians is, that no decree which the king hath made, may be altered. Then the king commanded, and they brought Daniel, and cast him into the den of the lions. And the king said to Daniel: Thy God, whom thou always servest, he will deliver thee. And the king went away to his house and laid himself down without taking supper, and meat was not set before him, and even sleep departed from him. Then the king rising very early in the morning, went in haste to the lions' den: and coming near to the den, cried with a lamentable voice to Daniel, and said to him: Daniel, servant of the living God, hath thy God, whom thou servest always, been able, thinkest thou, to deliver thee from the lions? And Daniel answering the king, said: O king, live forever: my God hath sent his Angel, and hath shut up the mouths of the lions, and they have not hurt me: forasmuch as before him justice hath been found in me: yea and before thee, O king, I have done no offence. Then was the king exceeding glad for him, and he commanded that Daniel should be taken out of the den: and Daniel was taken out of the den, and no hurt was found in him, because he believed in his God. And by the king's commandment, those men were brought that had accused Daniel: and they were cast into the lions' den, they and their children, and their wives: and they did not reach the bottom of the den, before the lions caught them, and broke all their bones in pieces. Then King Darius wrote to all people: It is decreed by me, that in all my empire and my kingdom all men dread and fear the God of Daniel. For he is the living and eternal God for ever: and his kingdom shall not be destroyed, and his power shall be forever. He is the deliverer and saviour, doing signs, and wonders in heaven, and in earth: who hath delivered Daniel out of the lions' den.

Q. Is prayer necessary to salvation?

See " L. of C.," p. 106, No. 9.

Q. At what particular times should we pray?

See " L. of C.," p. 40, No. 37; p. 44, No. 49.

(Num. 28. A. M. 2553.) The Lord said to Moses: Command the children of Israel, and thou shalt say to them: Offer ye my oblation and my bread, and burnt-sacrifice of most sweet odour, in their due seasons. These are the sacrifices which you shall offer: Two lambs of a year old without blemish every day for the perpetual holocaust: one you shall offer in the morning, and the other in the evening: and on the sabbath day you shall offer two lambs of a year old without blemish, and two tenths of flour tempered with oil in sacrifice, and the libations. And on the first day of the month you shall offer a holocaust to the Lord, two calves of the herd, one ram, and seven lambs of a year old, without blemish, so shall you do every day of the seven days for the food of the fire, and for a most sweet odour to the Lord, which shall rise from the holocaust, and from the libations of each. The seventh day also shall be most solemn and holy unto you: you shall do no servile work therein.

Q. How should we pray?
See "L. of C.," p. 33, No. 15; p. 68, No. 22; p. 80, Nos. 3, 4.

(Gen. 18. A. M. 2107). The Lord said: The cry of Sodom and Gomorrha is multiplied, and their sin is become exceedingly grievous. I will go down and see whether they have done according to the cry that is come to me; or whether it be not so, that I may know. And they turned themselves from thence, and went their way to Sodom: but Abraham as yet stood before the Lord. And drawing nigh he said: Wilt thou destroy the just with the wicked? If there be fifty just men in the city, shall they perish withal? and wilt thou not spare that place for the sake of the fifty just, if they be therein? Far be it from thee to do this thing, and to slay the just with the wicked, and for the just to be in like case as the wicked, this is not beseeming thee: thou who judgest all the earth, wilt not make this judgment. And the Lord said to him: If I find in Sodom fifty just within the city, I will spare the whole place for their sake. And Abraham answered, and said: Seeing I have once begun, I will speak to my Lord, whereas I am dust and ashes. What if there be five less than fifty just persons? wilt thou for five and forty destroy the whole city? And he said: I will not destroy it, if I find five and forty. And again he said to him: But if forty be found there, what wilt thou do? He said: I will not destroy it for the sake of forty. Lord, saith he, be not angry, I beseech thee, if I speak: What if thirty shall be found there? He answered: I will not do it, if I find thirty there. Seeing, saith he, I have once begun, I will speak to my Lord. What if twenty be found there? He said: I will not destroy it for the sake of twenty. I beseech thee, saith he, be not angry, Lord, if I speak yet once more: What if ten should be found there? And he said: I will not destroy it for the sake of ten. And the Lord departed, after he had left speaking to Abraham: and Abraham returned to his place.

(Ex. 17. A. M. 2514.) Josue did as Moses had spoken, and he fought against Amalec; but Moses, and Aaron, and Hur went up upon the top of the hill. And when Moses lifted up his hands, Israel overcame: but if he let them down a little, Amalec overcame. And Moses's hands were heavy: so they took a stone, and put under him, and he sat on it: and Aaron and Hur stayed up his hands on both sides. And it came to pass that his hands were not weary until sunset. And Josue put Amalec and his people to flight, by the edge of the sword.

(Judg. 20. A. M. 2887.) The children of Israel rising in the morning, camped by Gabaa; and going out from thence to fight against Benjamin, began to assault the city. And the children of Benjamin coming out of Gabaa, slew of the children of Israel that day two and twenty thousand men. Again Israel trusting in their strength and their number, set their army in array in the same place, where they had fought before: yet so that they first went up and wept before the Lord until night: and consulted him and said: Shall I go out any more to fight against the children of Benjamin my brethren, or no? And he answered them: Go up against them, and join battle. And when the children of Israel went out the next day to fight against the children of Benjamin, the children of Benjamin sallied forth out of the gates of Gabaa: and meeting them made so great a slaughter of them, as to kill eighteen thousand men that drew the sword. Where-fore all the children of Israel came to the house of God, and sat and wept before the Lord: and they fasted that day till the evening, and offered to him holocausts, and victims of peace-offerings, and inquired of him concerning their state. At that time the ark of the covenant of the Lord was there, and Phinees the son of Eleazar the son of Aaron was over the house. So they consulted the Lord and said: Shall we go out any more to fight against the children of Benjamin our brethren, or shall we cease? And the Lord said to them: Go up, for to-morrow I will deliver them into your hands. And the Lord defeated them before the children of Israel, and they slew of them in that day five and twenty thousand, and one hundred, all fighting men and that drew the sword.

(III. Kings 18.) Achab went up to eat and drink: and Elias went up to the top of Carmel, and casting himself down upon the earth put his face beeween his knees, and he said to his servant: Go up, and look toward the sea. And he went up, and looked, and said: There is nothing. And again he said to him: Return seven times. And at the seventh time: Behold a little cloud arose out of the sea like a man's foot. And he said: Go up and say to Achab: Prepare thy chariot and go down, lest the rain prevent thee. And while he turned himself this way and that way, behold the heavens grew dark, with clouds, and wind, and there fell a great rain.

Q. Which are the prayers most recommended to us?
See "L. of C.," p. 75, No. 15.

Q. Are prayers said with distractions of any avail?
See "L. of C.," p. 47, No. 2; p. 88, No. 28.

(Num. 15. A. M. 2530.) The Lord also said to Moses: Speak to the children of Israel, and thou shalt tell them to make to themselves fringes in the corners of their garments, putting in them ribands of blue: that when they shall see them, they may remember all the commandments of the Lord, and not follow their own thoughts and eyes going astray after divers things, but rather being mindful of the precepts of the Lord, may do them and be holy to their God. I am the Lord your God, who brought you out of the land of Egypt, that I might be your God.

LESSON TWENTY-NINTH.

ON THE COMMANDMENTS OF GOD.

Q. Is it enough to belong to God's Church in order to be saved?
See "L. of C.," p. 34, No. 22; p. 65, No. 27; p. 70, No. 2.

(Rom. 2.) Circumcision profiteth indeed, if thou keep the law; but if thou be a transgressor of the law, thy circumcision is made uncircumcision. If, then, the uncircumcised keep the justices of the law, shall not this uncircumcision be counted for circumcision? And shall not that which by nature is uncircumcision, if it fulfil the law, judge thee, who by the letter and circumcision art a transgressor of the law? For it is not he is a Jew, that is so outwardly; nor is that circumcision, which is outward in the flesh. But he is a Jew, that is one inwardly; and the circumcision is that of the heart, in the spirit, not in the letter; whose praise is not of men, but of God.

Q. Which are the Commandments that contain the whole law of God?
See "L. of C.," p. 32, No. 13.

(I. John 4.) Let us love God, because God first hath loved us. If any man say, I love God, and hateth his brother; he is a liar. For he that loveth not his brother, whom he seeth, how can he love God, whom he seeth not? And this commandment we have from God, that he, who loveth God, love also his brother.

(Deut. 22.) Thou shalt not pass by if thou seest thy

brother's ox, or his sheep go astray: but thou shalt bring them back to thy brother. And if thy brother be not nigh, or thou know him not: thou shalt bring *them* to thy house, and they shall be with thee until thy brother seek them, and receive them. Thou shalt do in like manner with his ass, and with his raiment, and with every thing that is thy brother's, which is lost: if thou find it, neglect it not as pertaining to another. If thou see thy brother's ass or his ox to be fallen down in the way, thou shalt not slight it, but shalt lift it up with him. A woman shall not be clothed with man's apparel, neither shall a man use woman's apparel: for he that doeth these things is abominable before God. If thou find as thou walkest by the way, a bird's nest in a tree, or on the ground, and the dam sitting upon the young or upon the eggs: thou shalt not take her with her young: but shalt let her go, keeping the young which thou hast caught: that it may be well with thee, and thou mayest live a long time.

Q. **Why do these two Commandments of the love of God and of our neighbor contain the whole law of God?**

See "L. of C.," p. 91, No. 32; p. 102, No. 7.

Q. **Which are the Commandments of God?**

(Dan. 14. A. M. 3398.) Daniel was the king's guest, and was honoured above all his friends. Now the Babylonians had an idol called Bel: and there were spent upon him every day twelve great measures of fine flour, and forty sheep, and sixty vessels of wine. The king also worshipped him, and went every day to adore him: but Daniel adored his God. And the king said to him: Why dost thou not adore Bel? And he answered, and said to him: Because I do not worship idols made with hands, but the living God, that created heaven and earth, and hath power over all flesh. And the king said to him: Doth not Bel seem to thee to be a living god? Seest thou not how much he eateth and drinketh every day? Then Daniel smiled and said: O king, be not deceived: for this is but clay within, and brass without, neither hath he eaten at any time. And the king being angry called for his priests, and said to them: If you tell me not, who it is that eateth up these expenses, you shall die. But if you can shew that Bel eateth these things, Daniel shall die, because he hath blasphemed against Bel. And Daniel said to the king: Be it done according to thy word. So it came to pass after they were gone out, the king set the meats before Bel: and Daniel commanded his servants, and they brought ashes, and he sifted them all over the temple before the king: and going forth they shut the door, and having sealed it with the king's ring, they departed. But the priests went in by night, according to their custom, with their wives and their children: and they eat and drank up all. And the king arose early in the morning, and Daniel with him. And the king said: are the seals whole, Daniel? And he answered: They are whole, O king. And as soon as he had opened the door, the king looked upon the table, and cried out with a loud voice: Great art thou O Bel, and there is not any deceit with thee. And Daniel laughed: and he held the king that he should not go in: and he said: Behold the pavement, mark whose foot-steps these are. And the king said: I see the foot-steps of men, and women, and children. And the king was angry. Then he took the priests, and their wives, and their children: and they shewed him the private doors by which they came in, and consumed the things that were on the table. The king therefore put them to death, and delivered Bel into the power of Daniel: who destroyed him, and his temple.

(Eccltus. 23.) Let not thy mouth be accustomed to swearing: for in it there are many falls. And let not the naming of God be usual in thy mouth, and meddle not with the names of saints, for thou shalt not escape free from them. For as a slave daily put to the question, is never without a blue mark: so every one that sweareth, and nameth, shall not be wholly pure from sin. A man that sweareth much, shall be filled with iniquity, and a scourge shall not depart from his house. And if he make it void, his sin shall be upon him: and if he dissemble it, he offendeth double: and if he swear in vain, he shall not be justified: for his house shall be filled with his punishment.

(Isa. 56.) Blessed is the man that doth this, and the son of man that shall lay hold on this: that keepeth the sabbath from profaning it, for thus saith the Lord: They that shall keep my sabbaths, and shall choose the things that please me, and shall hold fast my covenant: I will give to them in my house, and within my walls, a place, and a name better than sons and daughters: I will give them an everlasting name which shall never perish. And the children of the stranger that adhere to the Lord, to worship him, and to love his name, to be his servants: every one that keepeth the sabbath from profaning it, and that holdeth fast my covenant: I will bring them into my holy mount, and will make them joyful in my house of prayer: their holocausts, and their victims shall please me upon my altar: for my house shall be called the house of prayer, for all nations.

(Eccltus. 3.) Children, hear

the judgment of your father, and so do that you may be saved. For God hath made the father honourable to the children: and seeking the judgment of the mothers, hath confirmed *it* upon the children. And he that honoureth his mother is as one that layeth up a treasure. He that honoureth his father shall have joy in *his own* children, and in the day of his prayer he shall be heard. He that honoureth his father shall enjoy a long life: and he that obeyeth the father, shall be a comfort to his mother. He that feareth the Lord, honoreuth his parents, and will serve them as his masters that brought him into the world. Honour thy father, in work and word, and all patience, that a blessing may come upon thee from him, and his blessing may remain in the latter end. The father's blessing establisheth the houses of the children: but the mother's curse rooteth up the foundation. Glory not in the dishonour of thy father: for his shame is no glory to thee. For the glory of a man is from the honour of his father, and a father without honour is the disgrace of the son. Son, support the old age of thy father, and grieve him not in his life; and if his understanding fail, have patience with him, and despise him not when thou art in thy strength: for the relieving of the father shall not be forgotten.

(Gen. 9.) I will require the blood of your lives at the hand of every beast, and at the hand of man, at the hand of every man, and of his brother, will I require the life of man. Whosoever shall shed man's blood, his blood shall be shed: for man was made to the image of God.

(Gen. 12. A. M. 2084.) There came a famine in the country; and Abram went down into Egypt, to sojourn there: for the famine was very grievous in the land. And when he was near to enter into Egypt, he said to Sarai his wife: I know that thou art a beautiful woman: and that when the Egyptians shall see thee, they will say: She is his wife; and they will kill me, and keep thee. Say, therefore, I pray thee, that thou art my sister: that I may be well used for thee, and that my soul may live for thy sake. And when Abram was come into Egypt, the Egyptians saw the woman that she was very beautiful. And the princes told Pharao, and praised her before him: and the woman was taken into the house of Pharao. And they used Abram well for her sake: And he had sheep and oxen, and he-asses and men-servants and maid-servants, and she-asses, and camels. But the Lord scourged Pharao and his house with most grievous stripes for Sarai, Abram's wife. And Pharao called Abram, and said to him: What is this that thou hast done to me? Why didst thou not tell *me* that she was thy wife? For what cause didst thou say, she was thy sister, that I might take her to my wife? Now, therefore, there is thy wife, take her and go thy way.

(Josh. 7. A. M. 2553.) Achan answered Josue, and said to him: indeed I have sinned against the Lord the God of Israel, and thus and thus have I done. For I saw among the spoils a scarlet garment exceeding good, and two hundred sicles of silver, and a golden rule of fifty sicles: and I coveted them, and I took them away, and hid them in the ground in the midst of my tent, and the silver I covered with the earth that I dug up. Josue therefore sent ministers: who running to his tent, found all hidden in the same place, together with the silver. And taking them away out of the tent, they brought them to Josue, and to all the children of Israel, and threw them down before the Lord. Then Josue and all Israel with him took Achan the son of Zare, and the silver and the garments, and the golden rule, his sons also and his daughters, his oxen and asses and sheep, the tent also, and all the goods: and brought them to the valley of Achor: where Josue said: Because thou hast troubled us, the Lord trouble thee this day. And all Israel stoned him: and all things that were his, were consumed with fire. And they gathered together upon him a great heap of stones, which remaineth until this present day. And the wrath of the Lord was turned away from them.

(III. Kings 21. A. M. 3105.) Naboth the Jezrahelite, who was in Jezrahel had at that time a vineyard near the palace of Achab king of Samaria. And Achab spoke to Naboth, saying: Give me thy vineyard, that I may make me a garden of herbs, because it is nigh, and joining to my house, and I will give thee for it a better vineyard: or if thou think it more convenient for thee, I will give thee the worth of it in money. Naboth answered him: The Lord be merciful to me, and not let me give thee the inheritance of my fathers. And Achab came into his house angry and fretting, because of the word that Naboth had said. Then Jezabel his wife said to him: be of good cheer, I will give thee the vineyard of Naboth the Jezrahelite. So she wrote letters in Achab's name, and sealed them with his ring, and sent them to the ancients, and the chief men that were in his city, and that dwelt with Naboth. And this was the tenor of the letters: Proclaim a fast, and make Naboth sit among the chief of the people, and suborn two men, sons of Belial against him, and let them bear false witness: that he hath blasphemed God and the king: and then carry him out, and stone him, and so let him die. And they sent to Jezabel, saying: Naboth is stoned, and is dead. And the word of the Lord came to Elias the Thesbite, saying: Arise, and go down to meet Achab king of Israel, who is in Samaria: behold he is going down to the vineyard of Naboth, to take possession of it: and thou shalt speak to him, saying: Thus saith the Lord: Thou hast slain, moreover also thou hast taken possession. And after these words thou shalt add: Thus saith the Lord: In this place, wherein the dogs have licked the blood of Naboth, they shall lick thy blood also. And of Jezabel also the Lord spoke, saying: The dogs shall eat Jezabel in the field of Jezrahel.

(II. Kings 11. A. M. 2969.) It happened that David arose from his bed after noon, and walked upon the roof of the king's house: and he saw from the roof of his house a woman washing herself, over-against him: and the woman was very beautiful. And the king sent, and inquired who the woman was. And it was told him, that she was Bethsabee the daughter of Eliam, the wife of Urias the Hethite. And David sent messengers, and took her, and this thing which David had done, was displeasing to the Lord.

(Eph. 5.) But covetousness, let it not so much as be named among you, as becometh saints: For know you this and understand, that no covetous person hath inheritance in the kingdom of Christ and of God.

Q. Who gave the Ten Commandments?

(Ex. 19. A. M. 2513.) In the third month of the departure of Israel out of the land of Egypt, on this day they came into the wilderness of Sinai: for departing out of Raphidim, and coming to the desert of Sinai, they camped in the same place, and there Israel pitched their tents over-against the mountain. And Moses went up to God: and the Lord, when he had ended his words in mount Sinai, gave to Moses two stone-tables of testimony, written with the finger of God. And the people seeing that Moses delayed to come down from the mount, gathering together against Aaron, said: Arise, make us gods, that may go before us: For as to this Moses, the man that brought us out of the land of Egypt, we know not what has befallen him. And Aaron said to them: Take the golden ear-rings from the ears of your wives, and your sons and daughters, and bring them to me. And the people did what he had commanded, bringing the ear-rings to Aaron. And when he had received them, he fashioned them by founders' work, and made of them a molten calf. And they said: These are thy gods, O Israel, that have brought thee out of the land of Egypt. And the Lord spoke to Moses, saying: Go, get thee down: thy people, which thou hast brought out of the land of Egypt, hath sinned. And Moses returned from the mount, carrying the two tables of the testimony in his hand, written on both sides, and made by the work of God: the writing also of God was graven in the tables. And when he came nigh to the camp, he saw the calf, and the dances: and being very angry, he threw the tables out of his hand, and broke them at the foot of the mount: and after this God said: Hew thee two tables of stone like unto the former, and I will write upon them the words which were in the tables, which thou brokest. Then he cut out two tables of stone, such as had been before: and rising very early he went up into the mount Sinai, as the Lord had commanded him, carrying with him the tables. And when the Lord was come down in a cloud, Moses stood with him, calling upon the name of the Lord. And the Lord said to Moses: Write thee these words by which I have made a covenant both with thee and with Israel. And he was there with the Lord forty days and forty nights: he neither ate bread nor drank water, and he wrote upon the tables the ten words of the covenant. And when Moses came down from the mount Sinai, he held the two tables of the testimony, and he knew not that his face was horned from the conversation of the Lord.

LESSON THIRTIETH.

ON THE FIRST COMMANDMENT.

Q. What is the first Commandment?

(Ex. 20. A. M. 2513.) The Lord spoke all these words: I am the Lord thy God, who brought thee out of the land of Egypt, out of house of bondage. Thou shalt not have strange gods before me. Thou shalt not make to thyself a graven thing, nor the likeness of anything that is in heaven above, or in the earth beneath, nor of those things that are in the waters under the earth. Thou shalt not adore them, nor serve *them:* I am the Lord thy God, mighty, jealous, visiting the iniquity of the fathers upon the children, unto the third and fourth generation of them that hate me: and shewing mercy unto thousands to them that love me, and keep my commandments.

Q. How does the first Commandment help us to keep the great Commandment of the love of God?

See "L. of C.," p. 72, No. 7.

Q. How do we adore God?
See "L. of C.," p. 88, No. 27.

Q. How may the first Commandment be broken?

(Acts 12. A. D. 42.) Upon a day appointed, Herod being arrayed in kingly apparel, sat in the judgment-seat, and made an oration to them. And the people made acclamation, saying: It is the voice of a God, and not of a man. And forthwith an Angel of the Lord struck him, because he had not given the honour to God: and being eaten up by worms, he gave up the ghost.

(Acts 14. A. D. 43.) There sat a certain man at Lystra, impotent in his feet, a cripple from his mother's womb, who never had walked. This same heard Paul speaking. Who looking upon him, and seeing that he had faith to be healed, said with a loud voice: Stand upright on thy feet. And he leaped up, and walked. And when the multitudes had seen what Paul had done, they lifted up their voice in the Lycaonian tongue, saying: The gods are come down to us in the likeness of men; and they called Barnabas, Jupiter: but Paul, Mercury; because he was chief speaker. The priest also of Jupiter that was before the city, bringing oxen and garlands before the gate, would have offered sacrifice with the people. Which, when the apostles Barnabas and Paul had heard, rending their clothes, they leaped out among the people crying, and saying: Ye men, why do ye these things? We also are mortal men like unto you.

(Judg.17. A. M. 2886.) There was at that time a man of mount Ephraim whose name was Michas, who said to his mother: The eleven hundred pieces of silver, which thou hadst put aside for thyself, and concerning which thou didst swear in my hearing, behold I have, and they are with me. And she said to him: Blessed be my son by the Lord. So he restored them to his mother, who said to him: I have consecrated and vowed this silver to the Lord, that my son may receive it at my hand, and make a graven and a molten *god*, so now I deliver it to thee. And he restored them to his mother: and she took two hundred pieces of silver and gave them to the silversmith, to make of them a graven and a molten *god*, which was in the house of Michas. There was also another young man of Bethlehem Juda, of the kindred thereof: and he was a Levite, and dwelt there. Now he went out from the city of Bethlehem, and desired to sojourn wheresoever he should find it convenient for him. And when he was come to mount Ephraim, as he was on his journey, and had turned aside a little into the house of Michas, he was asked by him whence he came. And he answered: I am a Levite of Bethlehem Juda, and I am going to dwell where I can, and where I shall find a place to my advantage. And Michas said: Stay with me, and be unto me a father and a priest, and I will give thee every year ten pieces of silver, and a double suit of apparel, and thy victuals. He was content, and abode with the man, and was unto him as one of his sons. There went therefore of the kindred of Dan, to wit, from Saraa and Esthaol, six hundred men, furnished with arms for war, and going up they lodged in Cariathiarim of Juda: which place from that time is called the camp of Dan, and is behind Cariathiarim. From thence they passed into mount Ephraim. And when they were come to the house of Michas, and when they had turned a little aside, they went into the house of the young man the Levite, who was in the house of Michas: and they saluted him with words of peace. And the six hundred men stood before the door, appointed with their arms. So they that were gone in took away the graven thing, the ephod, and the idols, and the molten *god*. And the priest said to them: What are you doing? And they said to him: Hold thy peace and put thy finger on thy mouth and come with us, that we may have thee for a father, and a priest. Whether is better for thee, to be a priest in the house of one man, or in a tribe and family in Israel? When he had heard this, he agreed to their words, and took the ephod, and the idols, and the graven *god*, and departed with them. And the six hundred men took the priest, and the things we spoke of before, and came to Lais to a people that was quiet and secure, and smote them with the edge of the sword: and the city was burnt with fire.

Q. Do those who make use of spells and charms, or who believe in dreams, in mediums, spiritists, fortunetellers, and the like, sin against the first Commandment?

(Gen. 40, 41. A. M. 2287.) After this, it came to pass, that two servants, the butler and the baker, of the king of Egypt, offended their lord. And Pharao being angry with them (now the one was chief butler, the other chief baker) he sent them to the prison of the commander of the soldiers, in which Joseph also was prisoner. But the keeper of the prison delivered them to Joseph, and he served them. Some little time passed, and they were kept in custody. And they both dreamed a dream the same night, according to the interpretation agreeing to themselves: and when Joseph was come in to them in the morning, and saw them sad, he asked them, saying: Why is your countenance sadder to-day than usual? They answered:

We have dreamed a dream, and there is nobody to interpret it to us. And Joseph said to them: Doth not interpretation belong to God? Tell me what you have dreamed? The chief butler first told his dream: I saw before me a vine, on which were three branches, which by little and little sent out buds, and after the blossoms brought forth ripe grapes: and the cup of Pharao was in my hand: and I took the grapes, and pressed them into the cup which I held, and I gave the cup to Pharao. Joseph answered: This is the interpretation of the dream: The three branches are yet three days: after which Pharao will remember thy service, and will restore thee to thy former place: and thou shalt present him the cup according to thy office, as before thou wast wont to do. Only remember me, when it shall be well with thee, and do me this kindness: to put Pharao in mind to take me out of this prison: for I was stolen away out of the land of the Hebrews, and here without any fault was cast into the dungeon. The chief baker seeing that he had wisely interpreted the dream, said: I also dreamed a dream: That I had three baskets of meal upon my head: and that in one basket which was uppermost, I carried all meats that are made by the art of baking, and that the birds ate out of it. Joseph answered: This is the interpretation of the dream: The three baskets, are yet three days: after which Pharao will take thy head from thee, and hang thee on a cross, and the birds shall tear thy flesh. The third day after this was the birthday of Pharao: and he made a great feast for his servants, and at the banquet remembered the chief butler, and the chief baker, and he restored the one to his place to present him the cup: the other he hanged on a gibbet, that the truth of the interpreter might be shewn. But the chief butler, when things prospered with him, forgot his interpreter. After two years Pharao had a dream. He thought he stood by the river, out of which came up seven kine, very beautiful and fat: and they fed in marshy places. Other seven also came up out of the river, ill-favoured, and lean fleshed: and they fed on the very bank of the river, in green places: and they devoured them, whose bodies were very beautiful and well conditioned. So Pharao awoke. He slept again, and dreamed another dream: Seven ears of corn came up upon one stalk full and fair: then seven other ears sprung up thin and blasted, and devoured all the beauty of the former. Pharao awaked after his rest: and when morning was come, being struck with fear, he sent to all the interpreters of Egypt, and to all the wise men: and they being called for, he told them his dream, and there was not any one that could interpret it. Then at length the chief butler remembering, said: There was a young man a Hebrew, servant to the captain of the soldiers: to whom we told our dreams, and we heard what afterwards the event of the thing proved to be so. For I was restored to my office: and he was hanged upon a gibbet. Forthwith at the king's command, Joseph was brought out of the prison, and they shaved him, and changing his apparel, brought him in to him. Joseph answered: The king's dream is one: God hath shewn to Pharao what he is about to do. The seven beautiful kine, and the seven full ears, are seven years of plenty: and *both* contain the same meaning of the dream. And the seven lean and thin kine that came up after them, and the seven thin ears that were blasted with the burning wind, are seven years of famine to come. And Pharao said to Joseph: Behold, I have appointed thee over the whole land of Egypt. And he took his ring from his own hand, and gave it into his hand: and he put upon him a robe of silk, and put a chain of gold about his neck. And he made him go up into his second chariot, the crier proclaiming that all should bow their knee before him, and that they should know he was made governor over the whole land of Egypt. And the king said to Joseph: I am Pharao; without thy commandment no man shall move hand or foot in all the land of Egypt. And he turned his name, and called him in the Egyptian tongue the saviour of the world.

(Ex. 7. A. M. 2513.) The Lord said to Moses and Aaron: When Pharao shall say to you, shew signs: thou shalt say to Aaron: Take thy rod, and cast it down before Pharao, and it shall be turned into a serpent. So Moses and Aaron went in unto Pharao, and did as the Lord had commanded. And Aaron took the rod before Pharao, and his servants, and it was turned into a serpent. And Pharao called the wise men and the magicians: and they also by Egyptian enchantments and certain secrets did in like manner, but Aaron's rod devoured theirs.

(Deut. 18.) When thou art come into the land which the Lord thy God shall give thee, beware lest thou have a mind to imitate the abominations of those nations. Neither let there be found among you any one that shall expiate his son or daughter, making them to pass through the fire: or that consulteth soothsayers, or observeth dreams and omens, neither let there be any wizard, nor charmer, nor any one that consulteth pythonic spirits, or fortune-tellers, or that seeketh the truth from the dead. For the Lord abhorreth all these things, and for these abominations he will destroy them at thy coming. And if in silent thought thou answer: How shall I know the word that the Lord hath not spoken? Thou shalt have this sign: Whatsoever that same prophet foretelleth in the name of the Lord, and it cometh not to pass: that thing the Lord hath not spoken, but the prophet hath forged it by the pride of his mind: and therefore thou shalt not fear him.

(Deut. 13.) If there rise in the midst of thee a prophet or one that saith he hath dreamed a dream, and he foretell a sign and a wonder, and that come to pass which he spoke, and he say to thee: Let us go and follow strange gods, which thou knowest not, and let us serve them: Thou shalt not hear the words of that prophet or dreamer: for the Lord your God trieth you, that it may appear whether you love him with all your heart, and with all your soul, or no. Follow the Lord your God, and fear him, and keep his commandments, and hear his voice: him you shall serve, and to him you shall cleave. And that prophet or forger of dreams shall be slain: because he spoke to draw you away from the Lord your God.

(I. Kings 28. A. M. 2949.) Saul saw the army of the Philistines, and was afraid, and his heart was very much dismayed. And he consulted the Lord, and he answered him not, neither by dreams, nor by priests, nor by prophets. And Saul said to his servants: Seek me a woman that hath a divining spirit, and I will go to her, and inquire by her. And his servants said to him: There is a woman that hath a divining spirit at Endor. Then he disguised himself: and put on other clothes, and he went, and two men with him, and they came to the woman by night. And the woman said to him: Whom shall I bring up to thee? And he said. Bring me up Samuel. And when the woman saw Samuel, she cried out with a loud voice, and said to Saul: Why hast thou deceived me? for thou art Saul. And the king said to her: Fear not: what hast thou seen? And the woman said to Saul: I saw gods ascending out of the earth. And he said to her: What form is he of? And she said: An old man cometh up, and he is covered with a mantle. And Saul understood that it was Samuel, and he bowed himself with his face to the ground, and adored. And Samuel said to Saul: Why hast thou disturbed my rest, that I should be brought up? And Saul said, I am in great distress: for the Philistines fight against me, and God is departed from me, and would not hear me, neither by the hand of prophets, nor by dreams: therefore I have called thee, that thou mayest show me what I shall do. And Samuel said: Why askest thou me, seeing the Lord has departed from thee, and is gone over to thy rival: for the

Lord will do to thee as he spoke by me, and he will rend thy kingdom out of thy hand, and will give it to thy neighbour David.

(IV. Kings I. A. M. 3108.) Ochozias fell through the lattices of his upper chamber which he had in Samaria, and was sick: and he sent messengers, saying to them: Go, consult Beelzebub, the god of Accaron, whether I shall recover of this my illness. And an angel of the Lord spoke to Elias the Thesbite, saying: Arise, and go up to meet the messengers of the king of Samaria, and say to them: Is there not a God in Israel, that ye go to consult Beelzebub the God of Accaron? Wherefore thus saith the Lord: From the bed, on which thou art gone up, thou shalt not come down, but thou shalt surely die. And Elias went away. And the messengers turned back to Ochozias. And he said to them: Why are you come back? But they answered him: A man met us, and said to us: Go, and return to the king, that sent you, and you shall say to him: Thus saith the Lord: Is it because there was no God in Israel that thou sendest to Beelzebub the God of Accaron? And he said: It is Elias the Thesbite. And he sent to him a captain of fifty, and the fifty men that were under him. And he went up to him, and as he was sitting on the top of a hill, said to him: Man of God, the king hath commanded that thou come down. And Elias answering, said to the captain of fifty: If I be a man of God, let fire come down from heaven, and consume thee, and thy fifty. And there came down fire from heaven, and consumed him, and the fifty that were with him. And again he sent to him another captain of fifty men, and his fifty with him. And he said to him: Man of God, thus saith the king: Make haste and come down. Elias answering, said: If I be a man of God, let fire come down from heaven, and consume thee and thy fifty. And fire came down from heaven, and consumed him and his fifty. Again he sent a third captain of fifty men, and the fifty that were with him. And when he was come, he fell upon his knees, before Elias, and besought him and said: Man of God, despise not my life, and the lives of thy servants that are with me. Behold fire came down from heaven, and consumed the two first captains of fifty men, and the fifties that were with them: but now I beseech thee to spare my life. And the angel of the Lord spoke to Elias, saying: Go down with him, fear not. He arose therefore, and went down with him to the king, and said to him: Thus saith the Lord: Because thou hast sent messengers to consult Beelzebub the god of Accaron, as though there were not a God in Israel, of whom thou mightest inquire the word, therefore from the bed on which thou art gone up, thou shalt not come down, but thou shalt surely die. So he died according to the word of the Lord which Elias spoke.

(Eccltus. 34.) The hopes of a man that is void of understanding are vain and deceitful; and dreams lift up fools. The man that giveth heed to lying visions, is like to him that catcheth at a shadow, and followeth after the wind. The vision of dreams is the resemblance of one thing to another: as when a man's likeness is before the face of a man. What can be made clean by the unclean? and what truth can come from that which is false? Deceitful divinations and lying omens and the dreams of evil doers, are vanity. And the heart fancieth as that of a woman in travail: except it be a vision sent forth from the most High, set not thy heart upon them. For dreams have deceived many, and they have failed that put their trust in them.

Q. Are sins against faith, hope, and charity also sins against the first Commandment?

See "L. of C.," p. 104, No. 6.

Q. How does a person sin against faith?

See "L. of C.," p. 88, No. 30; p. 71, No. 6.

(Acts 13. A. D. 42.) Sergius Paulus, a prudent man, sending for Barnabas and Saul, desired to hear the word of God. But Elymas the magician (for so his name is interpreted) withstood them, seeking to turn away the proconsul from the faith. Then Saul, otherwise Paul, filled with the Holy Ghost, looking upon him, said: O full of all guile, and of all deceit, child of the devil, enemy of all justice, thou ceasest not to pervert the right ways of the Lord. And now behold, the hand of the Lord is upon thee, and thou shalt be blind, not seeing the sun for a time. And immediately there fell a mist and darkness upon him, and going about, he sought some one to lead him by the hand. Then the proconsul, when he had seen what was done, believed, admiring at the doctrine of the Lord.

Q. How do we fail to try to know what God has taught?

See "L. of C.," p. 88, No. 32.

(II. Tim. 2.) Avoid foolish and unlearned questions, knowing that they beget strifes. But the servant of the Lord must not wrangle: but be mild towards all men, apt to teach, patient, with modesty admonishing them that resist the truth: if peradventure God may give them repentance to know the truth, and they may recover themselves from the snares of the devil, by whom they are held captive at his will.

(III. Kings 10. A. M. 3023.) The queen of Saba, having heard of the fame of Solomon in the name of the Lord, came to try him with hard questions. And entering into Jerusalem with a great train, and riches, and camels that carried spices, and an immense quantity of gold, and precious stones, she came to king Solomon, and spoke to him all that she had in her heart. And Solomon informed her of all the things she proposed to him: there was not any word the king was ignorant of, and which he could not answer her. And when the queen of Saba saw all the wisdom of Solomon, and the house which he had built, and the meat of his table, and the apartments of his servants, and the order of his ministers, and their apparel, and the cup-bearers, and the holocaust, which he offered in the house of the Lord: she had no longer any spirit in her, and she said to the king: The report is true, which I heard in my own country, concerning thy words, and concerning thy wisdom. And I did not believe them that told me, till I came myself, and saw with my own eyes, and have found that the half hath not been told me: thy wisdom and thy works, exceed the fame which I heard. Blessed are thy men, and blessed are thy servants, who stand before thee always, and hear thy wisdom. Blessed be the Lord thy God, whom thou hast pleased, and who hath set thee upon the throne of Israel, because the Lord hath loved Israel for ever, and hath appointed thee king, to do judgment and justice. And she gave the king a hundred and twenty talents of gold, and of spices a very great store, and precious stones: there was brought no more such abundance of spices as these which the queen of Saba gave to king Solomon.

Q. Who are they who do not believe all that God has taught?

See "L. of C.," p. 23, Nos. 7, 8; p. 60, No. 20; p. 64, No. 26; p. 69, No. 40.

Q. Who are they who neglect to profess their belief in what God has taught?

See "L. of C.," p. 88, No. 31; p. 93, No. 38.

Q. Can they who fail to profess their faith in the true Church in which they believe expect to be saved while in that state?

See "L. of C.," p. 39, No. 33.

(Rom. 10.) If thou confess with thy mouth the Lord Jesus, and believe in thy heart that God hath raised him up from the dead, thou shalt be saved. For, with the heart, we believe unto justice; but, with the mouth, confession is made unto salvation.

Q. Are we obliged to make open profession of our faith?

See "L. of C.," p. 65, No. 29.

(II. Kings 6. A. M. 2960.) When the ark of the Lord was come into the city of David, Michol the daughter of Saul, looking out through a window, saw king David leaping and dancing before the Lord: and she despised him in her heart. And they brought the ark of the Lord, and set it in its place in the midst of the tabernacle, which David had pitched for it: and David offered holocausts, and peace-offerings before the Lord. And when he had made an end of offering holocausts and peace-offerings, he blessed the people in the name of the Lord of hosts. And he distributed to all the multitude of Israel, both men and women, to every one, a cake of bread, and a piece of roasted beef, and fine flour fried with oil: and all the people departed every one to his house. And David returned to bless his own house: and Michol the daughter of Saul coming out to meet David, said: How glorious was the king of Israel to-day, uncovering himself before the handmaids of his servants, and was naked, as if one of the buffoons should be naked. And David said to Michol: Before the Lord, who chose me rather than thy father, and than all his house, and commanded me to be ruler over the people of the Lord in Israel, I will both play and make myself meaner than I have done: and I will be little in my own eyes: and with the handmaids of whom thou speakest, I shall appear more glorious. Therefore Michol the daughter of Saul had no child to the day of her death.

Q. Which are the sins against hope?

(Rom. 2.) Thinkest thou this, O man, that judgest them who do such things, and dost the same, that thou shalt escape the judgment of God? Or despisest thou the riches of his goodness, and patience, and long-suffering? Knowest thou not, that the benignity of God leadeth thee to penance? But according to thy hardness and impenitent heart, thou treasurest up to thyself wrath, against the day of wrath, and revelation of the just judgment of God, who will render to every man according to his works.

Q. What is persumption?

(Eccltus. 5.) Follow not in thy strength the desires of thy heart: and say not: How mighty am I? and who shall bring me under for my deeds? for God will surely take revenge. Say not: I have sinned, and what harm hath befallen me? for the most High is a patient rewarder. Be not without fear about sin forgiven, and add not sin upon sin: and say not: The mercy of the Lord is great, he will have mercy on the multitude of my sins. For mercy and wrath quickly come from him, and his wrath looketh upon sinners. Delay not to be converted to the Lord, and defer it not from day to day. For his wrath shall come on a sudden, and in the time of vengeance he will destroy thee.

Q. What is despair?

See "L. of C.," p. 111, No. 8.

(Ex. 4. A. M. 2513.) Moses said: I beseech thee, Lord, I am not eloquent from yesterday and the day before: and since thou hast spoken to thy servant, I have more impediment and slowness of tongue. The Lord said to him: Who made man's mouth? or who made the dumb and the deaf, the seeing and the blind? did not I. Go therefore, and I will be in thy mouth: and I will teach thee what thou shalt speak. But he said: I beseech thee, Lord, send whom thou wilt send. The Lord being angry at Moses, said: Aaron the Levite is thy brother, I know that he is eloquent: behold he cometh forth to meet thee, and seeing thee shall be glad at heart. Speak to him, and put my words in his mouth: and I will be in thy mouth, and in his mouth, and will show you what you must do. He shall speak in thy stead to the people, and shall be thy mouth: but thou shalt be to him in those things that pertain to God.

(IV. Kings 6-7. A. M. 3117.) There was a great famine in Samaria: and so long did the siege continue, till the head of an ass was sold for fourscore pieces of silver. And Eliscus said: Hear ye the word of the Lord: Thus saith the Lord: To-morrow about this time a bushel of fine flour shall be sold for a stater, and two bushels of barley for a stater, in the gate of Samaria. Then one of the lords, upon whose hand the king leaned, answering the man of God, said: If the Lord should make flood-gates in heaven, can that possibly be which thou sayest? And he said: Thou shalt see it with thy eyes, but shalt not eat thereof. Now the Lord had made them hear, in the camp of Syria, the noise of chariots, and of horses, and of a very great army, and they said one to another: Behold the king of Israel hath hired against us the kings of the Hethites, and of the Egyptians, and they are come upon us. Wherefore they arose, and fled away in the dark, and left their tents, and their horses and asses in the camp, and fled, desiring to save their lives. And the people going out pillaged the camp of the Syrians: and a bushel of fine flour was sold for a stater, and two bushels of barley for a stater, according to the word of the Lord. And the king appointed that lord on whose hand he leaned, to stand at the gate: and the people trod upon him in the entrance of the gate; and he died, as the man of God had said, when the king came down to him. And it came to pass according to the word of the man of God, which he spoke to the king, when he said: Two bushels of barley shall be for a stater, and a bushel of fine flour for a stater, at this very time to-morrow in the gate of Samaria. When that lord answered the man of God, and said: Although the Lord should make flood-gates in heaven, could this come to pass which thou sayest? And he said to him: Thou shalt see with thy eyes, and shalt not eat thereof. And so it fell out to him as it was foretold, and the people trod upon him in the gate, and he died.

Q. How do we sin against the love of God?

See "L. of C.," p. 59, No. 17.

LESSON THIRTY-FIRST.

THE FIRST COMMANDMENT—ON THE HONOR AND INVOCATION OF SAINTS.

Q. Does the first Commandment forbid the honoring of the saints?

(Acts 5. A. D. 33.) Now the multitude of men and women who believed in the Lord, was more increased insomuch that they brought forth the sick into the streets, and laid them on beds and couches, that when Peter came, his shadow at the least, might overshadow any of them, and they might be delivered from their infirmities.

Q. Does the first Commandment forbid us to pray to the saints?

(Job 5.) Call now if there be any that will answer thee, and turn to some of the saints.

Q. What do we mean by praying to the saints?

(Esther 1. A. M. 3485.) In the days of Assuerus, the city Susan was the capital of his kingdom. Now in the third year of his reign he made a great feast for all the princes, and for his servants, also Vasthi the queen made a feast for the women in the palace, where king Assuerus was used to dwell. Now on the seventh day, when the king was merry, and after very much drinking was well warmed with wine, he commanded, the seven servants that served in his presence, to bring in queen Vasthi before the king, with the crown set upon her head, to shew her beauty to all the people and the princes: for she was exceeding beautiful. But she refused, and would not come at the king's commandment, which he had signified to her by these servants. Whereupon the king, being angry, and inflamed with a very great fury, ordered: that Vasthi come in no more to the king, but another, that is better than her, be made queen in her place. There was a man in the city of Susan, a Jew, named Mardochai, the son of Jair, the son of Semei, the son of Cis, of the race of Jemini, who had been carried away from Jerusalem at the time that Nabuchodonosor king of Babylon carried away Jechonias king of

Juda, and he had brought up his brother's daughter Edissa, who by another name was called Esther: now she had lost both her parents: and was exceeding fair and beautiful. And her father and mother being dead, Mardochai adopted her for his daughter. And the king loved her more than all the women, and she had favour and kindness before him above all the women, and he set the royal crown on her head, and made her queen instead of Vasthi. And she would not tell him her people nor her country. For Mardochai had charged her to say nothing at all of that: and he walked every day before the court of the house, in which the chosen virgins were kept, having a care for Esther's welfare, and desiring to know what would befall her. Now Mardochai the son of Jair, had a dream. And this was his dream: Behold there were voices, and tumults, and thunders, and earthquakes, and a disturbance upon the earth. And behold two great dragons came forth ready to fight one against another. And at their cry all nations were stirred up to fight against the nation of the just. And that was a day of darkness and danger, of tribulation and distress, and great fear upon the earth. And the nation of the just was troubled fearing their own evils, and was prepared for death. And they cried to God: and as they were crying, a little fountain grew into a very great river, and abounded into many waters. The light and the sun rose up, and the humble were exalted, and they devoured the glorious. And when Mardochai had seen this, and arose out of his bed, he was thinking what God would do: and he kept it fixed in his mind, desirous to know what the dream should signify. At the time therefore, when Mardochai abode at the king's gate, two of the king's servants, who were porters, and presided in the first entry of the palace, were angry: and they designed to rise up against the king, and to kill him. And Mardochai had notice of it, and immediately he told it to queen Esther: and she to the king in Mardochai's name, who had reported the thing unto her. It was inquired into, and found out: and they were both hanged on a gibbet. And it was put in the histories, and recorded in the chronicles before the king. After these things, king Assuerus advanced Aman, the son of Amadathi, who was of the race of Agag: and he set his throne above all the princes that were with him. And all the king's servants, that were at the doors of the palace, bent their knees, and worshipped Aman: for so the emperor had commanded them, only Mardochai did not bend his knee, nor worship him. Now when Aman had heard this, and had proved by experience that Mardochai did not bend his knee to him, nor worship him, he was exceeding angry. And he counted it nothing to lay his hands upon Mardochai alone: for he had heard that he was of the nation of the Jews, and he chose rather to destroy all the nation of the Jews that were in the kingdom of Assuerus. And Aman said to king Assuerus: There is a people scattered through all the provinces of thy kingdom, and separated one from another, that use new laws and ceremonies, and moreover despise the king's ordinances: and thou knowest very well that it is not expedient for thy kingdom that they should grow insolent by impunity. And the king took the ring that he used, from his own hand, and gave it to Aman, the son of Amadathi of the race of Agag, the enemy of the Jews, and he said to him: As to the money which thou promisest, keep it for thyself: and as to the people do with them as seemeth good to thee. And the king's scribes were called in the first month Nisan, on the thirteenth day of the same month: and they wrote, as Aman had commanded, to all the king's lieutenants, and to the judges of the provinces, and of divers nations, as every nation could read, and hear according to their different languages, in the name of king Assuerus: and the letters sealed with his ring were sent by the king's messengers to all provinces, to kill and destroy all the Jews, both young and old, little children, and women, in one day, that is, on the thirteenth of the twelfth month, which is called Adar, and to make a spoil of their goods. And when Mardochai had heard this, he sent word to Esther, saying: Think not that thou mayst save thy life only, because thou art in the king's house, more than all the Jews: for if thou wilt now hold thy peace, the Jews shall be delivered by some other occasion: and thou, and thy father's house shall perish. And who knoweth whether thou art not therefore come to the kingdom, that thou mightest be ready in such a time as this? And Esther sent to Mardochai in these words: Go, and gather together all the Jews whom thou shalt find in Susan, and pray ye for me. Neither eat nor drink for three days and three nights: and I with my handmaids will fast in like manner, and then I will go in to the king, against the law, not being called, and expose myself to death and to danger. So Mardochai went, and did all that Esther had commanded him. And on the third day Esther put on her royal apparel, and stood in the inner court of the king's house, over-against the king's hall: now he sat upon his throne in the hall of the palace, over-against the door of the house. And when he saw Esther the queen standing, she pleased his eyes, and he held out toward her the golden sceptre, which he held in his hand: and she drew near, and kissed the top of his sceptre. And the king said to her: What wilt thou, queen Esther? what is thy request? if thou shouldst even ask one half of the kingdom, it shall be given to thee. And Esther answered: My petition and request is this: if I have found favour in the king's sight, and if it please the king to give me what I ask, and to fulfil my petition: let the king and Aman come to the banquet which I have prepared them, and to-morrow I will open my mind to the king. That night the king passed without sleep, and he commanded the histories and chronicles of former times to be brought him. And when they were reading them before him, they came to that place where it was written, how Mardochai had discovered the treason of the servants, who sought to kill king Assuerus. And when the king heard this, he said: What honour and reward hath Mardochai received for this fidelity? His servants and ministers said to him: He hath received no reward at all. And the king said immediately: Who is in the court? for Aman was coming in to the inner court of the king's house, to speak to the king, that he might order Mardochai to be hanged upon the gibbet which was prepared for him. The servants answered: Aman standeth in the court, and the king said: Let him come in. And when he was come in, he said to him: What ought to be done to the man whom the king is desirous to honour? But Aman thinking in his heart, and supposing that the king would honour no other but himself, answered: The man whom the king desireth to honour, ought to be clothed with the king's apparel, and to be set upon the horse that the king rideth upon, and to have the royal crown upon his head, and let the first of the king's princes and nobles hold his horse, and going through the street of the city, proclaim before him and say: Thus shall he be honoured, whom the king hath a mind to honour. And the king said to him: Make haste and take the robe and the horse, and do as thou hast spoken to Mardochai the Jew, who sitteth before the gates of the palace. Beware thou pass over any of those things which thou hast spoken. So Aman took the robe and the horse, and arraying Mardochai in the street of the city, and setting him on the horse, went before him, and proclaimed: This honour is he worthy of, whom the king hath a mind to honour. And Mardochai returned to the palace gate: And Aman made haste to go to his house, mourning and having his head covered: and he told Zares his wife, and his friends, all that had befallen him. And the king said forthwith: Call ye Aman quickly, that he may obey Esther's will.

So the king and Aman went in, to drink with the queen. And the king said to her again the second day, after he was warm with wine: What is thy petition, Esther, that it may be granted thee? and what wilt thou have done: although thou ask the half of my kingdom, thou shalt have it. Then she answered: If I have found favour in thy sight, O king, and if it please thee, give me my life for which I ask, and my people for which I request. For we are given up, I and my people, to be destroyed, to be slain, and to perish. And would God we were sold for bond-men and bond-women: the evil might be borne with, and I would have mourned in silence: but now we have an enemy, whose cruelty redoundeth upon the king. And king Assuerus answered and said: Who is this, and of what power, that he should do these things? And Esther said: It is this Aman that is our adversary and most wicked enemy. Aman hearing this was forthwith astonished, not being able to bear the countenance of the king and of the queen. But the king being angry rose up, and went from the place of the banquet into the garden set with trees. Aman also rose up to entreat Esther the queen for his life, for he understood that evil was prepared for him by the king. And Harbona, one of the servants that stood waiting on the king, said: Behold the gibbet which he hath prepared for Mardochai, who spoke for the king, standeth in Aman's house, being fifty cubits high. And the king said to him: Hang him upon it. So Aman was hanged on the gibbet, which he had prepared for Mardochai: and the king's wrath ceased. On that day king Assuerus gave the house of Aman, the Jews' enemy, to queen Esther, and Mardochai came in before the king. For Esther had confessed to him that he was her uncle. And the king took the ring which he had commanded to be taken again from Aman, and gave it to Mardochai. And Esther set Mardochai over her house. And not content with these things, she fell down at the king's feet and wept, and speaking to him besought him, that he would give orders that the malice of Aman the Agagite, and his most wicked devices which he had invented against the Jews, should be of no effect. And the king gave orders to them, to speak to the Jews in every city, and to command them to gather themselves together, and to stand for their lives, and to kill and destroy all their enemies with their wives. So the Jews made a great slaughter of their enemies, and killed them, repaying according to what they had prepared to do to them: then Mardochai said: God hath done these things. I remember a dream that I saw, which signified these same things: and nothing thereof hath failed. The little fountain which grew into a river, and was turned into a light, and into the sun, and abounded into many waters, is Esther, whom the king married, and made queen. But the two dragons: are I, and Aman. The nations that were assembled: are they that endeavoured to destroy the name of the Jews. And my nation: is Israel, who cried to the Lord, and the Lord saved his people: and he delivered us from all evils, and hath wrought great signs and wonders among the nations.

Q. How do we know that the saints hear us?

(Acts 9. A. D. 39.) It came to pass that Peter, as he passed through, visiting all, came to the saints who dwelt at Lydda. And he found there a certain man named Eneas, who had kept his bed for eight years, who was ill of the palsy. And Peter said to him: Enens, the Lord Jesus Christ healeth thee: arise, and make thy bed. And immediately he arose.

(II. Mach. 15. A. M. 3843.) Now when Nicanor understood that Judas was in the places of Samaria, he purposed to set upon him with all violence on the sabbath day. But Machabeus ever trusted with all hope that God would help them. And he exhorted his people not to fear the coming of the nations, and told them a dream worthy to be believed, whereby he rejoiced them all. Now the vision was in this manner: Onias who had been high priest, a good and virtuous man, modest in his looks, gentle in his manners, and graceful in his speech, and who from a child was exercised in virtues, holding up his hands, prayed for all the people of the Jews: after this there appeared also another man, admirable for age, and glory, and environed with great beauty and majesty: then Onias answering, said: This is a lover of his brethren, and of the people of Israel: this is he that prayeth much for the people, and for all the holy city, Jeremias the prophet of God. Whereupon Jeremias stretched forth his right hand, and gave to Judas a sword of gold, saying: Take this holy sword a gift from God, wherewith thou shalt overthrow the adversaries of my people Israel.

Q. Why do we believe that the saints will help us?

(Gal. 3.) You are all the children of God by faith, in Christ Jesus. For as many of you as have been baptized in Christ, have put on Christ. There is neither Jew nor Greek: there is neither bond nor free: there is neither male nor female. For you are all one in Christ Jesus. And if you be Christ's, then are you the seed of Abraham, heirs according to the promise.

(Heb. 12.) You are not come to a mountain that might

be touched, and a burning fire, and a whirlwind, and darkness, and storm, and the sound of a trumpet, and the voice of words, which they that heard excused themselves, that the word might not be spoken to them: for they did not endure that which was said: *And if so much as a beast shall touch the mount, it shall be stoned.* And so terrible was that which was seen, Moses said: *I am frighted, and tremble.* But you are come to mount Sion, and to the city of the living God, the heavenly Jerusalem, and to the company of many thousands of angels, and to the church of the first-born, who are written in the heavens, and to God the judge of all, and to the spirits of the just made perfect, and to Jesus the mediator of the new testament, and to the sprinkling of blood which speaketh better than that of Abel.

Q. How are the saints and we members of the same Church?

(Rom. 12.) I beseech you, brethren, by the mercy of God, that you present your bodies a living sacrifice, holy, pleasing unto God, your reasonable service. And be not conformed to this world; but be reformed in the newness of your mind, that you may prove what is the good, and the acceptable, and the perfect will of God. For I say, by the grace that is given me, to all that are among you, not to be more wise than it behoveth to be wise, but to be wise unto sobriety, and according as God hath divided to every one the measure of faith. For as in one body we have many members, but all the members have not the same office: so we being many, are one body in Christ, and every one members one of another.

Q. What is the communion of the members of the Church called?

(Eph. 2.) Now therefore you are no more strangers and foreigners; but you are fellow-citizens with the saints, and the domestics of God, built upon the foundation of the apostles and prophets, Jesus Christ himself being the chief corner-stone.

Q. What does the communion of saints mean?

(I. Cor. 12.) As the body is one, and hath many members; and all the members of the body, whereas they are many, yet are one body, so also *is* Christ. For in one Spirit were we all baptized into one body, whether Jews or Gentiles, whether bond or free; and in one Spirit we have all been made to drink. For the body also is not one member, but many. If the foot should say, because I am not the hand, I am not of the body; is it therefore not of the body? And if the ear should say, because I am not the eye, I am not the body; is it therefore not of the body? If the whole body were the eye, where would be the hearing? If the whole were hearing, where would be the smelling? But now God hath set the members every one of them in the body as it hath pleased him. And if they all were one member, where would be the body? But now *there are* many members indeed, yet one body. And the eye cannot say to the hand: I need not thy help; nor again the head to the feet: I have no need of you. Yea, much more those that seem to be the more feeble members of the body, are more necessary.

Q. What benefits are derived from the communion of saints?

(Rom. 15.) I beseech you, brethren, through our Lord Jesus Christ, and by the charity of the Holy Ghost, that you help me in your prayers for me to God, that I may be delivered from the unbelievers that are in Judea, and that the oblation of my service may be acceptable in Jerusalem to the saints. That I may come to you with joy, by the will of God, and may be refreshed with you. Now the God of peace be with you all. Amen.

(I. Tim. 2.) I desire therefore, first of all, that supplications, prayers, intercessions, and thanksgivings be made for all men: for kings, and for all that are in high station: that we may lead a quiet and a peaceable life in all piety and chastity. For this is good and acceptable in the sight of God our Saviour, who will have all men to be saved, and to come to the knowledge of the truth.

Q. Does the first Commandment forbid us to honour relics?

(Acts 19. A. D. 56.) God wrought by the hand of Paul more than common miracles. So that even there were brought from his body to the sick, handkerchiefs and aprons, and the diseases departed from them, and the wicked spirits went out of them.

Q. Does the first Commandment forbid the making of images?

(Dan. 3. A. M. 3417.) King Nabuchodonosor made a statue of gold, of sixty cubits high, and six cubits broad, and he set it up in the plain of Dura of the province of Babylon. Then Nabuchodonosor the king sent to call together the nobles, the magistrates, and the judges, the captains, the rulers, and governors, and all the chief men of the provinces, to come to the dedication of the statue which king Nabuchodonosor had set up. Then a herald cried with a strong voice: To you it is commanded, O nations, tribes, and languages: That in the hour that you shall hear the sound of the trumpet, ye fall down and adore the golden statue which king Nabuchodonosor hath set up. But if any man shall not fall down and adore, he shall the same hour be cast into a furnace of burning fire. Upon this therefore, at the time when all the people heard the sound of the trumpet, all the nations, tribes, and languages fell down and adored the golden statue which king Nabuchodonosor had set up. And presently at that very time some Chaldeans came and accused the Jews, and said to king Nabuchodonosor: O king, live for ever: there are certain Jews whom thou hast set over the works of the province of Babylon, Sidrach, Misach, and Abdenago: these men, O king, have slighted thy decree: they worship not thy gods, nor do they adore the golden statue which thou hast set up. Then Nabuchodonosor in fury, and in wrath, commanded that Sidrach, Misach, and Abdenago should be brought: who immediately were brought before the king. And Nabuchodonosor the king spoke to them, and said: Is it true, O Sidrach, Misach, and Abdenago, that you do not worship my gods, nor adore the golden statue that I have set up? Sidrach, Misach, and Abdenago answered and said to king Nabuchodonosor: We have no occasion to answer thee concerning this matter. For behold our God, whom we worship, is able to save us from the furnace of burning fire, and to deliver us out of thy hands, O king. But if he will not, be it known to thee, O king, that we will not worship thy gods, nor adore the golden statue which thou hast set up. Then was Nabuchodonosor filled with fury: and immediately these men were bound and were cast into the furnace of burning fire, with their coats, and their caps, and their shoes, and their garments. For the king's commandment was urgent, and the furnace was heated exceedingly. And the flame of the fire slew those men that had cast in Sidrach, Misach, and Abdenago. But these three men, that is, Sidrach, Misach, and Abdenago, fell down bound in the midst of the furnace of burning fire. And they walked in the midst of the flame, praising God and blessing the Lord. Then Nabuchodonosor the king was astonished, and rose up in haste, and said to his nobles: Did we not cast three men bound into the midst of the fire? They answered the king, and said: True, O king. He answered, and said: Behold I see four men loose, and walking in the midst of the fire, and there is no hurt in them, and the form of the fourth is like the son of God. Then Nabuchodonosor came to the door of the burning fiery furnace, and said: Sidrach, Misach, and Abdenago, ye servants of the most high God, go ye forth, and come. And immediately Sidrach, Misach, and Abdenago went out from the midst of the fire. And the nobles, and the magistrates, and the judges, and the great men of the king being gathered together, considered these men, that the fire had no power on their bodies, and that not a hair of their head had been singed, nor their garments altered, nor the smell of the fire had passed on them. Then Nabuchodonosor breaking forth, said: Blessed be the God of them, to wit, of Sidrach, Misach, and Abdenago, who hath sent his Angel, and delivered his servants that believed in him: and they changed the king's word, and delivered up their bodies that they might not serve, nor adore any god, except their own God. By me therefore this decree is made, that every people, tribe, and tongue, which shall speak blasphemy against the God of Sidrach, Misach, and Abdenago, shall be destroyed, and their houses laid waste: for there is no other God that can save in this manner. Then the king promoted Sidrach, Misach, and Abdenago, in the province of Babylon.

(Acts 19. A. D. 57.) Now at that time there arose no small disturbance about the way of the Lord. For a certain man named Demetrius, a silversmith, who made silver temples for Diana, brought no small gain to the craftsmen; whom he calling together, with the workmen of like occupation, said: Sirs, you know that our gain is by this trade; and you see and hear, that this Paul by persuasion hath drawn away a great multitude, not only of Ephesus, but almost of all Asia, saying: They are not gods which are made by hands. So that not only this our craft is in danger to be set at nought, but also the temple of great Diana shall be reputed for nothing; yea, and her majesty shall begin to be destroyed, whom all Asia and the world worshippeth. Having heard these things, they were full of anger, and cried out, saying: Great is Diana of the Ephesians.

Q. Is it right to show respect to the pictures and images of Christ and His saints?

See "L. of C.," p 31, No. 3.

Q. Is it allowed to pray to the crucifix or to the images and relics of the saints?

See "L. of C.," p. 41, No. 40.

(IV. Kings 13. A. M. 3165.) Eliseus died, and they buried him. And the rovers from Moab came into the land the same year. And some that were burying a man, saw the rovers, and cast the body into the sepulchre of Eliseus. And when it had touched the bones of Eliseus, the man came to life, and stood upon his feet.

Q. Why do we pray before the crucifix and the images and relics of the saints?

(Gal. 6.) God forbid that I should glory, save in the cross of our Lord Jesus Christ; by whom the world is crucified to me, and I to the world.

LESSON THIRTY-SECOND.

FROM THE SECOND TO THE FOURTH COMMANDMENT.

Q. What is the second Commandment?

See "L. of C.," p. 32, No. 11.

(Ex. 20.) Thou shalt not take the name of the Lord thy God in vain: for the Lord will not hold him guiltless that shall take the name of the Lord his God in vain.

(Phil. 2.) Let nothing be done through contention, neither by vain-glory: but in humility, let each esteem others better than themselves: each one not considering the things that are his own, but those that are other men's. For let this mind be in you, which was also in Christ Jesus: who being in the form of God, thought it not robbery to be equal with God: but emptied himself, taking the form of a servant, being made in the likeness of men, and in habit found as a man. He humbled himself, becoming obedient unto death, even to the death of the cross. For which cause God also hath exalted him, and hath given him a name which is above all names: that in the name of Jesus every knee should bow, of those that are in heaven, on earth, and under the earth: and that every tongue should confess that the Lord Jesus Christ is in the glory of God the Father.

Q. What are we commanded by the second Commandment?

See "L. of C.," p. 92, No. 35.

Q. What is an oath?

(Heb. 6.) God making promise to Abraham, because he had no one greater by whom he might swear, swore by himself, saying: *Unless blessing I shall bless thee, and multiplying I shall multiply thee.* And so patiently enduring he obtained the promise. For men swear by one greater than themselves: and an oath for confirmation is the end of all their controversy. Wherein God, meaning more abundantly to shew to the heirs of the promise the immutability of his counsel, interposed an oath: that by two immutable things, in which it is impossible for God to lie, we may have the strongest comfort, who have fled for refuge to hold fast the hope set before us.

Q. When may we take an oath?

(James 5.) Above all things, my brethren, swear not, neither by heaven, nor by the earth, nor by any other oath. But let your speech be, yea, yea: no, no: that you fall not under judgment.

(Jer. 4.) And thou shalt swear: As the Lord liveth, in truth, and in judgment, and in justice: and the Gentiles shall bless him, and shall praise him.

Q. What is necessary to make an oath lawful?

(Eccltus. 23.) A man that

sweareth much, shall be filled with iniquity, and a scourge shall not depart from his house. And if he make it void, his sin shall be upon him: and if he dissemble it, he offendeth double: and if he swear in vain, he shall not be justified: for his house shall be filled with his punishment.

Q. What is a vow?

(Eccltus. 5.) If thou hast vowed any thing to God, defer not to pay it: for an unfaithful and foolish promise displeaseth him: but whatsoever thou hast vowed, pay it. And it is much better not to vow, than after a vow not to perform the things promised.

Q. Is it a sin not to fulfil our vows?

(Lev. 27. A. M. 2514.) The Lord spoke to Moses, saying: Speak to the children of Israel, and thou shalt say to them: The man that shall have made a vow, and promised his soul to God, shall give the price according to estimation. Any thing that is devoted to the Lord, whether it be man, or beast, or field, shall not be sold, neither may it be redeemed. Whatsoever is once consecrated shall be holy of holies to the Lord.

(Num. 30.) Moses said to the princes of the tribes of the children of Israel: This is the word that the Lord hath commanded: if any man make a vow to the Lord, or bind himself by an oath: he shall not make his word void but shall fulfil all that he promised. If a woman vow any thing, and bind herself by an oath, being in her father's house, and but yet a girl in age: if her father knew the vow that she hath promised, and the oath wherewith she hath bound her soul, and held his peace, she shall be bound by the vow: whatsoever she promised and swore, she shall fulfil in deed. But if her father, immediately as soon as he heard it, gain-said it, both her vows and her oaths shall be void, neither shall she be bound to what she promised, because her father hath gain-said it. If she have a husband, and shall vow any thing, and the word once going out of her mouth shall bind her soul by an oath: the day that her husband shall hear it, and not gain-say it, she shall be bound to the vow, and shall give whatsoever she promised. But if as soon as he heareth he gain-say it, and make her promises and the words wherewith she had bound her soul of no effect: the Lord will forgive her. If she vow and bind herself by oath, to afflict her soul by fasting, or abstinence from other things, it shall depend on the will of her husband, whether she shall do it, or not do it. But if the husband hearing it hold his peace, and defer the declaring his mind till another day: whatsoever she had vowed and promised, she shall fulfil: because immediately as he heard it, he held his peace. But if he gain-say it after that he knew it, he shall bear her iniquity.

(Deut. 23.) When thou hast made a vow to the Lord thy God, thou shalt not delay to pay it: because the Lord thy God will require it. And if thou delay, it shall be imputed to thee for a sin. If thou wilt not promise, thou shalt be without sin. But that which is once gone out of thy lips, thou shalt observe, and shalt do as thou hast promised to the Lord thy God, and hast spoken with thy own will and with thy own mouth.

Q. What is forbidden by the second Commandment?

See "L. of C.," p. 32, No. 11.

(Lev. 24. A. M. 2514.) Behold there went out the son of a woman of Israel, whom she had of an Egyptian, among the children of Israel, and fell at words in the camp with a man of Israel. And when he had blasphemed the name, and had cursed it, he was brought to Moses: (now his mother was called Salumith, the daughter of Dabri, of the tribe of Dan:) and they put him into prison, till they might know what the Lord would command. And the Lord spoke to Moses, saying: Bring forth the blasphemer without the camp, and let them that heard him, put their hands upon his head, and let all the people stone him. And thou shalt speak to the children of Israel: the man that curseth his God, shall bear his sin: and he that blasphemeth the name of the Lord, dying let him die: all the multitude shall stone him, whether he be a native or a stranger. He that blasphemeth the name of the Lord, dying let him die.

Q. What is the third Commandment?

(Gen. 2. A. M. 1.) So the heavens and the earth were finished, and all the furniture of them. And on the seventh day God ended his work which he had made: and he rested on the seventh day from all his work which he had done. And he blessed the seventh day, and sanctified it: because in it he had rested from all his work which God created and made.

Q. What are we commanded by the third Commandment?

(Ex. 20.) Remember that thou keep holy the sabbath day. Six days shalt thou labour, and shalt do all thy works. But on the seventh day is the sabbath of the Lord thy God: thou shalt do no work on it, thou nor thy son, nor thy daughter, nor thy man-servant, nor thy maid servant, nor thy beast, nor the stranger that is within thy gates. For in six days the Lord made heaven and earth, and the sea, and all things that are in them, and rested on the seventh day: therefore the Lord blessed the seventh day, and sanctified it.

Q. How are we to worship God on Sundays and holydays of obligation?
See "L. of C.," p. 68, No. 38.

Q. Are the Sabbath day and the Sunday the same?
See "L. of C.," p. 28, No. 1.

Q. Why does the Church command us to keep the Sunday holy instead of the Sabbath?
See "L. of C.," p. 124, No. 18; p. 125, No. 23.

Q. What is forbidden by the third commandment?

(Lev. 23. A. M. 2514.) The Lord spoke to Moses, saying: Speak to the children of Israel, and thou shalt say to them: These are the feasts of the Lord, which you shall call holy. Six days shall ye do work: the seventh day, because it is the rest of the sabbath, shall be called holy. You shall do no work on that day: it is the sabbath of the Lord in all your habitations. These also are the holy-days of the Lord, which you must celebrate in their seasons.

Q. What are servile works?
See "L. of C.," p. 71, No. 4.

Q. Are servile works on Sunday ever lawful?
See "L. of C.," p. 30, Nos. 3, 4.

LESSON THIRTY-THIRD.

FROM THE FOURTH TO THE SEVENTH COMMANDMENT.

Q. What is the fourth Commandment?

(Ex. 20.) Honour **thy father and thy mother,** that thou mayest be long-lived upon the land which the Lord thy God will give thee.

Q. What are we commanded by the fourth Commandment?
See "L. of C.." p. 91, No. 34.

(Deut. 21.) If a man have a stubborn and unruly son, who will not hear the commandments of his father or mother, and being corrected, slighteth obedience: they shall take him and bring him to the ancients of his city, and to the gate of judgment, and shall say to them: This our son is rebellious and stubborn, he slighteth hearing our admonitions, he giveth himself to revelling, and to debauchery and banquetings: the people of the city shall stone him; and he shall die, that you may take away the evil out of the midst of you, and all Israel hearing it may be afraid.

Q. Are we bound to honour and obey others than our parents?

(I. Kings 14. A. M. 2911.) Now it came to pass one day

that Jonathan the son of Saul said to the young man that bore his armour: Come, and let us go over to the garrison of the Philistines, which is on the other side of yonder place. But he told not this to his father. And Jonathan went up creeping on his hands and feet, and his armour-bearer after him. And some fell before Jonathan, others his armour-bearer slew as he followed him. And the watchmen of Saul, who were in Gabaa of Benjamin looked and behold a multitude overthrown, and fleeing this way and that. Then Saul and all the people that were with him, shouted together, and they came to the place of the fight: and behold every man's sword was turned upon his neighbour, and there was a very great slaughter. And the Lord saved Israel that day. And the fight went on as far as Beth-aven. And the men of Israel were joined together that day; and Saul adjured the people, saying: Cursed be the man that shall eat food till evening, till I be revenged of my enemies. So none of the people tasted any food: and all the common people came into a forest, in which there was honey upon the ground. And when the people came into the forest, behold the honey dropped, but no man put his hand to his mouth. For the people feared the oath. But Jonathan had not heard when his father adjured the people: and he put forth the end of the rod, which he had in his hand, and dipt it in a honey comb: and he carried his hand to his mouth, and his eyes were enlightened. And one of the people answering, said: Thy father hath bound the people with an oath, saying: Cursed be the man that shall eat any food this day. (And the people were faint.) And Jonathan said: My father hath troubled the land: you have seen yourselves that my eyes are enlightened, because I tasted a little of this honey: how much if more the people had eaten of the prey of their enemies, which they found? had there not been made a greater slaughter among the Philistines? And Saul consulted the Lord: Shall I pursue after the Philistines? wilt thou deliver them into the hands of Israel? And he answered him not that day. And Saul said: Bring hither all the corners of the people: and know, and see by whom this sin hath happened to-day. As the Lord liveth who is the saviour of Israel, if it was done by Jonathan my son, he shall surely die. In this none of the people gain-said him. And Saul said to the Lord: O Lord God of Israel, give a sign, by *which we may know*, what the meaning is, that thou answerest not thy servant to-day: If this iniquity be in me, or in my son Jonathan, give a proof: or if this iniquity be in thy people, give holiness. And Jonathan and Saul were taken, and the people escaped. And Saul said: Cast lots between me, and Jonathan my son. And Jonathan was taken. And Saul said to Jonathan: Tell me what thou hast done. And Jonathan told him, and said: I did but taste a little honey with the end of the rod, which was in my hand, and behold I *must* die. And Saul said: May God do so and so to me, and add still more: for dying thou shalt die, O Jonathan. And the people said to Saul: Shall Jonathan then die, who hath wrought this great salvation in Israel? this must not be: as the Lord liveth, there shall not one hair of his head fall to the ground, for he hath wrought with God this day. So the people delivered Jonathan, that he should not die.

(IV. Kings 2. A. M. 3108.) Eliseus went up to Bethel: and as he was going up by the way, little boys came out of the city and mocked him, saying: Go up, thou bald-head; go up, thou bald-head. And looking back, he saw them, and cursed them in the name of the Lord: and there came forth two bears out of the forest, and tore of them two and forty boys.

Q. Have parents and superiors any duties towards those who are under their charge?

(Eph. 6.) Children, obey your parents in the Lord, for this is just. *Honour thy father and thy mother* which is the first commandment with a promise: *that it may be well with thee, and thou mayest be long-lived upon earth.* And you, fathers, provoke not your children to anger; but bring them up in the discipline and correction of the Lord. Servants, be obedient to them that are your lords according to the flesh, with fear and trembling, in the simplicity of your heart, as to Christ: not serving to the eye, as it were pleasing men, but, as the servants of Christ, doing the will of God from the heart, with a good will serving, as to the Lord, and not to men. Knowing that whatsoever good thing any man shall do, the same shall he receive from the Lord, whether he be bond, or free. And you, masters, do the same things to them, forbearing threatenings, knowing that the Lord both of them and you is in heaven; and there is no respect of persons with him.

(I. Tim. 5.) But if any man have not care of his own, and especially of those of his house, he hath denied the faith, and is worse than an infidel.

Q. What is forbidden by the fourth Commandment?

See "L of C.," p. 90, No. 30.

(Rom. 13.) Let every soul be subject to higher powers: for there is no power but from God: and those that are, are ordained of God. Therefore he that resisteth the power, resisteth the ordinance of God. And they that resist, purchase to themselves damnation. For princes are not a terror to the good work, but to the evil. Wilt thou then not be afraid of the power? Do that which is good: and thou shalt have praise from the same. For he is God's minister to thee, for good. But if thou do that which is evil, fear: for he beareth not the sword in vain. For he is God's minister: an avenger to execute wrath upon him that doth evil. Wherefore be subject of necessity, not only for wrath, but also for conscience'-sake. For therefore also you pay tribute. For they are the ministers of God, serving unto this purpose. Render therefore to all men their dues. Tribute, to whom tribute is due: custom, to whom custom: fear, to whom fear: honour, to whom honour.

Q. What is the fifth Commandment?

See "L. of C.," p. 112, No. 1.

(I. John 3.) Whosoever hateth his brother is a murderer. And you know that no murderer hath eternal life abiding in himself. In this we have known the charity of God, because he hath laid down his life for us: and we ought to lay down our lives for the brethren. He that hath the substance of this world, and shall see his brother in need, and shall shut up his bowels from him: how doth the charity of God abide in him? My little children, let us not love in word, nor in tongue, but in deed, and in truth.

Q. What are we commanded by the fifth Commandment?

See "L. of C.," p. 81, No. 9.

Q. What is forbidden by the fifth Commandment?

See "L. of C.," p. 32, No. 12; p. 54, No. 1.

(Judg. 11. A. M. 2817.) The Spirit of the Lord came upon Jephte, and going round Galaad, and Manasses, and Maspha of Galaad, and passing over from thence to the children of Ammon, he made a vow to the Lord, saying: If thou wilt deliver the children of Ammon into my hands, whosoever shall first come forth out of the doors of my house, and shall meet me when I return in peace from the children of Ammon, the same will I offer a holocaust to the Lord. And Jephte passed over to the children of Ammon, to fight against them: and the Lord delivered them into his hands. And he smote *them* from Aroer till you come to Mennith, twenty cities, and as far as Abel, which is set with vineyards, with a very great slaughter: and the children of Ammon were humbled by the children of Israel. And when Jephte returned into Maspha to his house, his only daughter met him with timbrels and with dances: for he had no other children. And when he saw her, he rent his garments, and said: Alas! my daughter, thou hast deceived me, and thou thyself art deceived: for I have opened my mouth to the Lord, and I can do no other thing. And she answered him: My father, if thou hast opened thy mouth to the Lord, do unto me whatsoever thou hast promised, since the victory hath been granted to thee, and revenge of thy enemies. And she said to her father: Grant me only this which I desire: Let me go, that I may go about the mountains for two months, and may bewail my virginity with my companions. And he answered her: Go. And he sent her away for two months. And when she was gone with her comrades and companions, she mourned her virginity in the mountains. And the two months being expired, she returned to her father, and he did to her as he had vowed, and she knew no man.

(I. Kings 18. A. M. 2942.) Now when David returned, after he slew the Philistine, the women came out of all the cities of Israel, singing and dancing, to meet king Saul, with timbrels of joy, and cornets. And the women sung as they played, and they said: Saul slew his thousands, and David his ten thousands. And Saul was exceeding angry, and this word was displeasing in his eyes, and he said: They have given David ten thousands, and to me they have given *but* a thousand, what can he have more but the kingdom? And Saul did not look on David with a good eye from that day and forward. And the day after the evil spirit from God came upon Saul, and he prophesied in the midst of his house. And David played with his hand as at other times. And Saul held a spear in his hand, and threw it, thinking to nail David to the wall: and David stept aside out of his presence twice. And Saul feared David, because the Lord was with him, and was departed from himself.

Q. What is the sixth Commandment?

(Gen. 20. A. M. 2107.) Abraham removed from thence to the south country, and dwelt between Cades and Sur, and sojourned in Gerara. And he said of Sara his wife: She is my sister. So Abimelech the king of Gerara sent, and took her. And God came to Abimelech in a dream by night, and he said to him: Lo thou shalt die for the woman thou hast taken: for she hath a husband. Now therefore restore the man his wife, for he is a prophet: and he shall pray for thee, and thou shalt live: but if thou wilt not restore her, know that thou shalt surely die, thou and all that are thine. And Abimelech forthwith rising up in the night, called all his servants: and spoke all these words in their hearing, and all the men were exceedingly afraid. And Abimelech called also for Abraham, and said to him: What hast thou done to us? what have we offended thee in, that thou hast brought upon me and upon my kingdom a great sin? Abraham answered: I thought with myself, saying: Perhaps there is not the fear of God in this place: and they will kill me for the sake of my wife: howbeit, otherwise also she is truly my sister, the daughter of my father, and not the daughter of my mother, and I took her to wife. And after God brought me out of my father's house, I said to her: Thou shalt do me this kindness: In every place, to which we shall come, thou shalt say that I am thy brother. And Abimelech took sheep and oxen, and servants and handmaids, and gave to Abraham: and restored to him Sara, his wife. And when Abraham prayed, God healed Abimelech and his wife, and his handmaids.

Q. What are we commanded by the sixth Commandment?

See "L. of C.," p. 58, No. 13.

(I. Cor. 3.) Know you not, that you are the temple of God, and that the Spirit of God dwelleth in you? But if any man violate the temple of God, him shall God destroy. For the temple of God is holy, which you are.

(Apoc. 14.) I beheld, and lo a lamb stood upon Mount Sion, and with him an hundred forty-four thousand, having his name, and the name of his Father, written on their foreheads. And I heard a voice from heaven, as the noise of many waters, and as the voice of great thunder; and the voice which I heard, was as the voice of harpers, harping on their harps. And they sung as it were a new canticle, before the throne, and before the four living creatures, and the ancients; and no man could say the canticle, but those hundred forty-four thousand, who were purchased from the earth. These are they who were not defiled with women: for they are virgins. These follow the Lamb whithersoever he goeth. These were purchased from among men, the first-fruits to God and to the Lamb: and in their mouth there was found no lie; for they are without spot before the throne of God.

(Dan. 5. A. M. 3398.) In the third year of the reign of Joakim king of Juda, Nabuchodonosor king of Babylon came to Jerusalem, and besieged it. And the Lord delivered into his hands Joakim the king of Juda, and part of the vessels of the house of God.

(A. M. 3466.) And when Baltassar his son was king he made a great feast for a thousand of his nobles: and every one drank according to his age. Then were the golden and silver vessels brought, which he had brought away out of the temple that was in Jerusalem: and the king and his nobles, his wives and his concubines, drank in them. In the same hour there appeared fingers, as it were of the hand of a man, writing over-against the candlestick upon the surface of the wall of the king's palace: and the king beheld the joints of the hand that wrote. Then was the king's countenance changed, and his thoughts troubled him: and the joints of his loins were loosed, and his knees struck one against the other. Then came in all the king's wise men, but they could neither read the writing, nor declare the interpretation to the king. Then Daniel was brought in before the king. And the king spoke, and said to him: Art thou Daniel of the children of the captivity of Juda, whom my father the king brought out of Judea? I have heard of thee, that thou canst interpret obscure things, and resolve difficult things: now if thou art able to read the writing, and to shew me the interpretation thereof, thou shalt be clothed with purple, and shalt have a chain of gold about thy neck, and shalt be the third prince in my kingdom. To which Daniel made answer, and said before the king: Thy rewards be to thyself and the gifts of thy house give to another: but the writing I will read to thee, O king and shew thee the interpretation thereof. Thou hast lifted thyself up against the Lord of heaven: and the vessels of his house have been brought before thee: and thou, and thy nobles, and thy wives, and thy concubines have drunk wine in them: and thou hast praised the gods of silver, and of gold, and of brass, of iron, and of wood, and of stone, that neither see, nor hear, nor feel: but the God who hath thy breath in his hand, and all thy ways, thou hast not glorified. Wherefore he hath sent the part of the hand which hath written this that is set down. And this is the writing that is written: Mane, Thecel, Phares. And this is the interpretation of the word. Mane: God hath numbered thy kingdom, and hath finished it. Thecel: thou art weighed in the balance and art found wanting. Phares: thy kingdom is divided, and is given to the Medes and Persians. Then by the king's command Daniel was clothed with purple, and a chain of gold was put about his neck: and it was proclaimed of him that he had power *as* the third man in the kingdom. The same night Baltassar the Chaldean king was slain.

Q. What is forbidden by the sixth Commandment?

See " L. of C.," p. 32, No. 10.

(Judg. 16. A. M. 2385.) After this Samson loved a woman, who dwelt in the valley of Sorec, and she was called Dalila. And the princes of the Philistines came to her, and said: Deceive him, and learn of him wherein his great strength lieth, and how we may be able to overcome him, to bind and afflict him: which if thou shalt do, we will give thee every one of us eleven hundred pieces of silver. And Dalila said to Samson: Tell me, I beseech thee, wherein thy greatest strength lieth, and what it is wherewith if thou wert bound thou couldst not break loose. Then opening the truth of the thing, he said to her: The razor hath never come upon my head, for I am a Nazarite, that is to say, consecrated to God from my mother's womb: If my head be shaven, my strength shall depart from me, and I shall become weak, and shall be like other men. Then seeing that he had discovered to her all his mind, she sent to the princes of the Philistines, saying: Come up this once more, for now he hath opened his heart to me. And they went up taking with them the money which they had promised. But she made him sleep upon her knees, and lay his head in her bosom. And she called a barber, and shaved his seven locks, and began to drive him away, and thrust him from her: for immediately his strength departed from him. Then the Philistines seized upon him, and forthwith pulled out his eyes, and led him bound in chains to Gaza, and shutting him up in prison made him grind. And rejoicing in their feasts, when they had now taken their good cheer, they commanded that Samson should be called, and should play before them. And being brought out of prison he played before them, and they made him stand between two pillars. And he said to the lad that guided his steps: Suffer me to touch the pillars which support the whole house, and let me lean upon them, and rest a little. Now the house was full of men and women, and all the princes of the Philistines were there. Moreover about three thousand persons of both sexes from the roof and the higher part of the house, were beholding Samson's play. But he called upon the Lord, saying: O Lord God, remember me, and restore to me now my former strength, O my God, that I may revenge myself on my enemies, and for the loss of my two eyes I may take one revenge. And laying hold on both the pillars on which the house rested, and holding the one with his right hand, and the other with his left, he said: Let me die with the Philistines. And when he had strongly shook the pillars, the house fell upon all the princes, and the rest of the multitude that was there: and he killed many more at his death, than he had killed before in his life.

(Dan. 13. A. M. 3398.) Now there was a man that dwelt in Babylon, and his name was Joakim: and he took a wife whose name was Susanna, the daughter of Helcias, a very beautiful woman, and one that feared God. For her parents being just, had instructed their daughter according to the law of Moses. Now Joakim was very rich, and had an orchard near his house: and the Jews resorted to him, because he was the most honourable of them all. And there were two of the ancients of the people appointed judges that year, of whom the Lord said: Iniquity came out from Babylon from the ancient judges, that seemed to govern the people. These men frequented the house of Joakim, and all that had any matters of judgment came to them. And when the people departed away at noon, Susanna went in, and walked in her husband's orchard. And the old men saw her going in every day, and walking. So they were both wounded with the love of her, yet they did not make known their grief one to the other. And one said to another: Let us now go home, for it is dinner time. So going out they departed one from another. And turning back again, they came both to the same place: and asking one another the cause, they acknowledged their love; and then they agreed upon a time, when they might find her alone. And it fell out, as they watched a fit day, she went in on a time, as yesterday and the day before, with two maids only. Now when the maids were gone forth, the two elders arose, and ran to her, and said: Behold the doors of the orchard are shut, and nobody seeth us, and we are in love with thee: wherefore consent to us. But if thou wilt not, we will bear witness against thee, that a young man was with thee, and therefore thou didst send away thy maids from thee. Susanna sighed, and said: I am straitened on every side: for if I do this thing, it is death to me: and if I do it not, I shall not escape your hands. But it is better to fall into your hands without doing it, than to sin in the sight of the Lord. With that Susanna cried out with a loud voice: and the elders also cried out against her. So when the servants of the house heard the cry in the orchard, they rushed in by the back door to see what was the matter. And the elders said: As we walked in the orchard alone, this woman came in with two maids, and shut the doors of the orchard, and sent away the maids from her. Then a young man that was there hid came to her. And him indeed we could not take, because he was stronger than us, and opening the doors he leaped out: but having taken this woman, we asked who the young man was, but she would not tell us: of this thing we are witnesses. The multitude believed them as being the elders and the judges of the people, and they condemned her to death. Then Susanna cried out with a loud voice, to the Lord. And the Lord heard her voice. And when she was led to be put to death, the Lord raised up the holy spirit of a young boy, whose name was Daniel. And he standing in the midst of them, said: Are ye so foolish, ye children of Israel, that without examination or knowledge of the truth, you have condemned a daughter of Israel? Return to judgment, for they have borne false witness against her. And Daniel said to the people: Separate these two far from one another, and I will examine them. So when they were put asunder one from the other, he called one of them, and said to him: Now then, if thou sawest her, tell me under what tree thou sawest them conversing together. He said: Under a mastic tree. And Daniel said: Well hast thou lied against thy own head: for behold the Angel of God having received the sentence of him, shall cut thee in two. And having put him aside, he commanded that the other should come, and he said to him: Now therefore tell me, under what tree didst thou take them conversing together. And he answered: Under a holm tree. And Daniel said to him: Well hast thou also lied against thy own head: for the Angel of the Lord waiteth with a sword to cut thee in two, and to destroy you. And they rose up against the two elders (for Daniel had convicted them of false witness by their own mouth) and they did to them as they had maliciously dealt against their neighbour, to fulfil the law of Moses: and they put them to death, and innocent blood was saved in that day. And Daniel became great in the sight of the people from that day, and thence forward.

Q. Does the sixth Commandment forbid the reading of bad and immodest books and newspapers?

See " L. of C.," p. 50, No. 8.

(Eph. 5.) Be ye followers of God, as most dear children; and walk in love, as Christ also hath loved us, and hath delivered himself for us, an oblation and a sacrifice to God for an odor of sweetness. But fornication, and all uncleanness, or covetousness, let it not so much as be named among you, as becometh saints: or obscenity, or foolish talking, or scurrility, which is to no purpose; but rather giving of thanks. For know you this and understand, that no fornicator, or unclean, or covetous person (which is a serving of idols), hath inheritance in the kingdom of Christ and of God. Let no man deceive you with vain words. For because of these things cometh the anger of God upon the children of unbelief.

LESSON THIRTY-FOURTH.

FROM THE SEVENTH TO THE END OF THE TENTH COMMANDMENT.

Q. What is the seventh Commandment?

(Tob. 2. A. M. 3283.) Tobias fearing God more than the king, carried off the bodies of them that were slain, and hid them in his house, and at midnight buried them. Now it happened one day, that being wearied with burying, he came to his house, and cast himself down by the wall and slept. And as he was sleeping a swallow's nest fell upon his eyes, and he was made blind. Now this trial the Lord therefore permitted to happen to him, that an example might be given to posterity of his patience. Now Anna, his wife, went daily to weaving work and she brought home what she could get for their living by the labor of her hands. Whereby it came to pass, that she received a young kid, and brought it home: and when her husband heard it bleating, he said: Take heed, lest perhaps it be stolen, restore ye it to its owners, for it is not lawful for us either to eat or to touch any thing that cometh by theft.

Q. What are we commanded by the seventh Commandment?

(Gen. 23. A. M. 2148.) Abraham bowed down before the people of the land, and he spoke to Ephron, in the presence of the people: I beseech thee to hear me: I will give money for the field: take it, and so I will bury my dead in it. And Ephron answered: My Lord, hear me. The ground which thou desirest, is worth four hundred sicles of silver: this is the price between me and thee: but what is this? bury thy dead. And when Abraham had heard this, he weighed out the money that Ephron had asked, in the hearing of the children of Heth, four hundred sicles of silver of common current money. And the field that before was Ephron's, wherein was the double cave, looking towards Mambre, both it and the cave, and all the trees thereof in all its limits round about, was made sure to Abraham for a possession, in the sight of the children of Heth, and of all that went in at the gate of his city.

(Deut. 24.) When thou shalt demand of thy neighbor any thing that he oweth thee, thou shalt not go into his house to take away a pledge: but thou shalt stand without, and he shall bring out to thee what he hath. But if he be poor, the pledge shall not lodge with thee that night, but thou shalt restore it to him presently before the going down of the sun: that he may sleep in his own raiment and bless thee, and thou mayst have justice before the Lord thy God. Thou shalt not refuse the hire of the needy, and the poor, whether he be thy brother, or a stranger that dwelleth with thee in the land, and is within thy gates: but thou shalt pay him the price of his labour the same day, before the going down of the sun, because he is poor, and with it maintaineth his life: lest he cry against thee to the Lord, and it be refuted to thee for a sin.

Q. What is forbidden by the seventh Commandment?

(Ex. 12. A. M. 2513.) The children of Israel did as Moses had commanded: and they asked of the Egyptians vessels of silver and gold, and very much raiment. And the Lord gave favor to the people in the sight of the Egyptians, so that they lent unto them: and they stripped the Egyptians.

(Deut. 25.) Thou shalt not have divers weights in thy bag, a greater and a less: neither shall there be in thy house a greater bushel and a less. Thou shalt have a just and a true weight, and thy bushel shall be equal and true: that thou mayest live a long time upon the land which the Lord thy God shall give thee. For the Lord thy God abhorreth him that doth these things, and he hateth all injustice.

(Jer. 32. A. M. 3415.) Jeremias said: The word of the Lord came to me, saying: Behold, Hanameel the son of Sellum thy cousin shall come to thee, saying: Buy thee my field, which is in Anathoth, for it is thy right to buy it being next akin. And Hanameel my uncle's son came to me, according to the word of the Lord, to the entry of the prison, and said to me: Buy my field, which is in Anathoth in the land of Benjamin: for the right of inheritance is thine, and thou art next of kin to possess it. And I understood that this was the word of the Lord. And I bought the field of Hanameel my uncle's son, that is in Anathoth: and I weighed him the money, seven staters, and ten pieces of silver. And I wrote it in a book and sealed it, and took witnesses: and I weighed him the money in the balances. And I took the deed of the purchase that was sealed, and the stipulations, and the ratifications with the seals that were on the outside. And I gave the deed of the purchase to Baruch the son of Neri the son of Maasias in the sight of Hanameel my uncle's son, in the presence of the witnesses that subscribed the book of the purchase, and before all the Jews that sat in the court of the prison. And I charged Baruch before them, saying: Thus saith the Lord of hosts the God of Israel: Take these writings, this deed of the purchase that is sealed up, and this deed that is open: and put them in an earthen vessel, that they may continue many days. For thus saith the Lord of hosts the God of Israel: Houses, and fields, and vineyards shall be possessed again in this land.

Q. Are we bound to restore ill-gotten goods?

See "L. of C.," p. 83, No. 12.

Q. Are we obliged to repair the damage we have unjustly caused?

(James 5.) Go to now, ye rich men, weep and howl in your miseries, which shall come upon you. Your riches are corrupted: and your garments are moth-eaten. Your gold and silver is cankered: and the rust of them shall be for a testimony against you, and shall eat your flesh like fire. You have stored up to yourself wrath against the last days. Behold the hire of the labourers, who have reaped down your fields, which by fraud has been kept back by you, crieth: and the cry of them hath entered into the ears of the Lord of sabaoth. You have feasted upon earth: and in riotousness you have nourished your hearts, in the day of slaughter. You have condemned and put to death the just one, and he resisted you not. Be patient therefore, brethren, until the coming of the Lord. Behold, the husbandman waiteth for the precious fruit of the earth: patiently bearing till he receive the early and latter *rain*. Be you therefore also patient, and strengthen your hearts: for the coming of the Lord is at hand.

Q. What is the eighth Commandment?

(Deut 19.) If a lying witness stand against a man, accusing him of transgression, both of them, between whom the controversy is, shall stand before the Lord in the sight of the priests and the judges that shall be in those days. And when after most diligent inquisition, they shall find that the false witness hath told a lie against his brother: they shall render to him as he meant to do to his brother, and thou shalt take away the evil out of the midst of thee: that others hearing may fear, and may not dare to do such things. Thou shalt not pity him, but shalt require life for life, eye for eye, tooth for tooth, hand for hand, foot for foot.

Q. What are we commanded by the eighth Commandment?

See "L. of C.," p. 110, No. 4.

Q. What is forbidden by the eighth Commandment?

See "L. of C.," p. 33, No. 17.

Q. What must they do who have lied about their neighbour and seriously injured his character?

See "L. of C.," p. 112, No. 2; p. 120, No. 5.

Q. What is the ninth Commandment?

(Ex. 20.) Thou shalt not covet thy neighbour's house: neither shalt thou desire his wife, nor his servant, nor his handmaid, nor his ox, nor his ass, nor any thing that is his.

Q. What are we commanded by the ninth Commandment?

(I. Peter 2.) Dearly beloved, I beseech you as strangers and pilgrims, to refrain yourselves from carnal desires which war against the soul, having your conversation good among the gentiles: that whereas they speak against you as evil-doers, they may, by the good works, which they shall behold in you, glorify God in the day of visitation.

Q. What is forbidden by the ninth Commandment?

(I. Cor. 5.) It is absolutely heard, that there is fornication among you, and such fornication as the like is not among the heathens; that one should have his father's wife. And you are puffed up; and have not rather mourned, that he might be taken away from among you, that hath done this deed. I indeed, absent in body, but present in spirit, have already judged, as though I were present, him that hath so done. In the name of our Lord Jesus Christ, you being gathered together, and my spirit, with the power of our Lord Jesus, deliver such a one to satan for the destruction of the flesh, that the spirit may be saved in the day of our Lord Jesus Christ.

Q. Are impure thoughts and desires always sins?

See "L. of C.," p. 48, No. 3.

Q. What is the tenth Commandment?

(I. Tim. 6.) Godliness with contentment is great gain. For we brought nothing into this world: and certainly we can carry nothing out. But having food, and wherewith to be covered, with these we are content. For they that will become rich, fall into temptation, and into the snare of the devil, and into many unprofitable and hurtful desires, which drown men into destruction and perdition. For the desire of money is the root of all evils; which some coveting have erred from the faith, and have entangled themselves in many sorrows.

Q. What are we commanded by the tenth Commandment?

(Num. 22-24. A. M. 2553.) Now Balac the son of Sephor, saw all that Israel had done to the Amorrhite, and that the Moabites were in great fear of him, and were not able to sustain his assault. He sent therefore messengers to Balaam the son of Beor, a soothsayer, who dwelt by the river of the land of the children of Ammon, to call him, and to say: Behold a people is come out of Egypt, that hath covered the face of the earth, sitting over-against me. Come therefore, and curse this people, because it is mightier than I: if by any means I may beat them and drive them out of my land: for I know that he whom thou shalt bless is blessed, and he whom thou shalt curse is cursed. And the ancients of Moab, and the elders of Madian, went with the price of divination in their hands. And when they were come to Balaam, and had told him all the words of Balac, he answered: Tarry here this night, and I will answer whatsoever the Lord shall say to me. And while they stayed with Balaam, God came and said to him: Thou shalt not go with them, nor shalt thou curse the people: because it is blessed. And he rose in the morning and said to the princes: Go into your country, because the Lord hath forbid me to come with you. Then he sent many more and more noble than he had sent before: saying: I am ready to honour thee, and will give thee whatsoever thou wilt: come and curse this people. Balaam answered: If Balac would give me his house full of silver and gold, I cannot alter the word of the Lord my God, to speak either more or less. I pray you to stay here this night also, that I may know what the Lord will answer me once more. God therefore came to Balaam in the night, and said to him: If these men be come to call thee, arise and go with them: yet so, that thou do what I shall command thee. Balaam arose in the morning, and saddling his ass went with them. And God was angry. And an angel of the Lord stood in the way against Balaam, who sat on the ass, and had two servants with him. The ass seeing the angel standing in the way, with a drawn sword, turned herself out of the way, and went into the field. And when Balaam beat her, and had a mind to bring her again to the way, the Lord opened the mouth of the ass, and she said: What have I done to thee? Why strikest thou me, lo, now this third time? Balaam answered: Because thou hast deserved it, and hast served me ill: I would I had a sword that I might kill thee. Forthwith the Lord opened the eyes of Balaam, and he saw the angel standing in the way with a drawn sword, and he worshipped him falling flat on the ground. Balaam said: I have sinned, not knowing that thou didst stand against me: and now if it displease thee that I go, I will return. The angel said: Go with these men, and see thou speak no other thing than what I shall command thee. He went therefore with the princes. And when morning was come, they brought him to the high places of Baal, and he beheld the uttermost part of the people. And taking up his parable, he said: Balac king of the Moabites hath brought me from Aram, from the mountains of the east: Come, said he, and curse Jacob: make haste and detest Israel. How shall I curse *him*, whom God hath not cursed? By what means should I detest *him*, whom the Lord detesteth not? I shall see him, but not now: I shall behold him, but not near. A star shall rise out of Jacob and a sceptre shall spring up from Israel: and shall strike the chiefs of Moab, and shall waste all the children of Seth. And Balac said to Balaam: What is this that thou dost? I sent for thee to curse my enemies: and thou contrary wise blessest them. And Balaam rose, and returned to his place: Balac also returned the way that he came.

Q. **What is forbidden by the tenth Commandment?**
See "L. of C.," p. 66, No. 30.

LESSON THIRTY-FIFTH.

ON THE FIRST AND SECOND COMMANDMENTS OF THE CHURCH.

Q. **Which are the chief Commandments of the Church?**
See "L. of C.," p. 54, No. 5.

(Heb. 13.) Obey your prelates, and be subject to them. For they watch as being to render an account of your souls; that they may do this with joy, and not with grief. For this is not expedient for you.

Q. **Is it a mortal sin not to hear Mass on a Sunday or a holy-day of obligation?**

(Ex. 7-11. A. M. 2513.) The Lord said to Moses: Behold I have appointed thee the God of Pharao: and Aaron thy brother shall be thy prophet. Thou shalt speak to him all that I command thee; and he shall speak to Pharao, that he let the children of Israel go out of his land. And thou shalt say to him: The Lord God of the Hebrews sent me to thee, saying: Let my people go to sacrifice to me in the desert: and hitherto thou wouldst not hear. Thus therefore saith the Lord: In this thou shalt know that I am the Lord: behold I will strike with the rod, that is in my hand, the water of the river, and it shall be turned into blood. But if thou wilt not let them go, behold I will strike all thy coasts with frogs. And the river shall bring forth an abundance of frogs: which shall come up, and enter into thy house, and thy bed-chamber, and upon thy bed, and into the houses of thy servants, and to thy people, and into thy ovens, and into the remains of thy meats; and the frogs shall come in to thee, and to thy people, and to all thy servants. And the Lord said to Moses: Say to Aaron, Stretch forth thy rod, and strike the dust of the earth: and may there be sciniphs in all the land of Egypt. And the Lord said to Moses: Arise in the morning, and stand before Pharao, and thou shalt say to him: Thus saith the Lord the God of the Hebrews: Let my people go to sacrifice to me. But if thou wilt not let them go, behold I will send in upon thee, and upon thy servants, and upon thy houses all kind of flies: and the houses of the Egyptians shall be filled with flies of divers kinds, and the whole land wherein they shall be. And Pharao called Moses and Aaron, and said to them: Go, and sacrifice to your God in this land. And Moses said: It cannot be so: for we shall sacrifice the abominations of the Egyptians to the Lord our God: now if we kill those things which the Egyptians worship, in their presence, they will stone us. And the Lord said to Moses: Go in to Pharao, and speak to him: Thus saith the Lord God of the Hebrews: Let my people go to sacrifice to me. But if thou refuse, and withhold them still: behold my hand shall be upon thy fields: and a very grievous murrain upon thy horses, and asses, and camels, and oxen, and sheep. And the Lord said to Moses and Aaron: Take to you handfuls of ashes out of the chimney, and let Moses sprinkle it in the air in the presence of Pharao. And be there dust upon all the land of Egypt: for there shall be boils and swelling blains both in men and beasts, in the whole land of Egypt. And the Lord said to Moses: Stretch forth thy hand towards heaven, that there may be hail in the whole land of Egypt, upon men, and upon beasts, and upon every herb of the field in the land of Egypt. And the Lord said to Moses: Stretch forth thy hand upon the land of Egypt unto the locust, that it come upon it, and devour every herb that is left after the hail. And the Lord hardened Pharao's heart, neither did he let the children of Israel go. And the Lord said to Moses: Stretch out thy hand towards heaven: and may there be darkness upon the land of Egypt, so thick that it may be felt. And it came to pass at midnight, the Lord slew every first-born in the land of Egypt, from the first-born of Pharao, who sat on his throne, unto the first-born of the captive woman that was in the prison, and all the first-born of cattle. And Pharao arose in the night, and all his servants, and all Egypt; and there arose a great cry in Egypt: for there was not a house wherein there lay not one dead. And Pharao calling Moses and Aaron, in the night, said: Arise and go forth from among my people, you and the children of Israel: go, sacrifice to the Lord as you say. And the children of Israel set forward from Ramesse to Socoth, being about six hundred thousand men on foot, beside children.

Q. Why were holy-days instituted by the Church?

(Lev. 23. A. M. 2514.) The Lord spoke to Moses, saying: Speak to the children of Israel, and thou shalt say to them: These are the feasts of the Lord, which you shall call holy. Six days shall ye do work: the seventh day, because it is the rest of the sabbath, shall be called holy. You shall do no work on that day: it is the sabbath of the Lord in all your habitations. These also are the holy-days of the Lord, which you must celebrate in their seasons. The first month, the fourteenth day of the month at evening, is the phase of the Lord: and the fifteenth day of the same month is the solemnity of the unleavened bread of the Lord. Seven days shall you eat unleavened bread. The first day shall be most solemn unto you, and holy: you shall do no servile work therein: but you shall offer sacrifice in fire to the Lord seven days. And the seventh day shall be more solemn, and more holy: and you shall do no servile work therein. And the Lord spoke to Moses, saying: Speak to the children of Israel, and thou shalt say to them: When you shall have entered into the land which I will give you, and shall reap your corn, you shall bring sheaves of ears, the first-fruits of your harvest to the priest: you shall count therefore from the morrow after the sabbath, wherein you offered the sheaf of the first-fruits, seven full weeks. Even unto the morrow after the seventh week be expired, that is to say, fifty days, and so you shall offer a new sacrifice to the Lord. And you shall call this day most solemn, and most holy. You shall do no servile work therein. It shall be an everlasting ordinance in all your dwellings and generations. And the Lord spoke to Moses, saying: Say to the children of Israel: The seventh month, on the first day of the month, you shall keep a sabbath, a memorial, with the sound of trumpets, and it shall be called holy. You shall do no servile work therein, and you shall offer a holocaust to the Lord. And the Lord spoke to Moses, saying: Upon the tenth day of this seventh month shall be the day of atonement, it shall be most solemn, and shall be called holy: and you shall afflict your souls on that day, and shall offer a holocaust to the Lord. You shall do no servile work in the time of this day: because it is a day of propitiation, that the Lord your God may be merciful unto you. It is a sabbath of rest, and you shall afflict your souls *beginning on* the ninth day of the month: from evening until evening you shall celebrate your sabbaths. And the Lord spoke to Moses, saying: Say to the children of Israel: From the fifteenth day of this same seventh month, shall be kept the feast of tabernacles' seven days to the Lord. The first day shall be called most solemn and most holy: you shall do no servile work therein. And seven days you shall offer holocausts to the Lord. The eighth day also shall be most solemn and most holy, and you shall offer holocausts to the Lord: for it is the day of assembly and congregation: you shall do no servile work therein. These are the feasts of the Lord, which you shall call most solemn and most holy, and shall offer on them oblations to the Lord, holocausts and libations according to the rite of every day.

Q. How should we keep the holy-days of obligation?

(James 1.) Be ye doers of the word, and not hearers only, deceiving your own selves. For if a man be a hearer of the word, and not a doer, he shall be compared to a man beholding his own countenance in a glass. For he beheld himself, and went his way, and presently forgot what manner of man he was. But he that hath looked into the perfect law of liberty, and hath continued therein, not becoming a forgetful hearer, but a doer of the work; this man shall be blessed in his deed. And if any man think himself to be religious, not bridling his tongue, but deceiving his own heart, this man's religion is vain. Religion clean and undefiled before God and the Father, is this: to visit the fatherless and widows in their tribulation: and to keep one's self unspotted from this world.

Q. What do you mean by fast-days?

(Zach. 7. A. M. 3487.) It came to pass in the fourth year of king Darius, that the word of the Lord came to Zacharias, in the fourth day of the ninth month, which is Casleu. When Sarasar, and Rogommelech, and the men that were with him, sent to the house of God, to entreat the face of the Lord: to speak to the priests of the house of the Lord of hosts, and to the prophets, saying: Must I weep in the fifth month, or must I sanctify myself as I have now done for many years? And the word of the Lord of hosts came to me, saying: Speak to all the people of the land, and to the priests, saying: When you fasted, and mourned in the fifth and the seventh month for these seventy years: did you keep a fast unto me? And when you did eat and drink, did you not eat for yourselves, and drink for yourselves? And the word of the Lord came to Zacharias, saying: Thus saith the Lord of hosts, saying: Judge ye true judgment, and shew ye mercy and compassion every man to his brother. And oppress not the widow, and the fatherless, and the stranger, and the poor: and let not a man devise evil in his heart against his brother. Thus saith the Lord of hosts: The fast of the fourth month, and the fast of the fifth, and the fast of the seventh, and the fast of the tenth shall be to the house of Juda, joy, and gladness, and great solemnities: only love ye truth and peace.

Q. What do you mean by days of abstinence?

(1 Cor. 9.) Know you not that they that run in the race, all run indeed, but one receiveth the prize? So run that you may obtain. And every one that striveth for the mastery, refraineth himself from all things: and they indeed that they may receive a corruptible crown; but we an incorruptible one. I therefore so run, not as an uncertainty: I so fight, not as one beating the air: but I chastise my body, and bring it into subjection: lest perhaps, when I have preached to others, I myself should become a castaway.

Q. Why does the Church command us to abstain from flesh-meat on Fridays?

See "L. of C.," p. 16, No. 5.

(Esdras 7–8. A. M. 3537.) I Esdras went up from Babylon, and I was a ready scribe in the law of Moses, which the Lord God had given to Israel: and the king granted me all my requests, according to the hand of the Lord his God upon him. For I Esdras had prepared my heart to seek the law of the Lord, and to do and to teach in Israel the commandments and judgment. And I proclaimed there a fast by the river Ahava, that we might afflict ourselves before the Lord our God, and might ask of him a right way for us and for our children, and for all our substance. For I was ashamed to ask the king for aid and for horsemen, to defend us from the enemy in the way: because we had said to the king: The hand of our God is upon all them that seek him in goodness: and his power and strength, and wrath upon all them that forsake him. And we fasted, and besought our God for this: and it fell out prosperously unto us.

(Dan. 1. A. M. 3398.) Nabuchodonosor, king of Babylon came to Jerusalem, and besieged it. And the Lord delivered into his hands Joakim the king of Juda. And the king spoke to Asphenez the master of the servants, that he should bring in *some* of the children of Israel, children in whom there was no blemish, well favoured, and skilful in all wisdom, acute in knowledge, and instructed in science, and such as might stand in the king's palace, that he might teach them the learning, and the tongue of the Chaldeans. And the king appointed them a daily provision, of his own meat, and of the wine of which he drank himself, that being nourished three years, afterwards they might stand before the king. Now there were among them of the children of Juda, Daniel, Ananias, Misael, and Azarias. But Daniel purposed in his heart that he would not be defiled with the king's table, nor with the wine which he drank: and he requested the master of the servants that he might not be defiled. And God gave to Daniel grace and mercy in the sight of the prince of the servants. And the prince of the servants said to Daniel: I fear my lord the king, who hath appointed you meat and drink: who if he should see your faces leaner than those of the other youths your equals, you shall endanger my head to the king. And Daniel said to Malasar, whom the prince of the servants had appointed over Daniel, Ananias, Misael, and Azarias: Try, I beseech thee, thy servants for ten days, and let pulse be given us to eat, and water to drink: and look upon our faces, and the faces of the children that eat of the king's meat: and as thou shalt see, deal with thy servants. And when he had heard these words, he tried them for ten days. And after ten days their faces appeared fairer and fatter than all the children that eat of the king's meat. So Malasar took their portions, and the wine that they should drink: and he gave them pulse. And to these children God gave knowledge, and understanding in every book, and wisdom: but to Daniel the understanding *also* of all visions and dreams. And when the days were ended, after which the king had ordered they should be brought in: the prince of the servants brought them in before Nabuchodonosor. And when the king had spoken to them, there were not found among them all such as Daniel, Ananias, Misael, and Azarias: and they stood in the king's presence. And in all matters of wisdom and understanding, that the king inquired of them, he found them ten times better than all the diviners, and wise men, that were in all his kingdom.

(Dan. 10. A. M. 3478.) In the third year of Cyrus king of the Persians, a word was revealed to Daniel surnamed Baltassar, and a true word, and great strength: and he understood the word: for there is need of understanding in a vision. In those days I Daniel mourned the days of three weeks. I eat no desirable bread, and neither flesh, nor wine entered into my mouth, neither was I anointed with ointment: till the days of three weeks were accomplished. And in the four and twentieth day of the first month I was by the great river which is the Tigris. And I lifted up my eyes, and I saw: and behold a man clothed in linen, and his loins were girded with the finest gold: and his body was like the chrysolite, and his face as the appearance of lightning, and his eyes as a burning lamp: and his arms, and all downward even to the feet, like in appearance to glittering brass: and the voice of his word like the voice of a multitude. And I Daniel alone saw the vision: for the men that were with me saw it not: but an exceeding great terror fell upon them, and they fled away, and hid themselves. And I being left alone saw this great vision: and there remained no strength in me, and the appearance of my countenance was changed in me, and I fainted away, and retained no strength. And I heard the voice of his words: and when I heard, I lay in a consternation upon my face, and my face was close to the ground. And behold a hand touched me, and lifted me up upon my knees, and upon the joints of my hands. And he said to me: Daniel, thou man of desires, understand the words that I speak to thee, and stand upright: for I am sent now to thee. And when he had said this word to me, I stood trembling. And he said to me: Fear not, Daniel: for from the first day that thou didst set thy heart to understand, to afflict thyself in the sight of the God, thy words have been heard: and I am come for thy words.

Q. Why does the Church command us to fast and abstain?

(II. Mach. 7. A. M. 3837.) It came to pass, that seven brethren, together with their mother, were apprehended, and compelled by the king to eat swine's flesh against the law, for which end they were tormented with whips and scourges. But one of them, who was the eldest, said thus: What wouldst thou ask, or learn of us? we are ready to die rather than to transgress the laws of God, received from our fathers. Then the king being angry commanded frying-pans, and brazen caldrons to be made hot: which forthwith being heated, he commanded to cut out the tongue of him that had spoken first: and the skin of his head being drawn off, to chop off also the extremities of his hands and feet, the rest of his brethren, and his mother, looking on. And when he was now maimed in all parts, he commanded him, being yet alive, to be brought to the fire, and to be fried in the frying-pan: and while he was suffering therein long torments, the rest, together with the mother, exhorted one another to die manfully. So when the first was dead after this manner, they brought the next to make him a mocking-stock: and when they had pulled off the skin of his head with the hair, they asked him if he would eat, before he were punished throughout the whole body in every limb. But he answered in his own language, and said: I will not do it. Wherefore he also in the next place, received the torments of the first: after him the third was made a mocking-stock, and when he was required, he quickly put forth his tongue, and courageously stretched out his hands: and after he was thus dead, they tormented the fourth in the like manner. And when they had brought the fifth, they tormented him. After him they brought the sixth, and he being ready to die, spoke thus: Do not think that thou shalt escape unpunished, for that thou hast attempted to fight against God. Now the mother was to be admired above measure, and worthy to be remembered by good men, who beheld her seven sons slain in the space of one day, and bore it with a good courage, for the hope that she had in God: and she bravely exhorted every one of them in her own language, being filled with wisdom: and joining a man's heart to a woman's thought. Now Antiochus, thinking himself despised, and withal despising the voice of the upbraider, when the youngest was yet alive, did not only exhort him by words, but also assured him with an oath, that he would make him a rich and a happy man, and, if he would turn from the laws of his fathers, would take him for a friend, and furnish him with things necessary. But when the young man was not moved with these things, the king called the mother, and counselled her to deal with the young man to save his life. And when he had exhorted her with many words, she promised that she would counsel her son. So bending herself towards him, mocking the cruel tyrant, she said in her own language: I beseech *thee*, my son, look upon heaven and earth, and all that is in them: and consider that God made them out of nothing, and mankind also: so thou shalt not fear this tormentor, but being made a worthy partner with thy brethren, receive death, that in that mercy I may receive thee again with thy brethren. While she was yet speaking these words, the young man said: For whom do you stay? I will not obey the commandment of the king, but the commandment of the law, which was given us by Moses. Then the king being incensed with anger, raged against him more cruelly than all the rest, taking it grievously that he was mocked. So this man also died undefiled, wholly trusting in the Lord. And last of all after the sons the mother also was consumed.

LESSON THIRTY-SIXTH.

ON THE THIRD, FOURTH, FIFTH, AND SIXTH COMMANDMENTS OF THE CHURCH.

Q. What is meant by the command of confessing at least once a year?

See "L. of C.," p. 67, No 31; p. 72, No. 7; p. 95, No. 43.

Q. Should we confess only once a year?

(Eccltus. 5.) Say not: How mighty am I? and who shall bring me under for my deeds? for God will surely take revenge. Say not: I have sinned, and what harm hath befallen me? for the most High is a patient rewarder. Be not without fear about sin forgiven, and add not sin upon sin: and say not: The mercy of the Lord is great, he will have mercy on the multitude of my sins. For mercy and wrath quickly come from him, and his wrath looketh upon sinners. Delay not to be converted to the Lord, and defer it not from day to day. For his wrath shall come on a sudden, and in the time of vengeance he will destroy thee.

Q. Should children go to confession?

See "L. of C.," p. 81, No. 6.

Q. What sin does he commit who neglects to receive Communion during the Easter time?

See "L. of C.," p. 71, No. 6.

Q. What is the Easter time?

(Jonas 3. A. M. 3197.) The word of the Lord came to Jonas the second time, saying: Arise, and go to Ninive the great city: and preach in it the preaching that I bid thee. And Jonas arose, and went to Ninive, according to the word of the Lord: now Ninive was a great city of three days' journey. And Jonas began to enter into the city one day's journey: and he cried, and said: Yet forty days, and Ninive shall be destroyed. And the men of Ninive believed in God: and they proclaimed a fast, and put on sackcloth from the greatest to the least. And the word came to the king of Ninive; and he rose up out of his throne, and cast away his robe from him, and was clothed with sackcloth, and sat in ashes. And he caused it to be proclaimed and published in Ninive from the mouth of the king and of his princes, saying: Let neither men nor beasts, oxen nor sheep, taste any thing: let them not feed, nor drink water. And let men and beasts be covered with sackcloth, and cry to the Lord with all their strength, and let them turn every one from his evil way, and from the iniquity that is in their hands. Who can tell if God will turn, and forgive: and will turn away from his fierce anger, and we shall not perish? And God saw their works, that they were turned from their evil way: and God had mercy with regard to the evil which he had said that he would do to them, and he did it not.

Q. Are we obliged to contribute to the support of our pastors?

See "L. of C.," p. 52, No. 15; p. 93, No. 37.

(I. Cor. 9.) Know you not, that they who work in the holy place, eat the things that are of the holy place; and they that serve the altar, partake with the altar? So also the Lord ordained that they who preach the gospel, should live by the gospel.

(Deut. 16.) Three times in a year shall all thy males appear before the Lord thy God in the place which he shall choose: in the feast of unleavened bread, in the feast of weeks, and in the feast of tabernacles. No one shall appear with his hands empty before the Lord: but every one shall offer according to what he hath, according to the blessing of the Lord his God, which he shall give him.

(IV. Kings 12. A. M. 3148.) Joiada the high priest took a chest and bored a hole in the top, and set it by the altar at the right hand of them that came into the house of the Lord, and the priests that kept the doors put therein all the money that was brought to the temple of the Lord. And when they saw that there was very much money in the chest, the king's scribe and the high priest came up, and poured it out, and counted the money that was found in the house of the Lord: and they gave it out by number and measure into the hands of them that were over the builders of the house of the Lord: and they laid it out to the carpenters, and the masons that wrought in the house of the Lord, and made the repairs: and to them that cut stones, and to buy timber, and stones, to be hewed, that the repairs of the house of the Lord might be completely finished, wheresoever there was need of expenses to uphold the house. For it was given to them that did the work, that the temple of the Lord might be repaired.

Q. What is the meaning of the commandment not to marry within the fourth degree of kindred?

See "L. of C.," p. 21, No. 5; p. 48, No. 47.

Q. What is the meaning of the command not to marry privately?

(I. Cor. 4.) Let a man so account of us as of the ministers of Christ, and the dispensers of the mysteries of God.

Q. What is the meaning of the precept not to solemnize marriage at forbidden times?

(Eccltus. 3.) All things have their season, and in their times all things pass under heaven. A time to be born and a time to die. A time to plant, and a time to pluck up that which is planted. A time to kill, and a time to heal. A time to destroy, and a time to build. A time to weep, and a time to laugh. A time to mourn, and a time to dance. A time to scatter stones, and a time to gather. A time to embrace, and a time to be far from embraces. A time to get, and a time to lose. A time to keep, and a time to cast away. A time to rend, and a time to sew. A time to keep silence, and a time to speak. A time of love, and a time of hatred. A time of war, and a time of peace.

Q. What is the nuptial Mass?
See " L. of C.," p. 18, No. 3.

Q. Should Catholics be married at a nuptial Mass?
See " L. of C.," p. 89, No. 29.

LESSON THIRTY-SEVENTH.

ON THE LAST JUDGMENT AND THE RESURRECTION, HELL, PURGATORY, AND HEAVEN.

Q. When will Christ judge us?
See " L. of C.," p. 67, No. 31; p. 79, No. 2.

(II. Peter 3.) Of this one thing be not ignorant, my beloved, that one day with the Lord is as a thousand years, and a thousand years as one day. The Lord delayeth not his promise, as some imagine, but dealeth patiently for your sake, not willing that any should perish, but that all should return to penance. But the day of the Lord shall come as a thief, in which the heavens shall pass away with great violence, and the elements shall be melted with heat, and the earth and the works which are in it, shall be burnt up. Seeing then that all these things are to be dissolved, what manner of people ought you to be in holy conversation and godliness? Looking for and hasting unto the coming of the day of the Lord, by which the heavens being on fire shall be dissolved, and the elements shall melt with the burning heat? But we look for new heavens and a new earth according to his promises, in which justice dwelleth. Wherefore, dearly beloved, seeing that you look for these things, be diligent that ye may be found undefiled and unspotted to him in peace.

(I. Thess. 5.) Of the times and moments, brethren, you need not, that we should write to you; for yourselves know perfectly, that the day of the Lord shall so come, as a thief in the night. For when they shall say, peace and security; then shall sudden destruction come upon them, as the pains upon her that is with child, and they shall not escape. But you, brethren, are not in darkness, that that day should overtake you as a thief. For all you are the children of light, and children of the day; we are not of the night, nor of darkness. Therefore, let us not sleep, as others do: but let us watch, and be sober.

(Eccltus. 41.) O death, how bitter is the remembrance of thee to a man that hath peace in his possessions. To a man that is at rest, and whose ways are prosperous in all things, and that is yet able to take meat! O death, thy sentence is welcome to the man that is in need, and to him whose strength faileth. Who is in a decrepit age, and that is in care about all things, and to the distrustful that looseth patience! Fear not the sentence of death. Remember what things have been before thee, and what shall come after thee: this sentence is from the Lord upon all flesh.

(Jer. 4. A. M. 3375.) I beheld the earth, and lo it was void, and nothing: and the heavens, and there was no light in them. I looked upon the mountains, and behold they trembled: and all the hills were troubled. I beheld, and lo there was no man: and all the birds of the air were gone. I looked, and behold Carmel was a wilderness: and all its cities were destroyed at the presence of the Lord, and at the presence of the wrath of his indignation.

(Dan. 12.) At that time shall Michael rise up, the great prince, who standeth for the children of thy people: and a time shall come such as never was from the time that nations began even until that time. And at that time shall thy people be saved, every one that shall be found written in the book. And many of those that sleep in the dust of the earth, shall awake: some unto life everlasting, and others unto reproach, to see it always. But they that are learned shall shine as the brightness of the firmament: and they that instruct many to justice, as stars for all eternity.

Q. What is the judgment called which we have to undergo immediately after death?
See "L. of C.," p. 95, Nos. 42, 43.

Q. What is the judgment called which all men have to undergo on the last day?
See "L. of C.," p. 94, No 41.

(Joel 3.) I will gather together all nations, and will bring them down into the valley of Josaphat: and I will plead with them there for my people, and for my inheritance Israel, whom they have scattered among the nations, and have parted my land. Break forth, and come, all ye nations, from round about, and gather yourselves together: there will the Lord cause all thy strong ones to fall down. Let them arise, and let the nations come up into the valley of Josaphat:

for there I will sit to judge all nations round about.

Q. Why does Christ judge men immediately after death?

(Rom. 2.) Thou art inexcusable, O man, whosoever thou art that judgest. For wherein thou judgest another, thou condemnest thyself. For thou dost the same things which thou judgest. For we know that the judgment of God is, according to truth, against them that do such things. And thinkest thou this, O man, that judgest them who do such things, and dost the same, that thou shalt escape the judgment of God? Or despisest thou the riches of his goodness, and patience, and long-suffering? Knowest thou not, that the benignity of God leadeth thee to penance? But according to thy hardness and impenitent heart, thou treasurest up to thyself wrath, against the day of wrath, and revelation of the just judgment of God, who will render to every man according to his works. To them indeed, who according to patience in good work, seek glory, and honour, and incorruption: eternal life: but to them that are contentious, and who obey not the truth, but give credit to iniquity: wrath and indignation, tribulation and anguish upon every soul.

Q. What are the rewards or punishments appointed for men's souls after the Particular Judgment?

(II. Thess. 1.) We are bound to give thanks always to God for you, brethren, as it is fitting, because your faith groweth exceedingly, and the charity of every one of you towards each other, aboundeth: so that we ourselves also glory in you in the churches of God, for your patience and faith, and in all your persecutions and tribulations, which you endure. For an example of the just judgment of God, that you may be counted worthy of the kingdom of God, for which also you suffer. Seeing it is a just thing with God, to repay tribulation to them that trouble you: and to you who are troubled, rest with us when the Lord Jesus shall be revealed from heaven, with the angels of his power: in a flame of fire, yielding vengeance to them who know not God, and who obey not the gospel of our Lord Jesus Christ. Who shall suffer eternal punishment in destruction, from the face of the Lord, and from the glory of his power: when he shall come to be glorified in his saints, and to be made wonderful in all them who have believed; because our testimony was believed upon you in that day.

(Gen. 15. A. M. 2092.) Now when these things were done, the word of the Lord came to Abram by a vision, saying: Fear not, Abram, I am thy protector, and thy reward exceeding great. And Abram said: Lord God, what wilt thou give me? And he said to him: I am the Lord who brought thee out from Ur of the Chaldees, to give thee this land, and that thou mightest possess it. Abram believed God, and it was reputed to him unto justice. And when the sun was set, there arose a dark mist, and there appeared a smoking furnace and a lamp of fire passing between those divisions. That day God made a covenant with Abram, saying: To thy seed will I give this land, from the river of Egypt even to the great river Euphrates.

(Ex. 13. A. M. 2513.) The children of Israel set forward from Ramesse to Socoth, being about six hundred thousand men on foot, beside children. And marching from Socoth they encamped in Etham in the utmost coasts of the wilderness. And the Lord went before them to shew the way by day in a pillar of a cloud, and by night in a pillar of fire: that he might be the guide of their journey at both times. There never failed the pillar of the cloud by day, nor the pillar of fire by night, before the people.

Q. What is Hell?

(Wisd. 5.) Then shall the just stand with great constancy against those that have afflicted them, and taken away their labors. These seeing it, shall be troubled with terrible fear, and shall be amazed at the suddenness of their unexpected salvation. Saying within themselves, repenting, and groaning for anguish of spirit: These are they, whom we had some time in derision, and for a parable of reproach. We fools esteemed their life madness, and their end without honor. Behold how they are numbered among the children of God, and their lot is among the saints. Therefore we have erred from the way of truth, and the light of justice hath not shined unto us, and the sun of understanding hath not risen upon us. We wearied ourselves in the way of iniquity and destruction, and have walked through hard ways, but the way of the Lord we have not known. What hath pride profited us? or what advantage hath the boasting of riches brought us? All those things are passed away like a shadow, and like a post that runneth on, and as a ship that passeth through the waves: whereof when it is gone by, the trace cannot be found, nor the path of its keel in the waters: or as when a bird flieth through the air, of the passage of which no mark can be found, but only the sound of the wings beating the light air, and parting it by the force of her flight; she moved her wings, and hath flown through, and there is no mark found afterwards of her way: or as when an arrow is shot at a mark, the divided air presently cometh together again, so that the passage thereof is not known: so we also being born, forthwith ceased to be: and have been able to shew no mark of virtue: but are consumed in our wickedness. Such things as these the sinners said in hell: for the hope of the wicked is as dust, which is blown away with the wind, and as a thin froth which is dispersed by the storm: and a smoke that is scattered abroad by the wind: and as the remembrance of a guest of one day that passeth by. But the just shall live for evermore: and their reward is with the Lord, and the care of them with the most High. Therefore shall they receive a kingdom of glory, and a crown of beauty at the hand of the Lord.

(Nahum 1.) The Lord is a jealous God, and a revenger: the Lord is a revenger, and hath wrath: the Lord taketh vengeance on his adversaries, and he is angry with his enemies. The Lord is patient, and great in power, and will not cleanse and acquit *the guilty*. The Lord's ways *are* in a tempest, and a whirlwind, and clouds *are* the dust of his feet. He rebuketh the sea, and drieth it up: and bringeth all the rivers to be a desert. The mountains tremble at him, and the hills are made desolate: and the earth hath quaked at his presence, and the world, and all that dwell therein. Who can stand before the face of his indignation? and who shall resist in the fierceness of his anger? his indignation is poured out like fire: and the rocks are melted by him.

Q. What is Purgatory?
See "L. of C.," p. 68, No. 34.

(I. Cor. 3.) Other foundation no man can lay, but that which is laid; which is Christ Jesus. Now if any man build upon this foundation, gold, silver, precious stones, wood, hay, stubble: every man's work shall be manifest; for the day of the Lord shall declare *it*, because it shall be revealed in fire; and the fire shall try every man's work, of what sort it is. If any man's work abide, which he hath built thereupon, he shall receive a reward. If any man's work burn, he shall suffer loss; but he himself shall be saved, yet so as by fire.

(Zach. 13.) There shall be in all the earth, saith the Lord, two parts in it shall be scattered, and shall perish: but the third part shall be left therein. And I will bring the third part through the fire, and will refine them as silver is refined: and I will try them as gold is tried. They shall call on my name, and I will hear them. I will say: Thou art my people: and they shall say: The Lord is my God.

Q. Can the faithful on earth help the souls in Purgatory?

(II. Mach. 12. A. M. 3841.) After Pentecost Judas marched against Gorgias the governor of Idumea. And when they had joined battle, it happened that a few of the Jews were slain. And the day following Judas came with his company, to take away the bodies of them that were slain, and to bury them with their kinsmen, in the sepulchres of their fathers. And they found under the coats of the slain some of the donaries of the idols of Jamnia, which the law forbiddeth to the Jews: so that all plainly saw, that for this cause they were slain. Then they all blessed the just judgment of the Lord, who had discovered the things that were hidden. And so betaking themselves to prayers, they besought him, that the sin which had been committed might be forgotten. But the most valiant Judas exhorted the people to keep themselves from sin, forasmuch as they saw before their eyes what had happened, because of the sins of those that were slain. And making a gathering, he sent twelve thousand drachms of silver to Jerusalem for sacrifice to be offered for the sins of the dead, thinking well and religiously concerning the resurrection. (For if he had not hoped that they that were slain should rise again, it would have seemed superfluous and vain to pray for the dead,) and because he considered that they who had fallen asleep with godliness, had great grace laid up for them. It is therefore a holy and wholesome thought to pray for the dead, that they may be loosed from sins.

Q. If every one is judged immediately after death, what need is there of a general judgment?

See " L. of C," p. 75, No. 13; p. 82, No. 8; p. 97, No. 44.

Q. Will our bodies share in the reward or punishment of our souls?

See " L. of C.," p. 77, Nos. 19-21.

(I. Thess. 4.) We will not have you ignorant, brethren, concerning them that are asleep, that you be not sorrowful, even as others who have no hope. For if we believe that Jesus died, and rose again; even so them who have slept through Jesus, will God bring with him. For this we say unto you in the word of the Lord, that we who are alive, who remain unto the coming of the Lord, shall not prevent them who have slept. For the Lord himself shall come down from heaven with commandment, and with the voice of an Archangel, and with the trumpet of God: and the dead who are in Christ, shall rise first. Then we who are alive, who are left, shall be taken up together with them in the clouds to meet Christ, into the air, and so shall we be always with the Lord. Wherefore, comfort ye one another with these words.

(Ezek. 37. A. M. 3417.) The hand of the Lord was upon me, and brought me forth in the spirit of the Lord: and set me down in the midst of a plain that was full of bones. And he led me about through them on every side: now they were very many upon the face of the plain, and they were exceeding dry. And he said to me: Son of man, dost thou think these bones shall live? And I answered: O Lord God, thou knowest. And he said to me: Prophesy concerning these bones; and say to them: Ye dry bones, hear the word of the Lord. Thus saith the Lord God to these bones: Behold, I will send spirit into you, and you shall live. And I will lay sinews upon you, and will cause flesh to grow over you, and will cover you with skin: and I will give you spirit and you shall live, and you shall know that I am the Lord. And I prophesied as he had commanded me: and as I prophesied there was a noise, and behold a commotion: and the bones came together, each one to its joint. And I saw; and behold the sinews, and the flesh came up upon them: and the skin was stretched out over them, but there was no spirit in them. And he said to me: Prophesy to the spirit, prophesy, O son of man, and say to the spirit: Thus saith the Lord God: Come, spirit, from the four winds, and blow upon these slain, and let them live again. And I prophesied as he had commanded me: and the spirit came into them, and they lived: and they stood up upon their feet, an exceeding great army. And he said to me: Son of man: All these bones are the house of Israel: they say: Our bones are dried up, and our hope is lost, and we are cut off. Therefore prophesy, and say to them: Thus saith the Lord God: Behold I will open your graves, and will bring you out of your sepulchres, O my people: and will bring you into the land of Israel.

Q. In what state will the bodies of the just rise?
See "L. of C.," p. 90, No. 31.

(Gen. 15. A. M. 2092.) Now when these things were done, the word of the Lord came to Abram by a vision, saying: Fear not, Abram, I am thy protector, and thy reward exceeding great. And Abram said: Lord God what wilt thou give me? And he brought him forth abroad, and said to him: Look up to heaven and number the stars, if thou canst. And he said to him: So shall thy seed be.

Q. Will the bodies of the damned also rise?

(I. Cor. 15.) Now if Christ be preached, that he arose again from the dead, how do some among you say, that there is no resurrection of the dead? But if there be no resurrection of the dead, then Christ is not risen again. And if Christ be not risen again, then is our preaching vain, and your faith is also vain. Yea, and we are found false witnesses of God: because we have given testimony against God, that he hath raised up Christ; whom he hath not raised up, if the dead rise not again. For if the dead rise not again, neither is Christ risen again. And if Christ be not risen again, your faith is vain, for you are yet in your sins. Then they also that are fallen asleep in Christ, are perished. If in this life only we have hope in Christ, we are of all men most miserable. But now Christ is risen from the dead, the first-fruits of them that sleep: for by a man came death, and by a man the resurrection of the dead. And as in Adam all die, so also in Christ all shall be made alive. But every one in his own order: the first-fruits Christ, then they that are of Christ, who have believed in his coming. Afterwards the end, when he shall have delivered up the kingdom to God and the Father, when he shall have brought to nought all principality, and power, and virtue. But some man will say: How do the dead rise again? or with what manner of body shall they come? Senseless man, that which thou sowest is not quickened, except it die first. And that which thou sowest, thou sowest not the body that shall be; but bare grain, as of wheat, or of some of the rest. But God giveth it a body as he will: and to every seed its proper body. All flesh *is* not the same flesh: but one *is the flesh* of men, another of beasts, another of birds, another of fishes. And *there are* bodies celestial, and bodies terrestrial: but, one *is the* glory of the celestial, and another of the terrestrial. One *is the* glory of the sun, another the glory of the moon, and another the glory of the stars. For star differeth from star in glory. So also is the resurrection of the dead. It is sown in corruption, it shall rise in incorruption. It is sown in dishonour, it shall rise in glory. It is sown in weakness, it shall rise in power. It is sown a natural body, it shall rise a spiritual body. Behold, I tell you a mystery. We shall all indeed rise again: but we shall not all be changed. In a moment, in the twinkling of an eye, at the last trumpet: for the trumpet shall sound, and the dead shall rise again incorruptible: and we shall be changed. For this corruptible must put on incorruption; and this mortal must put on immortality. And when this mortal hath put on immortality, then shall come to pass the saying that is written: *Death is swallowed up in victory. O death, where is thy victory? O death, where is thy sting?* Now the sting of death is sin: and the strength of sin *is* the law. But thanks be to God, who hath given us the victory through our Lord Jesus Christ.

Q. What is Heaven?
See "L. of C.," p. 34, No. 20.

(II. Tim. 4.) I am even now ready to be sacrificed: and the time of my dissolution is at hand. I have fought a good fight, I have finished my course, I have kept the faith. As to the rest, there is laid up for me a crown of justice, which the Lord the just judge will render to me in that day: and not only to me, but to them also that love his coming. Make haste to come to me quickly.

(Apoc. 7. A. D. 64.) After this I saw a great multitude, which no man could number, of all nations, and tribes, and peoples, and tongues, standing before the throne, and in sight of the Lamb, clothed with white robes, and palms in their hands: and they cried with a loud voice, saying: Salvation to our God, who sitteth upon the throne, and to the Lamb. And all the Angels stood round about the throne, and the ancients, and the four living creatures; and they fell down before the throne upon their faces, and adored God, saying: Amen. Benediction, and glory, and wisdom, and thanksgiving, honour, and power, and strength to our God for ever and ever. Amen. And one of the ancients answered, and said to me: These that are clothed in white robes, who are they? and whence came they? And I said to him: My Lord, thou knowest. And he said to me: These are they who are come out of great tribulation, and have washed their robes, and have made them white in the blood of the Lamb. Therefore they are before the throne of God, and they serve him day and night in his temple: and he, that sitteth on the throne, shall dwell over them. They shall no more hunger nor thirst, neither shall the sun fall on them, nor any heat. For the Lamb, which is in the midst of the throne, shall rule them, and shall lead them to the fountains of the waters of life, and God shall wipe away all tears from their eyes.

(Apoc. 21.) I saw a new heaven and a new earth. For the first heaven and the first earth was gone, and the sea is now no more. And I John saw the holy city, the new Jerusalem, coming down out of heaven from God, prepared as a bride adorned for her husband. And the building of the wall thereof was of jasper-stone: but the city itself pure gold, like to clear glass. And the foundations of the wall of the city were adorned with all manner of precious stones. And the twelve gates are twelve pearls, one to each: and every several gate was of one several pearl. And the street of the city was pure gold, as it were transparent glass. And I saw no temple therein. For the Lord God Almighty is the temple thereof, and the Lamb. And the city hath no need of the sun, nor of the moon, to shine in it. For the glory of God hath enlightened it, and the Lamb is the lamp thereof. And I heard a great voice from the throne, saying: Behold the tabernacle of God with men, and he will dwell with them. And they shall be his people; and God himself with them shall be their God. And God shall wipe away all tears from their eyes: and death shall be no more, nor mourning, nor crying, nor sorrow shall be any more, for the former things are passed away. And he that sat on the throne, said: Behold, I make all things new. And he said to me: Write, for these words are most faithful and true. And he said to me: It is done. I am Alpha and Omega; the beginning and the end. To him that thirsteth, I will give of the fountain of the water of life, freely. He that shall overcome shall possess these things, and I will be his God; and he shall be my son.

(Isa. 65.) There shall not enter into it any thing defiled, or that worketh abomination or maketh a lie, but they that are written in the book of life of the Lamb. For behold I create new heavens, and a new earth: and the former things shall not be in remembrance, and they shall not come upon the heart. But you shall be glad and rejoice for ever in these things, which I create: for behold I create Jerusalem a rejoicing, and the people thereof joy. And I will rejoice in Jerusalem, and joy in my people, and the voice of weeping shall no more be heard in her, nor the voice of crying.

Q. What words should we bear always in mind?
See "L. of C.," p. 50, No. 11.

(Ex. 15. A. M. 2513.) Moses brought Israel from the Red Sea, and they went forth into the wilderness of Sur: and they marched three days through the wilderness, and found no water. And they came into Mara, and they could not drink the waters of Mara, because they were bitter: whereupon he gave a name also agreeable to the place, calling it Mara, that is, bitterness. And the people murmured against Moses, saying: What shall we drink? But he cried to the Lord, and he shewed him a tree, which when he had cast into the waters, they were turned into sweetness. There he appointed him ordinances, and judgments, and there he proved him, saying: If thou wilt hear the voice of the Lord thy God, and do what is right before him, and obey his commandments, and keep all his precepts, none of the evils that I laid upon Egypt, will I bring upon thee: for I am the Lord thy healer.

PREFACE.

(Luke 1.) FORASMUCH as many have taken in hand to set forth in order a narration of the things that have been accomplished among us; According as they have delivered them unto us, who from the beginning, were eyewitnesses and ministers of the word. It seemed good to me also, having diligently attained to all things from the beginning, to write to thee in order, most excellent Theophilus, That thou mayest know the verity of those words in which thou hast been instructed.

(John 1.) In the beginning was the Word, and the Word was with God, and the Word was God. The same was in the beginning with God. All things were made by him: and without him was made nothing that was made. In him was life, and the life was the light of men. And the light shineth in darkness, and the darkness did not comprehend it. There was a man sent from God, whose name was John. This man came for a witness, to give testimony of the light, that all men might believe through him. He was not the light, but was to give testimony of the light. That was the true light, which enlighteneth every man that cometh into this world. He was in the world, and the world was made by him, and the world knew him not. He came unto his own, and his own received him not. But as many as received him, he gave them power to be made the sons of God, to them that believe in his name. Who are born, not of blood, nor of the will of the flesh, nor of the will of man, but of God. And the Word was made flesh, and dwelt among us, (and we saw his glory, the glory as it were of the only-begotten of the Father) full of grace and truth.

LIFE OF CHRIST.

PART I.

CHRIST'S BIRTH AND CHILDHOOD.

1. (Oct., 15 ms. B. B. C. Luke 1.) There was in the days of Herod, the king of Judea, a certain priest named Zachary, of the course of Abia; and his wife was of the daughters of Aaron, and her name Elizabeth. And they were both just before God, walking in all the commandments and justifications of the Lord without blame. And they had no son, for that Elizabeth was barren, and they both were well advanced in years. And it came to pass, when he executed the priestly function in the order of his course before God, According to the custom of the priestly office, it was his lot to offer incense, going into the temple of the Lord. And all the multitude of the people was praying without, at the hour of incense. And there appeared to him an angel of the Lord, standing on the right side of the altar of incense. And Zachary seeing him, was troubled, and fear fell upon him. But the angel said to him: Fear not, Zachary, for thy prayer is heard; and thy wife Elizabeth shall bear thee a son, and thou shalt call his name John: And thou shalt have joy and gladness, and many shall rejoice in his nativity.

2. For he shall be great before the Lord; and shall drink no wine nor strong drink: and he shall be filled with the Holy Ghost, even from his mother's womb. And he shall convert many of the children of Israel to the Lord their God. And he shall go before him in the spirit and power of Elias; that he may turn the hearts of the fathers unto the children, and the incredulous to the wisdom of the just, to prepare unto the Lord a perfect people.

3. And Zachary said to the Angel: Whereby shall I know this? for I am an old man, and my wife is advanced in years. And the angel answering, said to him: I am Gabriel, who stand before God; and am sent to speak to thee, and to bring thee these good tidings. And behold, thou shalt be dumb, and shalt not be able to speak until the day wherein these things shall come to pass, because thou hast not believed my words, which shall be fulfilled in their time. And the people was waiting for Zachary; and they wondered that he tarried so long in the temple. And when he came out, he could not speak to them: and they understood that he had seen a vision in the temple. And he made signs to them, and remained dumb. And it came to pass, after the days of his office were accomplished, he departed to his own house. And after those days, Elizabeth his wife conceived, and hid herself five months, saying: Thus hath the Lord dealt with me in the days wherein he hath had regard to take away my reproach among men.

4. (Mar., 9 ms. B. B. C.) And in the sixth month, the angel Gabriel was sent from God into a city of Galilee, called Nazareth, To a virgin espoused to a man whose name was Joseph, of the house of David; and the virgin's name was Mary. And the Angel being come in, said unto her: Hail, full of grace, the Lord is with thee: blessed art thou among women. Who having heard, was troubled at his saying, and thought with herself what manner of salutation this should be. And the Angel said to her: Fear not Mary, for thou hast found grace with God. Behold thou shalt conceive in thy womb, and shalt bring forth a son; and thou shalt call his name Jesus. He shall be great, and shall be called the son of the most High; and the Lord God shall give unto him the throne of David his father; and he shall reign in the house of Jacob for ever. And of his kingdom there shall be no end. And Mary said to the Angel: How shall this be done, because I know not man? And the Angel answering, said to her: the Holy Ghost shall come upon thee, and the power of the most High shall overshadow thee: And therefore also the Holy which shall be born of thee shall be called the Son of God. And behold thy cousin Elizabeth, she also hath conceived a son in her old age; and this is the sixth month with her that is called barren: Because no word shall be impossible with God. And Mary said: Behold the handmaid of the Lord; be it done to me according to thy word. And the Angel departed from her.

5. And Mary rising up in those days, went into the hill country with haste into a city of Juda. And she entered into the house of Zachary, and saluted Elizabeth. And it came to pass, that when Eliza-

beth heard the salutation of Mary, the infant leaped in her womb. And Elizabeth was filled with the Holy Ghost: And she cried out with a loud voice, and said: Blessed art thou among women, and blessed is the fruit of thy womb. And whence is this to me, that the mother of my Lord should come to me? For behold as soon as the voice of thy salutation sounded in my ears, the infant in my womb leaped for joy. And blessed art thou that hast believed, because those things shall be accomplished that were spoken to thee by the Lord. And Mary said: My soul doth magnify the Lord. And my spirit hath rejoiced in God my Saviour. Because he hath regarded the humility of his handmaid; for behold from henceforth all generations shall call me blessed. Because he that is mighty, hath done great things to me; and holy is his name. And his mercy is from generation unto generations, to them that fear him. He hath shewed might in his arm: he hath scattered the proud in the conceit of their heart. He hath put down the mighty from their seat, and hath exalted the humble. He hath filled the hungry with good things; and the rich he hath sent empty away. He hath received Israel his servant, being mindful of his mercy. As he spoke to our fathers, to Abraham and to his seed for ever. And Mary abode with her about three months; and she returned to her own house.

6. (June, 6 ms. B. B. C.) Now Elizabeth's full time of being delivered was come, and she brought forth a son. And her neighbors and kinsfolks heard that the Lord had shewed his great mercy towards her, and they congratulated with her.

7. Now it came to pass, that on the eighth day they came to circumcise the child, and they called him by his father's name Zachary. And his mother answering, said: Not so; but he shall be called John. And they said to her: There is none of thy kindred that is called by this name. And they made signs to his father, how he would have him called. And demanding a writing-table, he wrote, saying: John is his name. And they all wondered. And immediately his mouth was opened, and his tongue *loosed*, and he spoke, blessing God. And fear came upon all their neighbors; and all these things were noised abroad over all the hill-country of Judea. And all they that had heard them laid them up in their heart, saying: What an one, think ye, shall this child be? For the hand of the Lord was with him. And Zachary his father was filled with the Holy Ghost; and he prophesied, saying: Blessed be the Lord God of Israel; because he hath visited and wrought the redemption of his people: And hath raised up an horn of salvation to us,

in the house of David his servant. As he spoke by the mouth of his holy prophets, who are from the beginning. Salvation from our enemies, and from the hand of all that hate us. To perform mercy to our fathers, and to remember his holy testament. The oath, which he swore to Abraham our father, that he would grant to us, That being delivered from the hand of our enemies, we may serve him without fear, In holiness and justice before him, all our days. And thou, child, shall be called the prophet of the Highest: for thou shalt go before the face of the Lord to prepare his ways. To give knowledge of salvation to his people, unto the remission of their sins. Through the bowels of the mercy of our God, in which the Orient from on high hath visited us. To enlighten them that sit in darkness, and in the shadow of death: to direct our feet into the way of peace. And the child grew, and was strengthened in spirit; and was in the deserts until the day of his manifestation to Israel.

8. (Mat. 1.) Now the generation of Christ was in this wise. When as his mother Mary was espoused to Joseph, before they came together, she was found with child, of the Holy Ghost. Whereupon Joseph her husband, being a just man, and not willing publicly to expose her, was minded to put her away privately. But while he thought on these things, behold the Angel of the Lord appeared to him in his sleep, saying: Joseph, son of David, fear not to take unto thee Mary thy wife, for that which is conceived in her, is of the Holy Ghost. And she shall bring forth a son: and thou shalt call his name Jesus. For he shall save his people from their sins. Now all this was done that it might be fulfilled which the Lord spoke by the prophet, saying: *Behold a virgin - shall be with child, and bring forth a son, and they shall call his name Emmanuel*, which being interpreted is, *God with us.* And Joseph rising up from sleep, did as the Angel of the Lord had commanded him, and took unto him his wife. And he knew her not till she brought forth her first-born son: and he called his name Jesus.

9. (Luke 2.) And it came to pass, that in those days there went out a decree from Cesar Augustus, that the whole world should be enrolled. This enrolling was first made by Cyrinius, the governor of Syria. And all went to be enrolled, every one into his own city. And Joseph also went up from Galilee, out of the city of Nazareth into Judea, to the city of David, which is called Bethlehem, because he was of the house and family of David, to be enrolled with Mary his espoused wife, who was with child. And it came to pass, that when they were there, her days were accomplished, that

she should be delivered. And she brought forth her first-born son, and wrapped him up in swaddling clothes, and laid him in a manger; because there was no room for them in the inn. And there were in the same country shepherds watching, and keeping the night-watches over their flock. And behold an angel of the Lord stood by them, and the brightness of God shone round about them; and they feared with a great fear. And the Angel said to them: Fear not; for, behold, I bring you good tidings of great joy, that shall be to all the people: For, this day, is born to you a Saviour, who is Christ the Lord, in the city of David. And this shall be a sign unto you. You shall find the infant wrapped in swaddling-clothes, and laid in a manger. And suddenly there was with the angel a multitude of the heavenly army, praising God, and saying: Glory to God in the highest; and on earth peace to men of good-will. And it came to pass, after the angels departed from them into heaven, the shepherds said one to another: Let us go over to Bethlehem, and let us see this word that is come to pass, which the Lord hath shewed to us. And they came with haste; and they found Mary and Joseph, and the infant lying in the manger. And seeing, they understood of the word that had been spoken to them concerning this child. And all that heard, wondered; and at those things that were told them by the shepherds. But Mary kept all these words, pondering *them* in her heart. And the shepherds returned, glorifying and praising God, for all the things they had heard and seen, as it was told unto them.

10. (1 Jan., A. D. 1.) And after eight days were accomplished, that the child should be circumcised, his name was called Jesus, which was called by the angel, before he was conceived in the womb. And after the days of her purification according to the law of Moses, were accomplished, they carried him to Jerusalem, to present him to the Lord. As it is written in the law of the Lord: *Every male opening the womb shall be called holy to the Lord.* And to offer a sacrifice, according as it is written in the law of the Lord, a pair of turtle doves, or two young pigeons.

11. And behold there was a man in Jerusalem named Simeon, and this man was just and devout, waiting for the consolation of Israel; and the Holy Ghost was in him. And he had received an answer from the Holy Ghost, that he should not see death, before he had seen the Christ of the Lord. And he came by the Spirit into the temple. And when his parents brought in the child Jesus, to do for him according to the custom of the law, He also took him into his arms, and blessed God, and said:

Now thou dost dismiss thy servant, O Lord, according to thy word in peace; Because my eyes have seen thy salvation, Which thou hast prepared before the face of all peoples: A light to the revelation of the Gentiles, and the glory of thy people Israel. And his father and mother were wondering at those things which were spoken concerning him. And Simeon blessed them, and said to Mary his mother: Behold this *child* is set for the fall, and for the resurrection of many in Israel, and for a sign which shall be contradicted; And thy own soul a sword shall pierce, that, out of many hearts, thoughts may be revealed. And there was one Anna, a prophetess, the daughter of Phanuel, of the tribe of Aser; she was far advanced in years, and had lived with her husband seven years from her virginity. And she was a widow until fourscore and four years; who departed not from the temple, by fastings and prayers serving night and day. Now she, at the same hour, coming in, confessed to the Lord; and spoke of him to all that looked for the redemption of Israel. And after they had performed all things according to the law of the Lord, they returned into Galilee, to their city Nazareth.

12. (6 Jan., A. D. 2. Mat. 2.) When Jesus therefore was born in Bethlehem of Juda, in the days of king Herod, behold, there came wise men from the East to Jerusalem. Saying, Where is he that is born King of the Jews? For we have seen his star in the East, and are come to adore him. And king Herod hearing this, was troubled, and all Jerusalem with him. And assembling together all the chief priests and the Scribes of the people, he inquired of them where Christ should be born. But they said to him: In Bethlehem of Juda. For so it is written by the prophet: *And thou Bethlehem the land of Juda art not the least among the princes of Juda: for out of thee shall come forth the captain that shall rule my people Israel.* Then Herod, privately calling the wise men, learned diligently of them the time of the star which appeared to them; And sending them into Bethlehem, said: Go and diligently inquire after the child, and when you have found him, bring me word again, that I also may come and adore him. Who having heard the king, went their way; and behold the star which they had seen in the East, went before them, until it came and stood over where the child was. And seeing the star they rejoiced with exceeding great joy. And entering into the house, they found the child with Mary his mother, and falling down they adored him; and opening their treasures, they offered him gifts; gold, frankincense, and myrrh. And having received an answer in sleep that they should not return to Herod, they went back another way into their country.

13. Now after they were departed, behold an Angel of the Lord appeared in sleep to Joseph, saying: Arise, and take the child and his mother, and fly into Egypt: and be there until I shall tell thee. For it will come to pass that Herod will seek the child to destroy him. Who arose, and took the child and his mother by night, and retired into Egypt: and he was there until the death of Herod: That it might be fulfilled which the Lord spoke by the prophet, saying: *Out of Egypt have I called my son.*

14. Then Herod perceiving that he was deluded by the wise men, was exceeding angry; and sending killed all the men-children that were in Bethlehem, and in all the borders thereof, from two years old and under, according to the time which he had diligently inquired of the wise men. Then was fulfilled that which was spoken by Jeremias the prophet, saying: *A voice in Rama was heard, lamentation and great mourning; Rachel bewailing her children, and would not be comforted, because they are not.*

15. (A. D. 7 or 8.) But when Herod was dead, behold an Angel of the Lord appeared in sleep to Joseph in Egypt, Saying: Arise, and take the child and his mother, and go into the land of Israel. For they are dead that sought the life of the child. Who arose, and took the child and his mother, and came into the land of Israel. But hearing that Archelaus reigned in Judea in the room of Herod his father, he was afraid to go thither: and being warned in sleep retired into the quarters of Galilee. And coming he dwelt in a city called Nazareth: that it might be fulfilled which was said by the prophets: That he shall be called a Nazarite. And the child grew, and waxed strong, full of wisdom; and the grace of God was in him.

16. (Luke 2. A. D. 12.) Now his parents went every year to Jerusalem, at the solemn day of the pasch, And when he was twelve years old, they going up into Jerusalem, according to the custom of the feast, and having fulfilled the days, when they returned, the child Jesus remained in Jerusalem; and his parents knew it not. And thinking that he was in the company, they came a day's journey, and sought him among their kinsfolks and acquaintance. And not finding him, they returned into Jerusalem, seeking him. And it came to pass, that, after three days, they found him in the temple, sitting in the midst of the doctors, hearing them, and asking them questions. And all that heard him were astonished at his wisdom and his answers. And seeing *him*, they wondered. And his mother said to him: Son, why hast thou done so to us? behold thy father and I have sought thee sorrowing. And he said to them: How is it that you sought me? did you not know, that I must be about my father's business? And they understood not the word that he had spoke unto them. And he went down with them, and came to Nazareth, and was subject to them. And his mother kept all these words in her heart. And Jesus advanced in wisdom, and age, and grace with God and men.

PART II.

CHRIST'S PUBLIC LIFE.

CHAPTER I.

PREPARATION.

1. (Luke 3. A. D. 30.) Now in the fifteenth year of the reign of Tiberius Cesar, Pontius Pilate being governor of Judea, and Herod being tetrarch of Galilee, and Philip his brother tetrarch of Iturea, and the country of Trachonitis, and Lysanias tetrarch of Abilina; Under the high-priests Annas and Caiphas; the word of the Lord was made unto John, the son of Zachary, in the desert. And he came into all the country about the Jordan, preaching the baptism of penance for the remission of sins; And saying: Do penance: for the kingdom of heaven is at hand. As it is written in Isaias the prophet: *Behold I send my angel before thy face, who shall prepare the way before thee. A voice of one crying in the desert: Prepare ye the way of the Lord, make straight his paths. Every valley shall be filled; and every mountain and hill shall be brought low; and the crooked shall be made straight; and the rough ways plain; And all flesh shall see the salvation of God.*

(Mat. 3.) And the same John had his garment of camels' hair, and a leathern girdle about his loins: and his meat was locusts and wild honey. Then went out to him Jerusalem and all Judea, and all the country about Jordan: And were baptized by him in the Jordan, confessing their sins.

2. And seeing many of the Pharisees and Sadducees coming to his baptism, he said to them: Ye brood of vipers, who hath shewed you to flee from the wrath to come? Bring forth therefore fruit worthy of penance. And think not to say within yourselves, We have Abraham for our father. For I tell you that God is able of these stones to raise up children to Abraham. For now the axe is laid to the root of the trees. Every tree therefore that doth not yield good fruit, shall be cut down, and cast into the fire.

(Luke 3.) And the people asked him, saying: What then shall we do? And he answering, said to them: he that hath two coats, let him give to him that hath none; and he that hath meat, let him do in like manner. And the publicans also came to be baptized, and said to him: Master, what shall we do? But he said to them: Do nothing more than that which is appointed you. And the soldiers also asked him, saying: and what shall we do? And he said to them: Do violence to no man; neither calumniate any man; and be content with your pay.

3. Now as the people was of opinion, and all were thinking in their hearts of John, that perhaps he might be the Christ; John answered, saying unto all: I indeed baptize you with water; but there shall come one mightier than I, the latchet of whose shoes I am not worthy to loose: he shall baptize you with the Holy Ghost, and with fire: Whose fan is in his hand, and he will purge his floor, and will gather the wheat into his barn; but the chaff he will burn with unquenchable fire. And many other things exhorting, did he preach to the people.

4. (Mat. 3.) Then cometh Jesus from Galilee to the Jordan, unto John, to be baptized by him. But John stayed him, saying: I ought to be baptized by thee, and comest thou to me? And Jesus answering, said to him: Suffer it to be so now. For so it becometh us to fulfill all justice. Then he suffered him. And Jesus being baptized, forthwith came out of the water: and lo, the heavens were opened to him: and he saw the Spirit of God descending as a dove, and coming upon him. And behold a voice from heaven, saying: This is my beloved Son, in whom I am well pleased.

5. (Mat. 4. A. D. 30.) Then Jesus was led by the spirit into the desert, to be tempted by the devil. And when he had fasted forty days and forty nights, afterwards he was hungry. And the tempter coming said to him: If thou be the Son of God, command that these stones be made bread. Who answered and said: It is written, *Not in bread alone doth man live, but in every word that proceedeth from the mouth of God.* Then the devil took him up into the holy city, and set him upon the pinnacle of the temple, And said to him: If thou be the Son of God, cast thyself down, for it is written: *That he hath given his Angels charge over thee, and in their hands shall they bear thee up,*

lest perhaps thou dash thy foot against a stone. Jesus said to him: *It is written again: Thou shalt not tempt the Lord thy God.* Again the devil took him up into a very high mountain, and shewed him all the kingdoms of the world, and the glory of them, And said to him: All these will I give thee, if falling down thou wilt adore me. Then Jesus saith to him: Be gone, satan: for it is written, *The Lord thy God shalt thou adore, and him only shalt thou serve.* Then the devil left him; and behold Angels came and ministered to him.

6. (John 1.) Now this is the testimony of John, when the Jews sent from Jerusalem priests and levites to him, to ask him: Who art thou? And he confessed, and did not deny: and he confessed: I am not the Christ. And then they asked him: What then? Art thou Elias? And he said: I am not. Art thou the prophet? And he answered: No. They said therefore unto him: Who art thou, that we may give an answer to them that sent us? What sayest thou of thyself? He said: *I am the voice of one crying in the wilderness, make straight the way of the Lord,* as said the prophet Isaias. And they that were sent, were of the Pharisees. And they asked him, and said to him: Why then dost thou baptize, if thou be not Christ, nor Elias, nor the prophet? John answered them, saying: I baptize with water; but there hath stood one in the midst of you, whom you know not. The same is he that shall come after me, who is preferred before me: the latchet of whose shoe I am not worthy to loose. These things were done in Bethania, beyond the Jordan, where John was baptizing.

CHAPTER II.

FIRST MANIFESTATIONS.

1. (John 1. A. D. 30.) The next day, John saw Jesus coming to him, and he saith: Behold the Lamb of God, behold him who taketh away the sin of the world. This is he, of whom I said: After me there cometh a man, who is preferred before me: because he was before me. And I knew him not, but that he may be made manifest in Israel, therefore am I come baptizing with water. And John gave testimony saying: I saw the spirit coming down, as a dove from heaven, and he remained upon him. And I knew him not; but he

who sent me to baptize with water, said to me: He upon whom thou shalt see the spirit descending, and remaining upon him, he it is that baptizeth with the Holy Ghost. And I saw, and I gave testimony, that this is the Son of God.

2. The next day again John stood, and two of his disciples. And beholding Jesus walking, he saith: Behold the Lamb of God. And the two disciples heard him speak and they followed Jesus. And Jesus turning and seeing them following him, saith to them: What seek you? Who said to him, Rabbi, (which is to say, being interpreted, Master,) where dwellest thou? He saith to them: Come and see. They came, and saw where he abode, and they staid with him that day: now it was about the tenth hour. And Andrew, the brother of Simon Peter, was one of the two who had heard of John, and followed him. He findeth first his brother Simon, and saith to him: We have found the Messias, which being interpreted, the Christ. And he brought him to Jesus. And Jesus looking upon him, said: Thou art Simon the son of Jona: Thou shalt be called Cephas, which is intrepreted Peter. On the following day, he would go forth into Galilee, and he findeth Philip. And Jesus saith unto him: Follow me. Now Philip was of Bethsaida, the city of Andrew and Peter. Philip findeth Nathanael, and saith to him: We have found him of whom Moses in the law, and the prophets did write, Jesus the Son of Joseph of Nazareth. And Nathanael said to him: Can any thing of good come from Nazareth? Philip saith to him: Come and see. Jesus saw Nathanael coming to him: and he saith of him: Behold an Israelite indeed, in whom there is no guile. Nathanael saith to him: Whence knowest thou me? Jesus answered, and said to him: Before that Philip called thee, when thou wast under the fig-tree, I saw thee. Nathanael answered him and said: Rabbi, thou art the Son of God, thou art the king of Israel. Jesus answered, and said to him: Because I said unto thee, I saw thee under the fig-tree, thou believest: greater things than these shalt thou see. And he saith to him: Amen, amen I say to you, you shall see the heaven opened, and the angels of God ascending and descending upon the son of man.

3. (John 2. A. D. 30.) Now the third day, there was a marriage in Cana of Galilee: and the mother of Jesus was there. And Jesus also was invited, and his disciples, to the marriage. And the wine failing, the mother of Jesus saith to him: They have no wine. And Jesus saith to her: Woman, what is it to me and to thee? my hour is not yet come. His mother saith to the waiters: Whatsoever he shall say,

to you, do ye. Now there were set there six water-pots of stone, according to the manner of the purifying of the Jews, containing two or three measures a piece. Jesus saith to them: Fill the water-pots with water. And they filled them up to the brim. And Jesus saith to them: Draw out now, and carry to the chief steward of the feast. And they carried it. And when the chief steward had tasted the water made wine, and knew not whence it was, but the waiters knew who had drawn the water; the chief steward calleth the bridegroom, And saith to him: Every man at first setteth forth good wine, and when men have well drunk, then that which is worse. But thou hast kept the good wine until now. This beginning of miracles did Jesus in Cana of Galilee; and manifested his glory, and his disciples believed in him. After this he went down to Capharnaum, he and his mother, and his brethren, and his disciples: and they remained there not many days. And the pasch of the Jews was at hand and Jesus went up to Jerusalem.

CHAPTER III.

JESUS AND JOHN.

1. (A. D. 81.) Now Jesus found in the temple them that sold oxen and sheep and doves, and the changers of money sitting. And when he had made, as it were, a scourge of little cords, he drove them all out of the temple, the sheep also and the oxen, and the money of the changers he poured out, and the tables he overthrew. And to them that sold doves he said: Take these things hence, and make not the house of my Father a house of traffic. And his disciples remembered, that it was written: *The zeal of thy house hath eaten me up.* The Jews, therefore, answered, and said to him: What sign dost thou show unto us, seeing thou dost these things? Jesus answered, and said to them: Destroy this temple, and in three days I will raise it up. The Jews then said: Six and forty years was this temple in building; and wilt thou raise it up in three days? But he spoke of the temple of his body. When therefore he was risen again from the dead, his disciples remembered, that he had said this, and they believed the scripture, and the word that Jesus had said.

2. Now when he was at Jerusalem, at the pasch, upon

the-festival day, many believed in his name, seeing his signs which he did. But Jesus did not trust himself unto them, for that he knew all men. And because he needed not that any should give testimony of man: for he knew what was in man.

3. (John 3. A. D. 31.) Now there was a man of the Pharisees, named Nicodemus, a ruler of the Jews. This man came to Jesus by night, and said to him: Rabbi, we know that thou art come a teacher from God; for no man can do these signs which thou dost, unless God be with him. Jesus answered and said to him: Amen, amen I say to thee, unless a man be born again, he cannot see the kingdom of God. Nicodemus saith to him: How can a man be born when he is old? can he enter a second time into his mother's womb, and be born again? Jesus answered: Amen, amen I say to thee, unless a man be born again of water and the Holy Ghost, he cannot enter into the kingdom of God. That which is born of the flesh, is flesh; and that which is born of the Spirit, is spirit. Wonder not, that I said to thee, you must be born again. The Spirit breatheth where he will; and thou hearest his voice, but thou knowest not whence he cometh, and whither he goeth: so is every one that is born of the Spirit. Nicodemus answered, and said to him: How can these things be done? Jesus answered, and said to him: Art thou a master in Israel, and knowest not these things? Amen, amen I say to thee, that we speak what we know, and we testify what we have seen, and you receive not our testimony. If I have spoken to you earthly things, and you believe not; how will you believe, if I shall speak to you heavenly things? And no man hath ascended into heaven, but he that descended from heaven, the son of man who is in heaven. And as Moses lifted up the serpent in the desert, so must the son of man be lifted up: That whosoever believeth in him, may not perish; but may have life everlasting. For God so loved the world, as to give his only-begotten Son; that whosoever believeth in him, may not perish, but may have life everlasting. For God sent not his son into the world, to judge the world, but that the world may be saved by him. He that believeth in him is not judged. But he that doth not believe, is already judged: because he believeth not in the name of the only begotten son of God. And this is the judgment: because the light is come into the world, and men love darkness rather than the light: for their works were evil. For every one that doth evil hateth the light, and cometh not to the light, that his works may not be reproved. But he that doth truth, cometh to the light, that his works may be made manifest, because they are done in

God. After these things Jesus and his disciples came into the land of Judea: and there he abode with them, and baptized.

4. Now John also was baptizing in Ennon near Salim; because there was much water there; and they came and were baptized. For John was not yet cast into prison. And there arose a question between some of John's disciples and the Jews concerning purification: And they came to John, and said to him: Rabbi, he that was with thee beyond the Jordan, to whom thou gavest testimony, behold he baptizeth, and all men come to him. John answered and said: A man cannot receive any thing, unless it be given him from heaven. You yourselves do bear me witness, that I said, I am not Christ, but that I am sent before him. He that hath the bride, is the bridegroom: but the friend of the bridegroom, who standeth and heareth him, rejoiceth with joy because of the bridegroom's voice. This my joy therefore is fulfilled. He must increase, but I must decrease. He that cometh from above, is above all. He that is of the earth, of the earth he is; and of the earth he speaketh. He that cometh from heaven, is above all. And what he hath seen and heard, that he testifieth: and no man receiveth his testimony. He that hath received his testimony, hath set to his seal that God is true. For he whom God hath sent, speaketh the words of God: for God doth not give the spirit by measure. The Father loveth the Son: and he hath given all things into his hand. He that believeth in the Son, hath life everlasting; but he that believeth not the Son, shall not see life; but the wrath of God abideth on him.

(John 4.) When Jesus therefore understood that the Pharisees had heard that Jesus maketh more disciples, and baptizeth *more* than John, (Though Jesus *himself* did not baptize, but his disciples,) He left Judea, and went again into Galilee.

5. (Luke 3.) But Herod the tetrarch, when he was reproved by John for Herodias, his brother's wife, and for all the evils which Herod had done; He added this also above all, and shut up John in prison.

6. (John 4. A. D. 31.) Now Jesus was of necessity to pass through Samaria. He cometh therefore to a city of Samaria, which is called Sichar, near the land which Jacob gave to his son Joseph. Now Jacob's well was there. Jesus therefore being wearied with his journey, sat thus on the well. It was about the sixth hour. There cometh a woman of Samaria, to draw water. Jesus saith to her: give me to drink. For his disciples were gone into the city to buy meats. Then that Samaritan woman saith to him: How dost thou, being a Jew,

ask of me to drink, who am a Samaritan woman? For the Jews do not communicate with the Samaritans. Jesus answered, and said to her: If thou didst know the gift of God, and who he is that saith to thee, Give me to drink; thou perhaps wouldst have asked of him, and he would have given thee living water. The woman saith to him: Sir, thou hast nothing wherein to draw, and the well is deep; from whence then hast thou living water? Art thou greater than our father Jacob, who gave us the well, and drank thereof himself, and his children, and his cattle? Jesus answered, and said to her: Whosoever drinketh of this water, shall thirst again; but he that shall drink of the water that I will give him, shall not thirst for ever: But the water that I will give him, shall become in him a fountain of water, springing up into life everlasting. The woman saith to him: Sir, give me this water, that I may not thirst, nor come hither to draw. Jesus saith to her: Go, call thy husband, and come hither. The woman answered, and said: I have no husband. Jesus said to her: Thou hast said well, I have no husband: For thou hast had five husbands: and he whom thou now hast, is not thy husband. This thou hast said truly. The woman saith to him: Sir, I perceive that thou art a prophet. Our fathers adored on this mountain, and you say, that at Jerusalem is the place where men must adore. Jesus saith to her: Woman, believe me, that the hour cometh, when you shall neither on this mountain, nor in Jerusalem, adore the Father. You adore that which you know not: we adore that which we know; for salvation is of the Jews. But the hour cometh, and now is, when the true adorers shall adore the Father in spirit and in truth. For the Father also seeketh such to adore him. God is a spirit; and they that adore him, must adore him in spirit and in truth. The woman saith to him: I know that the Messias cometh (who is called Christ); therefore, when he is come, he will tell us all things. Jesus saith to her: I am he, who am speaking with thee. And immediately his disciples came; and they wondered that he talked with the woman. Yet no man said: What seekest thou? or, why talkest thou with her? The woman therefore left her waterpot, and went her way into the city, and saith to the men there: Come, and see a man who has told me all things whatsoever I have done. Is not he the Christ? They went therefore out of the city, and came unto him. In the meantime the disciples prayed him, saying: Rabbi, eat. But he said to them: I have meat to eat, which you know not. The disciples therefore said one to another: Hath any man brought him to eat? Jesus saith to them: My meat is to do the will of him that sent me, that I may perfect his work. Do not you say, There are yet four months, and then the harvest cometh? Behold, I say to you, lift up your eyes, and see the countries; for they are white already to harvest. And he that reapeth receiveth wages, and gathereth fruit unto life everlasting: that both he that soweth, and he that reapeth, may rejoice together. For in this is the saying true: That it is one man that soweth, and it is another that reapeth. I have sent you to reap that in which you did not labour: others have laboured, and you have entered into their labours. Now of that city many of the Samaritans believed in him, for the word of the woman giving testimony: He told me all things whatsoever I have done. So when the Samaritans were come to him, they desired that he would tarry there. And he abode there two days. And many more believed in him because of his own word. And they said to the woman: We now believe, not for thy saying: for we ourselves have heard him, and know that this is indeed the Saviour of the world.

7. Now after two days, he departed thence, and went into Galilee. For Jesus himself gave testimony that a prophet hath no honour in his own country. And when he was come into Galilee, the Galileans received him, having seen all the things he had done at Jerusalem on the festival day; for they also went to the festival day. He came again therefore into Cana of Galilee, where he made the water wine. And there was a certain ruler, whose son was sick at Capharnaum. He having heard, that Jesus was come from Judea into Galilee, went to him, and prayed him to come down, and heal his son; for he was at the point of death. Jesus therefore said to him: Unless you see signs and wonders, you believe not. The ruler saith to him: Lord, come down before that my son die. Jesus saith to him: Go thy way; thy son liveth. The man believed the word which Jesus said to him, and went his way. And as he was going down, his servants met him; and they brought word, saying, that his son lived. He asked therefore of them the hour wherein he grew better. And they said to him: Yesterday, at the seventh hour, the fever left him. The father therefore knew, that it was at the same hour that Jesus said to him, Thy son liveth; and himself believed, and his whole house. This is again the second miracle that Jesus did, when he was come out of Judea into Galilee.

8. (Luke 4. A. D. 31.) And Jesus returned in the power of the spirit, into Galilee, and the fame of him went out through

the whole country. And he taught in their synagogues, saying: The time is accomplished, and the kingdom of God is at hand: repent, and believe the gospel. He was magnified by all. And he came to Nazareth, where he was brought up: and he went into the synagogue, according to his custom, on the sabbath day; and he rose up to read. And the book of Isaias the prophet was delivered unto him. And as he unfolded the book, he found the place where it was written: *The spirit of the Lord is upon me. Wherefore he hath anointed me to preach the gospel to the poor, he hath sent me to heal the contrite of heart, To preach deliverance to the captives, and sight to the blind, to set at liberty them that are bruised, to preach the acceptable year of the Lord, and the day of reward.* And when he had folded the book, he restored it to the minister, and sat down. And the eyes of all in the synagogue were fixed on him. And he began to say to them: This day is fulfilled this scripture in your ears. And all gave testimony to him: and they wondered at the words of grace that proceeded from his mouth, and they said: Is not this the son of Joseph? And he said to them: Doubtless you will say to me this similitude: Physician, heal thyself: as great things as we have heard done in Capharnaum, do also here in thy own country. And he said: Amen I say to you, that no prophet is accepted in his own country. In truth I say to you, there were many widows in the days of Elias in Israel, when heaven was shut up three years and six months, when there was a great famine throughout all the earth. And to none of them was Elias sent, but to 'Sarepta of Sidon, to a widow woman. And there were many lepers in Israel in the time of Eliseus the prophet: and none of them was cleansed but Naaman the Syrian. And all they in the synagogue, hearing these things, were filled with anger. And they rose up and thrust him out of the city; and they brought him to the brow of the hill, whereon their city was built, that they might cast him down headlong. But he passing through the midst of them, went his way.

9. (Mat. 4. A. D. 31.) Now when Jesus had heard that John was delivered up, he retired into Galilee: And leaving the city Nazareth, he came and dwelt in Capharnaum on the seacoast, in the borders of Zabulon and of Nephthalim; That it might be fulfilled which was said by Isaias the prophet: *Land of Zabulon and land of Nephthalim, the way of the sea beyond the Jordan, Galilee of the Gentiles: The people that sat in darkness, hath seen great light: and to them that sat in the region of the shadow of death, light is sprung up.*

(Mark 1.) And passing by

the sea of Galilee, he saw Simon and Andrew his brother, casting nets into the sea (for they were fishermen.) And Jesus said to them: Come after me, and I will make you to become fishers of men. And immediately leaving their nets, they followed him. And going on from thence a little farther, he saw James the son of Zebedee, and John his brother, who also were mending their nets in the ship: And forthwith he called them. And leaving their father Zebedee in the ship with his hired men, they followed him.

10. Now they entered into Capharnaum, and forthwith upon the sabbath days going into the synagogue, he taught them. And they were astonished at his doctrine. For he was teaching them as one having power, and not as the scribes. And there was in their synagogue a man with an unclean spirit; and he cried out. Saying: What have we to do with thee, Jesus of Nazareth? art thou come to destroy us? I know who thou art, the Holy one of God. And Jesus threatened him, saying: Speak no more, and go out of the man. And the unclean spirit tearing him, and crying out with a loud voice, went out of him. And they were all amazed, insomuch that they questioned among themselves, saying: What thing is this? what is this new doctrine? for with power he commandeth even the unclean spirits, and they obey him. And the fame of him was spread forthwith into all the country of Galilee.

11. But immediately going out of the synagogue they came into the house of Simon and Andrew, with James and John. And Simon's wife's mother lay in a fit of a fever: and forthwith they tell him of her. And coming to her, he lifted her up, taking her by the hand; and immediately the fever left her, and she ministered unto them. (Luke 4.) And when the sun was down, all they that had any sick with divers diseases, brought them to him. But he laying his hands on every one of them, healed them. And devils went out from many, crying out and saying: Thou art the son of God. And rebuking them he suffered them not to speak, for they knew that he was Christ. And when it was day, going out he went into a desert place, and the multitudes sought him, and came unto him: and they stayed him that he should not depart from them. To whom he said: To other cities also I must preach the kingdom of God: for therefore am I sent. And he was preaching in the synagogues of Galilee.

12. (Luke 5.) Now it came to pass, that when the multitudes pressed upon him to hear the word of God, he stood by the lake of Genesareth, And saw two ships standing by the lake: but the fishermen were gone out of them, and were washing their nets. And going into one of the ships that was Simon's, he desired him to draw back a little from the land. And sitting he taught the multitudes out of the ship. Now when he had ceased to speak, he said to Simon: Launch out into the deep, and let down your nets for a draught. And Simon answering said to him: Master, we have laboured all the night, and have taken nothing: but at thy word I will let down the net. And when they had done this, they enclosed a very great multitude of fishes, and their net broke. And they beckoned to their partners that were in the other ship, that they should come and help them. And they came, and filled both the ships, so that they were almost sinking. Which when Simon Peter saw, he fell down at Jesus's knees, saying: Depart from me, for I am a sinful man, O Lord. For he was wholly astonished, and all that were with him, at the draught of the fishes which they had taken. And so were also James and John the sons of Zebedee, who were Simon's partners. And Jesus saith to Simon: Fear not: from henceforth thou shalt catch men. And having brought their ships to land, leaving all things, they followed him.

13. (Mark 1.) Now there came a leper to him, beseeching him, and kneeling down said to him: If thou wilt, thou canst make me clean. And Jesus having compassion on him, stretched forth his hand; and touching him, saith to him: I will. Be thou made clean. And when he had spoken, immediately the leprosy departed from him, and he was made clean. And he strictly charged him, and forthwith sent him away. And he saith to him: See thou tell no one; but go, shew thyself to the high-priest, and offer for thy cleansing the things that Moses commanded, for a testimony to them. But he being gone out, began to publish and to blaze abroad the word: so that he could not openly go into the city, but was without in desert places: and they flocked to him from all sides.

14. (Luke 5.) Now it came to pass on a certain day, as he sat teaching, that there were also Pharisees and doctors of the law sitting by, that were come out of every town of Galilee, and Judea and Jerusalem: and the power of the Lord was to heal them. And behold, men brought in a bed a man, who had the palsy: and they sought means to bring him in, and to lay him before him. And when they could not find by what way they might bring him in, because of the multitude, they went up upon the roof, and let him down through the tiles with his bed into the midst before Jesus. Whose faith when he saw, he said: Man, thy sins are forgiven thee. And the scribes and Pharisees began to think, say-

ing; Who is this who speaketh blasphemies? Who can forgive sins, but God alone? And when Jesus knew their thoughts, answering, he said to them: What is it you think in your hearts? Which is easier to say, Thy sins are forgiven thee; or to say, Arise and walk? But that you may know that the son of man hath power on earth to forgive sins (he saith to the sick of the palsy) I say to thee, Arise, take up thy bed, and go into thy house. And immediately rising up before them, he took up the bed on which he lay; and he went away to his own house, glorifying God. And all were astonished; and they glorified God. And they were filled with fear, saying; We have seen wonderful things to-day.

15. (Mark 9.) And when Jesus passed on from thence, he saw a man sitting in the custom-house, named Matthew; and he saith to him: Follow me. And he arose up and followed him.

(Luke 5.) And Levi made him a great feast in his own house; and there was a great company of publicans, and of others, that were at table with them. But the Pharisees and scribes murmured, saying to his disciples: Why do you eat and drink with publicans and sinners? And Jesus answering, said to them: They that are whole, need not the physician: but they that are sick. I came not to call the just, but sinners to penance. And they said to him: Why do the disciples of John fast often, and make prayers, and the disciples of the Pharisees in like manner; but thine eat and drink? To whom he said: Can you make the children of the bridegroom fast, whilst the bridegroom is with them? But the days will come, when the bridegroom shall be taken away from them, then shall they fast in those days. And he spoke also a similitude to them: That no man putteth a piece from a new garment upon an old garment; otherwise he both rendeth the new, and the piece taken from the new agreeth not with the old. And no man putteth new wine into old bottles: otherwise the new wine will break the bottles, and it will be spilled, and the bottles will be lost. But new wine must be put into new bottles; and both are preserved. And no man drinking old, hath presently a mind to new: for he saith, The old is better.

CHAPTER IV.

MIRACLES, DOCTRINE AND PARABLES.

1. (John 5. A. D. 31.) AFTER these things was a festival day of the Jews, and Jesus went up to Jerusalem. Now there is at Jerusalem a pond, *called* Probatica, which in Hebrew is named Bethsaida, having five porches. In these lay a great multitude of sick, of blind, of lame, of withered; waiting for the moving of the water. And an Angel of the Lord descended at certain times into the pond; and the water was moved. And he that went down first into the pond after the motion of the water, was made whole, of whatsoever infirmity he lay under. And there was a certain man there, that had been eight and thirty years under his infirmity. Him when Jesus had seen lying, and knew that he had been now a long time, he saith to him: Wilt thou be made whole? The infirm man answered him: Sir, I have no man, when the water is troubled, to put me into the pond. For whilst I am coming, another goeth down before me. Jesus saith to him: Arise, take up thy bed, and walk. And immediately the man was made whole: and he took up his bed, and walked. And it was the sabbath that day. The Jews therefore said to him that was healed: It is the sabbath; it is not lawful for thee to take up thy bed. He answered them: He that made me whole, he said to me, Take up thy bed, and walk. They asked him therefore: Who is that man who said to thee, Take up thy bed, and walk? But he who was healed, knew not who it was; for Jesus went aside from the multitude standing in the place. Afterwards, Jesus findeth him in the temple, and saith to him: Behold thou art made whole: sin no more, lest some worse thing happen to thee. The man went his way, and told the Jews, that it was Jesus who had made him whole. Therefore did the Jews persecute Jesus, because he did these things on the sabbath. But Jesus answered them: My Father worketh until now; and I work. Hereupon therefore the Jews sought the more to kill him, because he did not only break the sabbath, but also said God was his Father, making himself equal to God.

2. Then Jesus answered, and said to them: Amen, amen, I say unto you, the Son cannot do any thing of himself, but what he seeth the father doing: for what things soever he doth, these the Son also doth in like manner. For the Father loveth the Son, and sheweth him all things which himself doth: and greater works than these will he shew him, that you may wonder. For as the Father raiseth up the dead, and giveth life: so the Son also giveth life to whom he will. For neither doth the Father judge any man, but hath given all judgment to the Son. That all men may honour the Son, as they honour the Father. He who honoureth not the Son, honoureth not the Father, who hath sent him. Amen, amen, I say unto you, that he who heareth my word, and believeth him that sent me, hath life everlasting; and cometh not into judgment, but is passed from death to life. Amen, amen, I say unto you, that the hour cometh, and now is, when the dead shall hear the voice of the Son of God, and they that hear shall live. For as the Father hath life in himself, so he hath given to the Son also to have life in himself: And he hath given him power to do judgment, because he is the son of man. Wonder not at this; for the hour cometh, wherein all that are in the graves shall hear the voice of the Son of God. And they that have done good things, shall come forth unto the resurrection of life; but they that have done evil, unto the resurrection of judgment. I cannot of myself do any thing. As I hear, so I judge: and my judgment is just; because I seek not my own will, but the will of him that sent me. If I bear witness of myself, my witness is not true. There is another that beareth witness of me; and I know that the witness which he witnesseth of me is true. You sent to John, and he gave testimony to the truth. But I receive not testimony from man; but I say these things, that you may be saved. He was a burning and a shining light; and you were willing for a time to rejoice in his light. But I have a greater testimony than that of John: for the works which the Father hath given me to perfect; the works themselves, which I do, give testimony of me, that the Father hath sent me. And the Father himself who hath sent me, hath given testimony of me: neither have you heard his voice at any time, nor seen his shape. And you have not his word abiding in you: for whom he hath sent, him you believe not. Search the Scriptures, for you think in them to have life everlasting; and the same are they that give testimony of me. And you will not come to me that you may have life. I receive not glory from men. But I know you, that you have not the love of God in you. I am come in the name of my Father, and you receive me not: if another shall come in his own name, him you will receive. How can you believe, who receive glory one from another: and the glory which is from God alone, you do not seek? Think not that I will accuse you to the Father. There is one that accuseth you, Moses, in whom you trust. For if you did believe Moses you would perhaps believe me also; for he wrote of me. But if you do not believe his writings, how will you believe my words?

3. (Mat. 12.) At that time Jesus went through the corn on the sabbath: and his disciples being hungry, began to pluck the ears, and to eat. And the Pharisees seeing them, said to him: Behold thy disciples do that which is not lawful to do on the sabbath days. But he said to them: have you not read what David did when he was hungry, and they that were with him: How he entered into the house of God, and did eat the loaves of proposition, which it was not lawful for him to eat, nor for them that were with him, but for the priests only? Or have ye not read in the law, that on the sabbath days the priests in the temple break the sabbath, and are without blame? But I tell you that there is here a greater than the temple. And if you knew what this meaneth: *I will have mercy, and not sacrifice:* you would never have condemned the innocent. For the son of man is Lord even of the sabbath.

4. (A. D. 31.) Now when he had passed from thence, he came into their synagogues. And behold there was a man who had a withered hand, and they asked him, saying: Is it lawful to heal on the sabbath days? that they might accuse him. But he said to them: What man shall there be among you, that hath one sheep: and if the same fall into a pit on the sabbath day, will he not take hold on it and lift it up? How much better is a man than a sheep? Therefore it is lawful to do a good deed on the sabbath days. Then he saith to the man: Stretch forth thy hand; and he stretched it forth, and it was restored to health even as the other. And the Pharisees going out made a consultation against him, how they might destroy him. But Jesus knowing it, retired from thence: and many followed him, and he healed them all. And he charged them that they should not make him known. That it might be fulfilled which was spoken by Isaias the prophet, saying: *Behold my servant whom I have chosen, my beloved in whom my soul hath been well pleased. I will put my spirit upon him, and he shall shew judgment to the gentiles. He shall not contend, nor cry out, neither shall any man hear his voice in the streets. The bruised reed he shall not break: and smoking flax he shall not extinguish: till he send forth judgment unto victory. And in his name the gentiles shall hope.*

5. (Luke 6.) Now it came to pass in those days, that he went out into a mountain to pray, and he passed the whole

night in the prayer of God. And when day was come, he called unto him his disciples; And he chose twelve of them (whom also he named Apostles): Simon, whom he surnamed Peter, and Andrew his brother, James and John, Philip and Bartholomew, Matthew and Thomas, James *the son* of Alpheus, and Simon who is called Zelotes, And Jude, *the brother* of James, and Judas Iscariot, who was the traitor.

6. Now coming down with them, he stood in a plain place, and the company of his disciples, and a very great multitude of people from all Judea and Jerusalem, and the seacoast both of Tyre and Sidon, who were come to hear him, and to be healed of their diseases. And they that were troubled with unclean spirits, were cured. And all the multitude sought to touch him, for virtue went out from him, and healed all.

7. (Mat. 5.) But he, lifting up his eyes on his disciples, said: Blessed are the poor in spirit: for theirs is the kingdom of heaven. Blessed are the meek: for they shall possess the land. Blessed are they that mourn: for they shall be comforted. Blessed are they that hunger and thirst after justice: for they shall have their fill. Blessed are the merciful: for they shall obtain mercy. Blessed are the clean of heart: for they shall see God. Blessed are the peacemakers: for they shall be called the children of God. Blessed are they that suffer persecution for justice' sake: for theirs is the kingdom of heaven. Blessed are ye when they shall revile you, and persecute you, and speak all that is evil against you, untruly, for my sake: Be glad and rejoice, for your reward is very great in heaven. For so they persecuted the prophets that were before you.

8. You are the salt of the earth. But if the salt lose its savour, wherewith shall it be salted? It is good for nothing any more but to be cast out and to be trodden on by men. You are the light of the world. A city seated on a mountain cannot be hid. Neither do men light a candle and put it under a bushel, but upon a candlestick, that it may shine to all that are in the house. So let your light shine before men, that they may see your good works, and glorify your Father who is in heaven.

9. Do not think that I am come to destroy the law, or the prophets. I am not come to destroy, but to fulfill. For amen I say unto you, till heaven and earth pass, one jot, or one tittle shall not pass of the law, till all be fulfilled. He therefore that shall break one of these least commandments, and shall so teach men, shall be called the least in the kingdom of heaven. But he that shall do and teach, he shall be called great in the kingdom of heaven.

For I tell you, that unless your justice abound more than that of the Scribes and Pharisees, you shall not enter into the kingdom of heaven. You have heard that it was said to them of old: thou shall not kill. And whosoever shall kill shall be in danger of the judgment. But I say to you, that whosoever is angry with his brother, shall be in danger of the judgment. And whosoever shall say to his brother, Raca, shall be in danger of the council. And whosoever shall say, Thou fool, shall be in danger of hell fire. If therefore thou offer thy gift at the altar, and there thou remember that thy brother hath any thing against thee; Leave there thy offering before the altar, and go first to be reconciled to thy brother: and then coming thou shalt offer thy gift. Be at agreement with thy adversary betimes, whilst thou art in the way with him: lest perhaps the adversary deliver thee to the judge, and the judge deliver thee to the officer, and thou be cast into prison. Amen I say to thee, thou shalt not go out from thence till thou rè-pay the last farthing.

10. You have heard that it was said to them of old: Thou shalt not commit adultery. But I say to you, that whosoever shall look on a woman to lust after her, hath already committed adultery with her in his heart. And if thy right eye scandalize thee, pluck it out and cast it from thee. For it is expedient for thee that one of thy members should perish, rather than thy whole body be cast into hell. And if thy right hand scandalize thee, cut it off, and cast it from thee: for it is expedient for thee that one of thy members should perish, rather than that thy whole body go into hell.

11. Again you have heard that it was said to them of old, Thou shalt not forswear thyself: but thou shalt perform thy oaths to the Lord. But I say to you not to swear at all, neither by heaven, for it is the throne of God: Nor by the earth, for it is his footstool: nor by Jerusalem, for it is the city of the great king: Neither shalt thou swear by thy head, because thou canst not make one hair white or black. But let your speech be yea, yea: no, no: and that which is over and above these, is of evil.

12. You have heard that it hath been said, An eye for an eye, and a tooth for a tooth. But I say to you not to resist evil: but if one strike thee on thy right cheek, turn to him also the other: And if a man will contend with thee in judgment, and take away thy coat, let go thy cloak also unto him. And whosoever will force thee one mile, go with him other two. Give to him that asketh of thee, and from him that would borrow of thee turn not away.

13. (A. D. 31.) You have heard that it hath been said, Thou shalt love thy

neighbour, and hate thy enemy. But I say to you, Love your enemies: do good to them that hate you: and pray for them that persecute and calumniate you: That you may be the children of your Father who is in heaven, who maketh his sun to rise upon the good, and bad, and raineth upon the just and the unjust. For if you love them that love you, what reward shall you have? do not even the publicans this? And if you salute your brethren only, what do you more? do not also the heathens this? Be you therefore perfect, as also your heavenly Father is perfect.

14. (Mat. 6.) Take heed that you do not your justice before men, to be seen by them: otherwise you shall not have a reward of your Father who is in heaven. Therefore when thou dost an alms-deed, sound not a trumpet before thee, as the hypocrites do in the synagogues and in the streets, that they may be honoured by men. Amen I say to you, they have received their reward. But when thou dost alms, let not thy left hand know what thy right hand doth. That thy alms may be in secret, and thy Father who seeth in secret will repay thee.

15. And when ye pray, you shall not be as the hypocrites, that love to stand and pray in the synagogues and corners of the streets, that they may be seen by men: Amen I say to you, they have received their reward. But thou when thou shalt pray, enter into thy chamber, and having shut the door, pray to thy Father in secret: and thy Father who seeth in secret will repay thee. And when you are praying, speak not much, as the heathens. For they think that in their much speaking they may be heard. Be not you therefore like to them, for your Father knoweth what is needful for you, before you ask him.

16. And when you fast, be not as the hypocrites, sad. For they disfigure their faces, that they may appear unto men to fast. Amen I say to you, they have received their reward. But thou, when thou fastest anoint thy head, and wash thy face; That thou appear not to men to fast, but to thy Father who is in secret: and thy Father who seeth in secret, will repay thee.

17. (Mat. 7.) Judge not, that you may not be judged. For with what judgment you judge, you shall be judged: and with what measure you mete, it shall be measured to you again. And why seest thou the mote that is in thy brother's eye; and seest not the beam that is in thy own eye? Or how sayest thou to thy brother: Let me cast the mote out of thy eye; and behold a beam is in thy own eye? Thou hypocrite, cast out first the beam out of thy own eye, and then shalt thou see to cast out the mote out of thy brother's eye.

18. (Luke 6.) Give, and it shall be given to you: good measure and pressed down and shaken together and running over shall they give into your bosom. For with the same measure that you shall mete withal, it shall be measured to you again. And he spoke also to them a similitude: Can the blind lead the blind? do they not both fall into the ditch? The disciple is not above his master: but every one shall be perfect, if he be as his master.

19. (Mat. 7.) Give not that which is holy to dogs; neither cast ye your pearls before swine, lest perhaps they trample them under their feet, and turning upon you, they tear you. All things therefore whatsoever you would that men should do to you, do you also to them. For this is the law and the prophets.

20. Enter ye in at the narrow gate: for wide is the gate, and broad is the way that leadeth to destruction, and many there are who go in thereat. How narrow is the gate, and strait is the way that leadeth to life: and few there are that find it!

21. Beware of false prophets, who come to you in the clothing of sheep, but inwardly they are ravening wolves. By their fruits you shall know them. Do men gather grapes of thorns, or figs of thistles? Even so every good tree bringeth forth good fruit, and the evil tree bringeth forth evil fruit. A good tree cannot bring forth evil fruit, neither can an evil tree bring forth good fruit. Every tree that bringeth not forth good fruit, shall be cut down, and shall be cast into the fire. Wherefore by their fruits you shall know them. Not every one that saith to me, Lord, Lord, shall enter into the kingdom of heaven: but he that doth the will of my Father who is in heaven, he shall enter into the kingdom of heaven. Many will say to me in that day: Lord, Lord, have not we prophesied in thy name, and cast out devils in thy name, and done many miracles in thy name? And then will I profess unto them, I never knew you: depart from me, you that work iniquity.

22. Every one therefore that heareth these my words, and doth them, shall be likened to a wise man that built his house upon a rock, And the rain fell, and the floods came, and the winds blew, and they beat upon that house, and it fell not, for it was founded on a rock. And every one that heareth these my words, and doth them not, shall be like a foolish man that built his house upon the sand, And the rain fell, and the floods came, and the winds blew, and they beat upon that house, and it fell, and great was the fall thereof. And it came to pass when Jesus had fully ended these words, the people were in admiration at his doctrine. For he was teaching them as one having power, and not as the scribes and Pharisees.

23. (Luke 7.) Now when he had finished all his words in the hearing of the people, he entered into Capharnaum. And the servant of a certain centurion, who was dear to him, being sick, was ready to die. And when he had heard of Jesus, he sent unto him the ancients of the Jews, desiring him to come and heal his servant. And when they came to Jesus, they besought him earnestly, saying to him: He is worthy that thou shouldest do this for him. For he loveth our nation; and he hath built us a synagogue. And Jesus went with them. And when he was now not far from the house, the centurion sent his friends to him, saying: Lord, trouble not thyself; for I am not worthy that thou shouldest enter under my roof. For which cause neither did I think myself worthy to come to thee; but say the word, and my servant shall be healed. For I also am a man subject to authority, having under me soldiers: and I say to one, Go, and he goeth; and to another, Come, and he cometh; and to my servant, Do this, and he doth it. Which Jesus hearing, marvelled: and turning about to the multitude that followed him, he said: Amen I say to you, I have not found so great faith, not even in Israel. And they who were sent, being returned to the house, found the servant whole who had been sick.

24. Now it came to pass afterwards, that he went into a city that is called Naim; and there went with him his disciples, and a great multitude. And when he came nigh to the gate of the city, behold a dead man was carried out, the only son of his mother; and she was a widow: and a great multitude of the city was with her. Whom when the Lord had seen, being moved with mercy towards her, he said to her: Weep not. And he came near and touched the bier. And they that carried it, stood still. And he said: Young man, I say to thee, arise. And he that was dead, sat up, and began to speak. And he gave him to his mother. And there came a fear on them all: and they glorified God, saying: A great prophet is risen up among us: and, God hath visited his people. And this rumour of him went forth throughout all Judea, and throughout all the country round about. And John's disciples told him of all these things.

25. Now John called to him two of his disciples, and sent them to Jesus, saying: Art thou he that art to come; or look we for another? And when the men were come unto him, they said: John the Baptist hath sent us to thee, saying: art thou he that art to come; or look we for another? (And in that same hour, he cured many of their diseases, and hurts, and evil spirits: and to many that were blind he gave sight.) And answering, he said to them: Go and relate to John what you have heard and seen: The blind see, the lame walk, the lepers are made clean, the deaf hear, the dead rise again, to the poor the gospel is preached: And blessed is he whosoever shall not be scandalized in me.

26. (A. D. 31.) Now when the messengers of John were departed, he began to speak to the multitudes concerning John. What went ye out into the desert to see? a reed shaken with the wind? But what went you out to see? a man clothed in soft garments? Behold they that are in costly apparel and live delicately, are in the houses of kings. But what went you out to see? a prophet? Yea, I say to you, and more than a prophet. This is he of whom it is written: *Behold I send my angel before thy face, who shall prepare thy way before thee.* For I say to you: Amongst those that are born of women, there is not a greater prophet than John the Baptist. But he that is the lesser in the kingdom of God, is greater than he. And all the people hearing, and the publicans, justified God, being baptized with John's baptism. But the Pharisees and the lawyers despised the counsel of God against themselves, being not baptized by him. And the Lord said: Whereunto then shall I liken the men of this generation? and to what are they like? They are like to children sitting in the market-place, and speaking one to another, and saying: We have piped to you, and you have not danced: we have mourned, and you have not wept. For John the Baptist came neither eating bread nor drinking wine; and you say: He hath a devil. The Son of man is come eating and drinking: and you say: Behold a man that is a glutton and a drinker of wine, a friend of publicans and sinners. And wisdom is justified by all her children.

27. Now one of the Pharisees desired him to eat with him. And he went into the house of the Pharisee, and sat down to meat. And behold a woman that was in the city, a sinner, when she knew that he sat at meat in the Pharisee's house, brought an alabaster-box of ointment; And standing behind at his feet, she began to wash his feet, with tears, and wiped them with the hairs of her head, and kissed his feet, and anointed them with the ointment. And the Pharisee, who had invited him, seeing it, spoke within himself, saying: This man, if he were a prophet, would know surely who and what manner of woman this is that toucheth him, that she is a sinner. And Jesus answering, said to him: Simon, I have somewhat to say to thee.

But he said: Master, say *it*. A certain creditor had two debtors, the one owed five hundred pence, and the other fifty. And whereas they had not wherewith to pay, he forgave them both. Which therefore of the two loveth him most? Simon answering said: I suppose that he to whom he forgave most. And he said to him: Thou hast judged rightly. And turning to the woman, he said unto Simon: Dost thou see this woman? I entered into thy house, thou gavest me no water for my feet; but she with tears hath washed my feet, and with her hairs hath wiped them. Thou gavest me no kiss; but she, since she came in, hath not ceased to kiss my feet. My head with oil thou didst not anoint; but she with ointment hath anointed my feet. Wherefore I say to thee: Many sins are forgiven her, because she hath loved much. But to whom less is forgiven, he loveth less. And he said to her: Thy sins are forgiven thee. And they that sat at meat with him began to say within themselves: Who is this that forgiveth sins also? And he said to the woman: Thy faith hath made thee safe, go in peace.

28. (Luke 8.) Now it came to pass afterwards, that he travelled through the cities and towns, preaching and evangelizing the kingdom of God; and the twelve with him. And certain women who had been healed of evil spirits and infirmities; Mary who is called Magdalen, out of whom seven devils were gone forth, And Joanna the wife of Chusa, Herod's steward, and Susanna, and many others who ministered unto him of their substance followed him.

(Mark 3.) And they come to a house, and the multitude cometh together again, so that they could not so much as eat bread. And when his friends had heard of it, they went out to lay hold on him. For they said: He is become mad. And the scribes who were come down from Jerusalem, said: He hath Beelzebub, and by the prince of devils he casteth out devils. And after he had called them together, he said to them in parables: How can satan cast out satan? And if a kingdom be divided against itself, that kingdom cannot stand. And if a house be divided against itself, that house cannot stand. And if satan be risen up against himself, he is divided, and cannot stand, but hath an end. No man can enter into the house of a strong man and rob him of his goods, unless he first bind the strong man, and then shall he plunder his house. Amen I say to you, that all sins shall be forgiven unto the sons of men, and the blasphemies wherewith they shall blaspheme: But he that shall blaspheme against the Holy Ghost, shall never have forgiveness, but shall be guilty of an everlasting sin. Because they said: He hath an unclean spirit.

29. Now his mother and his brethren came; and standing without, sent unto him, calling him. And the multitude sat about him; and they say to him: Behold thy mother and thy brethren without seek for thee. And answering them, he said: Who is my mother and my brethren? And looking round about on them who sat about him, he saith: Behold my mother and my brethren. For whosoever shall do the will of God, he is my brother, and my sister, and mother.

30. (Luke 8.) Now when a very great multitude was gathered together, and hastened out of the cities unto him, he spoke by a similitude. The sower went out to sow his seed. And as he sowed, some fell by the wayside, and it was trodden down, and the fowls of the air devoured it. And other some fell upon a rock: and as soon as it was sprung up, it withered away, because it had no moisture. And other some fell among thorns, and the thorns growing up with it, choked it. And other some fell upon good ground; and being sprung up, yielded fruit a hundredfold. Saying these things, he cried out: He that hath ears to hear, let him hear. And his disciples asked him what this parable might be. To whom he said: To you it is given to know the mystery of the kingdom of God; but to the rest in parables, that seeing they may not see, and hearing may not understand. Now the parable is this: The seed is the word of God. And they by the wayside are they that hear, then the devil cometh, and taketh the word out of their heart, lest believing they should be saved. Now they upon the rock; *are they* who when they hear, receive the word with joy: and these have no roots; for they believe for a while, and in time of temptation, they fall away. And that which fell among thorns, are they who have heard, and going their way are choked with the cares and riches and pleasures of this life, and yield no fruit. But that on the good ground, are they who in a good and very good heart, hearing the word, keep it, and bring forth fruit in patience.

31. Now no man lighting a candle covereth it with a vessel, or putteth it under a bed; but setteth it upon a candlestick, that they who come in may see the light. For there is not any thing secret that shall not be made manifest, nor hidden, that shall not be known and come abroad. Take heed therefore how you hear. For whosoever hath, to him shall be given: and whosoever hath not, that also which he thinketh he hath, shall be taken away from him.

32. (Mark 4.) And he said:

So is the kingdom of God, as if a man should cast seed into the earth, And should sleep, and rise, night and day, and the seed should spring, and grow up whilst he knoweth not. For the earth of itself bringeth forth fruit, first the blade, then the ear, afterwards the full corn in the ear. And when the fruit is brought forth, immediately he putteth in the sickle, because the harvest is come.

33. (Mat. 13.) Another parable he proposed to them, saying: The kingdom of heaven is likened to a man that sowed good seed in his field. But while men were asleep, his enemy came and oversowed cockle among the wheat and went his way. And when the blade was sprung up, and had brought forth fruit, then appeared also the cockle. And the servants of the goodman of the house coming said to him: Sir, didst thou not sow good seed in thy field? whence then hath it cockle? And he said to them: An enemy hath done this. And the servants said to him: Wilt thou that we go and gather it up? And he said: No, lest perhaps gathering up the cockle, you root up the wheat also together with it. Suffer both to grow until the harvest, and in the time of the harvest I will say to the reapers: Gather up first the cockle, and bind it into bundles to burn, but the wheat gather ye into my barn. All these things Jesus spoke in parables to the multitudes: and without parables he did not speak to them. That it might be fulfilled which was spoken by the prophet, saying: *I will open my mouth in parables, I will utter things hidden from the foundation of the world.* Then having sent away the multitudes, he came into the house, and his disciples came to him, saying: Expound to us the parable of the cockle of the field. Who made answer and said to them: He that soweth the good seed, is the son of man. And the field, is the world. And the good seed are the children of the kingdom. And the cockle, are the children of the wicked one. And the enemy that sowed them, is the devil. But the harvest is the end of the world. And the reapers are the angels. Even as cockle therefore is gathered up, and burnt with fire: so shall it be at the end of the world. The son of man shall send his Angels, and they shall gather out of his kingdom all scandals, and them that work iniquity, and shall cast them into the furnace of fire: there shall be weeping and gnashing of teeth. Then shall the just shine as the sun, in the kingdom of their Father. He that hath ears to hear, let him hear.

34. The kingdom of heaven is like unto a treasure hidden in a field. Which a man having found, hid it, and for joy thereof goeth, and selleth all that he hath, and buyeth that field.

35. Again the kingdom of heaven is like to a merchant seeking good pearls. Who when he had found one pearl of great price, went his way, and sold all that he had, and bought it.

36. Again the kingdom of heaven is like to a net cast into the sea, and gathering together of all kind of fishes. Which, when it was filled, they drew out, and sitting by the shore, they chose out the good into vessels, but the bad they cast forth. So shall it be at the end of the world. The Angels shall go out, and shall separate the wicked from among the just. And shall cast them into the furnace of fire: there shall be weeping and gnashing of teeth. Have ye understood all these things? They say to him: Yes. He said unto them: Therefore every scribe instructed in the kingdom of heaven, is like to a man that is a householder, who bringeth forth out of his treasure new things and old.

37. (Luke 8.) Now it came to pass on a certain day that he went into a little ship with his disciples, and he said to them: Let us go over to the other side of the lake. And they launched forth. And when they were sailing, he slept: and there came down a storm of wind upon the lake, and they were filled, and were in danger. And they came and awaked him, saying: Master, we perish. But he arising, rebuked the wind and the rage of the water; and it ceased, and there was a calm. And he said to them: Where is your faith? Who being afraid, wondered, saying one to another: Who is this (think you) that he commandeth both the winds and the sea, and they obey him?

38. Now they sailed to the country of the Gerasens, which is over-against Galilee. And when he was come forth to the land, there met him a certain man who had a devil now a very long time, and he wore no clothes, neither did he abide in a house, but in the sepulchres. And when he saw Jesus, he fell down before him; and crying out with a loud voice, he said: What have I to do with thee, Jesus, Son of the most high God? I beseech thee do not torment me. For he commanded the unclean spirit to go out of the man. For many times it seized him, and he was bound with chains, and kept in fetters; and breaking the bonds, he was driven by the devil into the deserts. And Jesus asked him, saying: What is thy name? But he said: Legion; because many devils were entered into him. And they besought him that he would not command them to go into the abyss. And there was there a herd of many swine feeding on the mountain; and they besought him that he would suffer them to enter into them. And he suffered them. The devils therefore went out

of the man, and entered into the swine; and the herd ran violently down a steep place into the lake, and was stifled. Which when they that fed them saw done, they fled, and told it in the city and in the villages. And they went out to see what was done; and they came to Jesus, and found the man, out of whom the devils were departed, sitting at his feet, clothed, and in his right mind; and they were afraid. And they also that had seen, told them how he had been healed from the legion. And all the multitude of the country of the Gerasens besought him to depart from them; for they were taken with great fear: And he, going up into the ship, returned back again. Now the man, out of whom the devils were departed, besought him that he might be with him. But Jesus sent him away, saying: Return to thy house, and tell how great things God hath done to thee. And he went through the whole city, publishing how great things Jesus had done to him.

39. Now it came to pass, that when Jesus was returned, the multitude received him: for they were all waiting for him. And behold there came a man whose name was Jairus, and he was a ruler of the synagogue: and he fell down at the feet of Jesus, beseeching him that he would come into his house: For he had an only daughter, almost twelve years old, and she was dying. And it happened as he went, that he was thronged by the multitudes.

40. (A. D. 31.) Now there was a certain woman having an issue of blood twelve years, who had bestowed all her substance on physicians, and could not be healed by any. She came behind him, and touched the hem of his garment; and immediately the issue of her blood stopped. And Jesus said: Who is it that touched me? And all denying, Peter and they that were with him said: Master, the multitudes throng and press thee, and dost thou say, Who touched me? And Jesus said: Some body hath touched me; for I know that virtue is gone out from me. And the woman seeing that she was not hid, came trembling, and fell down before his feet, and declared before all the people for what cause she had touched him, and how she was immediately healed. But he said to her: Daughter, thy faith hath made thee whole; go thy way in peace.

41. And as he was yet speaking, there cometh one to the ruler of the synagogue, saying to him: Thy daughter is dead, trouble him not. And Jesus hearing this word, answered the father of the maid: Fear not; believe only, and she shall be safe. And when he was come to the house, he suffered not any man to go in with him, but Peter and James and John, and the father and mother of the

maiden. And all wept and mourned for her. But he said: Weep not; the maid is not dead, but sleepeth. And they laughed him to scorn, knowing that she was dead. But he taking her by the hand, cried out, saying: Maid, arise. And her spirit returned, and she arose immediately. And he bid them give her to eat. And her parents were astonished, whom he charged to tell no man what was done.

42. (Mat. 9.) Now as Jesus passed from thence, there followed him two blind men crying out and saying, Have mercy on us, O Son of David. And when he was come to the house, the blind men came to him. And Jesus saith to them, Do you believe, that I can do this unto you? They say to him, Yea, Lord. Then he touched their eyes, saying, According to your faith, be it done unto you. And their eyes were opened, and Jesus strictly charged them, saying, See that no man know this. But they going out, spread his fame abroad in all that country.

43. Now when they were gone out, behold they brought him a dumb man, possessed with a devil. And after the devil was cast out, the dumb man spoke, and the multitudes wondered, saying, Never was the like seen in Israel. But the Pharisees said, By the prince of devils he casteth out devils.

44. (Mark 6.) Now going out from thence, he went into his own country; and his disciples followed him. And when the sabbath was come, he began to teach in the synagogue: and many hearing him were in admiration at his doctrine, saying: How came this man by all these things? and what wisdom is this that is given to him, and such mighty works as are wrought by his hands? Is not this the carpenter, the son of Mary, the brother of James, and Joseph, and Jude, and Simon? are not also his sisters here with us? And they were scandalized in regard of him. And Jesus said to them: A prophet is not without honour, but in his own country, and in his own house, and among his own kindred.

45. Now he could not do any miracles there, only that he cured a few that were sick, laying his hands upon them, And he wondered because of their unbelief, and he went through the villages round about teaching.

46. Now he called the twelve; and began to send them two and two, and gave them power over unclean spirits. And he commanded them that they should take nothing for the way, but a staff only: no scrip, no bread, nor money in their purse, But to be shod with sandals, and that they should not put on two coats. And he said to them: Wheresoever you shall enter into an house, there abide till you depart from that place. And whosoever shall not receive you, nor hear you; going forth from thence, shake off the dust from your feet for a testimony to them. And going forth they preached that *men* should do penance: And they cast out many devils, and anointed with oil many that were sick, and healed them.

47. Now king Herod heard: (for his name was made manifest) and he said: John the Baptist is risen again from the dead, and therefore mighty works shew forth themselves in him. And others said: It is Elias. But others said: It is a prophet, as one of the prophets. Which Herod hearing, said: John whom I beheaded, he is risen again from the dead. For Herod himself had sent and apprehended John, and bound him in prison for the sake of Herodias the wife of Philip his brother, because he had married her. For John said to Herod: It is not lawful for thee to have thy brother's wife. Now Herodias laid snares for him: and was desirous to put him to death, and could not. For Herod feared John, knowing him to be a just and holy man: and kept him, and when he heard him, did many things: and he heard him willingly. And when a convenient day was come, Herod made a supper for his birth-day, for the princes, and tribunes, and chief men of Galilee. And when the daughter of the same Herodias had come in, and had danced, and pleased Herod, and them that were at table with him, the king said to the damsel: Ask of me what thou wilt, and I will give it thee. And he swore to her: Whatsoever thou shalt ask I will give thee, though *it be* the half of my kingdom. Who when she was gone out, said to her mother, What shall I ask? But she said: The head of John the Baptist. And when she was come in immediately with haste to the king, she asked, saying: I will that forthwith thou give me in a dish, the head of John the Baptist. And the king was struck sad. *Yet* because of his oath, and because of them that were with him at table, he would not displease her: But sending an executioner, he commanded that his head should be brought in a dish. And he beheaded him in the prison, and brought his head in a dish: and gave it to the damsel, and the damsel gave it to her mother. Which his disciples hearing came, and took his body, and laid it in a tomb.

48. Now the apostles coming together unto Jesus, related to him all things that they had done and taught. And he said to them: Come apart into a desert place, and rest a little. For there were many coming and going: and they had not so much as time to eat. And going up into a ship, they went into a desert place apart.

(John 6.) And a great multitude followed him, because they saw the miracles which he did on them that were diseased. Jesus therefore went up into a mountain, and there he sat with his disciples. Now the pasch, the festival day of the Jews, was near at hand. When Jesus therefore had lifted up his eyes, and seen, that a very great multitude cometh to him, he said to Philip: Whence shall we buy bread, that these may eat? And this he said to try him; for he himself knew what he would do. Philip answered him: Two hundred pennyworths of bread are not sufficient for them, that every one may take a little. One of his disciples, Andrew, the brother of Simon Peter, saith to him: There is a boy here that hath five barley loaves, and two fishes; but what are these among so many? Then Jesus said: Make the men sit down. Now there was much grass in the place. The men therefore sat down, in number about five thousand. And Jesus took the loaves: and when he had given thanks, he distributed to them that were sat down. In like manner also of the fishes, as much as they would. And when they were filled, he said to his disciples: Gather up the fragments that remain, lest they be lost. They gathered up therefore, and filled twelve baskets with the fragments of the five barley loaves, which remained over and above to them that had eaten. Now those men, when they had seen what a miracle Jesus had done, said: This is of a truth the prophet, that is to come into the world. Jesus therefore, when he knew that they would come to take him by force, and make him king, fled again into the mountain himself alone.

49. Now when evening was come, his disciples went down to the sea. And when they had gone up into a ship, they went over the sea to Capharnaum; and it was now dark, and Jesus was not come unto them. And the sea arose, by reason of a great wind that blew.

(Mat. 14.) And having dismissed the multitude, Jesus went into a mountain alone to pray. And when it was evening, he was there alone. But the boat in the midst of the sea was tossed with the waves: for the wind was contrary. And in the fourth watch of the night, he came to them walking upon the sea. And they seeing him walking upon the sea, were troubled, saying: It is an apparition. And they cried out for fear. And immediately Jesus spoke to them, saying: Be of good heart: it is I, fear ye not. And Peter making answer, said: Lord, if it be thou, bid me come to thee upon the waters. And he said: Come. And Peter going down out of the boat, walked upon the water to come to Jesus. But seeing the wind strong, he was afraid:

and when he began to sink, he cried out, saying: Lord, save me. And immediately Jesus stretching forth his hand took hold of him, and said to him: O thou of little faith, why didst thou doubt? And when they were come up into the boat, the wind ceased. And they that were in the boat came and adored him, saying: Indeed thou art the son of God.

(John 6.) The next day, the multitude that stood on the other side of the sea, saw that there was no other ship there but one, and that Jesus had not entered into the ship with his disciples, but that his disciples were gone away alone. But other ships came in from Tiberias; nigh unto the place where they had eaten the bread, the Lord giving thanks. When therefore the multitude saw that Jesus was not there, nor his disciples, they took shipping, and came to Capharnaum, seeking for Jesus. And when they had found him on the other side of the sea, they said to him: Rabbi, when camest thou hither? Jesus answered them, and said: Amen, amen, I say to you, you seek me, not because you have seen miracles, but because you did eat of the loaves, and were filled.

50. Labour not for the meat which perisheth, but for that which endureth unto life everlasting, which the son of man will give you. For him hath God, the Father sealed. They said therefore unto him: What shall we do, that we may work the works of God? Jesus answered, and said to them: This is the work of God, that you believe in him whom he hath sent. They said therefore to him: What sign therefore dost thou shew, that we may see, and may believe thee? What dost thou work? Our Fathers did eat manna in the desert, as it is written: *He gave them bread from heaven to eat.* Then Jesus said to them: Amen, amen, I say to you; Moses gave you not bread from heaven, but my Father giveth you the true bread from heaven. For the bread of God is that which cometh down from heaven, and giveth life to the world. They said therefore unto him: Lord, give us always this bread. And Jesus said to them: I am the bread of life: he that cometh to me shall not hunger: and he that believeth in me shall never thirst. But I said unto you, that you also have seen me, and you believe not. All that the Father giveth to me shall come to me; and him that cometh to me, I will not cast out. Because I came down from heaven, not to do my own will, but the will of him that sent me. Now this is the will of the Father who sent me: that of all that he hath given me, I should lose nothing; but should raise it up again in the last day. And this is the will of my Father that sent me: that every one who seeth the Son, and believeth in him, may have life

everlasting, and I will raise him up in the last day. The Jews therefore murmured at him, because he had said: I am the living bread which came down from heaven. And they said: Is not this Jesus, the son of Joseph, whose father and mother we know? How then saith he, I came down from heaven? Jesus therefore answered, and said to them: Murmur not among yourselves. No man can come to me, except the Father, who hath sent me, draw him; and I will raise him up in the last day. It is written in the prophets: *And they shall all be taught of God.* Every one that hath heard of the Father, and hath learned, cometh to me. Not that any man hath seen the Father; but he who is of God, he hath seen the Father. Amen, amen, I say unto you: He that believeth in me, hath everlasting life.

51. (A. D. 31.) I am the bread of life. Your fathers did eat manna in the desert, and are dead. This is the bread which cometh down from heaven; that if any man eat of it, he may not die. I am the living bread which came down from heaven. If any man eat of this bread, he shall live for ever; and the bread that I will give, is my flesh, for the life of the world. The Jews therefore strove among themselves, saying: How can this man give us his flesh to eat? Then Jesus said to them: Amen, amen, I say unto you: Except you eat the flesh of the son of man, and drink his blood, you shall not have life in you. He that eateth my flesh, and drinketh my blood, hath everlasting life: and I will raise him up in the last day. For my flesh is meat indeed: and my blood is drink indeed. He that eateth my flesh, and drinketh my blood, abideth in me, and I in him. As the living Father hath sent me, and I live by the Father; so he that eateth me, the same also shall live by me. This is the bread that came down from heaven. Not as your fathers did eat manna, and are dead. He that eateth this bread, shall live for ever. These things he said, teaching in the synagogue, in Capharnaum. Many therefore of his disciples, hearing it, said: This saying is hard, and who can hear it? But Jesus, knowing in himself, that his disciples murmured at this, said to them: Doth this scandalize you? If then you shall see the son of man ascend up where he was before? It is the spirit that quickeneth: the flesh profiteth nothing. The words that I have spoken to you, are spirit and life. But there are some of you that believe not. For Jesus knew from the beginning, who they were that did not believe, and who he was, that would betray him. And he said: Therefore did I say to you, that no man can come to me, unless it be given him by my Father. After this many of his disciples went back; and

walked no more with him. Then Jesus said to the twelve: Will you also go away? And Simon Peter answered him: Lord, to whom shall we go? thou hast the words of eternal life. And we have believed and have known, that thou art the Christ, the Son of God. Jesus answered them: Have not I chosen you twelve; and one of you is a devil? Now he meant Judas Iscariot, the son of Simon: for this same was about to betray him, whereas he was one of the twelve.

CHAPTER V.

SHADOWS OF COMING EVENTS.

1. (John 7. A. D. 32.) AFTER these things Jesus walked in Galilee; for he would not walk in Judea, because the Jews sought to kill him.

(Mark 6.) And when they had passed over, they came into the land of Genezareth, and set to the shore. And when they were gone out of the ship, immediately they knew him: And running through that whole country, they began to carry about in beds those that were sick, where they heard he was. And whithersoever he entered, into towns or into villages or cities, they laid the sick in the streets, and besought him that they might touch but the hem of his garment: and as many as touched him were made whole.

2. (Mark. 7.) Now there assembled together unto him the Pharisees and some of the scribes, coming from Jerusalem. And when they had seen some of his disciples eat bread with common, that is, with unwashed hands, they found fault. For the Pharisees, and all the Jews eat not without often washing their hands, holding the tradition of the ancients: And when they come from the market, unless they be washed, they eat not: and many other things there are that have been delivered to them to observe, the washings of cups and of pots, and of brazen vessels, and of beds. And the Pharisees and scribes asked him: Why do not thy disciples walk according to the tradition of the ancients, but they eat bread with common hands? But he answering, said to them: Well did Isaias prophesy of you hypocrites, as it is written: *This people honoureth me with their lips, but their heart is far from me. And in vain do they worship me, teaching doctrines and precepts of men.* For leaving the commandment of God,

you hold the tradition of men, the washings of pots and of cups: and many other things you do like to these. And he said to them: Well do you make void the commandment of God, that you may keep your own tradition. For Moses said: *Honour thy father and thy mother;* and *He that shall curse father or mother, dying let him die.* But you say: If a man shall say to his father or mother, Corban (which is a gift,) whatsoever is from me, shall profit thee. And farther you suffer him not to do anything for his father or mother, making void the word of God by your own tradition, which you have given forth. And many other such like things you do.

3. Now calling again the multitude unto him, he said to them: Hear ye me all and understand. There is nothing from without a man that entering into him, can defile him. But the things which come from a man, those are they that defile a man. If any man have ears to hear, let him hear. And when he was come into the house from the multitude, his disciples asked him the parable. And he saith to them: So are you also without knowledge? understand you not that every thing from without, entering into a man cannot defile him: Because it entereth not into his heart, but goeth into the belly, and goeth out into the privy, purging all meats? But he said that the things which come out from a man, they defile a man. For from within out of the heart of men proceed evil thoughts, adulteries, fornications, murders, Thefts, covetousness, wickedness, deceit, lasciviousness, an evil eye, blasphemy, pride, foolishness. All these evil things come from within, and defile a man.

4. Now rising from thence he went into the coasts of Tyre and Sidon: and entering into a house, he would that no man should know it, and he could not be hid. For a woman as soon as she heard of him, whose daughter had an unclean spirit, came in and fell down at his feet. For the woman was a Gentile, a Syrophenician born. And she besought him that he would cast forth the devil out of her daughter. Who said to her: Suffer first the children to be filled: for it is not good to take the bread of the children, and cast it to the dogs. But she answered and said to him: Yea, Lord; for the whelps also eat under the table of the crumbs of the children. And he said to her: For this saying go thy way, the devil is gone out of thy daughter. And when she was come into her house, she found the girl lying upon the bed, and that the devil was gone out.

5. (A. D. 32.) But again going out of the coasts of Tyre, he came by Sidon to the sea of Galilee, through the midst of the coasts of Decapolis. And they

bring to him one deaf and dumb; and they besought him that he would lay his hand upon him. And taking him from the multitude apart, he put his fingers into his ears, and spitting, he touched his tongue: And looking up to heaven, he groaned, and said to him: Ephpheta, which is, Be thou opened. And immediately his ears were opened and the string of his tongue was loosed, and he spoke right. And he charged them that they should tell no man. But the more he charged them, so much the more a great deal did they publish it. And so much the more did they wonder, saying: He hath done all things well; he hath made both the deaf to hear, and the dumb to speak.

6. (Mat. 15.) Now when Jesus had passed away from thence, he came nigh the sea of Galilee. And going up into a mountain, he sat there. And there came to him great multitudes, having with them the dumb, the blind, the lame, the maimed, and many others: and they cast them down at his feet, and he healed them: So that the multitudes marvelled seeing the dumb speak, the lame walk, the blind see: and they glorified the God of Israel. And Jesus called together his disciples, and said: I have compassion on the multitudes, because they continue with me now three days, and have not what to eat, and I will not send them away fasting, lest they faint in the way. And the disciples say unto him: Whence then should we have so many loaves in the desert, as to fill so great a multitude? And Jesus said to them: how many loaves have you? But they said: Seven, and a few little fishes. And he commanded the multitude to sit down upon the ground. And taking the seven loaves and the fishes, and giving thanks, he brake, and gave to his disciples, and the disciples gave to the people. And they did all eat, and had their fill. And they took up seven baskets full, of what remained of the fragments. And they that did eat, were four thousand men, beside children and women. And having dismissed the multitude, he went up into a boat, and came into the coasts of Magedan.

7. (Mat. 16.) Now there came to him the Pharisees and Sadducees tempting: and they asked him to shew them a sign from heaven. But he answered and said to them: When it is evening, you say, It will be fair weather, for the sky is red. And in the morning: To-day *there will be* a storm, for the sky is red and lowering. You know then how to discern the face of the sky: and can you not know the signs of the times? A wicked and adulterous generation seeketh after a sign: and a sign shall not be given it, but the sign of Jonas the prophet. And leaving them, he went up again into the ship,

and passed to the other side of the water.

8. Now when his disciples were come over the water, they had forgotten to take bread. Who said to them: Take heed and beware of the leaven of the Pharisees and Sadducees. But they thought within themselves, saying: Because we have taken no bread. And Jesus knowing it, said: Why do you think within yourselves, O ye of little faith, for that you have no bread? Do you not yet understand, neither do you remember the five loaves among five thousand men, and how many baskets you took up? Nor the seven loaves among four thousand men, and how many baskets you took up? Why do you not understand that it was not concerning bread I said to you: Beware of the leaven of the Pharisees and Sadducees? Then they understood that he said not that they should beware of the leaven of bread, but of the doctrine of the Pharisees and Sadducees.

9. (Mark 8.) Now they came to Bethsaida; and they bring to him a blind man, and they besought him that he would touch him. And taking the blind man by the hand, he led him out of the town; and spitting upon his eyes, laying his hands on him, he asked him if he saw any thing. And looking up, he said: I see men as it were trees, walking. After that again he laid his hands upon his eyes, and he began to see, and was restored, so that he saw all things clearly. And he sent him into his house, saying: Go into thy house, and if thou enter into the town, tell nobody.

10. (Mat. 16. A. D. 32.) Now Jesus came into the quarters of Cesarea Philippi: and he asked his disciples, saying: Whom do men say that the son of man is? But they said: Some John the Baptist, and other some Elias, and others Jeremias, or one of the prophets. Jesus saith to them: But whom do you say that I am? Simon Peter answered and said: Thou art Christ, the Son of the living God. And Jesus answering, said to him: Blessed art thou, Simon Bar-Jona: because flesh and blood hath not revealed it to thee, but my father who is in heaven. And I say to thee: That thou art Peter; and upon this rock I will build my church, and the gates of hell shall not prevail against it. And I will give to thee the keys of the kingdom of heaven. And whatsoever thou shalt bind upon earth, it shall be bound also in heaven: and whatsoever thou shalt loose on earth, it shall be loosed also in heaven. Then he commanded his disciples, that they should tell no one that he was Jesus the Christ.

11. From that time Jesus began to shew to his disciples, that he must go to Jerusalem, and suffer many things from the ancients and scribes and chief-priests, and be put to death, and the third day rise again. And Peter taking him, began to rebuke him, saying: Lord, be it far from thee, this shall not be unto thee. Who turning said to Peter: Go behind me, satan, thou art a scandal unto me: because thou savourest not the things that are of God, but the things that are of men. Then Jesus said to his disciples: If any man will come after me, let him deny himself, and take up his cross, and follow me. For he that will save his life, shall lose it: and he that shall lose his life for my sake, shall find it. For what doth it profit a man, if he gain the whole world, and suffer the loss of his own soul? Or what exchange shall a man give for his soul? For the son of man shall come in the glory of his Father with his Angels: and then will he render to every man according to his works. Amen I say to you, there are some of them that stand here, that shall not taste death, till they see the son of man coming in his kingdom.

12. (Mat. 17.) Now after six days Jesus taketh unto him Peter and James, and John his brother, and bringeth them up into a high mountain apart: And he was transfigured before them. And his face did shine as the sun: and his garments became white as snow. And behold there appeared to them Moses and Elias talking with him. And Peter answering, said to Jesus: Lord, it is good for us to be here: if thou wilt, let us make here three tabernacles, one for thee, and one for Moses, and one for Elias. And as he was yet speaking, behold a bright cloud overshaded them. And lo a voice out of the cloud, saying: This is my beloved Son, in whom I am well pleased: hear ye him. And the disciples hearing, fell upon their face, and were very much afraid. And Jesus came and touched them: and said to them, Arise, and fear not. And they lifting up their eyes saw no one but only Jesus. And as they came down from the mountain, Jesus charged them, saying: Tell the vision to no man, till the son of man be risen from the dead. And his disciples asked him, saying: Why then do the Scribes say that Elias must come first? But he answering said to them: Elias indeed shall come, and restore all things. But I say to you, that Elias is already come, and they knew him not, but have done unto him whatsoever they had a mind. So also the Son of man shall suffer from them. Then the disciples understood, that he had spoken to them of John the Baptist.

13. (Luke 9. Mat. 17.) Now it came to pass the day following when they came down from the mountain, coming to his disciples, he saw a great multitude about them, and the scribes disputing with them. And presently all the people seeing Jesus, were astonished

and struck with fear; and running to him, they saluted him. And he asked them: What do you question about among you? And one of the multitude, answering, said: Master, I have brought my son to thee, having a dumb spirit, Who, wheresoever he taketh him, dasheth him, and he foameth, and gnasheth with the teeth, and pineth away; and I spoke to thy disciples to cast him out, and they could not. Who answering them, said: O incredulous generation, how long shall I be with you? how long shall I suffer you? bring him unto me. And they brought him. And when he had seen him, immediately the spirit troubled him; and being thrown down upon the ground, he rolled about foaming. And he asked his father: How long time is it since this hath happened unto him? But he said: From his infancy: And often times hath he cast him into the fire and into waters to destroy him. But if thou canst do any thing, help us, having compassion on us. And Jesus saith to him: If thou canst believe, all things are possible to him that believeth. And immediately the father of the boy crying out, with tears said: I do believe, Lord: help my unbelief. And when Jesus saw the multitude running together, he threatened the unclean spirit, saying to him: Deaf and dumb spirit, I command thee, go out of him; and enter not any more into him. And crying out, and greatly tearing him, he went out of him, and he became as dead, so that many said: He is dead. But Jesus taking him by the hand, lifted him up; and he arose. And when he was come into the house, his disciples secretly asked him: Why could not we cast him out? And he said to them: This kind can go out by nothing, but by prayer and fasting.

14. Now departing from thence, they passed through Galilee, and he would not that any man should know it. And he taught his disciples, and said to them: The son of man shall be betrayed into the hands of men, and they shall kill him; and after that he is killed, he shall rise again the third day. But they understood not the word, and they were afraid to ask him.

15. Now when they were come to Capharnaum, they that received the didrachmas, came to Peter and said to him: Doth not your master pay the didrachmas? He said: yes. And when he was come into the house, Jesus prevented him, saying: What is thy opinion, Simon? The kings of the earth, of whom do they receive tribute or custom? of their own children, or of strangers? And he said: Of strangers. Jesus said to him: Then the children are free. But that we may not scandalize them, go to the sea, and cast in a hook: and that fish which shall first come up, take: and when thou hast opened its mouth, thou shalt find a stater: take that, and give it to them for me and thee.

16. (Mark 9.) Now they came to Capharnaum. And when they were in the house, he asked them: What did you treat of in the way? But they held their peace, for in the way they had disputed among themselves, which of them should be the greatest. And sitting down, he called the twelve, and saith to them: If any man desire to be first, he shall be the last of all, and the minister of all. And taking a child, he set him in the midst of them. Whom when he had embraced, he saith to them: Whosoever shall receive one such child as this in my name, receiveth me. And whosoever shall receive me, receiveth not me, but him that sent me.

17. John answered him, saying: Master, we saw one casting out devils in thy name, who followeth not us, and we forbade him. But Jesus said: Do not forbid him. For there is no man that doth a miracle in my name, and can soon speak ill of me. For he that is not against you, is for you.

18. For whosoever shall give you to drink a cup of water in my name, because you belong to Christ: Amen I say to you, he shall not lose his reward.

19. And whosoever shall scandalize one of these little ones that believe in me; it were better for him that a millstone were hanged about his neck, and he were cast into the sea. And if thy hand scandalize thee, cut it off: it is better for thee to enter into life, maimed, than having two hands to go into hell, into unquenchable fire: Where their worm dieth not, and the fire is not extinguished. And if thy foot scandalize thee, cut it off. It is better for thee to enter lame into life everlasting, than having two feet, to be cast into the hell of unquenchable fire: Where their worm dieth not, and the fire is not extinguished. And if thy eye scandalize thee, pluck it out. It is better for thee with one eye to enter into the kingdom of God, than having two eyes to be cast into the hell of fire: Where their worm dieth not, and the fire is not extinguished. For every one shall be salted with fire: and every victim shall be salted with salt. Salt is good. But if the salt become unsavoury; wherewith will you season it? Have salt in you, and have peace among you.

20. (John 7. A. D. 32.) Now the Jews' feast of tabernacles was at hand. And his brethren said to him: Pass from hence, and go into Judea; that thy disciples also may see thy works which thou dost. For there is no man that doth any thing in secret, and he himself seeketh to be known openly. If thou do these things, manifest thyself to the world. For neither did his brethren believe in him. Then Jesus said to them: My time is not yet come; but your time is always ready. The world cannot hate you; but me it hateth: because I give testimony of it, that the works thereof are evil. Go you up to this festival day, but I go not up to this festival day: because my time is not accomplished. When he had said these things, he himself staid in Galilee.

CHAPTER VI.

BEHOLD WE GO UP TO JERUSALEM.

1. (Luke 9.) AND it came to pass, when the days of his assumption were accomplishing, that he steadfastly set his face to go to Jerusalem. And he sent messengers before his face; and going, they entered into a city of the Samaritans, to prepare for him. And they received him not, because his face was of one going to Jerusalem. And when his disciples James and John had seen this, they said: Lord, wilt thou that we command fire to come down from heaven, and consume them? And turning, he rebuked them, saying: You know not of what spirit you are. The son of man came not to destroy souls, but to save. And they went into another town.

2. Now it came to pass, as they walked in the way, that a certain man said to him: I will follow thee whithersoever thou goest. Jesus said to him: the foxes have holes, and the birds of the air nests; but the son of man hath not where to lay his head.

3. (A. D. 32.) But he said to another: Follow me. And he said: Lord, suffer me first to go, and to bury my father. And Jesus said to him: Let the dead bury their dead: but go thou, and preach the kingdom of God.

4. And another said: I will follow thee, Lord; but let me first take my leave of them that are at my house. Jesus said to him: No man putting his hand to the plough, and looking back, is fit for the kingdom of God.

5. (Luke 10.) Now after these things the Lord appointed also other seventy-two: and he sent them two and two before his face into every city and place whither he himself was to come. And he said to them: The harvest indeed is great, but the labourers are few. Pray ye therefore the

Lord of the harvest, that he send labourers into his harvest. Go: Behold I send you as lambs among wolves. Carry neither purse, nor scrip, nor shoes; and salute no man by the way. Into whatsoever house you enter, first say: Peace be to this house. And if the son of peace be there, your peace shall rest upon him; but if not, it shall return to you. And in the same house, remain, eating and drinking such things as they have: for the labourer is worthy of his hire. Remove not from house to house. And into what city soever you enter, and they receive you, eat such things as are set before you. And heal the sick that are therein, and say to them: The kingdom of God is come nigh unto you. But into whatsoever city you enter, and they receive you not, going forth into the streets thereof, say: Even the very dust of your city that cleaveth to us, we wipe off against you. Yet know this, that the kingdom of God is at hand. I say to you, it shall be more tolerable at that day for Sodom, than for that city. Wo to thee, Corozam, wo to thee, Bethsaida. For if in Tyre and Sidon had been wrought the mighty works that have been wrought in you, they would have done penance long ago, sitting in sackcloth and ashes. But it shall be more tolerable for Tyre and Sidon at the judgment, than for you. And thou, Capharnaum, which art exalted unto heaven, thou shalt be thrust down to hell. He that heareth you, heareth me; and he that despiseth you, despiseth me; and he that despiseth me, despiseth him that sent me.

6. (Mat. 11.) At that time Jesus answered and said: I confess to thee, O Father, Lord of heaven and earth, because thou hast hid these things from the wise and prudent, and hast revealed them to little ones. Yea, Father; for so hath it seemed good in thy sight. All things are delivered to me by my Father. And no one knoweth the Son, but the Father: neither doth any one know the Father, but the Son, and he to whom it shall please the Son to reveal *him*. Come to me, all you that labour, and are burdened, and I will refresh you. Take up my yoke upon you, and learn of me, because I am meek, and humble of heart: and you shall find rest to your souls. For my yoke is sweet and my burden light.

7. (Luke 10.) And behold a certain lawyer stood up tempting him, and saying, Master, what must I do to possess eternal life? But he said to him: What is written in the law? how readest thou? He answering, said: *Thou shall love the Lord thy God with thy whole heart, and with thy whole soul, and with all thy strength, and with all thy mind: and thy neighbour as thyself.* And he said to him: Thou

hast answered right: this do, and thou shalt live. But he willing to justify himself, said to Jesus: And who is my neighbour? And JESUS answering, said: A certain man went down from Jerusalem to Jericho, and fell among robbers, who also stripped him, and having wounded him went away leaving him half dead. And it chanced, that a certain priest went down the same way: and seeing him passed by. In like manner also a Levite, when he was near the place and saw him, passed by. But a certain Samaritan being on his journey, came near him; and seeing him, was moved with compassion. And going up to him, bound up his wounds, pouring in oil and wine: and setting him upon his own beast, brought him to an inn, and took care of him. And the next day he took out two pence, and gave to the host, and said: Take care of him; and whatsoever thou shalt spend over and above, I, at my return, will repay thee. Which of these three, in thy opinion, was neighbour to him that fell among the robbers? But he said: He that shewed mercy to him. And Jesus said to him: Go, and do thou in like manner.

8. Now it came to pass as they went, that he entered into a certain town: and a certain woman named Martha, received him into her house. And she had a sister called Mary, who sitting also at the Lord's feet, heard his word. But Martha was busy about much serving. Who stood and said: Lord, hast thou no care that my sister hath left me alone to serve? speak to her therefore, that she help me. And the Lord answering, said to her: Martha, Martha, thou art careful, and art troubled about many things. But one thing is necessary. Mary has chosen the best part, which shall not be taken away from her.

9. (John 7.) The Jews therefore sought him on the festival day, and said: Where is he? And there was much murmuring among the multitude concerning him. For some said: He is a good man. And others said: No, but he seduceth the people. Yet no man spoke openly of him, for fear of the Jews.

10. Now about the midst of the feast, Jesus went up into the temple, and taught. And the Jews wondered, saying: How doth this man know letters, having never learned? Jesus answered them, and said: My doctrine is not mine, but his that sent me. If any man will do the will of him; he shall know of the doctrine, whether it be of God, or whether I speak of myself. He that speaketh of himself, seeketh his own glory: but he that seeketh the glory of him that sent him, he is true, and there is no injustice in him. Did not Moses give you the law, and *yet* none of

you keepeth the law. Why seek you to kill me? The multitude answered, and said: Thou hast a devil; who seeketh to kill thee? Jesus answered, and said to them: One work I have done; and you all wonder: Therefore, Moses gave you circumcision, (not because it is of Moses, but of the fathers;) and on the sabbath day you circumcise a man. If a man receive circumcision on the sabbath day, that the law of Moses may not be broken; are you angry at me because I have healed the whole man on the sabbath day? Judge not according to the appearance, but judge just judgment. Some therefore of Jerusalem said: Is not this he whom they seek to kill? And behold, he speaketh openly, and they say nothing to him. Have the rulers known for a truth, that this is the Christ? But we know this man, whence he is: but when the Christ cometh, no man knoweth whence he is. Jesus therefore cried out in the temple, teaching, and saying: You both know me, and you know whence I am: and I am not come of myself; but he that sent me, is true, whom you know not. I know him, because I am from him, and he hath sent me. They sought therefore to apprehend him: and no man laid hands on him, because his hour was not yet come. But of the people many believed in him, and said: When the Christ cometh, shall he do more miracles, than these which this man doth? The Pharisees heard the people murmuring these things concerning him: and the rulers and Pharisees sent ministers to apprehend him. Jesus therefore said to them: Yet a little while I am with you: and *then* I go to him that sent me. You shall seek me, and shall not find me: and where I am, *thither* you cannot come. The Jews therefore said among themselves: Whither will he go, that we shall not find him? will he go unto the dispersed among the gentiles, and teach the gentiles? What is this saying that he hath said: You shall seek me, and shall not find me; and where I am, you cannot come?

11. And on the last, *and* great day of the festivity, Jesus stood and cried, saying: If any man thirst, let him come to me, and drink. He that believeth in me, as the scripture saith, *Out of his belly shall flow rivers of living water.* Now this he said of the spirit which they should receive, who believed in him: for as yet the spirit was not given, because Jesus was not yet glorified.

12. Of that multitude therefore, when they had heard these words of his, some said: This is the prophet indeed. Others said: this is the Christ. But some said: Doth the Christ come out of Galilee? Doth not the scripture say: That Christ cometh of the seed

of David, and from Bethlehem the town where David was? So there arose a dissension among the people because of him. And some of them would have apprehended him: but no man laid hands upon him. The ministers therefore came to the chief priests and the Pharisees. And they said to them: Why have you not brought him? The ministers answered: Never did man speak like this man. The Pharisees therefore answered them: Are you also seduced? Hath any one of the rulers believed in him, or of the Pharisees. But this multitude, that knoweth not the law, are accursed. Nicodemus said to them, (he that came to him by night, who was one of them:) Doth our law judge any man, unless it first hear him, and know what he doth? They answered, and said to him: Art thou also a Galilean? Search the scriptures, and see, that out of Galilee a prophet riseth not. And every man returned to his own house.

13. (A. D. 32. John 8.) Now Jesus went unto mount Olivet. And early in the morning he came again into the temple, and all the people came to him, and sitting down he taught them. And the scribes and Pharisees bring unto him a woman taken in adultery: and they set her in the midst, and said to him: Master, this woman was even now taken in adultery. Now Moses in the law commanded us to stone such a one. But what sayest thou? And this they said tempting him, that they might accuse. But Jesus bowing himself down, wrote with his finger on the ground. When therefore they continued asking him, he lifted up himself, and said to them: He that is without sin among you, let him first cast a stone at her. And again stooping down, he wrote on the ground. But they hearing *this*, went out one by one, beginning at the eldest. And Jesus alone remained, and the woman standing in the midst. Then Jesus lifting up himself, said to her: Woman, where are they that accused thee? Hath no man condemned thee? Who said: No man, Lord. And Jesus said: Neither will I condemn thee. Go, and now sin no more.

14. Again therefore, Jesus spoke to them, saying: I am the light of the world: He that followeth me, walketh not in darkness, but shall have the light of life. The Pharisees therefore said to him: Thou givest testimony of thyself: thy testimony is not true. Jesus answered, and said to them: Although I give testimony of myself, my testimony is true: for I know whence I came, and whither I go: but you know not whence I come, or whither I go. You judge according to the flesh: I judge not any man. And if I do judge, my judgment is true: because I am not alone, but I

and the Father that sent me. And in your law it is written, that the testimony of two men is true. I am one that give testimony of myself: and the Father that sent me giveth testimony of me. They said therefore to him: Where is thy Father? Jesus answered: Neither me do you know, nor my Father: if you did know me, perhaps you would know my Father also. These words Jesus spoke in the treasury, teaching in the temple: and no man laid hands on him, because his hour was not yet come.

15. Again therefore Jesus said to them: I go, and you shall seek me, and you shall die in your sin. Whither I go, you cannot come. The Jews therefore said: Will he kill himself, because he said: Whither I go, you cannot come? And he said to them: You are from beneath, I am from above. You are of this world, I am not of this world. Therefore I said to you, that you shall die in your sins. For if you believe not that I am he, you shall die in your sin. They said therefore to him: Who art thou? Jesus said to them: The beginning, who also speak unto you. Many things I have to speak, and to judge of you. But he that sent me, is true: and the things I have heard of him, these same I speak in the world. And they understood not, that he called God his Father.

16. Jesus therefore said to them: When you shall have lifted up the son of man, then shall you know, that I am he, and that I do nothing of myself, but as the Father hath taught me, these things I speak: And he that sent me, is with me, and he hath not left me alone: for I do always the things that please him. When he spoke these things, many believed in him.

17. Then Jesus said to those Jews, who believed him: If you continue in my word, you shall be my disciples indeed. And you shall know the truth, and the truth shall make you free. They answered him: We are the seed of Abraham, and we have never been slaves to any man: how sayest thou: you shall be free? Jesus answered them: Amen, amen, I say unto you: that whosoever committeth sin, is the servant of sin. Now the servant abideth not in the house for ever; but the son abideth for ever. If therefore the son shall make you free, you shall be free indeed. I know that you are the children of Abraham: but you seek to kill me, because my word hath no place in you. I speak that which I have seen with my Father: and you do the things that you have seen with your father. They answered, and said to him: Abraham is our father. Jesus saith to them: If you be the children of Abraham, do the works of Abraham. But now you seek to kill me, a man who

have spoken the truth to you, which I have heard of God. This Abraham did not. You do the works of your father. They said therefore to him: We are not born of fornication: We have one Father, *even* God. Jesus therefore said to them: if God were your father, you would indeed love me. For from God I proceeded, and came; for I came not of myself, but he sent me: Why do you not know my speech? Because you cannot hear my word. You are of *your* father the devil, and the desires of your father you will do. He was a murderer from the beginning, and he stood not in the truth; because truth is not in him. When he speaketh a lie, he speaketh of his own: for he is a liar, and the father thereof. But if I say the truth, you believe me not. Which of you shall convince me of sin? If I say the truth to you, why do you not believe me? He that is of God, heareth the words of God. Therefore you hear them not, because you are not of God. The Jews therefore answered, and said to him: Do not we say well that thou art a Samaritan, and hast a devil? Jesus answered: I have not a devil: but I honour my Father, and you have dishonoured me. But I seek not my own glory: there is one that seeketh and judgeth.

18. Amen, amen, I say to you: If any man keep my word, he shall not see death for ever. The Jews therefore said: Now we know that thou hast a devil. Abraham is dead, and the prophets; and thou sayest: If any man keep my word, he shall not taste death for ever. Art thou greater than our father Abraham, who is dead? and the prophets are dead. Whom dost thou make thyself? Jesus answered: If I glorify myself, my glory is nothing. It is my Father that glorifieth me, of whom you say that he is your God. And you have not known him, but I know him. And if I shall say that I know him not, I shall be like to you, a liar. But I do know him, and do keep his word. Abraham your father rejoiced that he might see my day: he saw it, and was glad. The Jews therefore said to him: Thou art not yet fifty years old, and hast thou seen Abraham?

19. Jesus said to them: Amen, amen, I say to you, before Abraham was made, I am. They took up stones therefore to cast at him. But Jesus hid himself, and went out of the temple.

20. (John 9. A. D. 32.) Now Jesus passing by, saw a man, who was blind from his birth: And his disciples asked him: Rabbi, who hath sinned, this man, or his parents, that he should be born blind? Jesus answered: Neither hath this man sinned, nor his parents; but that the works of God should be made manifest in him.

I must work the works of him that sent me, whilst it is day: the night cometh, when no man can work. As long as I am in the world, I am the light of the world. When he had said these things, he spat on the ground, and made clay of the spittle, and spread the clay upon his eyes, And said to him: Go, wash in the pool of Siloe, which is interpreted, Sent. He went therefore, and washed, and he came seeing. The neighbours therefore, and they who had seen him before that he was a beggar, said: Is not this he that sat and begged? Some said: This is he. But others said: No, but he is like him. But he said: I am he. They said therefore to him: How were thy eyes opened? He answered: That man that is called Jesus made clay, and anointed my eyes, and said to me: Go to the pool of Siloe, and wash. And I went, I washed, and I see. And they said to him: Where is he? He saith: I know not. They bring him that had been blind to the Pharisees. Now it was the sabbath, when Jesus made the clay, and opened his eyes. Again therefore the Pharisees asked him, how he had received his sight. But he said to them: He put clay upon my eyes, and I washed, and I see. Some therefore of the Pharisees said: This man is not of God, who keepeth not the sabbath. But others said: How can a man that is a sinner do such miracles? And there was a division among them. They say therefore to the blind man again: What sayest thou of him that hath opened thy eyes? And he said: He is a prophet. The Jews then did not believe concerning him, that he had been blind, and had received his sight, until they called the parents of him that had received his sight, and asked them, saying: Is this your son, who you say was born blind? How then doth he now see? His parents answered them, and said: We know that this is our son, and that he was born blind: But how he now seeth, we know not; or who hath opened his eyes, we know not: ask himself; he is of age, let him speak for himself. These things his parents said, because they feared the Jews: for the Jews had already agreed among themselves, that if any man should confess him to be Christ, he should be put out of the synagogue. Therefore did his parents say: He is of age, ask him. They therefore called the man again that had been blind, and said to him: Give glory to God. We know that this man is a sinner. He said therefore to them: If he be a sinner, I know not: one thing I know, that whereas I was blind, now I see. They said then to him: What did he to thee? How did he open thy eyes? He answered them: I have told you already, and you have heard: why would you hear it again? will you also become his disciples? They reviled him therefore, and said: Be thou his disciple; but we are the disciples of Moses. We know that God spoke to Moses: but as to this man, we know not from whence he is. The man answered, and said to them: Why, herein is a wonderful thing, that you know not from whence he is, and he hath opened my eyes. Now we know that God doth not hear sinners: but if a man be a server of God, and doth his will, him he heareth. From the beginning of the world it hath not been heard, that any man hath opened the eyes of one born blind. Unless this man were of God, he could not do anything. They answered, and said to him: Thou wast wholly born in sins, and dost thou teach us? And they cast him out. Jesus heard that they had cast him out; and when he had found him, he said to him: dost thou believe in the Son of God? He answered, and said: Who is he, Lord, that I may believe in him? And Jesus said to him: Thou hast both seen him; and it is he that talketh with thee. And he said: I believe, Lord. And falling down, he adored him. And Jesus said: For judgment I am come into this world; that they who see not, may see; and they who see, may become blind. And some of the Pharisees, who were with him, heard: and they said unto him: Are we also blind? Jesus said to them: If you were blind you should not have sin: but now you say: We see. Your sin remaineth.

21. (John 10.) Amen, amen, I say to you: he that entereth not by the door into the sheepfold, but climbeth up another way, the same is a thief and a robber. But he that entereth in by the door is the shepherd of the sheep. To him the porter openeth; and the sheep hear his voice: and he calleth his own sheep by name, and leadeth them out. And when he hath let out his own sheep, he goeth before them: and the sheep follow him, because they know his voice. But a stranger they follow not, but fly from him, because they know not the voice of strangers. This proverb Jesus spoke to them. But they understood not what he spoke to them. Jesus therefore said to them again: Amen, amen, I say to you, I am the door of the sheep. All *others*, as many as have come, are thieves and robbers: and the sheep heard them not. I am the door. By me, if any man enter in, he shall be saved: and he shall go in, and go out, and shall find pastures. The thief cometh not, but for to steal, and to kill, and to destroy. I am come that they may have life, and may have it more abundantly. I am the good shepherd. The good shepherd giveth his life for his sheep. But the hireling, and he that is not the shepherd, whose own the sheep are not, seeth the wolf coming, and leaveth the sheep, and flieth: and the wolf catcheth, and scattereth the sheep: And the hireling flieth, because he is a hireling: and he hath no care for the sheep. I am the good shepherd; and I know mine, and mine know me. As the Father knoweth me, and I know the Father: and I lay down my life for my sheep. And other sheep I have, that are not of this fold: them also I must bring, and they shall hear my voice, and there shall be one fold and one shepherd. Therefore doth the Father love me: because I lay down my life, that I may take it again. No man taketh it away from me: but I lay it down of myself, and I have power to lay it down: and I have power to take it up again. This commandment have I received of my Father. A dissension rose again among the Jews for these words. And many of them said: He hath a devil, and is mad: why hear you him? Others said: these are not the words of one that hath a devil: Can a devil open the eyes of the blind?

22. (Luke 11.) Now it came to pass, that as he was in a certain place praying, when he ceased, one of his disciples said to him: Lord, teach us to pray, as John also taught his disciples. And he said to them: When you pray, say: Father, hallowed be thy name. Thy kingdom come. Give us this day our daily bread. And forgive us our sins, for we also forgive every one that is indebted to us. And lead us not into temptation. And he said to them: Which of you shall have a friend, and shall go to him at midnight, and shall say to him: Friend, lend me three loaves, Because a friend of mine is come off his journey to me, and I have not what to set before him. And he from within should answer, and say: Trouble me not, the door is now shut, and my children are with me in bed; I cannot rise and give thee. Yet if he shall continue knocking, I say to you, although he will not rise and give him, because he is his friend; yet, because of his importunity, he will rise, and give him as many as he needeth. And I say to you, Ask, and it shall be given you: seek, and you shall find: knock, and it shall be opened to you. For every one that asketh, receiveth; and he that seeketh, findeth; and to him that knocketh, it shall be opened. And which of you if he ask his father bread, will he give him a stone? or a fish, will he for a fish give him a serpent? Or if he shall ask an egg, will he reach him a scorpion? If you then, being evil, know how to give good gifts to your children, how much more will your Father from heaven give the good Spirit to them that ask him?

23. (A. D. 32.) Now he was casting out a devil, and

the same was dumb: and when he had cast out the devil, the dumb spoke: and the multitudes were in admiration at it: But some of them said: He casteth out devils by Beelzebub, the prince of devils. And others tempting, asked of him a sign from heaven. But he seeing their thoughts, said to them: Every kingdom divided against itself, shall be brought to desolation, and house upon house shall fall. And if satan also be divided against himself, how shall his kingdom stand? because you say, that through Beelzebub I cast out devils. Now if I cast out devils by Beelzebub; by whom do your children cast them out? Therefore they shall be your judges. But if I by the finger of God cast out devils; doubtless the kingdom of God is come upon you. When a strong man armed keepeth his court, those things are in peace which he possesseth. But if a stronger than he come upon him, and overcome him; he will take away all his armour wherein he trusted, and will distribute his spoils. He that is not with me, is against me; and he that gathereth not with me, scattereth.

24. When the unclean spirit is gone out of a man, he walketh through places without water, seeking rest; and not finding, he saith: I will return into my house whence I came out. And when he is come, he findeth it swept and garnished. Then he goeth and taketh with him seven other spirits more wicked than himself, and entering in they dwell there. And the last state of that man becomes worse than the first.

25. Now it came to pass, as he spoke these things, a certain woman from the crowd, lifting up her voice, said to him: Blessed is the womb that bore thee, and the paps that gave thee suck. But he said: Yea rather, blessed are they who hear the word of God, and keep it.

26. Now the multitudes running together, he began to say: This generation is a wicked generation: it asketh a sign, and a sign shall not be given it, but the sign of Jonas the prophet. For as Jonas was a sign to the Ninivites; so shall the son of man also be to this generation. The queen of the south shall rise in the judgment with the men of this generation, and shall condemn them: because she came from the ends of the earth to hear the wisdom of Solomon; and behold more than Solomon here. The men of Ninive shall rise in the judgment with this generation, and shall condemn it; because they did penance at the preaching of Jonas; and behold more than Jonas here. No man lighteth a candle, and putteth it in a hidden place, nor under a bushel; but upon a candlestick, that they that come in, may see the light. The light of thy body is thy eye. If thy eye be single, thy whole body will be lightsome: but if it be evil, thy body also will be darksome. Take heed therefore, that the light which is in thee, be not darkness. If then thy whole body be lightsome, having no part of darkness; the whole shall be lightsome; and as a bright lamp, shall enlighten thee.

27. Now as he was speaking, a certain Pharisee prayed him, that he would dine with him. And he going in, sat down to eat. And the Pharisee began to say, thinking within himself, why he was not washed before dinner. And the Lord said to him: Now you Pharisees make clean the outside of the cup and of the platter; but your inside is full of rapine and iniquity. Ye fools, did not he that made that which is without, make also that which is within? But yet that which remaineth, give alms; and behold, all things are clean unto you. But wo to you Pharisees, because you tithe mint and rue and every herb; and pass over judgment, and the charity of God. Now these things you ought to have done, and not to leave the other undone. Wo to you, Pharisees, because you love the uppermost seats in the synagogues, and salutations in the market-place. Wo to you, because you are as sepulchres that appear not, and men that walk over, are not aware. And one of the lawyers answering, saith to him: Master, in saying these things, thou reproachest us also. And the Pharisees and the lawyers began violently to urge him, and to oppress his mouth about many things, lying in wait for him, and seeking to catch something from his mouth, that they might accuse him.

(Luke 12.) And when great multitudes stood about him, so that they trod one upon another, he began to say to his disciples: Beware ye of the leaven of the Pharisees, which is hypocrisy. For there is nothing covered, that shall not be revealed: nor hidden, that shall not be known. For whatsoever things you have spoken in darkness, shall be published in the light: and that which you have spoken in the ear in the chambers, shall be preached on the housetops.

28. Now I say to you, my friends: Be not afraid of them who kill the body, and after that have no more that they can do. But I will shew you whom you shall fear; fear ye him, who after he hath killed, hath power to cast into hell: Yea, I say to you, fear him. Are not five sparrows sold for two farthings, and not one of them is forgotten before God? Yea, the very hairs of your head are all numbered. Fear not therefore: You are of more value than many sparrows.

29. Now I say to you, Whosoever shall confess me be-

fore men, him shall the son of man also confess before the Angels of God. But he that shall deny me before men, shall be denied before the Angels of God. And whosoever speaketh a word against the son of man, it shall be forgiven him: but to him that shall blaspheme against the Holy Ghost, it shall not be forgiven. And when they shall bring you into the synagogues, and to magistrates and powers, be not solicitous how or what you shall answer, or what you shall say; For the Holy Ghost shall teach you in the same hour what you must say.

30. Now one of the multitude said to him: Master, speak to my brother that he divide the inheritance with me. But he said to him: Man, who hath appointed me judge, or divider, over you? And he said to them: Take heed, and beware of all covetousness; for a man's life doth not consist in the abundance of things which he possesseth. And he spoke a similitude to them, saying: The land of a certain rich man brought forth plenty of fruits. And he thought within himself, saying: What shall I do, because I have no room where to bestow my fruits? And he said: This will I do: I will pull down my barns, and will build greater; and into them will I gather all things that are grown to me, and my goods. And I will say to my soul: Soul, thou hast much goods laid up for many years, take thy rest; eat, drink, make good cheer. But God said to him: Thou fool, this night do they require thy soul of thee: and whose shall those things be which thou hast provided? So is he that layeth up treasure for himself, and is not rich towards God. And he said to his disciples: Therefore I say to you, be not solicitous for your life, what you shall eat; nor for your body, what you shall put on. The life is more than the meat, and the body is more than the raiment. Consider the ravens, for they sow not, neither do they reap, neither have they storehouse nor barn, and God feedeth them. How much are you more valuable than they? And which of you, by taking thought, can add to his stature one cubit? If then ye be not able to do so much as the least thing, why are you solicitous for the rest? Consider the lilies, how they grow: they labour not, neither do they spin. But I say to you, not even Solomon in all his glory was clothed like one of these. Now if God clothe in this manner the grass that is to-day in the field, and to-morrow is cast into the oven; how much more you, O ye of little faith? And seek not you what you shall eat, or what you shall drink: and be not lifted up on high. For all these things do the nations of the world seek. But your Father knoweth that you have need of these things. But

seek ye first the kingdom of God and his justice, and all these things shall be added unto you. Fear not, little flock, for it hath pleased your Father to give you a kingdom. Sell what you possess and give alms. Make to yourselves bags which grow not old, a treasure in heaven which faileth not: where no thief approacheth, nor moth corrupteth. For where your treasure is, there will your heart be also.

31. Let your loins be girt, and lamps burning in your hands. And you yourselves like to men who wait for their lord, when he shall return from the wedding; that when he cometh and knocketh, they may open to him immediately. Blessed are those servants, whom the Lord when he cometh, shall find watching. Amen I say to you, that he will gird himself, and make them sit down to meat, and passing will minister unto them. And if he shall come in the second watch, or come in the third watch, and find them so, blessed are those servants. But this know ye, that if the householder did know at what hour the thief would come, he would surely watch, and open, not suffer his house to be broken open. Be you then also ready: for at what hour you think not, the son of man will come. And Peter said to him: Lord, dost thou speak this parable to us, or likewise to all? And the Lord said: Who (thinkest thou) is the faithful and wise steward, whom his lord setteth over his family, to give them their measure of wheat in due season? Blessed is that servant, whom when his lord shall come, he shall find so doing. Verily I say to you, he will set him over all that he possesseth. But if that servant shall say in his heart: My lord is long a coming; and shall begin to strike the men servants and maidservants, and to eat and to drink and be drunk: The lord of that servant will come in the day that he hopeth not, and at the hour that he knoweth not, and shall separate him, and shall appoint him his portion with unbelievers, And that servant who knew the will of his lord, and prepared *not himself*, and did not according to his will, shall be beaten with many stripes. But he that knew not, and did things worthy of stripes, shall be beaten with few stripes. And unto whomsoever much is given, of him much shall be required: and to whom they have committed much, of him they will demand the more.

32. I am come to cast fire on the earth: and what will I, but that it be kindled? And I have a baptism wherewith I am to be baptised: and how am I straitened until it be accomplished? Think ye, that I am come to give peace on earth? I tell you, no; but separation. For there shall be from henceforth five in one house divided:

three against two, and two against three. The father *shall be divided* against the son, and the son against his father, the mother against the daughter, and the daughter against the mother, the mother-in-law against her daughter-in-law, and the daughter-in-law against her mother-in-law.

33. Then he said also to the multitudes: When you see a cloud rising from the west, presently you say: A shower is coming: and so it happeneth: And when *ye see* the south wind blow, you say: There will be heat: and it cometh to pass. You hypocrites, you know how to discern the face of the heaven and of the earth: but how is it that you do not discern this time? And why even of yourselves, do you not judge that which is just?

34. And when thou goest with thy adversary to the prince, whilst thou art in the way, endeavour to be delivered from him: lest perhaps he draw thee to the judge, and the judge deliver thee to the exacter, and the exacter cast thee into prison. I say to thee, thou shalt not go out thence, until thou pay the very last mite.

35. (Luke 13. A. D. 32.) Now there were present, at that very time, some that told him of the Galileans, whose blood Pilate had mingled with their sacrifices. And he answering, said to them: Think you, that these Galileans were sinners above all the men of Galilee, because they suffered such things? No, I say to you: but unless you shall do penance, you shall all likewise perish. Or those eighteen upon whom the tower fell in Siloe, and slew them: think you, that they also were debtors above all the men that dwelt in Jerusalem? No, I say to you; but except you do penance, you shall all likewise perish.

36. He spoke also this parable: A certain man had a fig-tree planted in his vineyard, and he came seeking fruit on it, and found none. And he said to the dresser of the vineyard: Behold, for these three years I come seeking fruit on this fig-tree, and I find none. Cut it down therefore: why cumbereth it the ground? But he answering said to him: Lord, let it alone this year also, until I dig about it, and dung it. And if happily it bear fruit: but if not, then after that thou shalt cut it down.

37. Now he was teaching in their synagogue on their sabbath. And behold there was a woman, who had a spirit of infirmity eighteen years: and she was bowed together, neither could she look upwards at all. Whom when Jesus saw, he called her unto him, and said to her: Woman, thou art delivered from thy infirmity. And he laid his hands upon her, and immediately she was made straight, and glorified God.

38. Now the ruler of the

synagogue (being angry that Jesus had healed on the sabbath,) answering said to the multitude: Six days there are wherein you ought to work. In them therefore come, and be healed; and not on the sabbath day. And the Lord answering him, said: Ye hypocrites, doth not every one of you, on the sabbath day, loose his ox or his ass from the manger, and lead them to water? And ought not this daughter of Abraham, whom satan hath bound, lo, these eighteen years, be loosed from this bond on the sabbath day? And when he said these things, all his adversaries were ashamed: and all the people rejoiced for all the things that were gloriously done by him.

39. He said therefore: To what is the kingdom of God like, and whereunto shall I resemble it? It is like to a grain of mustard-seed, which a man took and cast into his garden, and it grew and became a great tree, and the birds of the air lodged in the branches thereof. And again he said: Whereunto shall I esteem the kingdom of God to be like? It is like to leaven, which a woman took and hid in three measures of meal, till the whole was leavened. And he went through the cities and towns teaching, and making his journey to Jerusalem.

40. (John 10.) Now it was the feast of the dedication at Jerusalem: and it was winter. And Jesus walked in the temple, in Solomon's porch. The Jews therefore came round about him, and said to him: How long dost thou hold our souls in suspense? If thou be the Christ, tell us plainly. Jesus answered them: I speak to you, and you believe not: the works that I do in the name of my Father, they give testimony of me. But you do not believe, because you are not of my sheep. My sheep hear my voice: and I know them, and they follow me. And I give them life everlasting; and they shall not perish for ever, and no man shall pluck them out of my hand. That which my Father hath given me, is greater than all: and no one can snatch *them* out of the hand of my Father. I and the Father are one. The Jews then took up stones to stone him. Jesus answered them: Many good works I have shewed you from my Father; for which of those works do you stone me? The Jews answered him: For a good work we stone thee not, but for blasphemy; and because that thou, being a man, makest thyself God? Jesus answered them: Is it not written in your law: *I said you are gods?* If he called them gods, to whom the word of God was spoken, and the scripture cannot be broken; Do you say of him whom the Father hath sanctified and sent into the world: Thou blasphemest, because I said, I am the Son of God? If I do not the works of my Fa-

ther, believe me not. But if I do, though you will not believe me, believe the works: that you may know and believe that the Father is in me, and I in the Father. They sought therefore to take him; and he escaped out of their hands.

CHAPTER VII.

WARNINGS AND EXHORTATIONS.

1. (John 10. A. D. 32.) Now he went again beyond the Jordan, into that place where John was baptizing first; and there he abode. And many resorted to him, and they said: John indeed did no sign. But all things whatsoever John said of this man, were true. And many believed in him.

2. (Luke 13.) Now a certain man said to him: Lord, are they few that are saved? But he said to them: Strive to enter by the narrow gate; for many, I say to you, shall seek to enter, and shall not be able. But when the master of the house shall be gone in, and shall shut the door, you shall begin to stand without, and knock at the door, saying: Lord, open to us. And he answering, shall say to you: I know you not, whence you are. Then you shall begin to say: We have eaten and drunk in thy presence, and thou hast taught in our streets. And he shall say to you: I know you not, whence you are: depart from me, all ye workers of iniquity. There shall be weeping and gnashing of teeth, when you shall see Abraham and Isaac and Jacob, and all the prophets, in the kingdom of God, and you yourselves thrust out. And there shall come from the east and the west, and the north and the south; and shall sit down in the kingdom of God. And behold, they are last that shall be first; and they are first that shall be last.

3. The same day, there came some of the Pharisees, saying to him: Depart, and get thee hence, for Herod hath a mind to kill thee. And he said to them: Go and tell that fox, Behold, I cast out devils, and do cures to-day and to-morrow, and the third day I am consummated. Nevertheless I must walk to-day and to-morrow, and the day following, because it cannot be that a prophet perish out of Jerusalem. Jerusalem, Jerusalem, that killest the prophets, and stonest them that are sent to thee, how often would I have gathered thy children as the bird doth her brood under her wings, and thou wouldest not? Behold your house shall be left to you desolate. And I say to you, that you shall not see me till the time come, when you shall say: Blessed is he that cometh in the name of the Lord.

4. (Luke 14.) Now it came to pass, when Jesus went into the house of one of the chief of the Pharisees, on the sabbath-day, to eat bread, that they watched him. And behold, there was a certain man before him that had the dropsy. And Jesus answering, spoke to the lawyers and Pharisees, saying: Is it lawful to heal on the sabbath day? But they held their peace. But he taking him, healed him, and sent him away. And answering them, he said: Which of you shall have an ass or an ox fall into a pit, and will not immediately draw him out, on the sabbath-day? And they could not answer him to these things.

5. Now he spoke a parable also to them, that were invited, marking how they chose the first seats at the table, saying to them: When thou art invited to a wedding, sit not down in the first place, lest perhaps one more honourable than thou be invited by him: and he that invited thee and him, come and say to thee, give this man place: and then thou begin with shame to take the lowest place. But when thou art invited, go, sit down in the lowest place; that when he who invited thee, cometh, he may say to thee: Friend, go up higher. Then shalt thou have glory before them that sit at table with thee. Because every one that exalteth himself, shall be humbled; and he that humbleth himself, shall be exalted. And he said to him also that had invited him: When thou makest a dinner or a supper, call not thy friends, nor thy brethren, nor thy kinsmen, nor thy neighbours who are rich; lest perhaps they also invite thee again, and a recompense be made to thee. But when thou makest a feast, call the poor, the maimed, the lame, and the blind; And thou shalt be blessed, because they have not wherewith to make thee recompense: for recompense shall be made thee at the resurrection of the just.

6. When one of them that sat at table with him, had heard these things, he said to him: Blessed is he that shall eat bread in the kingdom of God. But he said to him: A certain man made a great supper, and invited many. And he sent his servant at the hour of supper to say to them that were invited, that they should come, for now all things are ready. And they began all at once to make excuse. The first said to him: I have bought a farm, and I must needs go out and see it: I pray thee, hold me excused. And another said: I have bought five yoke of oxen, and I go to try them: I pray thee,

hold me excused. And another said: I have married a wife, and therefore I cannot come. And the servant returning, told these things to his lord. Then the master of the house, being angry, said to his servant: Go out quickly into the streets and lanes of the city, and bring in hither the poor, and the feeble, and the blind, and the lame. And the servant said: Lord it is done as thou hast commanded, and yet there is room. And the Lord said to the servant: Go out into the highways and hedges, and compel them to come in, that my house may be filled. But I say unto you, that none of those men that were invited, shall taste of my supper.

7. Now there went great multitudes with him. And turning, he said to them: If any man come to me, and hate not his father, and mother, and wife, and children, and brethren, and sisters, yea and his own life also, he cannot be my disciple. And whosoever doth not carry his cross and come after me, cannot be my disciple. For which of you having a mind to build a tower, doth not first sit down, and reckon the charges that are necessary whether he have wherewithal to finish *it:* Lest, after he hath laid the foundation, and is not able to finish it, all that see it begin to mock him, Saying: This man began to build, and was not able to finish. Or what king, about to go to make war against another king, doth not first sit down, and think whether he be able, with ten thousand, to meet him that, with twenty thousand, cometh against him? Or else, whilst the other is yet afar off, sending an embassy, he desireth conditions of peace. So likewise every one of you that doth not renounce all that he possesseth, cannot be my disciple. Salt is good. But if the salt shall lose its savour, wherewith shall it be seasoned? It is neither profitable for the land nor for the dunghill, but shall be cast out. He that hath ears to hear, let him hear.

8. (Luke 15. A. D. 32.) Now the publicans and sinners drew near unto him to hear him. And the Pharisees and the scribes murmured, saying: This man receiveth sinners, and eateth with them. And he spoke to them this parable, saying: What man of you that hath an hundred sheep: and if he shall lose one of them, doth he not leave the ninety-nine in the desert, and go after that which was lost, until he find it? And when he hath found it, lay it upon his shoulders, rejoicing: And coming home, call together his friends and neighbours, saying to them: Rejoice with me, because I have found my sheep that was lost? I say to you, that even so there shall be joy in heaven upon one sinner that doth penance, more than upon ninety-nine just who need not penance. Or what woman having ten groats; if she lose

one groat, doth not light a candle, and sweep the house, and seek diligently until she find it? And when she hath found it, call together her friends and neighbours, saying: Rejoice with me, because I have found the groat which I had lost. So I say to you, there shall be joy before the Angels of God upon one sinner doing penance.

9. Then he said: A certain man had two sons: And the younger of them said to his father: Father, give me the portion of substance that falleth to me. And he divided unto them his substance. And not many days after, the younger son, gathering all together, went abroad into a far country: and there wasted his substance, living riotously. And after he had spent all, there came a mighty famine in that country; and he began to be in want. And he went and cleaved to one of the citizens of that country. And he sent him into his farm to feed swine. And he would fain have filled his belly with the husks the swine did eat; and no man gave unto him. And returning to himself, he said: How many hired servants in my father's house abound with bread, and I here perish with hunger? I will arise, and will go to my father, and say to him: Father, I have sinned against heaven, and before thee: I am not worthy to be called thy son: make me as one of thy hired servants. And rising up he came to his father. And when he was yet a great way off, his father saw him, and was moved with compassion, and running to him fell upon his neck, and kissed him. And the son said to him: Father, I have sinned against heaven, and before thee, I am not now worthy to be called thy son. And the father said to his servants: Bring forth quickly the first robe, and put it on him, and put a ring on his hand, and shoes on his feet: And bring hither the fatted calf, and kill it, and let us eat and make merry: Because this my son was dead, and is come to life again: was lost, and is found. And they began to be merry. Now his elder son was in the field, and when he came and drew nigh to the house, he heard music and dancing: And he called one of the servants, and asked, what these things meant. And he said to him: Thy brother is come, and thy father hath killed the fatted calf, because he hath received him safe. And he was angry, and would not go in. His father therefore coming out began to entreat him. And he answering, said to his father: Behold, for so many years do I serve thee, and I have never transgressed thy commandment, and yet thou hast never given me a kid to make merry with my friends: But as soon as this thy son is come, who hath devoured his substance with harlots, thou hast killed for him the fatted calf. But he said to him:

Son, thou art always with me, and all I have is thine. But it was fit that we should make merry and be glad, for this thy brother was dead and is come to life again; he was lost, and is found.

10. (Luke 16.) Now he said also to his disciples: There was a certain rich man who had a steward: and the same was accused unto him, that he had wasted his goods. And he called him, and said to him: How is it that I hear this of thee? give an account of thy stewardship: for now thou canst be steward no longer. And the steward said within himself: What shall I do, because my lord taketh away from me the stewardship? to dig I am not able; to beg I am ashamed. I know what I will do, that when I shall be removed from the stewardship, they may receive me into their houses. Therefore calling together every one of his lord's debtors, he said to the first: How much dost thou owe my lord? But he said: An hundred barrels of oil. And he said to him: Take thy bill and sit down quickly, and write fifty. Then he said to another: And how much dost thou owe? Who said: An hundred quarters of wheat. He said to him: Take thy bill, and write eighty. And the lord commended the unjust steward, forasmuch as he had done wisely; for the children of this world are wiser in their generation than the children of light. And I say to you: Make unto you friends of the mammon of iniquity; that when you shall fail, they may receive you into everlasting dwellings.

11. He that is faithful in that which is least, is faithful also in that which is greater: and he that is unjust in that which is little, is unjust also in that which is greater. If then you have not been faithful in the unjust mammon; who will trust you with that which is the true? And if you have not been faithful in that which is another's; who will give you that which is your own? No servant can serve two masters: for either he will hate the one, and love the other; or he will hold to the one, and despise the other. You cannot serve God and mammon.

12. Now the Pharisees, who were covetous, heard all these things: and they derided him. And he said to them: You are they who justify yourselves before men, but God knoweth your hearts; for that which is high to men, is an abomination before God. The law and the prophets *were* until John; from that time the kingdom of God is preached, and every one useth violence towards it. And it is easier for heaven and earth to pass, than one tittle of the law to fall. Every one that putteth away his wife, and marrieth another, committeth adultery: and he that marrieth her that is put away from her husband, committeth adultery.

13. There was a certain rich man, who was clothed in purple and fine linen; and feasted sumptuously every day. And there was a certain beggar, named Lazarus, who lay at his gate, full of sores, desiring to be filled with the crumbs that fell from the rich man's table, and no one did give him; moreover the dogs came, and licked his sores. And it came to pass, that the beggar died, and was carried by the angels into Abraham's bosom. And the rich man also died: and he was buried in hell. And lifting up his eyes when he was in torments, he saw Abraham afar off, and Lazarus in his bosom: And he cried, and said: Father Abraham, have mercy on me, and send Lazarus, that he may dip the tip of his finger in water, to cool my tongue: for I am tormented in this flame. And Abraham said to him: Son, remember that thou didst receive good things in thy lifetime, and likewise Lazarus evil things, but now he is comforted; and thou art tormented. And besides all this, between us and you, there is fixed a great chaos: so that they who would pass from hence to you, cannot, nor from thence come hither. And he said: Then, father, I beseech thee, that thou wouldst send him to my father's house, for I have five brethren. That he may testify unto them, lest they also come into this place of torments. And Abraham said to him: They have Moses and the prophets; let them hear them. But he said: No, father Abraham: but if one went to them from the dead, they will do penance. And he said to him: If they hear not Moses and the prophets, neither will they believe, if one arise again from the dead.

14. (Luke 17.) Now he said to his disciples: It is impossible that scandals should not come: but woe to him through whom they come. It were better for him, that a millstone were hanged about his neck, and he cast into the sea, than that he should scandalize one of these little ones. Take heed to yourselves. If thy brother sin against thee, reprove him: and if he do penance, forgive him.

(Mat. 18.) If he shall hear thee, thou shalt gain thy brother. And if he will not hear thee, take with thee one or two more: that in the mouth of two or three witnesses every word may stand. And if he will not hear them: tell the church. And if he will not hear the church, let him be to thee as the heathen and publican. Amen I say to you, whatsoever you shall bind upon earth, shall be bound also in heaven; and whatsoever you shall loose upon earth, shall be loosed also in heaven.

15. Again I say to you, that if two of you shall consent upon earth, concerning any thing whatsoever they shall ask, it shall be done to them by

my Father who is in heaven. For where there are two or three gathered together in my name, there am I in the midst of them.

16. Then came Peter unto him and said: Lord, how often shall my brother offend against me, and I forgive him? till seven times? Jesus saith to him: I say not to thee, till seven times; but till seventy times seven times? Therefore is the kingdom of heaven likened to a king, who would take an account of his servants. And when he had begun to take the account, one was brought to him, that owed him ten thousand talents. And as he had not wherewith to pay it, his lord commanded that he should be sold, and his wife and children and all that he had, and payment to be made. But that servant falling down, besought him, saying: Have patience with me, and I will pay thee all. And the lord of that servant being moved with pity, let him go and forgave him the debt. But when that servant was gone out, he found one of his fellow-servants that owed him an hundred pence: and laying hold of him, he throttled him, saying: Pay what thou owest. And his fellow-servant falling down, besought him, saying: Have patience with me, and I will pay thee all. And he would not: but went and cast him into prison, till he paid the debt. Now his fellow-servants seeing what was done, were very much grieved, and they came and told their lord all that was done. Then his lord called him; and said to him: Thou wicked servant, I forgave thee all the debt, because thou besoughtest me: Shouldst not thou then have had compassion also on thy fellow-servant, even as I had compassion on thee? And his lord being angry, delivered him to the torturers until he paid all the debt. So also shall my heavenly Father do to you, if you forgive not every one his brother from your hearts.

17. (Luke 17.) Now the apostles said to the Lord: Increase our faith. And the Lord said: If you had faith like to a grain of mustard-seed, you might say to this mulberry-tree, Be thou rooted up, and be thou transplanted into the sea: and it would obey you.

18. But which of you having a servant plowing, or feeding cattle, will say to him, when he is come from the field: Immediately go, sit down to meat: And will not *rather* say to him: Make ready my supper, and gird thyself, and serve me, whilst I eat and drink, and afterwards thou shalt eat and drink? Doth he thank that servant, for doing the things which he commanded him? I think not. So you also, when you shall have done all these things that are commanded you, say: We are unprofitable servants; we have done that which we ought to do.

19. (John 11.) Now there was a certain man sick, named Lazarus, of Bethania, of the town of Mary and of Martha her sister. (And Mary was she that anointed the Lord with ointment, and wiped his feet with her hair: whose brother Lazarus was sick.) His sisters therefore sent to him, saying: Lord, behold, he whom thou lovest is sick. And Jesus hearing it, said to them: This sickness is not unto death, but for the glory of God: that the Son of God may be glorified by it. Now Jesus loved Martha, and her sister Mary, and Lazarus. When he had heard therefore that he was sick, he still remained in the same place two days. Then after that, he said to his disciples: Let us go into Judea again. The disciples say to him: Rabbi, the Jews but now sought to stone thee: and goest thou thither again? Jesus answered: Are there not twelve hours of the day? If a man walk in the day, he stumbleth not, because he seeth the light of this world: But if he walk in the night, he stumbleth, because the light is not in him. These things he said; and after that he said to them: Lazarus our Friend sleepeth; but I go that I may awake him out of sleep. His disciples therefore said: Lord, if he sleep, he shall do well. But Jesus spoke of his death; and they thought that he spoke of the repose of sleep. Then therefore Jesus said to them plainly: Lazarus is dead. And I am glad, for your sakes, that I was not there, that you may believe: but let us go to him. Thomas therefore, who is called Didymus, said to his fellow-disciples: Let us also go, that we may die with him. Jesus therefore came, and found that he had been four days already in the grave. (Now Bethania was near Jerusalem, about fifteen furlongs off.) And many of the Jews were come to Martha and Mary, to comfort them concerning their brother. Martha therefore, as soon as she heard that Jesus was come, went to meet him: but Mary sat at home.

20. Martha therefore said to Jesus: Lord, if thou hadst been here, my brother had not died. But now also I know that whatsoever thou wilt ask of God, God will give it thee. Jesus saith to her: Thy brother shall rise again. Martha saith to him: I know that he shall rise again, in the resurrection at the last day. Jesus said to her: I am the resurrection and the life: he that believeth in me, although he be dead, shall live: And every one that liveth, and believeth in me, shall not die forever. Believest thou this? She saith to him: Yea, Lord, I have believed that thou art Christ the Son of the living God, who art come into this world.

21. And when she had said these things, she went, and called her sister Mary secretly, saying: the master is come, and calleth for thee. She, as soon as she heard *this*, riseth quickly and cometh to him. For Jesus was not yet come into the town: but he was still in that place where Martha had met him. The Jews therefore, who were with her in the house, and comforted her, when they saw Mary that she rose up speedily and went out, followed her, saying: She goeth to the grave to weep there. When Mary therefore was come where Jesus was, seeing him, she fell down at his feet, and saith to him: Lord, if thou hadst been here, my brother had not died. JESUS, therefore, when he saw her weeping, and the Jews that were come with her, weeping, groaned in the spirit, and troubled himself, and said: Where have you laid him? They say to him: Lord, come and see. And Jesus wept. The Jews therefore said: Behold how he loved him. But some of them said: Could not he that opened the eyes of the man born blind, have caused that this man should not die? Jesus therefore again groaning in himself, cometh to the sepulchre: Now it was a cave; and a stone was laid over it. Jesus saith: Take away the stone. Martha, the sister of him that was dead, saith to him: Lord, by this time he stinketh, for he is now of four days. Jesus saith to her: Did not I say to thee, that if thou believe, thou shalt see the glory of God? They took therefore the stone away, And Jesus lifting up his eyes said: Father, I give thee thanks that thou hast heard me. And I knew that thou hearest me always; but because of the people who stand about have I said it, that they may believe that thou hast sent me. When he had said these things, he cried with a loud voice: Lazarus, come forth. And presently he that had been dead came forth, bound feet and hands with winding bands; and his face was bound about with a napkin. Jesus said to them: Loose him, and let him go. Many therefore of the Jews, who were come to Mary and Martha, and had seen the things Jesus did, believed in him. But some of them went to the Pharisees, and told them the things that Jesus had done.

22. (A. D. 32.) The chief priests therefore, and the Pharisees, gathered a council, and said: What do we, for this man doth many miracles? If we let him alone so, all will believe in him; and the Romans will come, and take away our place and nation. But one of them, named Caiphas, being the highpriest that year, said to them: You know nothing. Neither do you consider that it is expedient for you that one man should die for the people, and that the whole nation perish not. And this he spoke not of himself: but being the highpriest of that year, he prophesied that Jesus should die for

the nation. And not only for the nation, but to gather together in one the children of God, that were dispersed. From that day therefore they devised to put him to death. Wherefore Jesus walked no more openly among the Jews; but he went into a country near the desert, unto a city that is called Ephrem, and there he abode with his disciples.

CHAPTER VIII.

THE LAST JOURNEY.

1. (Luke 17. A. D. 33.) Now it came to pass, as he was going to Jerusalem, he passed through the midst of Samaria and Galilee. And as he entered into a certain town, there met him ten men that were lepers, who stood afar off; and lifted up their voice saying: Jesus, master, have mercy on us. Whom when he saw, he said: Go, show yourselves to the priests. And it came to pass, as they went, they were made clean. And one of them, when he saw that he was made clean, went back, with a loud voice glorifying God. And he fell on his face before his feet, giving thanks: and this was a Samaritan. And Jesus answering, said, Were not ten made clean? and where are the nine? There is no one found to return and give glory to God, but this stranger. And he said to him: Arise, go thy way; for thy faith hath made thee whole.

2. Now being asked by the Pharisees, where the kingdom of God should come? he answered them, and said: The kingdom of God cometh not with observation: Neither shall they say: Behold here, or behold there. For lo, the kingdom of God is within you. And he said to his disciples: The days will come, when you shall desire to see one day of the son of man; and you shall not see it. And they will say to you: See here, and see there. Go ye not after, nor follow them: For as the lightning that lighteneth from under heaven, shineth unto the parts that are under heaven, so shall the son of man be in his day. But first he must suffer many things, and be rejected by this generation. And as it came to pass in the days of Noe, so shall it be also in the days of the son of man. They did eat and drink, they married wives, and were given in marriage, until the day that Noe entered into the ark: and the flood came and destroyed

them all. Likewise as it came to pass, in the days of Lot: they did eat and drink, they bought and sold, they planted and built. And in the day that Lot went out of Sodom, it rained fire and brimstone from heaven, and destroyed them all. Even thus shall it be in the day when the son of man shall be revealed. In that hour, he that shall be on the housetop, and his goods in the house, let him not go down to take them away: and he that shall be in the field, in like manner, let him not return back. Remember Lot's wife. Whosoever shall seek to save his life, shall lose it: and whosoever shall lose it, shall preserve it. I say to you: in that night there shall be two men in one bed; the one shall be taken, and the other shall be left: Two women shall be grinding together: the one shall be taken, and the other shall be left, two men shall be in the field; the one shall be taken, and the other shall be left. They answering say to him: Where, Lord? Who said to them: Wheresoever the body shall be, thither will the eagles also be gathered together.

3. (Luke 18.) Now he spoke also a parable to them, that we ought always to pray, and not to faint, Saying: There was a judge in a certain city, who feared not God, nor regarded man. And there was a certain widow in that city, and she came to him, saying: Avenge me of my adversary. And he would not for a long time. But afterwards he said within himself: Although I fear not God, nor regard man, yet because this widow is troublesome to me, I will avenge her, lest continually coming she weary me. And the Lord said: Hear what the unjust judge saith. And will not God revenge his elect who cry to him day and night: and will he have patience in their regard? I say to you, that he will quickly revenge them. But yet the son of man, when he cometh, shall he find, think you, faith on earth?

4. Now to some who trusted in themselves as just, and despised others, he spoke also this parable: Two men went up into the temple to pray: the one a Pharisee, and the other a publican. The Pharisee standing, prayed thus with himself: O God, I give thee thanks that I am not as the rest of men, extortioners, unjust, adulterers, as also is this publican. I fast twice in a week: I give tithes of all that I possess. And the publican standing afar off, would not so much as lift up his eyes towards heaven; but struck his breast, saying: O God, be merciful to me a sinner. I say to you, this man went down into his house justified rather than the other: because every one that exalteth himself, shall be humbled: and he that humbleth himself, shall be exalted.

5. (Mark 10.) Now rising up from thence, he cometh into the coasts of Judea beyond the

Jordan: and the multitudes flock to him again. And as he was accustomed, he taught them again. And the Pharisees coming to him asked him: Is it lawful for a man to put away his wife? tempting him. But he answering, saith to them: What did Moses command you? Who said: Moses permitted to write a bill of divorce, and to put *her* away. To whom Jesus answering, said: Because of the hardness of your heart he wrote you that precept. But from the beginning of the creation, God made them male and female. For this cause a man shall leave his father and mother; and shall cleave to his wife. And they two shall be in one flesh. Therefore now they are not two, but one flesh. What therefore God hath joined together, let not man put asunder. And in the house again his disciples asked him concerning the same thing. And he saith to them: Whosoever shall put away his wife and marry another, committeth adultery against her. And if the wife shall put away her husband, and be married to another, she committeth adultery.

6. Now they brought to him young children, that he might touch them. And the disciples rebuked them that brought them. Whom when Jesus saw, he was much displeased, and saith to them: Suffer the little children to come unto me, and forbid them not; For of such is the kingdom of God. Amen I say to you, whosoever shall not receive the kingdom of God as a little child, shall not enter into it. And embracing them, and laying his hands upon them, he blessed them.

7. Now when he was gone forth into the way, a certain man running up and kneeling before him, asked him, Good Master, what shall I do that I may receive life everlasting? And Jesus said to him, Why callest thou me good? None is good but one, *that is* God. Thou knowest the commandments: *Do not commit adultery, do not kill, do not steal, bear not false witness, do no fraud, honour thy father and mother*. But he answering said to him: Master, all these things I have observed from my youth. And Jesus looking on him, loved him, and said to him: One thing is wanting unto thee: go, sell whatsoever thou hast, and give to the poor, and thou shalt have treasure in heaven; and come, follow me. Who being struck sad at that saying, went away sorrowful: for he had great possessions. And Jesus looking round about, saith to his disciples: How hardly shall they that have riches, enter into the kingdom of God! And the disciples were astonished at his words. But Jesus again answering, saith to them: Children, how hard is it for them that trust in riches, to enter into the kingdom of God? It is easier for a camel to pass

through the eye of a needle, than for a rich man to enter into the kingdom of God. Who wondered the more, saying among themselves: Who then can be saved? And Jesus looking on them, saith: With men it is impossible; but not with God: for all things are possible with God. And Peter began to say unto him: Behold, we have left all things, and have followed thee. Jesus answering, said: Amen I say to you, there is no man who hath left house, or brethren, or sisters, or father, or mother, or children, or lands, for my sake and for the gospel. who shall not receive an hundred times as much, now in this time; houses, and brethren, and sisters, and mothers, and children, and lands, with persecutions: and in the world to come life everlasting. But many that are first, shall be last: and the last first.

8. (Mat. 20.) The kingdom of heaven is like to an householder, who went out early in the morning to hire labourers into his vineyard. And having agreed with the labourers for a penny a day, he sent them into his vineyard. And going out about the third hour, he saw others standing in the market-place idle. And he said to them: Go you also into my vineyard, and I will give you what shall be just. And they went their way. And again he went out about the sixth and the ninth hour, and did in like manner. But about the eleventh hour he went out and found others standing, and he saith to them: Why stand you here all the day idle? They say to him: because no man hath hired us. He saith to them: Go you also into my vineyard. And when evening was come, the lord of the vineyard saith to his steward: Call the labourers and pay them their hire, beginning from the last even to the first. When therefore they were come, that came about the eleventh hour, they received every man a penny. But when the first also came, they thought that they should receive more: and they also received every man a penny. And receiving *it* they murmured against the master of the house, saying: These last have worked but one hour, and thou hast made them equal to us, that have borne the burden of the day and the heats. But he answering said to one of them: Friend, I do thee no wrong: didst thou not agree with me for a penny? Take what is thine, and go thy way: I will also give to this last even as to thee. Or, is it not lawful for me to do what I will? is thy eye evil, because I am good? So shall the last be first, and the first last. For many are called, but few chosen.

9. (Mark 10. A. D. 33.) Now they were in the way going up to Jerusalem: and Jesus went before them, and

they were astonished: and following were afraid.

(Luke 18. A. D. 33.) Then Jesus took unto him the twelve, and said to them: Behold, we go up to Jerusalem, and all things shall be accomplished which were written by the prophets concerning the son of man. For he shall be delivered to the gentiles, and shall be mocked, and scourged, and spit upon: And after they have scourged him, they will put him to death; and the third day he shall rise again. And they understood none of these things, and this word was hid from them, and they understood not the things that were said.

10. (Mat. 20.) Then came to him the mother of the sons of Zebedee with her sons, adoring and asking something of him. Who said to her: What wilt thou? She saith to him: Say that these my two sons may sit, the one on thy right hand, and the other on thy left, in thy kingdom. And Jesus answering, said: You know not what you ask. Can you drink the chalice that I shall drink? They say to him: we can. He saith to them: My chalice indeed you shall drink; but to sit on my right or left hand, is not mine to give to you, but to them for whom it is prepared by my Father. And the ten hearing it, were moved with indignation against the two brethren. But Jesus called them to him, and said: You know that the princes of the gentiles lord it over them; and they that are the greater, exercise power upon them. It shall not be so among you: but whosoever will be the greater among you, let him be your minister: And he that will be first among you, shall be your servant. Even as the son of man is not come to be ministered unto, but to minister, and to give his life a redemption for many.

11. (Luke 18.) Now it came to pass, when he drew nigh to Jericho, that a certain blind man sat by the wayside, begging. And when he heard the multitude passing by, he asked what this meant. And they told him, that Jesus of Nazareth was passing by. And he cried out, saying: Jesus, son of David, have mercy on me. And they that went before, rebuked him, that he should hold his peace: but he cried out much more: Son of David, have mercy on me. And Jesus standing, commanded him to be brought unto him. And when he was come near, he asked him, Saying: What wilt thou that I do to thee? But he said: Lord, that I may see. And Jesus said to him: Receive thy sight: thy faith hath made thee whole. And immediately he saw, and followed him, glorifying God. And all the people, when they saw it, gave praise to God.

12. (Luke 19. A. D. 33.) Now entering in, he walked through Jericho. And behold, there was a man named Zacheus, who was the chief of the publicans, and he was rich. And he sought to see Jesus who he was, and he could not for the crowd, because he was low of stature. And running before, he climbed up into a sycamore tree, that he might see him; for he was to pass that way. And when Jesus was come to the place, looking up, he saw him, and said to him: Zacheus, make haste and come down; for this day I must abide in thy house. And he made haste and came down; and received him with joy. And when all saw it, they murmured, saying, that he was gone to be a guest with a man that was a sinner. But Zacheus standing, said to the Lord: Behold, Lord, the half of my goods I give to the poor; and if I have wronged any man of any thing, I restore him fourfold. Jesus said to him: This day is salvation come to this house, because he also is a son of Abraham. For the son of man is come to seek and to save that which was lost.

13. As they were hearing these things, he added and spoke a parable, because he was nigh to Jerusalem, and because they thought that the kingdom of God should immediately be manifested. He said therefore: A certain nobleman went into a far country, to receive for himself a kingdom, and to return. And calling his ten servants, he gave them ten pounds, and said to them: Trade till I come. But his citizens hated him; and they sent an embassage after him, saying: We will not have this man to reign over us. And it came to pass, that he returned, having received the kingdom: and he commanded his servants to be called, to whom he had given the money, that he might know how much every man had gained by trading. And the first came, saying: Lord, thy pound hath gained ten pounds. And he said to him: Well done, thou good servant, because thou hast been faithful in a little, thou shalt have power over ten cities. And the second came, saying: Lord, thy pound hath gained five pounds. And he said to him: Be thou also over five cities. And another came, saying: Lord, behold here is thy pound, which I have kept laid up in a napkin; For I feared thee, because thou art an austere man: thou takest up what thou didst not lay down, and thou reapest that which thou didst not sow. He saith to him: Out of thy own mouth I judge thee, thou wicked servant. Thou knewest that I was an austere man, taking up what I laid not down, and reaping that which I did not sow: And why then didst thou not give my money into the bank, that at my coming, I might have exacted it with usury? And he said to them that stood by: Take the pound away from him, and give it to him that hath ten pounds. And they said to him: Lord, he hath ten pounds. But I say to you, that to every one that hath shall be given, and he shall abound: and from him that hath not, even that which he hath, shall be taken from him. But as for those my enemies, who would not have me reign over them, bring them hither, and kill them before me. And having said these things, he went before, going up to Jerusalem.

14. (Mat. 20. A. D. 33.) Now when they went out from Jericho, a great multitude followed him. And behold two blind men sitting by the wayside, heard that Jesus passed by, and they cried out, saying: O Lord, thou son of David, have mercy on us. And the multitude rebuked them that they should hold their peace. But they cried out the more, saying: O Lord, thou son of David, have mercy on us. And Jesus stood, and called them, and said: What will ye that I do to you? They say to him: Lord, that our eyes be opened. And Jesus having compassion on them, touched their eyes. And immediately they saw, and followed him.

15. (John 11.) Now the pasch of the Jews was at hand; and many from the country went up to Jerusalem, before the pasch, to purify themselves. They sought therefore for Jesus; and they discoursed one with another, standing in the temple: What think you that he is not come to the festival day? And the chief priests and the Pharisees had given a commandment, that if any man knew where he was, he should tell, that they might apprehend him.

(John 12. A. D. 33.) Jesus therefore, six days before the pasch, came to Bethania, where Lazarus had been dead, whom Jesus raised to life. And they made him a supper there: and Martha served: but Lazarus was one of them that were at table with him. Mary therefore took a pound of ointment of right spikenard, of great price, and anointed the feet of Jesus, and wiped his feet with her hair; and the house was filled with the odour of the ointment. Then one of his disciples, Judas Iscariot, he that was about to betray him, said: Why was not this ointment sold for three hundred pence, and given to the poor? Now he said this, not because he cared for the poor; but because he was a thief, and having the purse, carried the things that were put therein. Jesus therefore said: Let her alone, that she may keep it against the day of my burial. For the poor you have always with you; but me you have not always. A great multitude therefore of the Jews knew that he was there; and they came, not for Jesus' sake only, but that they might see Lazarus, whom he had raised from the dead. But the chief priests thought to kill Lazarus also: because many of the Jews, by reason of him, went away, and believed in Jesus.

16. (Mark 11. Sunday,

April 2, A. D. 33.) Now on the next day, when they drew nigh to Jerusalem, and were come to Bethphage, unto Mount Olivet, then Jesus sent two disciples, Saying to them: Go ye into the village that is over against you, and immediately you shall find an ass tied, and a colt with her: loose *them* and bring *them* to me. And if any man shall say anything to you, say ye, that the Lord hath need of them: and forthwith he will let them go. And the disciples going, did as Jesus commanded them. They found the colt tied before the gate without, in the meeting of two ways: and they loose him. And some of them that stood there, said to them: What do you loosing the colt? Who said to them as Jesus had commanded them; and he let them go with them. And they brought the colt to Jesus; and they lay their garments on him, and he sat upon him.

(Mat. 21.) Now all this was done that it might be fulfilled which was spoken by the prophet, saying: *Tell ye the daughter of Sion: Behold thy king cometh to thee, meek, and sitting upon an ass, and a colt the foal of her that is used to the yoke.*

(Luke 19.) And as he went, they spread their clothes underneath in the way. And when he was now coming near the descent of Mount Olivet, the whole multitude of his disciples began with joy to praise God with a loud voice, for all the mighty works they had seen, Saying: Blessed be the king who cometh in the name of the Lord, peace in heaven, and glory on high! And some of the Pharisees, from amongst the multitude, said to him: Master, rebuke thy disciples. To whom he said: I say to you, that if these shall hold their peace, the stones will cry out.

17. (A. D. 33.) Now when he drew near, seeing the city, he wept over it, saying: If thou also hadst known, and that in this thy day, the things that are to thy peace; but now they are hidden from thy eyes. For the days shall come upon thee: and thy enemies shall cast a trench about thee, and compass thee round, and straiten thee on every side, And beat thee flat to the ground, and thy children who are in thee: and they shall not leave in thee a stone upon a stone: because thou hast not known the time of thy visitation.

18. (Mat. 21.) Now when he was come into Jerusalem, the whole city was moved, saying: Who is this? And the people said: This is Jesus the prophet, from Nazareth of Galilee. And there came to him the blind and the lame in the temple; and he healed them. And the chief priests and scribes, seeing the wonderful things that he did, and the children crying in the temple, and saying: *Hosanna to the son of David;* were moved with indignation, and said to him: Hearest thou what these say?

And Jesus said to them: Yea, have you never read: *Out of the mouth of infants and of sucklings thou hast perfected praise?* And leaving them, he went out of the city into Bethania, and remained there.

19. (John 12.) Now certain Gentiles had come to Jerusalem for the festival. These therefore came to Philip, who was of Bethsaida of Galilee, and desired him, saying: Sir, we would see Jesus. Philip cometh, and telleth Andrew. Again Andrew and Philip told Jesus. But Jesus answered them, saying: The hour is come, that the son of man should be glorified. Amen, amen, I say to you, unless the grain of wheat falling into the ground die, itself remaineth alone. But if it die, it bringeth forth much fruit. He that loveth his life shall lose it; and he that hateth his life in this world, keepeth it unto life eternal. If any man minister to me, let him follow me; and where I am, there also shall my minister be. If any man minister to me, him will my Father honour.

20. Now is my soul troubled. And what shall I say? Father, save me from this hour. But for this cause I came unto this hour. Father, glorify thy name. A voice therefore came from heaven: I have both glorified it, and will glorify it again. The multitude therefore that stood and heard, said that it thundered. Others said: An angel spoke to him. Jesus answered, and said: This voice came not because of me, but for your sakes.

21. Now is the judgment of the world: now shall the prince of this world be cast out. And I, if I be lifted up from the earth, will draw all things to myself. (Now this he said, signifying what death he should die.) The multitude answered him: We have heard out of the law, that Christ abideth for ever; and how sayest thou: The son of man must be lifted up? Who is this son of man? Jesus therefore said to them: Yet a little while, the light is among you. Walk whilst you have the light, that the darkness overtake you not. And he that walketh in darkness, knoweth not whither he goeth. Whilst you have the light, believe in the light, that you may be the children of light. These things Jesus spoke; and he went away, and hid himself from them.

22. (Mark 11. Monday, April 3, A. D. 33.) Now the next day when they came out from Bethania, he was hungry. And when he had seen afar off a fig-tree having leaves, he came if perhaps he might find anything on it. And when he was come to it, he found nothing but leaves. For it was not the time for figs. And answering he said to it: May no man hereafter eat fruit of thee any more for ever. And his disciples heard it. And immediately the fig-tree withered away.

23. Now they came to Jerusalem. And when he was entered into the temple, he began to cast out them that sold and bought in the temple, and overthrew the tables of the money-changers, and the chairs of them that sold doves. And he suffered not that any man should carry a vessel through the temple; And he taught, saying to them: Is it not written, *My house shall be called the house of prayer to all nations?* *But you have made it a den of thieves.* Which when the chief priests and the scribes had heard, they sought how they might destroy him. For they feared him, because the whole multitude was in admiration at his doctrine. And when evening was come, he went forth out of the city.

24. (Tuesday, April 4, A. D. 33.) Now when they passed by in the morning they saw the fig-tree dried up from the roots. And Peter remembering, said to him: Rabbi, behold the fig-tree, which thou didst curse, is withered away. And Jesus answering saith to them: Have the faith of God. Amen I say to you, that whosoever shall say to this mountain, Be thou removed and be cast into the sea, and shall not stagger in his heart, but believe, that whatsoever he saith shall be done; it shall be done unto him. Therefore I say unto you, all things, whatsoever you ask when ye pray, believe that you shall receive; and they shall come unto you.

25. And when you shall stand to pray, forgive, if you have aught against any man; that your Father also, who is in heaven, may forgive you your sins. But if you will not forgive, neither will your Father that is in heaven, forgive you your sins.

26. (Luke 20.) Now it came to pass, that on one of the days, as he was teaching the people in the temple, and preaching the gospel, the chief priests and the scribes, with the ancients, met together, And spoke to him, saying: Tell us, by what authority dost thou these things? or, Who is he that hath given thee this authority? And Jesus answering, said to them: I will also ask you one thing. Answer me: The baptism of John was it from heaven, or of men? But they thought within themselves, saying: If we shall say From heaven: he will say: Why then did you not believe him? But if we say, Of men, the whole people will stone us: for they are persuaded that John was a prophet. And they answered, that they knew not whence it was. And Jesus said to them: Neither do I tell thee by what authority I do these things.

27. (Mat. 21.) But what think you? A certain man had two sons; and coming to the first, he said: Son, go work to-day in my vineyard. And he answering, said: I will not.

But afterwards, being moved with repentance, he went. And coming to the other, he said in like manner. And he answering, said: I go, Sir; and he went not. Which of the two did the father's will? They say to him: The first. Jesus saith to them: Amen I say to you, that the publicans and the harlots shall go into the kingdom of God before you. For John came to you in the way of justice, and you did not believe him. But the publicans and the harlots believed him: but you, seeing it, did not even afterwards repent, that you might believe him.

28. Hear ye another parable. There was a man an householder, who planted a vineyard, and made a hedge round about it, and dug in it a press, and built a tower, and let it out to husbandmen; and went into a strange country. And when the time of the fruits drew nigh, he sent his servants to the husbandmen that they might receive the fruits thereof. And the husbandmen laying hands on his servants, beat one, and killed another, and stoned another. Again he sent other servants more than the former; and they did to them in like manner. And last of all he sent to them his son, saying: They will reverence my son. But the husbandmen seeing the son, said among themselves: This is the heir: come, let us kill him, and we shall have his inheritance. And taking him, they cast him forth out of the vineyard, and killed him. When therefore the lord of the vineyard shall come, what will he do to those husbandmen? They say to him: He will bring those evil men to an evil end; and will let out his vineyard to other husbandmen, that shall render him the fruit in due season. Jesus saith to them: Have you never read in the Scriptures: *The stone which the builders rejected, the same is become the head of the corner? By the Lord this has been done; and it is wonderful in our eyes.* Therefore I say to you, that the kingdom of God shall be taken from you, and shall be given to a nation yielding the fruits thereof. And whosoever shall fall on this stone, shall be broken: but on whomsoever it shall fall, it shall grind him to powder. And when the chief priests and Pharisees had heard his parables, they knew that he spoke of them. And seeking to lay hands on him, they feared the multitudes: because they held him as a prophet. And leaving him they went their way.

29. (Mat. 22.) Now Jesus answering, spoke again in parables to them, saying: The kingdom of heaven is likened to a king, who made a marriage for his son. And he sent his servants, to call them that were invited to the marriage; and they would not come. Again he sent other servants, saying: Tell them that were invited,

Behold, I have prepared my dinner; my beeves and fatlings are killed, and all things are ready: come ye to the marriage. But they neglected, and went their ways, one to his farm, and another to his merchandise. And the rest laid hands on his servants, and having treated them contumeliously, put them to death. But when the king had heard of it, he was angry, and sending his armies, he destroyed those murderers, and burnt their city. Then he saith to his servants: The marriage indeed is ready; but they that were invited were not worthy. Go ye therefore into the highways; and as many as you shall find, call to the marriage. And his servants going forth into the ways, gathered together all that they found, both bad and good: and the marriage was filled with guests. And the king went in to see the guests: and he saw there a man who had not on a wedding garment. And he saith to him: Friend, how camest thou in hither not having on a wedding garment? But he was silent. Then the king said to the waiters: Bind his hands and feet, and cast him into the exterior darkness: there shall be weeping and gnashing of teeth. For many are called, but few *are* chosen.

30. Then the Pharisees going, consulted among themselves how to insnare him in *his* speech. And they sent to him their disciples with the Herodians, saying: Master, we know that thou art a true speaker, and teachest the way of God in truth, neither carest thou for any man: for thou dost not regard the person of men. Tell us therefore what dost thou think, is it lawful to give tribute to Cesar, or not? But Jesus knowing their wickedness, said: Why do you tempt me, ye hypocrites? Shew me the coin of the tribute. And they offered him a penny. And Jesus saith to them: Whose image and inscription is this? They say to him: Cesar's. Then he saith to them: Render therefore to Cesar the things that are Cesar's; and to God, the things that are God's. And hearing *this* they wondered, and leaving him, went their ways.

31. That day there came to him the Sadducees, who say there is no resurrection; and asked him, saying: Master, Moses said: *If a man die having no son, his brother shall marry his wife, and raise up issue to his brother.* Now there were with us seven brethren: and the first having married a wife, died; and not having issue, left his wife to his brother. In like manner the second, and the third, and so on to the seventh. And last of all the woman died also. At the resurrection therefore whose wife of the seven shall she be? for they all had her. And Jesus answering, said to them: You err, not knowing the Scriptures, nor

the power of God. For in the resurrection they shall neither marry nor be married; but shall be as the Angels of God in heaven. And concerning the resurrection of the dead, have you not read that which was spoken by God, saying to you: *I am the God of Abraham, and the God of Isaac, and the God of Jacob?* He is not the God of the dead, but of the living. And the multitudes hearing it, were in admiration at his doctrine.

32. But the Pharisees hearing that he had silenced the Sadducees, came together: And one of them, a doctor of the law, asked him, tempting him: Master, which is the great commandment in the law? Jesus said to him: *Thou shalt love the Lord thy God with thy whole heart, and with thy whole soul, and with thy whole mind.* This is the greatest and the first commandment. And the second is like to this: *Thou shalt love thy neighbour as thyself.* On these two commandments dependeth the whole law and the prophets.

33. Now the Pharisees being gathered together, Jesus asked them, Saying: What think you of Christ? whose son is he? they say to him: David's. He saith to them: How then doth David in spirit call him Lord, saying: *The Lord said to my Lord, Sit on my right hand, until I make thy enemies thy footstool?* If David then call him lord, how is he his son? And no man was able to answer him a word; neither durst any man from that day forth ask him any more questions.

34. (Mat. 23.) Then Jesus spoke to the multitudes and to his disciples, Saying: The Scribes and the Pharisees have sitten on the chair of Moses. All things therefore whatsoever they shall say to you, observe and do: but according to their works do ye not; for they say, and do not. For they bind heavy and insupportable burdens, and lay them on men's shoulders; but with a finger of their own they will not move them. And all their works they do for to be seen of men. For they make their phylacteries broad, and enlarge their fringes. And they love the first places at feast, and the first chairs in the synagogues, and salutations in the marketplace, and to be called by men, Rabbi. But be not you called Rabbi. For one is your master; and all you are brethren. And call none your father upon earth; for one is your father, who is in heaven. Neither be ye called masters; for one is you master, Christ. He that is the greatest among you shall be your servant. And whosoever shall exalt himself shall be humbled: and he that shall humble himself shall be exalted. But wo to your scribes and Pharisees, hypocrites; because you shut the kingdom of heaven against men, for you yourselves

do not enter in; and those that are going in, you suffer not to enter. Wo to you scribes and Pharisees, hypocrites: because you devour the houses of widows, praying long prayers. For this you shall receive the greater judgment. Wo to you scribes and Pharisees, hypocrites; because you go round about the sea and the land to make one proselyte; and when he is made, you make him the child of hell twofold more than yourselves.

35. Wo to you blind guides, that say, whosoever shall swear by the temple, it is nothing; but he that shall swear by the gold of the temple, is a debtor. Ye foolish and blind; for whether is greater, the gold, or the temple that sanctifieth the gold? And whosoever shall swear by the altar, it is nothing; but whosoever shall swear by the gift that is upon it, is a debtor. Ye blind: for whether is greater, the gift, or the altar that sanctifieth the gift? He therefore that sweareth by the altar, sweareth by it, and by all things that are upon it: And whosoever shall swear by the temple, sweareth by it, and by him that dwelleth in it: And he that sweareth by heaven, sweareth by the throne of God, and by him that sitteth thereon.

36. Wo to you scribes and Pharisees, hypocrites; because you tithe mint, and anise, and cummin, and have left the weightier things of the law; judgment, and mercy, and faith. These things you ought to have done, and not leave those undone. Blind guides, who strain out a gnat, and swallow a camel. Wo to you scribes and Pharisees, hypocrites; because you make clean the outside of the cup and of the dish, but within you are full of rapine and uncleanness. Thou blind Pharisee, first make clean the inside of the cup and of the dish, that the outside may become clean. Wo to you scribes and Pharisees, hypocrites; because you are like to whited sepulchres, which outwardly appear to men beautiful, but within are full of dead men's bones, and of all filthiness. So you also outwardly indeed appear to men just; but inwardly you are full of hypocrisy and iniquity. Wo to you scribes and Pharisees, hypocrites; that build the sepulchres of the prophets, and adorn the monuments of the just, and say: If we had been in the days of our Fathers, we would not have been partakers with them in the blood of the prophets. Wherefore you are witnesses against yourselves, that you are the sons of them that killed the prophets. Fill ye up then the measure of your fathers. You serpents, generation of vipers, how will you flee from the judgment of hell? Therefore behold I send to you prophets, and wise men, and scribes: and some of them you will put to death and crucify,

and some you will scourge in your synagogues, and persecute from city to city: That upon you may come all the just blood that hath been shed upon the earth, from the blood of Abel the just, even unto the blood of Zacharias the son of Barachias, whom you killed between the temple and the altar. Amen I say to you, all these things shall come upon this generation. Jerusalem, Jerusalem, thou that killest the prophets, and stonest them that are sent unto thee, how often would I have gathered together thy children, as the hen doth gather her chickens under her wings, and thou wouldest not? Behold, your house shall be left to you, desolate. For I say to you, you shall not see me henceforth till you say: Blessed is he that cometh in the name of the Lord.

37. (Luke 21.) Now looking on, he saw the rich men cast their gifts into the treasury. And he saw also a certain poor widow casting in two brass mites. And he said: Verily I say to you, that this poor widow hath cast in more than they all: For all these have of their abundance cast into the offerings of God: but she of her want, hath cast in all the living that she had.

38. (John 12.) And whereas he had done so many miracles before them, they believed not in him: That the saying of Isaias the prophet might be fulfilled, which he said: *Lord, who hath believed our hearing? and to whom hath the arm of the Lord been revealed?* Therefore they could not believe, because Isaias said again: *He hath blinded their eyes, and hardened their heart, that they should not see with their eyes, nor understand with their heart, and be converted, and I should heal them.* These things said Isaias, when he saw his glory, and spoke of him. However many of the chief men also believed in him; but because of the Pharisees they did not confess him, that they might not be cast out of the synagogue. For they loved the glory of men more than the glory of God. But Jesus cried, and said: He that believeth in me, doth not believe in me, but in him that sent me. And he that seeth me, seeth him that sent me. I am come a light into the world; that whosoever believeth in me, may not remain in darkness. And if any man hear my words, and keep them not, I do not judge him: for I came not to judge the world, but to save the world. He that despiseth me, and receiveth not my words, hath one that judgeth him; the word that I have spoken, the same shall judge him in the last day. For I have not spoken of myself; but the Father who sent me, he gave me commandment what I should say, and what I should speak. And I know that his commandment is life everlasting. The things therefore that

I speak, even as the Father said unto me, so do I speak.

39. (Mat. 10.) Then to his Apostles he said: But beware of men. For they will deliver you up in councils, and they will scourge you in their synagogues. And you shall be brought before governors, and before kings for my sake, for a testimony to them and to the gentiles: But when they shall deliver you up, take no thought how or what to speak: for it shall be given you in that hour what to speak. For it is not you that speak, but the Spirit of your Father that speaketh in you. The brother also shall deliver up the brother to death, and the father the son, and the children shall rise up against their parents, and shall put them to death. And you shall be hated by all men for my name's sake: but he that shall persevere unto the end, he shall be saved. And when they shall persecute you in this city, flee into another. Amen I say to you, you shall not finish all the cities of Israel, till the son of man come.

40. (Mat. 24.) Now Jesus being come out of the temple, went away. And his disciples came to show him the buildings of the temple. And he answering, said to them: Do you see all these things? Amen I say to you there shall not be left here a stone upon a stone that shall not be destroyed.

41. Now when he was sitting on mount Olivet, the disciples came to him privately, saying: Tell us when shall these things be? and what shall be the sign of thy coming, and of the consummation of the world? And Jesus answering, said to them: Take heed that no man seduce you: For many will come in my name saying, I am Christ: and they will seduce many. And you shall hear of wars and rumors of wars. See that you be not troubled. For these things must come to pass, but the end is not yet. For nation shall rise against nation, and kingdom against kingdom; and there shall be pestilences, and famines, and earthquakes in places: Now all these are the beginnings of sorrows. Then shall they deliver you up to be afflicted, and shall put you to death: and you shall be hated by all nations for my name's sake. And then shall many be scandalized: and shall betray one another: and shall hate one another. And many false prophets shall rise, and shall seduce many. And because iniquity hath abounded, the charity of many shall grow cold. But he that shall persevere to the end, he shall be saved. And this gospel of the kingdom, shall be preached in the whole world, for a testimony to all nations, and then shall the consummation come. When therefore you shall see *the abomination of desolation*, which was spoken of by Daniel the prophet, standing in the holy place: he that readeth let

him understand. Then they that are in Judea, let them flee to the mountains: And he that is on the housetop, let him not come down to take any thing out of his house: And he that is in the field, let him not go back to take his coat. And wo to them that are with child, and that give suck in those days. But pray that your flight be not in the winter, or on the sabbath. For there shall be then great tribulation, such as hath not been from the beginning of the world until now, neither shall be. And unless those days had been shortened, no flesh should be saved: but for the sake of the elect those days shall be shortened.

(Mark 13.) And immediately after the tribulation of those days, the sun shall be darkened and the moon shall not give her light, and the stars shall fall from heaven, and the powers of heaven shall be moved: And then shall appear the sign of the son of man in heaven: and then shall all tribes of the earth mourn: and they shall see the son of man coming in the clouds of heaven with much power and majesty. And he shall send his Angels with a trumpet, and a great voice: and they shall gather together his elect from the four winds, from the farthest parts of the heavens to the utmost bounds of them. And from the fig-tree learn a parable: When the branch thereof is now tender, and the leaves come forth, you know that summer is nigh. So you also, when you shall see all these things, know ye that it is nigh *even* at the doors. Amen I say to you, that this generation shall not pass, till all these things be done. Heaven and earth shall pass, but my words shall not pass.

42. But of that day and hour no one knoweth, no not the Angels of heaven, but the Father alone. And as in the days of Noe, so shall also the coming of the son of man be. For as in the days before the flood, they were eating and drinking, marrying and giving in marriage, even till that day in which Noe entered into the ark. And they knew not till the flood came, and took them all away; so also shall the coming of the son of man be. Then two shall be in the field: one shall be taken, and one shall be left. Two women shall be grinding at the mill: one shall be taken, and one shall be left. Take ye heed, watch and pray. For ye know not when the time is. Even as a man who going into a far country, left his house; and gave authority to his servants over every work, and commanded the porter to watch. Watch ye therefore (for you know not when the lord of the house cometh: at even, or at midnight, or at the cockcrowing, or in the morning.) Lest coming on a sudden, he find you sleeping. And what I say to you, I say to all: Watch.

43. (Mat. 25.) Then shall

the kingdom of heaven be like to ten virgins, who taking their lamps went out to meet the bridegroom and the bride. And five of them were foolish, and five wise. But the five foolish, having taken their lamps, did not take oil with them: But the wise took oil in their vessels with the lamps. And the bridegroom tarrying, they all slumbered and slept. And at midnight there was a cry made: Behold the bridegroom cometh, go ye forth to meet him. Then all those virgins arose and trimmed their lamps. And the foolish said to the wise: Give us of your oil, for our lamps are gone out. The wise answered, saying: Lest perhaps there be not enough for us and for you, go ye rather to them that sell, and buy for yourselves. Now whilst they went to buy, the bridegroom came; and they that were ready, went in with him to the marriage, and the door was shut. But at last come also the other virgins, saying: Lord, Lord, open to us. But he answering said: Amen I say to you, I know you not. Watch ye therefore, because you know not the day nor the hour. For even as a man going into a far country, called his servants, and delivered to them his goods. And to one he gave five talents, and to another two, and to another one, to every one according to his proper ability: and immediately he took his journey. And he that had received the five talents, went his way, and traded with the same, and gained other five. And in like manner he that had received the two, gained other two. But he that had received the one, going his way digged into the earth, and hid his lord's money. But after a long time the lord of those servants came, and reckoned with them. And he that had received the five talents coming, brought other five talents, saying: Lord, thou didst deliver to me five talents, behold I have gained other five over and above. His lord said to him: Well done, good and faithful servant, because thou hast been faithful over a few things, I will place thee over many things: enter thou into the joy of thy lord. And he also that had received the two talents came and said: Lord, thou deliveredst two talents to me: behold I have gained other two. His lord said to him: Well done, good and faithful servant: because thou hast been faithful over a few things, I will place thee over many things: enter thou into the joy of thy lord. But he that had received the one talent, came and said: Lord, I know that thou art a hard man; thou reapest where thou hast not sown, and gatherest where thou hast not strewed. And being afraid I went and hid thy talent in the earth: behold here thou hast that which is thine. And his Lord answering, said to him: Wicked and slothful servant, thou knewest that I reap where I sow not, and gather where I have not strewed: Thou oughtest therefore to have committed my money to the bankers, and at my coming I should have received my own with usury. Take ye away therefore the talent from him, and give it him that hath ten talents. For to every one that hath shall be given, and he shall abound: but from him that hath not, that also which he seemeth to have shall be taken away. And the unprofitable servant cast ye out into the exterior darkness. There shall be weeping and gnashing of teeth.

44. Now when the son of man shall come in his majesty, and all the angels with him, then shall he sit upon the seat of his majesty: And all nations shall be gathered together before him, and he shall separate them one from another, as the shepherd separateth the sheep from the goats: And he shall set the sheep on his right hand, but the goats on his left. Then shall the king say to them that shall be on his right hand: Come, ye blessed of my Father, possess you the kingdom prepared for you from the foundation of the world. For I was hungry, and you gave me to eat; I was thirsty, and you gave me to drink; I was a stranger, and you took me in: Naked, and you covered me: sick, and you visited me: I was in prison, and you came to me.

Then shall the just answer him, saying: Lord, when did we see thee hungry, and fed thee; thirsty, and gave thee drink? And when did we see thee a stranger, and took thee in? or naked, and covered thee! Or when did we see thee sick or in prison, and came to thee? And the king answering, shall say to them: Amen I say to you, as long as you did it to one of these my least brethren, you did it to me. Then he shall say to them also that shall be on his left hand: Depart from me, you cursed, into everlasting fire which was prepared for the devil and his angels. For I was hungry, and you gave me not to eat: I was thirsty, and you gave me not to drink. I was a stranger, and you took me not in: naked, and you covered me not: sick and in prison, and you did not visit me. Then they also shall answer him, saying: Lord, when did we see thee hungry, or thirsty, or a stranger, or naked, or sick, or in prison, and did not minister to thee? Then he shall answer them, saying: Amen I say to you, as long as you did it not to one of these least, neither did you do it to me. And these shall go into everlasting punishment: but the just, into life everlasting.

45. (Mat. 26. Wednesday, April 5, A. D. 33.) Now it came to pass, when Jesus had ended all these words, he said to his disciples: You know that after two days shall be the pasch, and the son of man shall be delivered up to be crucified: Then were gathered together the chief priests and ancients of the people into the court of the high-priest, who was called Caiphas: And they consulted together, that by subtilty they might apprehend Jesus, and put him to death. But they said: Not on the festival day, lest perhaps there should be a tumult among the people. Then went one of the twelve, who was called Judas Iscariot, to the chief priests, and said to them: What will you give me, and I will deliver him unto you? But they appointed him thirty pieces of silver. And from thenceforth he sought opportunity to betray him.

PART III.

CHRIST'S PASSION AND DEATH.

CHAPTER I.

THE LAST SUPPER.

1. (Mark 14. Thursday, April 6, A. D. 33.) Now the feast of unleavened bread, which is called the pasch, was at hand, on which it was necessary that the pasch should be killed. And he sent Peter and John, saying: Go, and prepare for us the pasch, that we may eat. But they said: Where wilt thou that we prepare? And he said to them: Behold, as you go into the city, there shall meet you a man carrying a pitcher of water: follow him into the house where he entereth in. And you shall say to the goodman of the house: The master saith to thee, Where is the guest-chamber, where I may eat the pasch with my disciples? And he will shew you a large dining-room, furnished; and there prepare. And they going, found as he had said to them, and made ready the pasch.

2. And when evening was come, he cometh with the twelve. And when they were at table and eating, Jesus saith: Amen I say to you, one of you that eateth with me shall betray me. But they began to be sorrowful, and to say to him one by one: Is it I? Who saith to them: One of the twelve, who dippeth with me his hand in the dish. And the son of man indeed goeth, as it is written of him: but wo to that man by whom the son of man shall be betrayed. It were better for him, if that man had not been born.

3. (John 13.) Jesus knowing that his hour was come, that he should pass out of this world to the Father: having loved his own who were in the world, he loved them unto the end. And when supper was done, (the devil having now put into the heart of Judas Iscariot, the son of Simon, to betray him,) knowing that the Father had given him all things into his hands, and that he came from God, and goeth to God; He riseth from supper, and layeth aside his garments, and having taken a towel, girded himself. After that, he putteth water into a basin, and began to wash the feet of the disciples, and to wipe them with the towel wherewith he was girded. He cometh therefore to Simon Peter. And Peter saith to him: Lord, dost thou wash my feet? Jesus answered, and said to him: What I do thou knowest not now; but thou shalt know hereafter. Peter saith to him: Thou shalt never wash my feet. Jesus answered him: If I wash thee not, thou shalt have no part with me. Simon Peter saith to him: Lord, not only my feet, but also my hands and my head. Jesus saith to him: He that is washed, needeth not but to wash his feet, but is clean wholly. And you are clean, but not all. For he knew who he was that would betray him; therefore he said: You are not all clean. Then after he had washed their feet, and taken his garments, being sat down again, he said to them: Know you what I have done to you? You call me Master, and Lord; and you say well, for so I am. If then I being *your* Lord and Master, have washed your feet; you also ought to wash one another's feet. For I have given you an example, that as I have done to you, so you do also. Amen, amen, I say to you: The servant is not greater than his lord; neither is the apostle greater than he that sent him. If you know these things, you shall be blessed if you do them. I speak not of you all: I know whom I have chosen. But that the scripture may be fulfilled: *He that eateth bread with me, shall lift up his heel against me.* At present I tell you, before it come to pass: that when it shall come to pass, you may believe that I am he. Amen, amen, I say to you, he that receiveth whomsoever I send, receiveth me; and he that receiveth me, receiveth him that sent me.

4. (Luke 22.) Again he said to them: With desire I have desired to eat this pasch with you, before I suffer. For I say to you, that from this time I will not eat it, till it be fulfilled in the kingdom of God. And having taken the chalice, he gave thanks, and said: Take, and divide *it* among you: For I say to you, that I will not drink of the fruit of the vine, till the kingdom of God come. And taking bread, he gave thanks, and brake; and gave to them, saying: This is my body, which is given for you. Do this for a commemoration of me.

(I Cor. 11.) And taking the chalice he gave thanks, and gave to them, saying: Drink ye all of this. For this is my blood of the new testament, which shall be shed for many unto remission of sins. Therefore whosoever shall eat this bread, or drink the chalice of the Lord unworthily, shall be guilty of the body and of the blood of the Lord. But let a man prove himself: and so let him eat of that bread, and drink of the chalice. For he that eateth and drinketh unworthily, eateth and drinketh judgment to himself, not discerning the body of the Lord. But yet behold, the hand of him that betrayeth me is with me on the table. And the son of man indeed goeth, according to that which is determined: but yet, wo to that man by whom he shall be betrayed.

5. When Jesus had said these things, he was troubled in spirit; and he testified, and said: Amen, amen, I say to you, one of you shall betray me. The disciples therefore looked one upon another, doubting of whom he spoke. Now there was leaning on Jesus's bosom one of his disciples, whom Jesus loved. Simon Peter therefore beckoned to him, and said to him: Who is it of whom he speaketh? He therefore, leaning on the breast of Jesus, saith to him: Lord, who is it? Jesus answered: He it is to whom I shall reach bread dipped. And when he had dipped the bread, he gave it to Judas Iscariot, *the son* of Simon. And after the morsel, satan entered into him.

(John 13.) And Judas that betrayed him, answering said: Is it I, Rabbi? He saith to him: Thou hast said *it*. And Jesus said to him: That which thou dost, do quickly. Now no man at the table knew to what purpose he said this unto him. For some thought, because Judas had the purse, that Jesus had said to him: Buy those things which we have need of for the festival day: or that he should give something to the poor. He therefore having received the morsel, went out immediately. And it was night. When he therefore was gone out, Jesus said: Now is the Son of man glorified, and God is glorified in him. If God be glorified in him, God also will glorify him in himself; and immediately will he glorify him.

6. (Luke 22.) Now there was also a strife amongst them, which of them should seem to be the greater. And he said to them: The kings of the gentiles lord it over them; and they that have power over them, are called beneficent. But you not so: but he that is the greater among you, let him become as the younger; and he that is the leader, as he that serveth. For which is greater, he that sitteth at table, or he that serveth? Is not he that sitteth at table? But I am in the midst of you, as he that serveth: And you are they who have continued with me in my temptations: And I dispose to you, as my Father hath

disposed to me, a kingdom; That you may eat and drink at my table, in my kingdom: and may sit upon thrones, judging the twelve tribes of Israel.

7. Little children, yet a little while I am with you. You shall seek me; and as I said to the Jews: Whither I go you cannot come; so I say to you now. A new commandment I give unto you: That you love one another, as I have loved you, that you also love one another. By this shall all men know that you are my disciples, if you have love one for another.

8. (John 13.) Simon Peter saith to him: Lord, whither goest thou? Jesus answered: Whither I go, thou canst not follow me now; but thou shalt follow hereafter. Peter saith to him: Why cannot I follow thee now? I will lay down my life for thee. Jesus answered him: Wilt thou lay down thy life for me?

(Luke 22.) And the Lord said: Simon, Simon, behold satan hath desired to have you, that he may sift you as wheat: But I have prayed for thee, that thy faith fail not: and thou, being once converted, confirm thy brethren. Who said to him: Lord, I am ready to go with thee, both into prison, and to death. And he said: I say to thee, Peter, the cock shall not crow this day, till thou thrice deniest that thou knowest me. And he said to them: When I sent you without purse, and scrip, and shoes, did you want any thing? But they said: Nothing. Then said he unto them: But now he that hath a purse, let him take it, and likewise a scrip; and he that hath not, let him sell his coat, and buy a sword. For I say to you, that this that is written must yet be fulfilled in me: *And with the wicked was he reckoned.* For the things concerning me have an end. But they said: Lord, behold here *are* two swords. And he said to them, it is enough.

CHAPTER II.

EXHORTATION AND PRAYER.

1. (John 14.) CONTINUING Jesus said: Let not your heart be troubled. You believe in God, believe also in me. In my Father's house there are many mansions. If not, I would have told you, that I go to prepare a place for you. And if I shall go, and prepare a place for you, I will come again, and will take you to myself; that where I am, you also may be. And

whither I go you know, and the way you know. Thomas saith to him: Lord, we know not whither thou goest; and how can we know the way? Jesus saith to him: I am the way, and the truth, and the life. No man cometh to the Father, but by me. If you had known me, you would without doubt have known my Father also: and from henceforth you shall know him, and you have seen him. Philip saith to him: Lord, shew us the Father, and it is enough for us. Jesus saith to him: So long a time have I been with you, and have you not known me? Philip, he that seeth me, seeth the Father also. How sayest thou, shew us the Father? Do you not believe, that I am in the Father, and the Father in me? The words that I speak to you, I speak not of myself. But the Father who abideth in me, he doth the works. Believe you not that I am in the Father, and the Father in me? Otherwise believe for the very works' sake. Amen, amen, I say to you, he that believeth in me, the works that I do, he also shall do; and greater than these shall he do. Because I go to the Father: and whatsoever you shall ask the Father in my name, that will I do: that the Father may be glorified in the Son. If you shall ask me any thing in my name, that I will do.

2. If you love me, keep my commandments. And I will ask the Father, and he shall give you another Paraclete, that he may abide with you for ever. The spirit of truth, whom the world cannot receive, because it seeth him not, nor knoweth him: but you shall know him; because he shall abide with you, and shall be in you. I will not leave you orphans, I will come to you. Yet a little while: and the world seeth me no more. But you see me: because I live, and you shall live. In that day you shall know, that I am in my Father, and you in me, and I in you. He that hath my commandments, and keepeth them; he it is that loveth me. And he that loveth me, shall be loved of my Father: and I will love him, and will manifest myself to him. Judas saith to him, not the Iscariot: Lord, how is it, that thou wilt manifest thyself to us, and not to the world? Jesus answered, and said to him: If any one love me, he will keep my word, and my Father will love him, and we will come to him, and will make our abode with him. He that loveth me not, keepeth not my words. And the word which you have heard, is not mine; but the Father's who sent me. These things have I spoken to you, abiding with you. But the Paraclete, the Holy Ghost whom the Father will send in my name, he will teach you all things, and bring all things to your mind, whatsoever I shall have said to you.

3. Peace I leave with you, my peace I give unto you: not

as the world giveth, do I give unto you. Let not your heart be troubled, nor let it be afraid. You have heard that I said to you: I go away, and I come unto you. If you loved me, you would indeed be glad, because I go to the Father: for the Father is greater than I. And now I have told you before it come to pass: that when it shall come to pass, you may believe. I will not now speak many things with you. For the prince of this world cometh, and in me he hath not any thing. But that the world may know, that I love the Father: and as the Father hath given me commandment, so do I: Arise, let us go hence.

4. (John 15.) I am the true vine; and my Father is the husbandman. Every branch in me, that beareth not fruit, he will take away: and every one that beareth fruit, he will purge it, that it may bring forth more fruit. Now you are clean by reason of the word, which I have spoken to you. Abide in me, and I in you. As the branch cannot bear fruit of itself, unless it abide in the vine, so neither can you, unless you abide in me. I am the vine; you the branches: he that abideth in me, and I in him, the same beareth much fruit: for without me you can do nothing. If any one abide not in me, he shall be cast forth as a branch, and shall wither, and they shall gather him up, and cast him into the fire, and he burneth. If you abide in me, and my words abide in you, you shall ask whatever you will, and it shall be done unto you. In this is my Father glorified; that you bring forth very much fruit, and become my disciples. As the Father hath loved me, I also have loved you. Abide in my love. If you keep my commandments, you shall abide in my love; as I also have kept my Father's commandments, and do abide in his love. These things I have spoken to you, that my joy may be in you, and your joy may be filled. This is my commandment, that you love one another, as I have loved you. Greater love than this no man hath, that a man lay down his life for his friends. You are my friends, if you do the things that I command you. I will not now call you servants: for the servant knoweth not what his Lord doth. But I have called you friends: because all things whatsoever I have heard of my Father, I have made known to you.

5. You have not chosen me: but I have chosen you; and have appointed you, that you should go, and should bring forth fruit; and your fruit should remain: that whatsoever you shall ask of the Father in my name, he may give it you. These things I command you, that you love one another.

6. If the world hate you, know ye, that it hath hated me before you. If you had been

of the world, the world would love its own: but because you are not of the world, but I have chosen you out of the world, therefore the world hateth you. Remember my word that I said to you: The servant is not greater than his master. If they have persecuted me, they will also persecute you: if they have kept my word, they will keep yours also. But all these things they will do to you for my name's sake: because they know not him that sent me. If I had not come, and spoken to them, they would not have sin; but now they have no excuse for their sin. He that hateth me, hateth my Father also. If I had not done among them the works that no other man hath done, they would not have sin; but now they have both seen and hated both me and my Father. But that the word may be fulfilled which is written in their law: *They hated me without cause.*

7. But when the Paraclete cometh, whom I will send you from the Father, the Spirit of truth, who proceedeth from the Father, he shall give testimony of me. And you shall give testimony, because you are with me from the beginning.

(John 16.) These things have I spoken to you, that you may not be scandalized. They will put you out of the synagogues: yea, the hour cometh, that whosoever killeth you, will think that he doth a service to God. And these things will they do to you; because they have not known the Father, nor me. But these things I have told you, that when the hour shall come, you may remember that I told you of them. But I told you not these things from the beginning, because I was with you. And now I go to him that sent me, and none of you asketh me: Whither goest thou? But because I have spoken these things to you, sorrow hath filled your heart. But I tell you the truth: it is expedient to you that I go: for if I go not, the Paraclete will not come to you; but if I go, I will send him to you. And when he is come, he will convince the world of sin, and of justice, and of judgment. Of sin: because they believed not in me. And of justice: because I go to the Father; and you shall see me no longer. And of judgment: because the prince of this world is already judged. I have yet many things to say to you: but you cannot bear them now. But when he, the Spirit of truth, is come, he will teach you all truth. For he shall not speak of himself; but what things soever he shall hear, he shall speak; and the things that are to come, he shall shew you. He shall glorify me; because he shall receive of mine, and shall shew *it* to you. All things whatsoever the Father hath, are mine. Therefore I said, that he shall receive of mine, and shew *it* to you.

8. A little while, and now you shall not see me; and again a little while, and you shall see me: because I go to the Father. Then some of his disciples said one to another: What is this that he saith to us: A little while, and you shall not see me; and again a little while, and you shall see me, and, because I go to the Father? They said therefore: What is this that he saith, A little while? we know not what he speaketh. And Jesus knew that they had a mind to ask him; and he said to them: Of this do you inquire among yourselves, because I said: A little while, and you shall not see me; and again a little while, and you shall see me? Amen, amen, I say to you, that you shall lament and weep, but the world shall rejoice; and you shall be made sorrowful, but your sorrow shall be turned into joy. A woman, when she is in labour, hath sorrow, because her hour is come; but when she hath brought forth the child, she remembereth no more the anguish, for joy that a man is born into the world. So also you now indeed have sorrow; but I will see you again, and your heart shall rejoice; and your joy no man shall take from you.

9. And in that day you shall not ask me any thing. Amen, amen, I say to you: if you ask the Father any thing in my name, he will give it you. Hitherto you have not asked any thing in my name. Ask, and you shall receive; that your joy may be full. These things I have spoken to you in proverbs. The hour cometh, when I will no more speak to you in proverbs, but will shew you plainly of the Father. In that day you shall ask in my name; and I say not to you, that I will ask the Father for you: For the Father himself loveth you, because you have loved me, and have believed that I came out from God.

10. I came forth from the Father, and am come into the world: again I leave the world, and I go to the Father. His disciples say to him: Behold, now thou speakest plainly, and speakest no proverb. Now we know that thou knowest all things, and thou needest not that any man should ask thee. By this we believe that thou camest forth from God. Jesus answered them: Do you now believe? Behold, the hour cometh, and it is now come, that you shall be scattered every man to his own, and shall leave me alone; and yet I am not alone, because the Father is with me. These things I have spoken to you, that in me you may have peace. In the world you shall have distress: but have confidence, I have overcome the world.

11. (John 17.) These things Jesus spoke, and lifting up his eyes to heaven, he said: Father, the hour is come, glorify thy Son, that thy Son

may glorify thee. As thou hast given him power over all flesh, that he may give eternal life to all whom thou hast given him. Now this is eternal life: That they may know thee, the only true God, and Jesus Christ, whom thou hast sent. I have glorified thee on the earth; I have finished the work which thou gavest me to do. And now glorify thou me, O Father with thyself, with the glory which I had, before the world was, with thee. I have manifested thy name to the men whom thou hast given me out of the world. Thine they were, and to me thou gavest them; and they have kept thy word. Now they have known, that all things which thou hast given me, are from thee: Because the words which thou gavest me, I have given to them; and they have received them, and have known in very deed that I came out from thee, and they have believed that thou didst send me. I pray for them: I pray not for the world, but for them whom thou hast given me: because they are thine: And all my things are thine, and thine are mine; and I am glorified in them. And now I am not in the world, and these are in the world, and I come to thee. Holy Father, keep them in thy name whom thou hast given me; that they may be one, as we also are. While I was with them, I kept them in thy name. Those whom thou gavest me have I kept; and none of them is lost, but the son of perdition, that the scripture may be fulfilled. And now I come to thee; and these things I speak in the world, that they may have my joy filled in themselves. Sanctify them in truth. Thy word is truth. As thou hast sent me into the world, I also have sent them into the world. And for them do I sanctify myself, that they also may be sanctified in truth. And not for them only do I pray, but for them also who through their word shall believe in me; That they all may be one, as thou, Father, in me, and I in thee; that they also may be one in us; that the world may believe that thou hast sent me. And the glory which thou hast given me, I have given to them; that they may be one, as we also are one: I in them, and thou in me; that they may be made perfect in one: and the world may know that thou hast sent me, and hast loved them, as thou hast also loved me. Father, I will that where I am, they also whom thou hast given me may be with me; that they may see my glory which thou hast given me, because thou hast loved me before the creation of the world. Just Father, the world hath not known thee; but I have known thee: and these have known that thou hast sent me. And I have made known thy name to them, and will make it known; that the love wherewith thou hast loved me, may be in them, and I in them.

12. (Mark 14.) When Jesus had said these things, And when they had said an hymn, they went forth to the mount of olives. And Jesus saith to them: You will all be scandalized in my regard this night; for it is written, *I will strike the shepherd and the sheep shall be dispersed.* But after I shall be risen again, I will go before you into Galilee. But Peter saith to him: Although all shall be scandalized in thee, yet not I. And Jesus saith to him: Amen I say to thee, to-day, even in this night, before the cock crow twice, thou shalt deny me thrice. But he spoke the more vehemently: Although I should die together with thee, I will not deny thee. And in like manner also said they all.

CHAPTER III.

GETHSEMANI.

1. (Mat. 26.) Then Jesus came with them into a country place which is called Gethsemani; and he said to his disciples: Sit you here, till I go yonder and pray. And taking with him Peter and the two sons of Zebedee, he began to grow sorrowful and to be sad. Then he saith to them: My soul is sorrowful even unto death: Stay you here, and watch with me. And going a little further, he fell upon his face, praying, and saying: My Father, if it be possible, let this chalice pass from me. Nevertheless not as I will, but as thou *wilt.* And he cometh to his disciples, and findeth them asleep, and he saith to Peter: What? Could you not watch one hour with me? Watch ye, and pray that ye enter not into temptation. The spirit indeed is willing, but the flesh weak. Again the second time, he went and prayed, saying: My Father, if this chalice may not pass away, but I must drink it, thy will be done. And he cometh again, and findeth them sleeping: for their eyes were heavy. And leaving them, he went again: and he prayed the third time, saying the self-same word. Then he cometh to his disciples, and saith to them: Sleep ye now and take your rest; behold the hour is at hand, and the son of man shall be betrayed into the hands of sinners. Rise, let us go: behold he is at hand that will betray me.

2. As he yet spoke, behold Judas, one of the twelve came, and with him a great multitude with swords and clubs, sent from the chief priests and the ancients of the people. And he that betrayed him, gave them a sign, saying: Whomsoever I shall kiss, that is he, hold him fast. And forthwith coming to Jesus, he said: Hail Rabbi. And he kissed him. And Jesus said to him: Friend, whereto art thou come? Whom seek ye?

(John 18.) They answered him: Jesus of Nazareth. Jesus saith to them: I am he. And Judas also, who betrayed him, stood with them. As soon therefore as he had said to them: I am he; they went backward, and fell to the ground. Again therefore he asked them: Whom seek ye? And they said: Jesus of Nazareth. Jesus answered, I have told you that I am he. If therefore you seek me, let these go their way.

3. (Luke 22.) And they that were about him, seeing what would follow, said to him: Lord shall we strike with the sword?

(John 18.) Then Simon Peter, having a sword, drew it, and struck the servant of the high-priest, and cut off his right ear. And the name of the servant was Malchus. Jesus therefore said to Peter: Put up thy sword into the scabbard. The chalice which my Father hath given me, shall I not drink it?

(Mat. 26.) Put up again thy sword into its place: For all that take the sword shall perish with the sword. Thinkest thou that I cannot ask my Father, and he will give me presently more than twelve legions of Angels? How then shall the scriptures be fulfilled, that so it must be done?

(Luke 22.) And when he had touched his ear, he healed him.

4. And Jesus said to the chief priests, and magistrates of the temple, and the ancients, that were come unto him: Are ye come out, as it were against a thief, with swords and clubs? When I was daily with you in the temple, you did not stretch forth your hands against me: but this is your hour, and the power of darkness. And apprehending him, they led him to the high-priest's house. But Peter followed afar off. Then the disciples all leaving him, fled.

(Mark 14.) And a certain young man followed him, having a linen cloth cast about his naked *body;* and they laid hold on him. But he, casting off the linen cloth, fled from them naked.

CHAPTER IV.

BEFORE THE TRIBUNAL.

1. (John 18.) Then the band and the tribune, and the servants of the Jews, took Jesus, and bound him: And they led him away to Annas first, for he was father-in-law to Caiphas, who was the high-priest of that year. Now Caiphas was he who had given the counsel to the Jews: That it was expedient that one man should die for the people.

2. And Simon Peter followed Jesus, and so did another disciple. And that disciple was known to the high-priest, and went in with Jesus into the court of the high-priest. But Peter stood at the door without. The other disciple therefore, who was known to the high-priest, went out, and spoke to the portress, and brought in Peter.

(Luke 22.) And when they had kindled a fire in the midst of the hall, and were sitting about it, Peter was in the midst of them. Whom when a certain servant-maid had seen sitting at the light, and had earnestly beheld him: she said: This man also was with him. But he denied him, saying: Woman, I know him not. And he went forth before the court; and the cock crew.

3. (John 18.) The high-priest therefore asked Jesus of his disciples, and of his doctrine. Jesus answered him: I have spoken openly to the world: I have always taught in the synagogue, and in the temple, whither all the Jews resort; and in secret I have spoken nothing. Why askest thou me? ask them who have heard what I have spoken unto them: behold they know what things I have said. And when he had said these things, one of the servants standing by, gave Jesus a blow, saying: Answerest thou the high-priest so? Jesus answered him: If I have spoken evil, give testimony of the evil; but if well, why strikest thou me? And Annas sent him bound to Caiphas the high-priest, where the scribes and the ancients were assembled.

4. (Mat. 26.) Now the chief priests and the whole council sought false witness against Jesus, that they might put him to death: And they found not, whereas many false witnesses had come in. And last of all there came two false witnesses: And they said: This man said, I am able to destroy the temple of God, and after three days to rebuild it. And the high-priest rising up, said to him: Answerest thou nothing to the things which these witness against thee? But Jesus held his peace. And the high-priest said to him: I adjure thee by the living God, that thou tell us if thou be the Christ the Son of God. Jesus saith to him: Thou hast said *it*. Nevertheless I say to you, hereafter you shall see the son of man sitting on the right hand of the power of God, and coming in the clouds of heaven. Then the high-priest rent his garments, saying: He hath blasphemed; what further need have we of witnesses? Behold, now you have heard the blasphemy: What think you? But they answering, said: He is guilty of death.

5. But Peter sat without in the court: And as he went out of the gate, another maid saw him, and she saith to them that were there: This man also was with Jesus of Nazareth. And again he denied with an oath: That I know not the man. And after a little while they came that stood by, and said to Peter: Surely thou also art one of them; for even thy speech doth discover thee. Then he began to curse and to swear that he knew not the man. And immediately the cock crew. And Peter remembered the word of Jesus which he had said: Before the cock crow twice thou wilt deny me thrice. And going forth, he wept bitterly.

6. (Luke 22.) And the men that held Jesus, mocked him, and struck him. And they blindfolded him, and smote his face. And they asked him, saying: Prophesy, who is it that struck thee? And blaspheming, many other things they said against him.

7. And as soon as it was day, the ancients of the people, and the chief priests and scribes, came together; and they brought him into their council, saying: If thou be the Christ, tell us. And he saith to them: If I shall tell you, you will not believe me. And if I shall also ask you, you will not answer me, nor let me go. But hereafter the son of man shall be sitting on the right hand of the power of God. Then said they all: Art thou then the Son of God? Who said: You say, that I am. And they said: What need we any farther testimony? for we ourselves have heard it from his own mouth. Then they led Jesus from Caiphas to the governor's hall.

8. (Mat. 27.) Then Judas, who betrayed him, seeing that he was condemned, repenting himself, brought back the thirty pieces of silver to the chief priests and ancients, saying: I have sinned in betraying innocent blood. But they said: What is that to us? look thou to it. And casting down the pieces of silver in the temple, he departed: and went and hanged himself with an halter. But the chief priests having taken the pieces of silver, said: It is not lawful to put them into the corbona, because it is the price of blood. And after they

had consulted together, they bought with them the potter's field, to be a burying-place for strangers. For this cause that field was called haceldama, that is, the field of blood, even to this day. Then was fulfilled that which was spoken by Jeremias the prophet, saying: *And they took the thirty pieces of silver, the price of him that was prized, whom they prized of the children of Israel. And they gave them unto the potter's field, as the Lord appointed to me.*

CHAPTER V.

SCOURGE AND CROWN.

1. (John 18. Friday, April 7, A. D. 33.) Now it was morning; and they went not into the hall, that they might not be defiled, but that they might eat the pasch. Pilate therefore went out to them, and said: What accusation bring you against this man? They answered, and said to him: If he were not a malefactor, we would not have delivered him up to thee. Pilate therefore said to them: Take him you, and judge him according to your law. The Jews therefore said to him: It is not lawful for us to put any man to death; That the word of Jesus might be fulfilled, which he said, signifying what death he should die.

2. Pilate therefore went into the hall again, and called Jesus, and said to him: Art thou the king of the Jews? Jesus answered: Sayest thou this thing of thyself, or have others told it thee of me? Pilate answered: Am I a Jew? Thy own nation, and the chief priests, have delivered thee up to me: what hast thou done? Jesus answered: My kingdom is not of this world. If my kingdom were of this world, my servants would certainly strive that I should not be delivered to the Jews: but now my kingdom is not from hence. Pilate therefore said to him: Art thou a king then? Jesus answered: Thou sayest that I am a king. For this was I born, and for this came I into the world; that I should give testimony to the truth. Every one that is of the truth, heareth my voice. Pilate saith to him: What is truth? And when he said this, he went out again to the Jews, and saith to them: I find no cause in him.

(Mat. 27.) And Jesus stood before the governor, and the governor asked him, saying:

Art thou the king of the Jews? Jesus saith to him: Thou sayest it. And when he was accused by the chief priests and ancients, he answered nothing. Then Pilate saith to him: Dost not thou hear how great testimonies they allege against thee? And he answered him to never a word; so that the governor wondered exceedingly.

(Luke 23.) And they began to accuse him, saying: We have found this man perverting our nation, and forbidding to give tribute to Cesar, and saying that he is Christ the king. And Pilate asked him, saying: Art thou the king of the Jews? But he answering, said: Thou sayest it. And Pilate said to the chief priests and to the multitudes: I find no cause in this man. But they were more earnest, saying: He stirreth up the people, teaching throughout all Judea, beginning from Galilee to this place. But Pilate hearing Galilee, asked if the man were of Galilee? And when he understood that he was of Herod's jurisdiction, he sent him away to Herod, who was also himself at Jerusalem, in those days.

3. Now Herod seeing Jesus, was very glad; for he was desirous of a long time to see him, because he had heard many things of him; and he hoped to see some sign wrought by him. And he questioned him in many words. But he answered him nothing. And the chief priests and the scribes stood by, earnestly accusing him. And Herod with his army set him at nought, and mocked him, putting on him a white garment, and sent him back to Pilate. And Herod and Pilate were made friends, that same day; for before they were enemies one to another.

4. (Mat. 27.) Now upon the solemn day the governor was accustomed to release to the people one prisoner, whom they would. And he had then a notorious prisoner, that was called Barabbas. They therefore being gathered together, Pilate said: Whom will you that I release to you, Barabbas, or Jesus that is called Christ? For he knew that for envy they had delivered him. And as he was sitting in the place of judgment, his wife sent to him, saying: Have thou nothing to do with that just man; for I have suffered many things this day in a dream because of him. But the chief priests and ancients persuaded the people, that they should ask Barabbas, and make Jesus away. And the governor answering, said to them: Whether will you of the two to be released unto you? But they said, Barabbas. Pilate saith to them: What shall I do then with Jesus that is called Christ? they say all: Let him be crucified. The governor said to them: Why, what evil hath he done? But they cried out the more, saying: Let him be cru-

cified. And Pilate seeing that he prevailed nothing, but that rather a tumult was made; taking water washed his hands before the people, saying: I am innocent of the blood of this just man; look you to it. And the whole people answering, said: His blood be upon us and upon our children.

5. Then he released to them Barabbas and took Jesus, and scourged him. Then the soldiers of the governor taking Jesus into the hall, gathered together unto him the whole band; And stripping him, they put a scarlet cloak about him. And platting a crown of thorns, they put it upon his head, and a reed in his right hand. And bowing the knee before him, they mocked him, saying: Hail, king of the Jews. And spitting upon him, they took the reed, and struck his head.

6. (John 19.) Pilate therefore went forth again, and saith to them: Behold, I bring him forth unto you, that you may know that I find no cause in him. (Jesus therefore came forth, bearing the crown of thorns and the purple garment.) And he saith to them: Behold the Man. When the chief priests therefore, and the servants, had seen him, they cried out, saying: Crucify him, crucify him. Pilate saith to them: Take him you, and crucify him: for I find no cause in him. The Jews answered him: We have a law; and according to the law he ought to die, because he made himself the Son of God. When Pilate therefore had heard this saying, he feared the more. And he entered into the hall again, and he said to Jesus: Whence art thou? But Jesus gave him no answer. Pilate therefore saith to him: Speakest thou not to me? knowest thou not that I have power to crucify thee, and I have power to release thee? Jesus answered: Thou shouldst not have any power against me, unless it were given thee from above. Therefore, he that hath delivered me to thee, hath the greater sin. And from henceforth Pilate sought to release him. But the Jews cried out, saying: If thou release this man, thou art not Cesar's friend. For whosoever maketh himself a king, speaketh against Cesar. Now when Pilate had heard these words, he brought Jesus forth, and sat down in the judgment seat, in the place that is called Lithostrotos, and in Hebrew Gabbatha. And it was the parasceve of the pasch about the sixth hour, and he saith to the Jews: Behold your king. But they cried out: Away with him, away with him; crucify him. Pilate saith to them: shall I crucify your king? The chief priests answered: We have no king but Cesar. Then therefore he delivered him to them to be crucified. And they took Jesus and led him forth.

CHAPTER VI.

TAKE UP THY CROSS.

1. (Luke 23.) Now as they led him away, they laid hold of one Simon of Cyrene, coming from the country; and they laid the cross on him, to carry after Jesus. And there were also two other malefactors led with him to be put to death.

2. And there followed him a great multitude of people, and of women, who bewailed and lamented him. But Jesus turning to them, said: Daughters of Jerusalem, weep not over me; but weep for yourselves, and for your children. For behold, the days shall come, wherein they will say: Blessed are the barren, and the wombs that have not borne, and the paps that have not given suck. Then shall they begin to say to the mountains: Fall upon us; and to the hills: Cover us. For if in the green wood they do these things, what shall be done in the dry.

CHAPTER VII.

IT IS FINISHED.

1. (Mark 15.) AND they bring him into the place *called* Golgotha, which being interpreted is, the place of Calvary. And they gave him to drink wine mingled with myrrh; but he took it not. And with him they crucify two thieves; the one on his right hand, and the other on his left. And the Scripture was fulfilled, which saith: *And with the wicked he was reputed.*

2. And crucifying him, they divided his garments, casting lots upon them, what every man should take. And Jesus said: Father, forgive them, for they know not what they do.

3. (John 19.) Now Pilate wrote a title also, and he put it upon the cross. And the writing was: JESUS OF NAZARETH, THE KING OF THE JEWS. This title therefore many of the Jews did read: because the place where Jesus was crucified was nigh to the city: and it was written in Hebrew, in Greek, and in Latin. Then the chief priests of the Jews said to Pilate: Write not, The King of the Jews; but that he said, I am the king of the Jews. Pilate answered: What I have written, I have written.

4. The soldiers therefore, when they had crucified him, took his garments (and they made four parts, to every soldier a part,) and also his coat. Now the coat was without seam, woven from the top throughout. They said then one to another: Let us not cut it, but let us cast lots for it, whose it shall be; that the scripture might be fulfilled, saying: *They have parted my garments among them, and upon my vesture they have cast lot.* And the soldiers indeed did these things.

5. (Luke 23.) Now the people stood beholding, and the rulers with them derided him, saying: He saved others; let him save himself, if he be Christ, the elect of God. And the soldiers also mocked him, coming to him, and offering him vinegar, And saying: If thou be the king of the Jews, save thyself.

6. And one of those robbers who were hanged, blasphemed him, saying: If thou be Christ, save thyself and us. But the other answering, rebuked him, saying: Neither dost thou fear God, seeing thou art under the same condemnation? And we indeed justly, for we receive the due reward of our deeds; but this man hath done no evil. And he said to Jesus: Lord, remember me when thou shalt come into thy kingdom. And Jesus said to him: Amen I say to thee, this day thou shalt be with me in paradise.

7. (John 19.) Now there stood by the cross of Jesus, his mother, and his mother's sister, Mary of Cleophas, and Mary Magdalen. When Jesus therefore had seen his mother and the disciple standing whom he loved, he saith to his mother: Woman, behold thy son. After that, he saith to the disciple: Behold thy mother. And from that hour, the disciple took her to his own.

8. (Mat. 27.) Now from the sixth hour there was darkness over the whole earth, until the ninth hour. And about the ninth hour Jesus cried with a loud voice, saying: Eli, Eli, lamma sabacthani? that is, My God, my God, why hast thou forsaken me? And some that stood there and heard, said: This man calleth Elias. Afterwards, Jesus knowing that all things were now accomplished, that the scripture might be fulfilled, said: I thirst. And immediately one of them running took a sponge, and filled it with vinegar; and put it on a reed, and gave him to drink. Jesus therefore, when he had taken the vinegar, said: It is consummated. And the others said: Let be, let us see whether Elias will come to deliver him. And Jesus again crying with a loud voice, Father, into

Thy hands I commend my Spirit, yielded up the ghost. And behold the veil of the temple was rent in two from the top even to the bottom, and the earth quaked, and the rocks were rent. And the graves were opened: and many bodies of the saints that had slept arose, And coming out of the tombs after his resurrection, came into the holy city, and appeared to many. Now the centurion and they that were with him watching Jesus, having seen the earthquake and the things that were done, were sore afraid, saying: Indeed this was the Son of God. And there were there many women afar off, who had followed Jesus from Galilee, ministering unto him; Among whom was Mary Magdalen, and Mary the mother of James and Joseph, and the mother of the sons of Zebedee.

9. (John 19.) Then the Jews (because it was the parasoeve,) that the bodies might not remain upon the cross on the sabbath day (for that was a great sabbath day,) besought Pilate that their legs might be broken, and that they might be taken away. The soldiers therefore came; and they broke the legs of the first, and of the other that was crucified with him. But after they were come to Jesus, when they saw that he was already dead, they did not break his legs. But one of the soldiers with a spear opened His Side, and immediately there came out Blood and Water.—And he that saw it hath given testimony: and his testimony is true. And he knoweth that he saith true; that you also may believe.— For these things were done, that the Scripture might be fulfilled: You shall not break a bone of Him.—And again another Scripture saith: They shall look on Him Whom they pierced.—

10. Now after these things, Joseph of Arimathea (because he was a disciple of Jesus but secretly for fear of the Jews) besought Pilate that he might take away the body of Jesus. And Pilate gave leave. He came therefore, and took away the body of Jesus. And Nicodemus also came, (he who at the first came to Jesus by night,) bringing a mixture of myrrh and aloes, about an hundred pound *weight*. They took therefore the body of Jesus, and bound it in linen cloths, with the spices, as the manner of the Jews is to bury. Now there was in the place where he was crucified, a garden; and in the garden a new sepulchre, wherein no man yet had been laid. There, therefore, because of the parasceve of the Jews, they laid Jesus, because the sepulchre was nigh at hand. And they rolled a stone to the door of the sepulchre. And Mary Magdalen, and Mary *the mother* of Joseph, beheld where he was laid.

(Mat. 27.) And there was

there Mary Magdalen, and the other Mary sitting over against the sepulchre.

11. (Saturday, April 8, A. D. 33.) Now the next day, which followed the day of preparation, the chief priests and the Pharisees came together to Pilate, Saying: Sir, we have remembered, that that seducer said, while he was yet alive: After three days I will rise again. Command therefore the sepulchre to be guarded until the third day: lest perhaps his disciples come and steal him away, and say to the people: He is risen from the dead; and the last error shall be worse than the first. Pilate saith to them: You have a guard; go, guard it as you know. And they departing, made the sepulchre sure, sealing the stone, and setting guards.

12. (Mark 16. Sunday, April 9, A. D. 33.) Now when the sabbath was past, Mary Magdalen, and Mary *the mother* of James and Salome, bought sweet spices that coming, they might anoint Jesus.

PART IV.

CHRIST'S RESURRECTION AND ASCENSION.

1. (Mat. 28. Sunday, A. D. 33.) In the end of the sabbath, when it began to dawn towards the first day of the week, came Mary Magdalen and the other Mary, to see the sepulchre. And behold there was a great earthquake. For an angel of the Lord descended from heaven, and coming, rolled back the stone, and sat upon it. And his countenance was as lightning and his raiment as snow. And for fear of him, the guards were struck with terror, and became as dead men. And Mary Magdalen, and Mary the mother of James the less and of Joseph, and Salome: entering into the sepulchre, saw a young man sitting on the right side, clothed with a white robe: and they were astonished. Who saith to them: be not affrighted; you seek Jesus of Nazareth, who was crucified; he is risen, he is not here, behold the place where they laid him. But go, tell his disciples and Peter that he goeth before you into Galilee; there you shall see him, as he told you. But they going out, fled from the sepulchre. For a trembling and fear had seized them: and they said nothing to any man; for they were afraid.

2. (John 20.) Mary Magdalen ran, therefore, and cometh to Simon Peter, and to the other disciple whom Jesus loved, and saith to them: They have taken away the Lord out of the sepulchre, and we know not where they have laid him. Peter therefore went out, and that other disciple, and they came to the sepulchre. And they both ran together, and that other disciple did outrun Peter, and came first to the sepulchre. And when he stooped down, he saw the linen cloths lying; but yet he went not in. Then cometh Simon Peter, following him, and went into the sepulchre, and saw the linen cloths lying, And the napkin that had been about his head, not lying with the linen cloths, but apart, wrapt up into one place. Then that other disciple also went in, who came first to the sepulchre: and he saw, and believed. For as yet they knew not the scripture, that he must

rise again from the dead. The disciples therefore departed again to their home.

3. But Mary stood at the sepulchre without, weeping. Now as she was weeping, she stooped down, and looked into the sepulchre, And she saw two angels in white, sitting, one at the head, and one at the feet, where the body of Jesus had been laid. They say to her: Woman, why weepest thou? She saith to them: Because they have taken away my Lord; and I know not where they have laid him. When she had thus said, she turned herself back, and saw Jesus standing; and she knew not that it was Jesus. Jesus saith to her: Woman, why weepest thou? whom seekest thou? She, thinking that it was the gardener, saith to him: Sir, if thou hast taken him hence, tell me where thou hast laid him, and I will take him away. Jesus saith to her: Mary. She turning, saith to him: Rabboni, (which is to say, Master.) Jesus saith to her: Do not touch me, for I am not yet ascended to my Father. But go to my brethren, and say to them: I ascend to my Father and to your Father, to my God and your God. Mary Magdalen cometh, and telleth the disciples: I have seen the Lord, and these things he said to me. And they hearing that he was alive and had been seen by her, did not believe.

4. (Mat. 28.) Now the other women went out quickly from the sepulchre with fear and great joy, running to tell his disciples. And behold Jesus met them, saying: All hail. But they came up and took hold of his feet, and adored him. Then Jesus said to them: Fear not. Go, tell my brethren that they go into Galilee, there they shall see me.

(Luke 24.) And going back from the sepulchre, they told all these things to the eleven, and to all the rest. And it was Mary Magdalen, and Joanna, and Mary of James, and the other women that were with them, who told these things to the apostles. And these words seemed to them as idle tales; and they did not believe them.

5. (Mat. 28.) Who when they were departed, behold some of the guards came into the city, and told the chief priests all things that had been done. And they being assembled together with the ancients, taking counsel, gave a great sum of money to the soldiers, Saying: Say you, His disciples came by night, and stole him away when we were asleep. And if the governor shall hear of this, we will persuade him and secure you. So they taking the money, did as they were taught: and this word was spread abroad among the Jews even unto this day.

6. (Luke 24.) And behold, two disciples went, the same day, to a town which was sixty furlongs from Jerusalem, named

Emmaus. And they talked together of all these things which had happened. And it came to pass, that while they talked and reasoned with themselves, Jesus himself also drawing near, went with them. But their eyes were held, that they should not know him. And he said to them: What are these discourses that you hold one with another as you walk, and are sad? And the one of them, whose name was Cleophas, answering, said to him: Art thou only a stranger in Jerusalem, and hast not known the things that have been done there in these days? To whom he said: What things? And they said: Concerning Jesus of Nazareth, who was a prophet, mighty in work and word before God and all the people; And how our chief priests and princes delivered him to be condemned to death, and crucified him. But we hoped, that it was he that should have redeemed Israel: and now besides all this, to-day is the third day since these things were done. Yea and certain women also of our company affrighted us, who before it was light, were at the sepulchre, And not finding his body, came, saying, that they had also seen a vision of angels, who say that he is alive. And some of our people went to the sepulchre, and found it so as the women had said, but him they found not. Then he said to them: O foolish, and slow of heart to believe in all things which the prophets have spoken. Ought not Christ to have suffered these things, and so to enter into his glory? And beginning at Moses and all the prophets, he expounded to them in all the scriptures, the things that were concerning him. And they drew nigh to the town, whither they were going: and he made as though he would go farther. But they constrained him; saying: Stay with us, because it is towards evening, and the day is now far spent. And he went in with them. And it came to pass, whilst he was at table with them, he took bread, and blessed, and brake, and gave to them. And their eyes were opened, and they knew him: and he vanished out of their sight. And they said one to the other: Was not our heart burning within us, whilst he spoke in the way, and opened to us the scriptures? And rising up, the same hour, they went back to Jerusalem: and they found the eleven gathered together, and those that were with them, Saying: The Lord is risen indeed, and hath appeared to Simon. And they told what things were done in the way; and how they knew him in the breaking of bread, neither did they believe them.

7. Now whilst they were speaking these things, Jesus stood in the midst of them, and saith to them: Peace *be* to you; it is I, fear not. But they being troubled and fright-

ed, supposed that they saw a spirit. And he said to them: Why are you troubled, and why do thoughts arise in your hearts? See my hands and feet, that it is I myself; handle, and see: for a spirit hath not flesh and bones, as you see me to have. And when he had said this, he shewed them his hands and feet. But while they yet believed not, and wondered for joy, he said: Have you here any thing to eat? And they offered him a piece of a broiled fish, and a honeycomb. And when he had eaten before them, taking the remains, he gave to them.

8. (John 20.) The disciples therefore were glad, when they saw the Lord. He said therefore to them again: Peace be to you. As the Father hath sent me, I also send you. When he had said this, he breathed on them: and he said to them: Receive ye the Holy Ghost. Whose sins you shall forgive, they are forgiven them; and whose *sins* you shall retain, they are retained.

9. Now Thomas, one of the twelve, who is called Didymus, was not with them when Jesus came. The other disciples therefore said to him: We have seen the Lord. But he said to them: Except I shall see in his hands the print of the nails, and put my finger into the place of the nails, and put my hand into his side, I will not believe. And after eight days again his disciples were within, and Thomas with them. Jesus cometh, the doors being shut, and stood in the midst, and said: Peace be to you. Then he saith to Thomas: Put in thy finger hither, and see my hands; and bring hither thy hand, and put it into my side; and be not faithless, but believing. Thomas answered, and said to him: My Lord, and my God. Jesus saith to him: Because thou hast seen me, Thomas, thou hast believed: blessed are they that have not seen, and have believed.

10. (John 21.) After this, Jesus shewed himself again to the disciples at the sea of Tiberias. And he shewed *himself* after this manner. There were together Simon Peter, and Thomas, who is called Didymus, and Nathanael, who was of Cana of Galilee, and the sons of Zebedee, and two others of his disciples. Simon Peter saith to them: I go a fishing. They say to him: We also come with thee. And they went forth, and entered into the ship: and that night they caught nothing. But when the morning was come, Jesus stood on the shore: yet the disciples knew not that it was Jesus. Jesus therefore said to them: Children, have you any meat? They answered him: No. He saith to them: Cast the net on the right side of the ship, and you shall find. They cast therefore; and now they were not able to draw it, for the multitude of fishes. That disciple therefore whom

Jesus loved, said to Peter: It is the Lord. Simon Peter, when he heard that it was the Lord, girt his coat about him (for he was naked,) and cast himself into the sea. But the other disciples came in the ship (for they were not far from the land, but as it were two hundred cubits,) dragging the net with fishes. As soon then as they came to land, they saw hot coals lying, and a fish laid thereon, and bread. Jesus saith to them: Bring hither of the fishes which you have now caught. Simon Peter went up, and drew the net to land, full of great fishes, one hundred and fifty-three. And although there were so many, the net was not broken. Jesus saith to them: Come, and dine. And none of them who were at meat, durst ask him: Who art thou? knowing that it was the Lord. And Jesus cometh and taketh bread, and giveth them, and fish in like manner. This is now the third time that Jesus was manifested to his disciples, after he was risen from the dead.

11. When therefore they had dined, Jesus saith to Simon Peter: Simon, *son* of John, lovest thou me more than these? He saith to him: Yea, Lord, thou knowest that I love thee. He saith to him: Feed my lambs. He saith to him again: Simon, *son* of John, lovest thou me? He saith to him: Yea, Lord, thou knowest that I love thee. He saith to him: Feed my lambs. He said to him the third time: Simon, son of John, lovest thou me? Peter was grieved, because he had said to him the third time: Lovest thou me? And he said to him: Lord, thou knowest all things: thou knowest that I love thee. He said to him: Feed my sheep.

12. Amen, amen, I say to thee, when thou wast younger, thou didst gird thyself, and didst walk where thou wouldst. But when thou shalt be old, thou shalt stretch forth thy hands, and another shall gird thee, and lead thee whither thou wouldst not. And this he said, signifying by what death he should glorify God. And when he had said this, he saith to him: Follow me.

13. Peter turning about, saw that disciple whom Jesus loved following, who also leaned on his breast at supper, and said: Lord, who is he that shall betray thee? Him therefore when Peter had seen, he saith to Jesus: Lord, and what *shall* this man *do?* Jesus saith to him: So I will have him to remain till I come, what is it to thee? follow thou me. This saying therefore went abroad among the brethren, that that disciple should not die. And Jesus did not say to him: He should not die; but, So I will have him to remain till I come, what is it to thee? This is that disciple who giveth testimony of these things, and hath written these things; and we know that his testimony is true.

14. (Mat. 28.) Now the eleven disciples went into Galilee, unto the mountain where Jesus had appointed them. And seeing him they adored: but some doubted.

15. (1 Cor. 15.) Then was he seen by more than five hundred brethren at once: of whom many remain until this present, and some are fallen asleep.

16. After that, he was seen by James, then by all the apostles. To whom also he shewed himself alive after his passion, by many proofs, for forty days appearing to them, and speaking of the kingdom of God.

17. (Mark 16.) At length he appeared to the eleven as they were at table; and he upbraided them with their incredulity and hardness of heart, because they did not believe them who had seen him after he was risen again. And he said to them: Go ye into the whole world, and preach the gospel to every creature. He that believeth and is baptized, shall be saved: but he that believeth not shall be condemned. And these signs shall follow them that believe: In my name they shall cast out devils: they shall speak with new tongues. They shall take up serpents; and if they shall drink any deadly thing, it shall not hurt them: they shall lay their hands upon the sick, and they shall recover.

(Luke 24.) These are the words which I spoke to you, while I was yet with you, that all things must needs be fulfilled, which are written in the law of Moses, and in the prophets, and in the psalms, concerning me. Then he opened their understanding, that they might understand the scriptures. And he said to them: Thus it is written, and thus it behoved Christ to suffer, and to rise again from the dead, the third day: And that penance and remission of sins should be preached in his name, unto all nations, beginning at Jerusalem. And you are witnesses of these things. And I send the promise of my Father upon you: but stay you in the city, till you be endued with power from on high. For John indeed baptized with water, but you shall be baptized with the Holy Ghost, not many days hence.

18. Now he led them out as far as Bethania: and lifting up his hands, he blessed them.

(Acts 1.) They therefore who were come together, asked him, saying: Lord, wilt thou at this time restore again the kingdom to Israel? But he said to them: It is not for you to know the times or moments, which the Father hath put in his own power: But you shall receive the power of the Holy Ghost coming upon you, and you shall be witnesses unto me in Jerusalem, and in all Judea, and Samaria, and even to the uttermost part of the earth. And when he had said these things, while they looked on, he was raised up: and a cloud received him out of their sight.

19. Now while they were beholding him going up to heaven, behold two men stood by them in white garments. Who also said: Ye men of Galilee, why stand you looking up to heaven? This Jesus who is taken up from you into heaven, shall so come, as you have seen him going into heaven.

20. Then they returned to Jerusalem from the mount that is called Olivet, which is nigh Jerusalem, within a sabbath day's journey. And when they were come in, they went up into an upper room, where abode Peter and John, James and Andrew, Philip and Thomas, Bartholomew and Matthew, James of Alpheus, and Simon Zelotes, and Jude *the brother of James.* All these were persevering with one mind in prayer with the women, and Mary the mother of Jesus, and with his brethren.

21. (A. D. 33.) In those days Peter rising up in the midst of the brethren said: (now the number of persons together was about an hundred and twenty:) Men, brethren, the scripture must needs be fulfilled, which the Holy Ghost spoke before by the mouth of David concerning Judas, who was the leader of them that apprehended Jesus: Who was numbered with us, and had obtained part of this ministry. And he indeed hath possessed a field of the reward of iniquity, and being hanged, burst asunder in the midst: and all his bowels gushed out. And it became known to all the inhabitants of Jerusalem: so that the same field was called in their tongue, Haceldama, that is to say, The field of blood. For it is written in the book of psalms: *Let their habitation become desolate, and let there be none to dwell therein. And his bishoprick let another take.*

22. Wherefore of these men who have companied with us all the time that the Lord Jesus came in and went out among us, beginning from the baptism of John, until the day wherein he was taken up from us, one of these must be made a witness with us of his resurrection. And they appointed two, Joseph, called Barsabas, who was surnamed Justus, and Matthias. And praying, they said: Thou, Lord, who knowest the hearts of all men, shew whether of these two thou hast chosen, to take the place of this ministry and apostleship, from which Judas hath by transgression fallen, that he might go to his own place. And they gave them lots, and the lot fell upon Matthias, and he was numbered with the eleven apostles.

23. (Acts 2.) Now when the days of the pentecost were accomplished, they were all together in one place: And suddenly there came a sound from heaven, as of a mighty wind

coming, and it filled the whole house where they were sitting. And there appeared to them parted tongues as it were of fire, and it sat upon every one of them: And they were all filled with the Holy Ghost, and they began to speak with divers tongues, according as the Holy Ghost gave them to speak. Now there were dwelling at Jerusalem, Jews, devout men, out of every nation under heaven. And when this was noised abroad, the multitude came together, and were confounded in mind, because that every man heard them speak in his own tongue. And they were all amazed, and wondered, saying: Behold, are not all these, that speak, Galileans? And how have we heard, every man our own tongue wherein we were born? Parthians, and Medes, and Elamites, and inhabitants of Mesopotamia, Judea, and Cappadocia, Pontus and Asia, Phrygia, and Pamphilia, Egypt, and the parts of Lybia about Cyrene, and strangers of Rome, Jews also, and proselytes, Cretes, and Arabians: we have heard them speak in our own tongues the wonderful works of God. And they were all astonished, and wondered, saying one to another: What meaneth this? But others mocking, said: These men are full of new wine.

24. But Peter standing up with the eleven, lifted up his voice, and spoke to them: Ye men of Judea, and all you that dwell in Jerusalem, be this known to you, and with your ears receive my words. For these are not drunk, as you suppose, seeing it is but the third hour of the day: But this is that which was spoken of by the prophet Joel: *And it shall come to pass, in the last days (saith the Lord,) I will pour out of my Spirit upon all flesh: and your sons and your daughters shall prophesy, and your young men shall see visions, and your old men shall dream dreams. And upon my servants indeed, and upon my handmaids will I pour out in those days of my spirit, and they shall prophesy. And I will shew wonders in the heaven above, and signs on the earth beneath: blood and fire, and vapour of smoke. The sun shall be turned into darkness, and the moon into blood, before the great and manifest day of the Lord come. And it shall come to pass, that whosoever shall call upon the name of the Lord, shall be saved.*

25. Ye men of Israel, hear these words: Jesus of Nazareth, a man approved of God among you, by miracles, and wonders, and signs, which God did by him, in the midst of you, as you also know: This same being delivered up, by the determinate counsel and foreknowledge of God, you by the hands of wicked men have crucified and slain. Whom God had raised up, having loosed the sorrows of hell, as it was

impossible that he should be holden by it. For David saith concerning him: *I foresaw the Lord before my face: because he is at my right hand that I may not be moved. For this my heart hath been glad, and my tongue hath rejoiced: moreover my flesh also shall rest in hope. Because thou wilt not leave my soul in hell, nor suffer thy Holy one to see corruption. Thou hast made known to me the ways of life: Thou shalt make me full of joy with thy countenance.* Ye men, brethren, let me freely speak to you of the patriarch David; that he died, and was buried; and his sepulchre is with us to this present day. Whereas therefore he was a prophet, and knew that *God hath sworn to him with an oath, that of the fruit of his loins one should sit upon his throne.* Forseeing this he spoke of the resurrection of Christ. For neither was he left in hell, neither did his flesh see corruption. This Jesus hath God raised again, whereof all we are witnesses. Being exalted therefore by the right hand of God, and having received of the Father the promise of the Holy Ghost, he hath poured forth this which you see and hear. For David ascended not into heaven; but He himself said: *The Lord said to my Lord, sit thou on my right hand, Until I make thy enemies thy footstool.* Therefore let all the house of Israel know most certainly, that God hath made both Lord and Christ, this same Jesus, whom you have crucified.

26. Now when they had heard these things, they had compunction in their heart, and said to Peter, and to the rest of the apostles: What shall we do, men *and* brethren? But Peter said to them: Do penance, and be baptized every one of you in the name of Jesus Christ, for the remission of your sins: and you shall receive the gift of the Holy Ghost. For the promise is to you, and to your children, and to all that are far off, whomsoever the Lord our God shall call. And with very many other words did he testify and exhort them, saying: Save yourselves from this perverse generation. They therefore that received his word, were baptized; and there were added in that day about three thousand souls. And they were persevering in the doctrine of the apostles, and in the communication of the breaking of bread, and in prayers. And fear came upon every soul: many wonders also and signs were done by the apostles in Jerusalem, and there was great fear in all.

27. Now all they that believed, were together and had all things common. Their possessions and goods they sold, and divided them to all, according as every one had need. And continuing daily with one accord in the temple, and breaking bread from house to house,

they took their meat with gladness and simplicity of heart; praising God, and having favour with all the people. And the Lord increased daily together such as should be saved.

28. (John 20. A. D. 33.) Many other signs also did Jesus in the sight of his disciples, which are not written in this book. But these are written, that you may believe that Jesus is the Christ, the Son of God: and that believing, you may have life in his name.

(John 21.) But there are also many other things which Jesus did; which, if they were written every one, the world itself, I think, would not be able to contain the books that should be written.

(Mark 16.) But the apostles going forth preached every where: the Lord working withal, and confirming the word with signs that followed.

(Maccab 15.) I will here make an end of my narration. Which if I have done well, and as it becometh the history, it is what I desired: but if not so perfectly, it must be pardoned me.

(2 Cor. 13.) For the rest, brethren, rejoice, be perfect, take exhortation, be of one mind, have peace; and the God of peace and of love shall be with you. The grace of our Lord Jesus Christ, and the charity of God, and the communication of the Holy Ghost be with you all. Amen.

FINIS.

www.ingramcontent.com/pod-product-compliance
Lightning Source LLC
Chambersburg PA
CBHW030005240426
43672CB00007B/839